Encyclopedia of Feminist Literature

KATHY J. WHITSON

GREENWOOD PRESS
Westport, Connecticut • London

Library of Congress Cataloging-in-Publication Data

Whitson, Kathy J.
   Encyclopedia of feminist literature / Kathy J. Whitson.
       p. cm.
   Includes bibliographical references and index.
   ISBN 0–313–32731–9 (alk. paper)
     1. Women authors—Bio-bibliography. 2. Women and literature—Encyclopedias.
3. Feminist literature—Encyclopedias. 4. Feminism and literature—Encyclopedias.
5. Feminism in literature—Encyclopedias. 6. Women in literature—Encyclopedias.
I. Title.
PN471.W455 2004
809′.89287—dc22   2004042478

British Library Cataloguing in Publication Data is available.

Library of Congress Catalog Card Number: 2004042478
ISBN: 0–313–32731–9

First published in 2004

Greenwood Press, 88 Post Road West, Westport, CT 06881
An imprint of Greenwood Publishing Group, Inc.
www.greenwood.com

Printed in the United States of America

The paper used in this book complies with the
Permanent Paper Standard issued by the National
Information Standards Organization (Z39.48–1984).

10 9 8 7 6 5 4 3 2 1

Contents

List of Entries

Introduction

The purposes of this book are to put before a high school, undergraduate, and general audience the works of a representative number of feminist writers over the past several centuries and to have it serve as a reference companion for the student. While the volume focuses primarily on English and American writers, it also includes a number of world authors whose works might often be taught in the classroom. The volume addresses early writers, such as Christine de Pizan of the fourteenth century, to writers publishing in the twenty-first century. Works addressed in the volume are generally those written in English, but I include some significant works in translation, particularly if they have had an important impact on feminist studies in America and other English-speaking countries. Authors represent a number of nationalities including, among others, Chilean, Brazilian, Indian, South African, Australian, French, and German.

Readers may have instant recognition of some of the authors and will find others unfamiliar. The lack of familiarity with many of the writers underscores the need for a book such as this. Many women writers throughout the centuries have been marginalized and erased from the general canon of literature. It is to the credit of feminist scholars in particular that the works of many women have been recovered, reevaluated, and reintroduced into the literary canon. Through the work of recovery, many women writers are finding a place of visibility that they did not enjoy just a generation ago, and, concomitantly, many readers of literature have found a whole new body of written works to excite and challenge them. Excerpts from the work of many of these authors are now available in anthologies, and, thus, they are gaining an even greater recognition and readership.

Because the work of historical recovery of texts is ongoing, and because there is a great and growing number of contemporary feminist writers, this volume in no way pretends to be exhaustive in its listing of feminist writers worthy of study.

Doubtless, some readers will notice omissions that seem unthinkable; this author respectfully requests the indulgence of the reader in recognizing that a work of general reference such as this can never be as inclusive as all readers would want. That we are at a place now where one volume can in no measure respond to the great body of work by feminist writers is a tribute to the continuing work of countless writers and scholars who have labored long in the often hostile environment of creation and recovery. The volume is, however, an attempt to continue the important work of validating women writers by providing secondary sources for their study.

Each author entry includes biographical information concerning the author, an extensive summary treatment of at least one of her works, a list of her other major works, internal cross-references, and a list of works cited in the production of the entry. What distinguishes this work from many other volumes addressing feminist literature or literature by women is the interpretative summary. It is this author's hope that the summary will provide sufficient coverage of the work to entice readership of the work and other works by that author. Too long have these works been neglected in favor of more than adequate treatments of works by male authors. In addition to author entries, I have included a number of entries on topics of particular relevance to the study of feminist literature. All the topics entries were researched and written by Lisa R. Williams while she was a graduate student at Washington State University.

The volume focuses in the main on imaginative writers and does not attempt to provide a summary of the primary sources of feminist literary theory. Insofar as some feminist theorists are also practicing creative writers (e.g., Monique Wittig), some discussion of their theoretical works is included.

And now to the problematic term *feminist*. It is a word and an idea greatly misunderstood and much vilified, a concept at the center of the culture wars at the end of the twentieth century. Even within the field of feminist studies and within the larger community of feminists, there is much variation in the understanding of the term. The American feminist movement has, from its beginning, been sometimes guilty of foregrounding the concerns of one class, race, ethnicity, or sexual orientation over the concerns of others. There have been calls for separatism as well as calls for inclusion, but the common denominator in most of the manifestations of feminism is the call for the social, political, and economic equality of women. Though some would maintain, this writer included, that it is possible for men to be feminists, others would suggest that it is impossible for men to enter into the condition of the oppressed fully enough to be feminist. While a full treatment of that discussion does not fall within the purview of this introduction, I will say that all the writers represented in this *Encyclopedia of Feminist Literature* are women. Because this volume is celebrating and focusing on the empowerment of women's voices, and because the writing of men who share feminist sympathies has not had to overcome the obstacles for readership and publication that women's writing historically has had to, I do not include any male writers, even if they avow their feminism.

A necessary corollary to the preceding assertion is that not all women are feminists. Many women raised in a deeply entrenched patriarchy have absorbed the values—spoken and unspoken—of the culture and must make a deliberate attempt to reprogram themselves to the possibilities of having a voice and the power to use it. Furthermore, there are women who are thoroughgoing feminists and live the precepts of the ideology but who, for whatever reasons, would never name themselves feminists.

I have used the following criteria in determining whether a woman writer is also a feminist writer: Does she explore the theme of women's oppression? Does she present characters who challenge traditional gender roles? Does she critique the patriarchy and advocate for the social, political, and economic equality of women?

During the writing of this volume, I have had the able research and bibliographic assistance of Kristi Howe, Brian Ingrassia, Molly Taylor, and Lisa R. Williams. As noted earlier, I am particularly indebted to Lisa Williams for her contribution of a number of entries on topics related to the study of feminist literature. I am thankful for Mary Sheila Bartle, Ann McClellan, Val Perry, and Jami Hemmenway for their collegiality and insightful discussions about the wonderful body of feminist literature. Many thanks to George Butler, who has continued to support the idea of this project at Greenwood Press. And finally, thanks to Nancy Scott, who has always encouraged me in the writing and has never failed to believe that the end was in sight.

ABOLITION

As the abolitionist, or antislavery, movement gained momentum in nineteenth-century America, much of its humanist logic cross-pollinated with the rhetoric of the women's movement. Women and their male supporters, likening the subjugated position of women to that of slaves, argued generally that a country claiming God and liberty as its foundation could in no way justify its treatment of either group. Highly visible abolitionists, such as Frederick Douglass, William Lloyd Garrison, Sojourner Truth, Sarah Margaret Fuller, John Stuart Mill, and Elizabeth Cady Stanton, spoke out in support of the women's movement, adding to both its visibility and its viability.

Of course, white women could hardly align themselves with abolitionists without acknowledging somehow their own roles in the institution of slavery. In trying to bridge this racial gap, women called on their counterparts to recognize the particular abuses leveled against female slaves and accept that, unless they protested such injustices, they too were as guilty of perpetuating inequality as were the men. In some cases, supporters of the women's causes spoke out directly against slavery; Sarah Grimke, for example, wrote that "[t]here is another class of women in this country, to whom I cannot refer, without deepest feelings of shame and sorrow. I allude to our female slaves," though she then added as a sort of disclaimer that

> the colored woman [does not] suffer alone: the moral purity of the white woman is deeply contaminated. In the daily habit of seeing the virtue of her enslaved sister without hesitancy or remorse, she looks upon the crimes of seduction and illicit intercourse without horror, and although not personally involved in the guilt, she loses that value for innocence in her own, as well as the other sex, which is one of the strongest safeguards to virtue.

In other cases, advocates of sexual equality simply—and less presumptuously—incorporated abolitionist arguments in order to strengthen their feminist ones. Sojourner Truth, a woman who had been "forty years a slave and forty years free," knew well the parallels between the institutions of gender- and race-based inequality, and she often invoked their power in her speeches:

> It is a good consolation to know that when we have got this battle once fought we shall not be coming to you [men] any more. You have been having our rights so long, that you think, like a slaveholder, that you own us.

Truth also pointed to the necessity of inclusion of all women, testifying, "I have borne thirteen children, and seen most of them sold off to slavery, and when I cried out with my mother's grief, none but Jesus heard me! And ain't I a woman?"

In some cases, though, the reliance of the women's movement on the arguments of abolitionists simply created more opportunity for the privileging of white women's rights. John Stuart Mill and Harriet Taylor, for example, used the movement's parallels to show that women in England faced subjugation even greater than that of American slaves—an arguably dismissive treatment of abolitionist rhetoric. They wrote that "in some slave codes the slave could, under certain circumstances of ill usage, compel the master to sell him. But no amount of ill usage, without adultery superadded, will in England free a wife from her tormentor." Additionally, much of the early motivation for those participating in the women's movement centered on upper-class concerns, such as property inheritance and voting, which, of course, excluded the less capitalistic concerns of many women of color, particularly those who had been enslaved. The continued elevation of white women's concerns, long a subject of debate within the women's movement, surely has some root in these lopsided analogies.

Although comparing the positions of black women with white women was, of course, problematic because of institutionalized racial inequalities, the two groups certainly did unite in their direct attacks on male dominance. In her well-known work "Woman in the Nineteenth Century," Sarah Margaret Fuller criticizes men who, while fighting for the abolitionist cause, continued to assert their rights to ownership of women:

> As the friend of the negro assumes that one man cannot, by right, hold another in bondage, so should the friend of Woman assume that Man cannot, by right, lay even well-meant restrictions on Woman. If the negro be a soul, if the woman be a soul, apparelled in flesh, to one Master only are they accountable. There is but one law for souls, and if there is to be an interpreter of it, he must come not as a man, or son of man, but as son of God.

Both movements invoked the authority of their God; both pointed to the predominantly male institution of dominance; both called on their audiences to consider the Constitution and its complete lack of support for the enslavement of any person or group. The women's movement benefited greatly from this shared rhetoric and, as a result, gained sufficient momentum to be noted by Elizabeth Cady Stanton as "the greatest revolution the world has ever known."

References and Suggested Readings

Fuller, Sarah Margaret. "Woman in the Nineteenth Century." *The Heath Anthology of American Literature*. Ed. Paul Lauter. Boston: Houghton Mifflin, 1998. 1714–35.

Grimke, Sarah Moore. "Letters on the Equality of the Sexes, and the Condition of Woman." *The Heath Anthology of American Literature*. Ed. Paul Lauter. Boston: Houghton Mifflin, 1998. 2024–31.

Mill, John Stuart, and Harriet Taylor. "From the Subjection of Women." *Feminist Theory: A Reader*. Ed. Wendy Kolmar and Frances Bartkowski. London: Mayfield, 2000. 67–75.

Truth, Sojourner. "Address to the First Annual Meeting of the American Equal Rights Association." *The Heath Anthology of American Literature*. Ed. Paul Lauter. Boston: Houghton Mifflin, 1998. 2051–52.

Wellman, Judith. "Elizabeth Cady Stanton." *The Heath Anthology of American Literature*. Ed. Paul Lauter. Boston: Houghton Mifflin, 1998. 2031–33.

Lisa R. Williams

ALLENDE, ISABEL

Isabel Allende was born in 1942 in Lima, Peru, the daughter of a Chilean diplomat. By 1945, her parents had ended their marriage, and Isabel returned to Chile with her mother and siblings to live for a time with her maternal grandparents who become the models for Esteban and Clara Trueba in her first novel, *The House of the Spirits* (1982). She spent her formative years in Bolivia, Europe, and the Middle East with her mother and diplomat stepfather. Allende began her professional career as a TV journalist and a writer for a feminist magazine, but that career and life were interrupted by the overthrow of the Socialist government run by her uncle Salvador Allende in 1973. Soon after the takeover in Chile, she fled to Venezuela with her family. Allende now lives in California. In addition to her best-known work *The House of the Spirits* (1982), Allende has also written *Of Love and Shadows* (1984), *Eva Luna* (1985), *The Stories of Eva Luna* (1989), *The Infinite Plan* (1991), *Paula* (1994), *Aphrodite* (1997), *Daughter of Fortune* (1999), *Portrait in Sepia* (2001), a young adult novel, *City of the Beasts* (2002), and *My Invented Country: A Nostalgic Journey Through Chile* (2003).

Her first novel, *The House of the Spirits*, is the story of three generations of women and the man around whose life they revolve. Critics were quick to recognize the similarities of the novel to Gabriel García Márquez's *One Hundred Years of Solitude* and its multigenerational Buendía family. *The House of the Spirits* does begin as a tale of magical realism but shifts, as Robert Antoni notes, "from family saga (fantasy), to love story, to political history" (22) as the novel chronicles first Clara's story, then Blanca's, and finally Alba's.

The story opens with the line "Barrabás came to us by sea, the child Clara wrote in her delicate calligraphy" (Allende 1), and fifty years later the narrator—whom we learn is Alba, Clara's granddaughter—uses those journals to "reclaim the past and overcome terrors of [her] own" (1). The narration is also given over to the first person voice of Esteban Trueba. His comfort in perpetuating, and desire to perpetuate, an oppressive patriarchy is obvious from the beginning of his narration, and it is only because of the redemptive love of his granddaughter that the text can bear the intrusion of his voice.

The novel begins with the story of the prominent del Valle family and the political ambitions of the husband and father, Severo. He and his wife are both nominal Catholics attending mass for the potential political returns; Severo hopes to be elected to Congress one day, and Nívea, his wife, wishes to finally realize her lifelong dream—to win enfranchisement for women in her country. For her efforts toward women's equality, she wins the disapproval of the Church and recognition as the "first feminist in the country" (121).

Clara, the youngest del Valle child, is "extremely precocious and had inherited the run-away imagination of all the women in her family on her mother's side" (3–4). She incurs the wrath of the parish priest and a reputation for oddity when on feast day, during a sermon on hell, the child Clara responds to a silence in the Jesuit's dramatic delivery, "Psst! Father Restepo! If that story about hell is a lie, we're all fucked, aren't we. . . ." (7). The rattled priest shouts that Clara is "possessed by the devil!" (7). It is true that Clara has abilities of telekinesis and prophecy, but the family has always viewed them as simply idiosyncratic and assumes that she will outgrow her powers when she comes into her power as a woman, her first menstruation. But her powers do not diminish, and when she is nineteen she has a vision that she will marry Esteban Trueba, the former fiancé of her prematurely deceased sister, Rosa.

Esteban Trueba's path first crossed with the del Valles' when he saw the beautiful Rosa and fell in love with her. Rosa has had no other suitors because "no one felt strong enough to spend his life protecting her from other men's desires" (23–24). Trueba comes from a less than savory father and a mother of good name, and on her connections he secures a loan to go to the hills to mine gold. He works there for years trying to find enough gold to earn Rosa's hand in marriage, but his plan is foiled when Rosa is accidentally poisoned by brandy meant for her politically ambitious father. Trueba is devastated and angry that Rosa slips away from him before he can marry her; rather than go back to the mines where he worked with her image before himself, he goes to the long-neglected family farm, Tres Marías. He immediately establishes himself as *patrón* and becomes a heavy-handed master, raising the standard of living only to the point where his workers are more productive but not ambitious. He "gradually became a savage and began to forget words" and "became very demanding" (54). He works hard all day and takes his evening pleasure by raping young girls in the countryside. He first rapes Pancha Garcia, and soon after she gives birth to his first illegitimate and unacknowledged child, Esteban Garcia. In the years that follow, no young girl is safe; he rapes them all and kills their fathers or brothers who protest.

Only when his mother is dying does Trueba leave his self-constructed world of Tres Marías where he is a law unto himself to return to the city and its mitigating civility. His mother dies soon after his arrival but asks him to marry and bear children of his name. Trueba knows of no other place to look than the del Valle family who once accepted him as a prospective son-in-law, so he visits them to see if they have any other daughters of marriageable age.

Meanwhile, Clara del Valle has had a vision revealing that she will marry Esteban Trueba, though she knows she is not marrying for love. On her nineteenth birthday, Clara speaks for the first time in nine years and announces her marriage. Even in their marriage, Trueba's "habits of rape and whoring" are "very deeply ingrained" (96). Though Trueba wants "Clara to think of nothing but him" and "to be completely dependent" on him, she does not conform to his demands.

Clara has a social conscience that will forever distinguish her and will ultimately separate her and her children from Trueba. When Clara arrives at Tres Marías, she begins an agenda of social improvement at the practical and theoretical levels. She teaches the peasants the alphabet, how to "boil milk, cure diarrhea, and bleach clothes" (105), and how to treat mange and lice. She also repeats for them the slogans she heard her mother shout "when she chained herself to the gates of Congress" (106).

When Trueba sometimes resorts to the rape and whoring of his earlier days, it brings him no lasting pleasure, "particularly since he knew that if he told his wife . . . she would be appalled by his mistreatment of the other woman but not by his infidelity to her" (129). Clara has found her purpose in life, though it will take two more generations to live out her vision and understanding that the people "don't need charity; they need justice" (136).

It is the role of Clara to make clear the path for the next generation to have some social and political influence. Her first child, Blanca, provides the linchpin between both the class and the power structure. As a young child, Blanca forms a friendship with Pedro Tercero Garcia, the son of Esteban's foreman. The two children grow older and more steadily in love. In complete rebellion to her father's wishes, Blanca carries the child of the peasant but is forced to marry an aristocratic hanger-on at her father's hacienda, Count Jean de Satigny. The marriage is one in name only; Satigny has sexual tastes that range well beyond the accepted norm, but he never bothers Blanca and allows others to think that he is the child's father. Alba, the daughter of Pedro Tercero and Blanca, is stronger in will than either her mother or grandmother, and she becomes an active political dissident, waging a war of disruption against her beloved grandfather's Conservative Party and the revolutionary forces that overtake the country.

As Esteban Trueba goes on to accumulate more wealth and political power, Pedro Tercero Garcia becomes the mouthpiece for the people in their political rebellion. When he and Blanca were children, Pedro's grandfather told them the story of the fox and hens. Every night the fox would raid the hen house until finally the hens met the fox at the door one night and pecked him "half to death" (141) so that the fox no longer terrorizes the hens. Pedro Tercero takes the story deep into his heart, puts it to music, and, thus, begins his career as a folk singer and Marxist agitator. When Trueba learns of Pedro Tercero's involvement with his daughter Blanca and that she carries his child, he tries to kill Pedro. In his axe-wielding attempt, Trueba manages only to wound Pedro, chopping off three of his fingers.

The twin sons of Clara and Esteban, Jaime and Nicolás, pale in comparison to the forcefulness of Esteban's character and the multidimensional fullness of Clara and her female descendents. Each son resembles Clara in part; Nicolás has her interest in spiritualism, and Jaime embodies her devotion to social justice. Esteban values neither son, and he ultimately is responsible for their outcomes. Mortified by Nicolás's lifestyle as a spiritual ascetic, Esteban drives him out of the country. And Esteban is complicit in Jaime's death, though he is unaware of it at the time. A Socialist activist, Jaime is killed in the military coup that his father is the first to call for after the election of the Socialist president.

It is in Alba that the seeds of social justice sown by three previous generations of del Valle and Trueba women ripen most fully and yield the bitterest fruit. Alba's great-grandmother rallied for the women's right to vote, her grandmother ministered to the poor and needy, and her mother diverted food to the hungry. When Alba comes of age, the spirit of revolution and counterrevolution are on the land, and her involvement is more dangerous than demonstrating or ministering to the needy. Alba helps the counterrevolutionaries get arms; she smuggles enemies of the new state into embassies; she hides others in her own home. Finally she is captured by the secret police and is questioned, beaten, tortured, raped, and disfigured by Colonel Esteban Garcia, the illegitimate grandson of Esteban Trueba. Garcia is the product of Trueba's rape of Pancha Garcia, and he has always harbored and nurtured a great resentment against Trueba. Preternaturally malevolent (he tries to put nails through the eyes of his own dead grandfather, Pedro Garcia), Garcia vents his anger against Trueba on Alba. It is only through the agency of Tránsito Soto, the prostitute whom Trueba once befriended, that Alba is finally released by Garcia and returned home to her grandfather. Through most of the military coup, Trueba dismisses the stories of torture, murder, and disappearances as so much Communist propaganda. But with Alba's experience, Trueba must reevaluate the conditions under the new government as well as his own behaviors, past and present.

Trueba's love for Alba and her deep love for him finally humanizes him in a way that nothing else could do. By the end of the novel, Trueba has mellowed and he dies in peace. Having survived rape, torture, and a concentration camp, Alba's final struggle is not against the military regime but against her initial desire for vengeance. She begins to question her hatred and says, "It would be very difficult for me to avenge all those who should be avenged, because my revenge would be just another part of the same inexorable rite. I have to break that terrible chain" (432). Not only does Alba carry within her the seeds of reconciliation, she also carries a child in her womb who may be the "daughter of so many rapes or perhaps of Miguel [her lover], but above all, my own daughter" (432). Alba begins the healing by telling the story of her family; the novel ends as it begins with "Barrabás came to us by sea" (433).

References and Suggested Readings

Allende, Isabel. *The House of the Spirits*. 1982. New York: Bantam-Knopf, 1985.
Antoni, Robert. "Parody or Piracy: The Relationship of *The House of Spirits* to *One Hundred Years of Solitude*." *Latin American Literary Review* 16.32 (1988): 16–28.

ALLISON, DOROTHY

Dorothy Allison was born in Greenville, South Carolina, in 1949. She holds a BA degree from Florida Presbyterian College in St. Petersburg and a master's degree in anthropology from the New School for Social Research in New York (Moore 13). Being born poor, white, and Southern has had an impact on Allison, and class issues constitute a major thread in her growing body of work. In her memoir, *Two or Three Things I Know for Sure* (1995), Allison writes, "I was born trash in a land where the people all believe themselves natural aristocrats" (32). Allison also addresses the issues of sexual abuse and lesbianism. Allison's stepfather began abusing her when she was only five, and her mother's silent awareness of the abuse created a complicated web of pain, anger, and betrayal in their relationship. Of her semiautobiographical novel *Bastard Out of Carolina* (1992), Allison says that "in order to write Bone, the character I created, and to write her mother and to write those people, I had to forgive them, and I had to forgive myself, which is the hard thing" (16).

Allison asserts that it is her responsibility and debt to write the stories of her family, of the disenfranchised voices of the Southern "white trash," particularly of its women. In her memoir she writes,

> I am one woman but I carry in my body all the stories I have ever been told, women I have known, women who have taken damage until they tell themselves they can feel no pain at all. (38)

Though Allison wrote steadily for many years for feminist and lesbian audiences, it was not until *Bastard Out of Carolina* in 1992 that she won national acclaim. That book was a National Book Award finalist and won the Bay Area Book Reviewers Award for fiction. Her earlier works include *The Women Who Hate Me* (1983), which was republished in 1991 as *The Women Who Hate Me: Poetry 1980–1990*; *Two or Three Things I Know for Sure* (1995); and *Trash* (1988; revised and reissued in 2002), which won Lambda Literary Awards for Lesbian Fiction and Lesbian Small Press Book. Since her stunning success with *Bastard,* she has had another successful novel in *Cavedweller* (1998), which won the Lambda Literary Award for Fiction.

In *Bastard Out of Carolina*, Allison establishes a strong set of characters and places them in an authentic environment. She creates realistic portrayals of the young narrator Ruth Anne, called Bone, and her loving, brawling, dysfunctional family. The novel opens with the story of Bone's mother's (Anney) quest to get the word *illegitimate* purged from Bone's birth certificate. Her very action causes the townspeople to snicker when they see her coming, laughing at the futility of her embarrassing quest. Later, when the courthouse burns to the ground, Anney sees it as a blessing that the official records are gone.

Anney works as a waitress, cajoling the truckers who pass through, always keeping them at arm's length. When Bone is still a toddler, Anney falls in love with and finally marries Lyle Parsons, a sweet-natured man. She soon is pregnant and almost as soon after widowed when Lyle is killed in an auto crash. Anney is nineteen. After Lyle's death, Glen Waddell, the disappointing son of a locally prominent family, courts Anney. Glen is attracted to her not only because she is young and beautiful but primarily because he knows that he can get his father's attention by marrying into the infamous Boatwright family. Anney is from a large extended family of moonshiners, gamblers, and brawlers. Her beloved brothers spend time in jail, become estranged from their wives, and womanize around the countryside. They are passionate, violent, hard-living men. Earle Boatwright and his two brothers, Beau and Nevil, "had all gone to jail for causing other men serious damage" (12).

While Anney dates Waddell, Bone's Granny says about Glen, "He's always looking at me out the sides of his eyes like some old junkyard dog waiting to steal a bone. And you know Anney's the bone he wants" (37). Bone's remark about the wedding picture of Anney and Glen reveals her natural suspicion of Glen: "The man's image was as flat and empty as a sheet of tin in the sun, throwing back heat and light, but no details—not one clear line of who he really was behind those eyes" (43).

The man "behind those eyes" not only wants Anney but will "steal" Bone as well. When Anney and Glen marry, she is pregnant, and on the night she delivers a stillborn boy, Glen sexually abuses Bone. In her child's brave attempt to not increase her mother's sadness at losing a child, Bone feels she cannot tell what has happened. Bone dwells in the dark cave of secrecy as the family moves often, always seeking a better life where Glen's temper and sullenness will allow him to keep a job and pay the bills. Glen continues to abuse Bone, and when she is ten, he beats her brutally with his belt. Her multiple injuries can no longer be denied, and her mother must confront the truth that Glen is hitting Bone. Anney takes the girls and goes to her sister's house, but after only two weeks, Glen has wooed her back with repentance and promises. Bone heals physically but has an incredulous anger toward her mother who can know of Glen's abuses and still stay with him. She says,

> My shoulder had healed quickly under Mama's patient, watchful care, but I felt as if something inside me would never be all right. I woke up so angry my throat hurt. My teeth felt ground down to the nerves. (118)

Bone reaches out to religion and comes close to "being saved about fourteen times—fourteen Sundays in fourteen different Baptist churches" (151) but cannot cross the line of abandonment to Christ, preferring the "moment of sitting on the line between salvation and damnation with the preacher and the old women pulling bodily at my poor darkened soul" (151). Still she longs for something, "Jesus or God or orange-blossom scent or dark chocolate terror in my throat" (151). She fantasizes about becoming a gospel singer, being on the road, singing with a "family" (142–43). When she flirts with more Pentecostal churches, her mother has her baptized at the local Baptist church, but "Whatever magic Jesus' grace promised, I didn't feel it" (152).

Estranged and at the margins of her world, Bone befriends Shannon Pearl, an albino girl who is tormented by the other kids in school. Through Shannon, Bone gains entrance into the world of gospel music but is disillusioned when she learns that Shannon's father, a gospel agent, won't handle black singers. Her relationship with Shannon ends in a traumatic scene worthy of a fundamentalist hell, fire, and damnation revival. Bone attends a family barbeque at Shannon's home and arrives just in time to see Shannon squirt lighter fluid onto the coals. The can explodes, and Shannon is burned to death. Bone's flirtation with the gospel is over.

Because of the acknowledged tensions between Bone and her stepfather, she is sent to her Aunt Raylene's. Raylene has led an unconventional life, working with the carnival as if she were a man, dressing and acting as a man. Raylene shows an interest in Bone, encourages her, praises her, and gives her meaningful work. "Bone, I'm counting on you to get out there and do things, girl. Make people nervous and make your old aunt glad" (182).

In spite of the family's interventions, none as strong as Bone knows they should be, Daddy Glen continues to abuse Bone. In her helplessness, Bone longs for the power to stop the abusive cycle. She vows,

> If I had a razor, I would surely cut his throat in the dead of the night, then run away
> to live naked and alone in the western hills like someone in a Zane Grey novel.
> All I had to do was grow a little, grow into myself. (208)

But still the abuse escalates until Glen beats her in front of her mother. Anney's brothers exact a punishing revenge that puts Glen in the hospital and gives Anney a chance to move her children to safety. Though on one level she knows better, on another level Bone feels that the breakup of the family is her fault, that she somehow deserved to be beaten. Aunt Raylene assures her that it is not her fault, but Bone is too young to unravel the complicated nest of silence, guilt, and blame. When Anney once again returns to Glen, Bone refuses to accompany her, and it is Raylene who nurtures and counsels Bone.

Raylene tells Bone of her own story and admonishes Bone not to make similar mistakes. Raylene warns Bone:

I made my life, the same way it looks like you're gonna make yours—out of pride and stubbornness and too much anger. You better think hard, Ruth Anne, about what you want and who you're mad at. You better think hard. (263)

Thus begins Bone's slow shift away from Anney to Raylene.

One day, while Bone is at her Aunt Alma's, Daddy Glen drives up and forces his way into the kitchen with Bone. With Alma away from the house and no one to protect Bone, Glen demands that she return to the family. When she refuses, Glen grabs her. Bone realizes, "I had always been afraid to scream, afraid to fight. I had always felt like it was my fault, but now it didn't matter. I didn't care anymore what might happen. I wouldn't hold still anymore" (282). When she resists him, he grows angry, kicks her down, and then rapes her. He yells at her, "You'll keep your mouth shut. You'll do as you're told. You'll tell Anney what I want you to tell her" (285).

The struggle ends when Anney comes into Alma's kitchen and finds Glen on Bone on the floor. In the boiling exchange that follows, Anney is torn between her love for her child and her imprisoning love for Glen. As Anney tries to drive off with Bone, Glen breaks down, saying, "Kill me, Anney. Go on. I can't live without you. I won't. Kill me! Kill me!" (290). Bone realizes that they are at a moment of crisis. Her mother's emotions are being pulled back to Glen; she stoops down and cradles him, and Bone feels that the pendulum has shifted back to Glen in the horrible battle for her mother's love. Bone says, "I'd said I could never hate her, but I hated her now for the way she held him, the way she stood there crying over him. Could she love me and still hold him like that?" (291).

Raylene helps Bone through the difficult interrogations with the sheriff, takes her home, and nurses her. When Anney does come to see Bone, Bone will not speak. Instead, she acknowledges her own new status: "I had lost my mama. She was a stranger, and I was so old my insides had turned to dust and stone" (306). As she leaves, Anney gives Bone a copy of her birth certificate, but one without the stamp of the damning word *illegitimate*. For the present, Bone has lost her mother, but the book ends with the suggestion that Bone will grow in empathy and, with the help of Aunt Raylene, will move into understanding and forgiveness.

References and Suggested Readings

Allison, Dorothy. *Two or Three Things I Know for Sure*. New York: Plume-Penguin, 1995.
"Allison, Dorothy E." *Contemporary Authors: New Revision Series*. Ed. Daniel Jones and John D. Jorgenson. Vol. 66. Detroit: Gale Publishers, 1998.
Bronski, Michael. "Allison, Dorothy (E.)." *Gay and Lesbian Literature*. Ed. Sharon Malinowski. Detroit: St. James Press, 1994.
Moore, Lisa. "Dorothy Allison (1949–)." *Contemporary Lesbian Writers of the United States: A Bio-Bibliographical Critical Sourcebook*. Ed. Sandra Pollack and Denise D. Knight. Westport, CT: Greenwood, 1993. 13–18.

AMAZON

The term Amazon has been appropriated and reappropriated by men and women alike. Of Greek origin, Amazon originally referred to a race of women thought to exist in Scythia and elsewhere who removed one breast in order to be able to more easily maneuver their weapons during battle. The root of the word, *mazos*, literally means "breastless." In contemporary feminist literature, though, Amazon has a more general use: It refers to women who are, in any sense of the phrase, warriors, so that "woman warrior" and Amazon are often used interchangeably.

Women have appropriated the idea of the Amazon when discussing women's strength, independence, and centrality. Maxine Hong Kingston's well-known novel *The Woman Warrior* takes up this image; Kingston writes of her childhood aspiration to become a woman warrior. In the text, she succeeds and eventually becomes a military leader whose "female" distractions, such as menstruation and pregnancy, enhance rather than inhibit her skills: "Marriage and childbirth strengthen the swordswoman, who is not a maid like Joan of Arc," Kingston explains. "The swordswoman and I are not so dissimilar. She fights too, but her words are her weapons. The reporting is the vengeance."

This notion of warring by alternative means, especially through the use of language, can also be identified in the work of Audre Lorde, whom many critics have referred to as a woman warrior in response to both her bold activism and her loss of one breast to cancer. The biographical blurb on one of Lorde's books reads simply, "Audre Lorde—Black lesbian feminist warrior mother poet essayist educator activist—died on November 17, 1992, after a fourteen-year struggle with cancer." This hyphenated descriptor summarizes the role of the Amazonian reference in present-day feminist thought: It indicates the different but interconnected battles in which a modern woman warrior must engage in order to survive.

References and Suggesting Readings

Kingston, Maxine Hong. *The Woman Warrior: Memoirs of a Girlhood among Ghosts.* New York: Knopf, 1976.
Lorde, Audre. *A Burst of Light.* Ithaca, NY: Firebrand Books, 1988.

See also Kingston, Maxine Hong; Lorde, Audre.

Lisa R. Williams

ANDROGYNY

Virginia Woolf mused in *A Room of One's Own* that "[p]erhaps to think, as I had been thinking these two days, of one sex as distinct from the other is an effort. It interferes with the unity of the mind." She then went on to try and imagine a perfect joining of male and female, explaining,

> I went on amateurishly to sketch a plan of the soul so that in each of us two powers preside, one male, one female; and in the man's brain, the man predominates

over the woman, and in the woman's brain, the woman predominates over the man. The normal and comfortable state of being is that when the two live in harmony together, spiritually co-operating.

While this "amateurish" notion of androgyny would revolutionize 1960's feminist thought, it hardly articulated a new concept. Ancient Greek philosopher Aristophanes had postulated the existence of a Man-Woman, made up of both male and female, whose doubled strength led to a human uprising against heaven. Zeus, as punishment, split the attackers down the middle, resulting in man and woman as separate existences forever in search of their other halves. Native American cultures, too, have throughout history defined gender roles in varying ways, often outside the confines of Western notions of what those roles should be, and Jesuit missionaries, baffled by Iroquois men who seemed to at times act or dress like women, coined the term *berdache* to describe these differing interpretations. "Thus, whereas every human society has designations to recognize phenotypic sex characteristics of male and female," writes Beatrice Medicine, "a careful examination of the cultures of native North America reveals a wide variation in gender roles—for example, the *nadle* or *nedleeh* among the Navajos, the Mohave *hwame*, and the Tewa *kwedo*, all of which designate a person who has both male and female spirits within."

In spite of its long history, feminists only gradually reclaimed the concept of androgyny. Carolyn Heilbrun resuscitated the term in 1973 with her seminal work *Toward a Recognition of Androgyny*. She noted,

> Today [in the 1970s], even though we have emerged somewhat from the shadow of Victorianism and Freud's views on women, it is still commonly said that any woman acting apart from her "conventional" role is "masculine." Therefore, it is the more important to perceive that it is in those works where the roles of the male and female protagonist can be reversed without appearing ludicrous or perverted that the androgynous ideal is present.

People struggling within the confines of these gender roles, not previously supported by theories differentiating between sex and gender, found Heilbrun's concept of androgyny empowering, for it could explain the sexual, emotional, or intellectual variations that patriarchal society deemed contradictory. As a result, many women, particularly those invested in middle- and upper-class women's causes, embraced and politicized the notion of androgyny as a way to underpin their "masculine" aspirations. The politicization of androgyny led to an explosion of gender role experimentation in popular culture: *Victor/Victoria* and *Tootsie* hit the stage, and Boy George and Prince began to sell enough music to alarm conservatives who thought such sexual "confusion" damaging.

Many women, too, began to see the political application of androgyny as damaging and responded by debating its worth. After all, both Freud and Lacan had crafted analyses that maintained the oppression of women through the elevation of masculine traits. This debate continues and has even broadened alongside a growing consciousness of the inherent masculinity of language itself. Kari Weil, in response to these conflicts, proposed the use of the term *hermaphrodite* instead, where the male/female union is "forever incomplete, two bodies competing with, rather than completing, each other." This distinction—between competition and completion—continues to shape justifications of "variant" gender combinations, which, in turn, feeds the poststructuralist effort to reevaluate the very concept of gender.

References and Suggested Readings

Heilbrun, Carolyn G. *Toward a Recognition of Androgyny*. New York: Alfred A. Knopf, 1973.

Medicine, Beatrice. "Gender." *Encyclopedia of North American Indians*. Ed. Frederick E. Hoxie. Boston: Houghton Mifflin, 1996. 216–18.

Weil, Kari. *Androgyny and the Denial of Difference*. Charlottesville, VA: University Press of Virginia, 1992.

Woolf, Virginia. *A Room of One's Own*. New York: Harcourt & Brace, 1989.

See also Woolf, Virginia.

Lisa R. Williams

ANGELOU, MAYA

Born Marguerite Johnson in St. Louis, Missouri, in 1928, Angelou was raised in Stamps, Arkansas, by her Grandmother Johnson, affectionately called Momma. Her name "Maya" is the childhood name given to her by her brother, Bailey, in his attempt to say "mine." Her childhood was tragically marked when she was raped by her mother's boyfriend. When she reported the rape and then the boyfriend was killed, presumably by the vigilantism of her uncles, Maya was overwhelmed by the power of language. She responded to the trauma and to her sense of guilt by refusing to speak. During her five years of muteness, Angelou read voraciously and reconciled herself to the beautiful power of language. From that love of language, Angelou has forged a place in American letters and has become perhaps our most visible public poet.

Angelou's range as an artist is noteworthy: She is a poet, playwright, memoirist, actress, singer, and dancer. In her desire for social justice, Angelou has worked in the civil rights movement, serving as the Northern coordinator for the Southern Christian Leadership Conference, and has protested at the United Nations after the assassination of Patrice Lumumba of the Belgian Congo. In her later years, she has taught at many universities and now holds for life the Reynolds Chair at Wake Forest University in North Carolina, an endowed chair that offers her the chance to teach any subject in the field of Humanities.

At the request of her fellow Arkansan, President Bill Clinton, Angelou read "On the Pulse of the Morning" at his first inauguration on January 20, 1993. Continuing in her role as a public poet, Angelou read her "A Brave and Startling

Truth" at the celebration of the fiftieth anniversary of the United Nations on June 26, 1995. Her association with Oprah Winfrey has increased her visibility and has secured her role as the *mater familias* of America's popular literature.

Though Angelou is an important poetic voice, she is most impressive in her autobiographical work. She has said,

> I think I am the only serious writer who has chosen the autobiographical form as the main form to carry my work, my expression. I pray that in each book I am getting closer to finding the mystery of really manipulating and being manipulated by this medium, to pulling it open, stretching it.

Angelou's first autobiography, *I Know Why the Caged Bird Sings* (1969), has certainly secured her a place in the canon of American literature. *Caged Bird* is followed by a series of autobiographies—*Gather Together in My Name* (1974), *Singin' and Swingin' and Gettin' Merry Like Christmas* (1976), *The Heart of a Woman* (1981), and *All God's Children Need Traveling Shoes* (1986).

She has written several volumes of poetry, including *Just Give Me a Cool Drink of Water 'fore I Diiie: The Poetry of Maya Angelou* (1971), *Oh Pray My Wings Are Gonna Fit Me Well* (1975), *And Still I Rise* (1978), *Shaker, Why Don't You Sing?* (1983), *Now Sheba Sings the Song* (1987), *I Shall Not Be Moved* (1990), *The Complete Collected Poems of Maya Angelou* (1994), and *Phenomenal Woman: Four Poems for Women* (1995).

In addition to children's works, drama, and TV screenplays, Angelou has written two volumes of essays, *Wouldn't Take Nothing for My Journey Now* (1993) and *Even the Stars Look Lonesome* (1997). Of her writing, Angleou says, "I speak to the black experience, but am always talking about the human condition—about what we can endure, dream, fail at and still survive."

I Know Why the Caged Bird Sings is the most familiar and beloved of Angelou's autobiographies. As the book opens, Angelou declares, "If growing up is painful for the Southern Black girl, being aware of her displacement is the rust on the razor that threatens the throat. It is an unnecessary insult" (3).

The book is Angelou's testimony of that "unnecessary insult" and her journey beyond the pain and displacement of her beginnings. When Maya and her brother, Bailey, were ages three and four, respectively, they were sent by train from California to Stamps, Arkansas. Their parents divorced and sent the children to be raised by their grandmother, affectionately called "Momma." In Stamps, they experience familial stability, living with their imposing grandmother and their Uncle Willie. Their lives revolve around their grandmother's store, the church, and their love of learning. Both children are bright and love to read. Maya falls in love with Shakespeare, her "first white love" (11).

But in painful counterpoint to their stable family life is their awareness of the burden of being black in a racist land. They suffer the indignities of "learning their place" and the horror of watching even their pious and crippled Uncle Willie hide in fear as the Klan rides through the night. Living as she does in a segregated society, Maya confesses, "I remember never believing that whites were really real" (20). Her childlike ethnocentrism is not altered until her teenage years when she moves to California and experiences there a multicultural environment.

Even though her grandmother provides a nurturing home for them, both Maya and Bailey wonder about their birth parents and try to imagine why they have been abandoned. Bailey is the only family member whom Maya thinks she can safely claim, knowing that she might one day be called for by her parents would have to leave Momma and Uncle Willie. She says, "Of all the needs . . . a lonely child has, the one that must be satisfied, if there is going to be hope and a hope of wholeness, is the unshaking need for an unshakable God. My pretty Black brother was my Kingdom Come" (19).

The day of separation comes when Maya is seven; her father shows up with much "bombastic pressure" (46) and takes the children to St. Louis to be with their mother. There they stay with their Baxter side of the family and live with their mother and her boyfriend, Mr. Freeman. Maya becomes the object of Mr. Freeman's sexual abuse, and he warns her, "If you ever tell anybody what we did, I'll have to kill Bailey" (62). She has never kept a secret from Bailey before, but now fears for his life. The secret creates a distance between her and Bailey, and she spends more and more time away from him, reading at the public library. As she reads, she notices that boys are generally the protagonists and victors in books. They were always good, they always won, and they were always boys. She writes, "I could have developed the first two virtues, but becoming a boy was sure to be difficult, if not impossible" (63).

Maya is only eight years old when Mr. Freeman's abuse escalates to a violent rape. When her mother discovers the rape, Freeman is arrested. Maya is required to testify in court, and though he is convicted, Freeman is released from jail. The next day he is found dead, kicked to death presumably by Maya's uncles. From the trauma of the rape and, more especially, the unexpected outcome of her testimony, Maya escapes into a volitional muteness for five years.

The children return to Stamps, Arkansas, where Maya welcomes the quiet and slow pace of life, though the contrast from the bustling city is remarkable. Maya continues to dwell in silence, talking only to Bailey. Momma enlists the help of Mrs. Bertha Flowers, the "aristocrat of Black Stamps" (77). Maya is awed by Mrs. Flowers and credits her as "the measure of what a human being can be" (78). Mrs. Flowers reminds Maya that "language is man's way of communicating with his fellow man and it is language alone which separates him from the lower animals" (82), and thus begins Maya's fascination with the sounds and meanings of language.

As Maya begins her healing from her St. Louis experience, she develops a deepening appreciation for education and begins to imagine that education can be the American equalizer of race and class. However, at her eighth grade graduation, the white speaker can only praise the blacks who have gone on to become athletic stars and cannot imagine any other role for them. Maya is discouraged and sees that "It was awful to be Negro and have no control over my life" (153). She soon moves to the recognition that the articulators of the dream keep the people alive, that "we survive in exact relationship to the dedication of our poets (include preachers, musicians, and blues singers)" (156). This awareness and challenge enables her to move beyond a debilitating despair and to an attitude of possibility and triumph.

Though the film of racism is always present in the lives of the family, two incidents happen that convince Momma that she should send the children to California to live with their parents. Maya develops a painful toothache, and when Momma takes her to the white dentist in town, he says, "Annie, my policy is I'd rather stick my hand in a dog's mouth than in a nigger's" (160).

Bailey has seen some white men fishing a dead black man out of a pond, and he sees the way in which they treat his body with great disrespect. Bailey is troubled by the incident and becomes "locked in the enigma that young Southern Black boys start to unravel, start to try to unravel, from seven years old to death" (168). Momma hopes to provide an escape from the racist South by sending the children to California.

In California, Maya and Bailey stay with her mother and her new husband and make adjustments to their new surroundings. Maya continues to excel in school and studies dance as well. When she is invited to spend the summer with her father, the California panacea begins to unravel. Always charming and endearing, her father is nonetheless still irresponsible, and Maya's relationship with his girlfriend is less than congenial. Their incompatibilities intensify and end finally in a brawl in which Maya is knifed by her father's girlfriend. Maya leaves her father's home and lives with a group of homeless children in a junkyard for a month before calling her mother to bring her home. The month of homelessness was developmentally significant; Maya says, "The lack of criticism evidenced by our ad hoc community influenced me, and set a tone of tolerance for my life" (216).

For both Maya and Bailey, the summer apart was "youth-shattering" (217). As Maya gave up "some youth for knowledge," (217), Bailey and his "Mother Dear" moved from mutual devotion to a sarcastic antagonism. They had escaped the South, with its tentacles of racism, but even the California sunshine could not protect them from the dangerous passage through adolescence and familial strife.

As Maya continues through her adolescence, she begins to wonder about her sexuality and fears that she is a lesbian. Her mother provides her with information, but she is still not satisfied. She believes that if she is with a man, it will settle the questions of her orientation. She initiates a sexual encounter with a young man, a casual and unemotional exchange. What she doesn't factor in is the risk of pregnancy, and she conceives a child at age sixteen. She graduates from high school and soon after gives birth to her son. *I Know Why the Caged Bird Sings* ends on a note of rest and contentment, but, as Angelou's subsequent memoirs show, her life ahead will be ripe with other adventures and painful lessons.

References and Suggested Readings

Angelou, Maya. *I Know Why the Caged Bird Sings*. 1969. New York: Bantam, 1993.

———. Inteview with Aminatta Forna. "Kicking Ass." *Conversations with Maya Angelou*. Ed. Jeffrey M. Elliot. Jackson: University Press of Mississippi, 1989. 161–64.

———. Inteview with Jackie Kay. "The Maya Character." *Conversations with Maya Angelou*. Ed. Jeffrey M. Elliot. Jackson: University Press of Mississippi, 1989. 194–200.

———. Inteview with Sal Manna. "The West Interview: Maya Angelou." *Conversations with Maya Angelou*. Ed. Jeffrey M. Elliot. Jackson: University Press of Mississippi, 1989. 157–60.

Braxton, Joanne M. "Maya Angelou." *Modern American Women Writers*. Ed. Lea Baechler and A. Walton Litz. New York: Charles Scribner's Sons, 1991.

Sylvester, William. "Angelou, Maya." *Contemporary Poets*. Ed. Tracy Chevalier. 5th ed. Chicago: St. James Press, 1991.

ARNOW, HARRIETTE

Harriette Arnow was born in Wayne County, Kentucky, in 1908 and lived until 1986. A short-story writer, novelist, and social historian, Arnow attended Berea College from 1924 to 1926, taught in one-room school in Southeast Kentucky, and earned a BS degree from the University of Louisville in 1930. She moved to Cincinnati in 1934 and began writing. In 1939, she married Harold B. Arnow, and the couple had two children. They moved to Detroit in 1944, a migration route that is reflected in her most important work, *The Dollmaker* (1954). Arnow conducted research on the Cumberland area and wrote two volumes of social history, *Seedtime on the Cumberland* (1960) and *Flowering of the Cumberland* (1963). Other works include *The Weedkiller's Daughter* (1970) and her last novel, *The Kentucky Trace*, in 1974 (Eckley 1974, 41–42). *Mountain Path* (1936) is a novel that establishes a contrast between the Kentucky hill people of Cal Valley and the outside "civilized" world. According to Eckley, *The Mountain Path* "represents in Southern-mountain fiction a break with the sentimentalism that marked that genre for so long" (54). *Hunter's Horn* (1949), set in the Kentucky hills, is the story of a hunter's obsession and of the desire of the hill people for a better life for their children.

Glenda Hobbs assesses Arnow's contribution to American fiction: "Like Twain and Faulkner, she creates a private world whose inhabitants face dilemmas reaching beyond geographical boundaries." Nowhere do we see these dilemmas any more clearly than in *The Dollmaker*.

Dorothy Lee sees the critical nexus of *The Dollmaker* as the journey from the Edenic Kentucky hills to the urban hell of Detroit. Lee also notes that "[e]ven more agonizing" than the physical realities of the Detroit poverty "are the psychological traumas effected by the pressures toward conformity, mechanization, and competition."

The Dollmaker (1954) is a novel firmly set in the realistic palate of the mid-twentieth century. Gertie Nevels, the main character, who has an art that must constantly be subdued to the needs of her family, is heartbreakingly honest and true. She is a woman shaped by her dream of living in self-sufficiency and provision. The novel opens with a scene that establishes Gertie's doggedness, her capability, and her determination to survive. Her instinct to protect her children is strong. The first encounter with Gertie shows her to be strong beyond belief, resourceful, and able to reach straight into the mouth of death and snatch back her child. Amos is nearly dead from diphtheria, but Gertie's heroic efforts to save him cast her in a supernatural light. We next see her as a child of the land, in tune with the rhythms of the earth and skillful enough to plumb its secrets for nourishment and abundance.

Gertie's desire is to buy a neighboring farm and raise her five children there in a pastoral setting. Her husband, Clovis, is called up for an examination as a prelude to induction to the service and the call to World War II that is raging outside the small Kentucky community where they live in near isolation. But the war is big enough to have reached into their hollow; Gertie's brother, Henley, has been killed, and Clovis has a brother missing in action.

Clovis makes a living hauling coal, sharecropping, and "tinkering" with machinery. He is a skilled and careful worker, but there is no money to be made in the hills. Gertie is the true farmer and husbandman of the land, and she can raise enough food for the family to live comfortably. She has saved a stash of money to fund her dream of buying a neighboring farm. Clovis takes the opportunity of his call to the physical examination to leave the Kentucky hills and go to Detroit where he gets a factory job that suits his talents and mechanical inclinations. He is slow to adapt to the world of union coercions and struggles, though he eventually gets pulled into the vortex of a union clash that leads to violence and murder.

This is a wrenching story of poverty, of the lot of men and women so tied to their gender roles that they are dwarfed as human beings in the process of trying to live out those roles. Gertie is quite capable of earning and saving enough money to buy a farm of her own, but her hidebound mother shrills that she will court hellfire if she steps outside the role of biblical subjection to the husband. Against her better judgment, against her will, and in submission only to the law of a tenuous faith and an unassailable social custom, Gertie leaves her dream of the farm and follows her husband to Detroit where he has gotten a factory job providing materials for the hungry maw of the war machine.

The housing project where they live is a world apart from the fresh air and health of the Kentucky hills. The whole family is thrust into an environment that demands "adjustment" for survival. The teachers at school warn Gertie that her boy Rueben and her youngest girl, Cassie, have not made an attempt to "adjust," and until they do, they will not succeed. The lingua franca of the city is both literally and metaphorically different from what the Nevels family knows in Kentucky; they have truly entered another world.

When Gertie enters the world of Detroit, the unfamiliarity of the city and its way of life quickly suck the confidence out of her. She becomes an uncertain woman living in her strong and manlike frame. But for all her difficulties in adjustment, she quickly forms true and sincere friendships with the women in her "unit" of the project. She defies Mrs. Daly, the strutting ruler of the alley, by standing up for a "gospel" woman; the other women of the alley find in her a true and helpful friend. She is never talkative but is always solid and stalwart in defense of others. Joyce Carol Oates notes that "Gertie Nevels is inarticulate throughout most of this hallucination of her new life, and her only means of expression—her carving—must finally be sacrificed, so that her family can eat" (605).

Once the family arrives in Detroit, they are thrust into a world that is completely foreign to them. They are no longer in the homogeneous culture of white hill people but are confronted with social, economic, racial, and ethnic diversity that is overwhelming. The hills of Kentucky have prepared them in no way for the new rules of this urban landscape; all their skills are useless for their survival in this new land.

Rueben's ability to adapt is diminished by a growing lack of respect for his mother that began before they ever left Kentucky. He watches her knuckle under to her mother and give up her dream of owning the Tipton place. Once they move to Detroit and see the erosion of their self-respect and their inability to forge a decent living, he cannot reconcile his feelings for her. Finally he leaves the family and goes back to Kentucky. Gertie would be better off if she followed his example, and perhaps he is a better side of her own self. He has the same artistic bent that she does, but as a male, he can mark his own way in ways that she cannot.

Gertie stays in Detroit with Clovis and the rest of her children, but the family is pulled deeper into a vortex of poverty and tragedy. Cassie, the youngest daughter, is killed by a train, and her loss is compounded by the unscrupulous dealings of the undertaker who plays upon the family's grief to suck their savings dry. Clovis is caught up with union struggles and comes home in the middle of the night wounded from a fight. Because of a plant strike and of his complicity in the fight, Clovis cannot work. Gertie and the children try to make extra money by selling wooden dolls they fashion at night in their home.

Throughout their trial in Detroit, Gertie has carved on a statue that she alternately views as Christ or Judas. Her Catholic neighbors believe it to be the Virgin Mother. The work is her creative outlet in her otherwise cheerless environment; the statue is her confessor and her accuser, but always it is her confidante. Her work on the statue and the physical presence of the statue itself are a comfort to her.

When Gertie receives a large order for more dolls, she has no wood with which to make them. In a wrenching act of sacrifice, she takes the fine cherry wood statue to the woodlot and has it split into the planks she needs to carve the dolls. The novel ends with this gesture and underscores the painful losses of Gertie's life. Through the poor and impulsive decisions of her husband, through her felt need to submit to his will, through the vicissitudes of life in Detroit tenements, Gertie has lost a child, her own confidence, the respect of her oldest son, the hope of a future for her children, and her own sustaining art.

References and Suggested Readings

Arnow, Harriette. *The Dollmaker*. 1954. New York: Avon, 1972.

Blain, Virginia, Isobel Grundy, and Patricia Clements. "Arnow, Harriette." *The Feminist Companion to Literature in English*. New Haven: Yale University Press, 1990. 31.

Eckley, Wilton. *Harriette Arnow*. Boston: G.K. Hall, 1974.

———. "Arnow, Harriette Simpson." *American National Biography*. Ed. John A. Garraty and Mark C. Carnes. Vol. 1. New York: Oxford University Press, 1999.

Hobbs, Glenda. "Harriette Louisa Simpson Arnow." *American Women Writers: From Colonial Times to the Present*. Ed. Lina Mainiero. Vol. 1. New York: Frederick Ungar, 1979.

Lee, Dorothy H. "Harriette Arnow's *The Dollmaker*: A Journey to Awareness." *Critique: Studies in Modern Fiction* 20.2 (1978): 92–98.

Oates, Joyce Carol. "Joyce Carol Oates on Harriette Arnow's *The Dollmaker*." Afterword. *The Dollmaker*. By Harriette Arnow. New York: Avon, 1972. 601–8.

ATWOOD, MARGARET

Margaret Atwood was born in Ottawa, Ontario, Canada, in 1939. She earned a BA degree from the University of Toronto, and an AM degree from Radcliffe College in 1962. Atwood is a prolific poet, novelist, and short-story writer whose work is imbued with a social conscience. Stocks notes, "Since 1978's *Two-Headed Poems*, Atwood's poetry has increasingly addressed political issues on a national and international level." He also notes that her "involvement with Amnesty International has produced a searing sequence of poems."

Atwood's long list of works includes the following novels: *The Edible Woman* (1969), *Surfacing* (1972), *Lady Oracle* (1976), *Life Before Man* (1979), *Bodily Harm* (1981), *The Handmaid's Tale* (1985), *Cat's Eye* (1988), *The Robber Bride* (1993), *Alias Grace* (1996), and *The Blind Assassin* (2000).

Her volumes of poetry include *The Circle Game* (1964) *The Animals in That Country* (1969), *The Journals of Susanna Moodie* (1970), *Procedures for Underground* (1970), *Power Politics* (1971), *You Are Happy* (1974), *Selected Poems* (1976), *Two-Headed Poems* (1978), *True Stories* (1981), *Interlunar* (1984), *Selected Poems II: Poems Selected and New, 1976–1986* (1986), *Selected Poems 1966–1984* (1990), *Margaret Atwood Poems 1965–1975* (1991), *Morning in the Burned House* (1995), and *Eating Fire: Selected Poems, 1965–1995* (1998). Atwood also publishes criticism and children's books.

Atwood began writing at an early age, starting a novel about an ant when she was only seven. Though she didn't finish the book, she recalls "it started off quite well." That Atwood cast her central character as an ant perhaps owes something to growing up in the Canadian bush where her father worked as an entomologist. Whatever the case, Atwood's early experimentation in writing reveals the first fruits of a talent grown ripe with age and experience. She is a writer struck by language and its function as a shaper and reflector of society. Of the role of language in the creative process, Atwood says,

> I would say that the way we formulate things verbally—that's how we think. We think in images, but we think in words as well. Words are our value markers. The way you formulate something to yourself can be remarkably protective or remarkably destructive. ("Margaret Atwood" 200)

For all the horrors produced in Atwood's fiction—the dystopic view of society in *The Handmaid's Tale*, the corrosive and treacherous relationships in *Surfacing*, the grisly murder in *Alias Grace*—Atwood remains a hopeful writer. She says that "behind every act of writing . . . there is this belief in meaning and this hope that communication is a meaningful human activity" (201). Atwood offers as metaphoric proof of her hopefulness her habit of writing on a slant. "That tells what an optimist I am," she says. "I start at the left and I slant up" (203).

Perhaps the best known and most often taught of Atwood's novels is *The Handmaid's Tale* (1985), the fictional record of a futuristic dystopian society grounded in the symbiotic doctrines of patriarchy and misogyny. The Republic of Gilead is a pseudotheocracy established after the overthrow of the United States government in the late twentieth century. The president is assassinated, the Congress is "machine-gunned," the army declares a state of emergency, and all is "blamed . . . on the Islamic fanatics" (225). The Constitution is "suspended" (225), and in the uncertain weeks that follow, personal and civil rights are quickly eroded. The fear of the people freezes them in inaction, and by the time citizens realize what has happened, the new regime is firmly in place.

The Republic of Gilead is a society of fear; any who do not subscribe to the politics of the oligarchy are suspect, candidates for the Colonies where the presence of toxic wastes ensures a quick and certain death. It is noteworthy that in the misogynistic Gilead, there is a category of "Unwomen," though there is no corresponding category of "Unmen." The patriarchy of the Gileadean society feeds misogyny, and the misogyny sustains the patriarchy.

The society is strictly functionalized and ritualized for all members except the Commanders, those men who are in charge of the government and society. There are the Handmaids who wear red and are reduced to the function of reproduction; they are the "two-legged wombs, that's all: sacred vessels, ambulatory chalices" (176). Those women who have not committed the "treachery" of sterilization nor have been divorced in their former lives are counted acceptable for the role of Handmaid. Offred, the Handmaid narrator, says of her role, "There wasn't a lot of choice but there was some, and this is what I chose" (121). Though all others in the society view them as distasteful, the Handmaids are allowed to exist because they alone are able to help repopulate the country after an environmental disaster and the concomitant drops in fertility that threaten the continuation of their society.

The Aunts are older women in charge of indoctrinating the Handmaids into the party line. They dress in brown and carry electric cattle prods that they use with some delightful sadism on the young women in their charge. The Handmaids hate the Aunts because they have either become true believers in the new order or they are willing to ignore their personal values in return for the benefits bestowed on them by compliance with and participation in the new order. Aunt Lydia is the Aunt in charge of the narrator's training group.

The Marthas are the green-gowned women unable to give birth but who are entrusted with the care and nurture of the highly prized babies born in this culture. In this neobiblical culture, the Marthas are reminiscent of the biblical character Martha, the sister of Lazarus. It was Martha who cooked and cleaned in readiness for the arrival of the guest, Jesus. It was her sister Mary who was the truth seeker, sitting at the feet of Jesus, searching for the divine. It is not surprising that the Republic of Gilead has no Marys. As in all politically repressive regimes, there is no need for any truth other than that of the government's.

Offred is the first Handmaid we meet, and it takes a while to realize that her name is a patronymic of the Commander to whom she is assigned. With the sole function of getting pregnant and bearing children, the Handmaids are forced to wear red clothes, a semiotic reference to their connection with the blood of birthing and the illicitness of sexuality. There is the linguistic suggestion in her name (read "Off red" rather than "Of Fred") that confirms that the character never submits to the indoctrination and brainwashing of the new order.

One of the first actions of the new government is the dissolution of literacy. Certainly the story is about the limits of sexual freedom, but it is more importantly about the freedoms of language and what happens when people are denied the right to literacy. Truly the Word becomes Flesh in this story where the Commander orchestrates forbidden meetings with his Handmaid, not for sex but to play Scrabble. The Republic of Gilead is a place where penis envy is a nonissue and where "Pen Is Envy" is the true longing of women. Offred nearly swoons when the Commander allows her to use his pen to write down a phrase. She remembers that at the Red Center they were warned about the danger of handling such objects and thinks, "And they were right, it is envy. Just holding it is envy. I envy the Commander his pen" (241).

In *The Handmaid's Tale* the narrative belongs to Offred, a character who, before the overthrow of the government, functioned in her multifaceted wholeness. She worked outside of the home and had a husband and a daughter. She had a college life with a best friend, Moira. Her own mother was a single mother who raised the narrator in a home of heightened feminist consciousness. Some of her earliest memories are of the protests and marches in which her mother was involved. She grew up as the recipient of the hard-earned rights that previous generations of women had been denied. Perhaps as a result, she carries her freedoms and privileges a little too lightly. She is unaware of their cost and of their evanescence. She is very much the image of a late-twentieth-century young woman who enjoys but does not guard her freedoms.

In her role as a Handmaid, Offred must submit to a monthly insemination ritual with the Commander and his wife. In her former life, Serena Joy, the wife of the Commander to whom Offred is appointed, was a Tammy Faye Bakker–like TV evangelist. Her message called for traditional gender roles and for woman to only work within the home. The narrator says, "How furious she must be, now that she's been taken at her word" (61).

Serena Joy is humiliated by her childlessness and the need for a handmaid. In the misogynistic Gilead, the failure to provide children is the fault of the women and not the men. Therefore, the presence of Offred in her house is a daily reminder not only that her husband is ritually copulating with the Handmaid but also that she herself has proved to be a failure as a woman.

Each Handmaid is given three postings with Commanders in which to produce a child. Offred is now in her third posting, and if she fails to become pregnant, she will be shipped to the Colonies where radiation sickness will quickly claim her life. It is a measure of Serena Joy's desperation for a child, and the validation that it will bring to her, that she offers to arrange meetings between Offred and Nick, the chauffeur, to increase the possibilities of conception. Though their offense is punishable by death, Offred consents to meet Nick and she even dares to establish a relationship with him. She tells him her name from her life before, a dangerous intimacy she never shares with her readers. Her relationship with Nick restores to her a sense of humanity, and she moves once again to the status of *person* rather than *function*. But her flirtation with the spirit of freedom is short lived, and Offred's narrative ends with the arrival of the black van of the security force. Nick quickly tells her that she will be safe, and she wonders if he is a double agent working as an operative for the resistance force, May Day. She says, "Whether this is my end or a new beginning I have no way of knowing: I have given myself over into the hands of strangers, because it can't be helped" (378).

Through Offred, Atwood spins a chronologically discontinuous narrative, which we learn only at the end, in the "Historical Notes," is reconstructed by late-twenty-second-century scholars. The "Notes" seem to confirm the reader's wish, tantalized by the ambiguous ending of the novel, that Offred does indeed escape the oppression of the Republic of Gilead.

Like so much afterbirth, the historical notes, given at a conference dated 2195, bear the distinct flavor of academic discourse, still flourishing after two centuries. The chair of the conference is Professor Maryann Crescent Moon of the Department of Caucasian Anthropology. Her name and department suggest an ascendancy of Native or aboriginal peoples and presumably the demise of white western hegemonic control, for often those who study others are those who are in power. The name "University of Denay Nunavit," with its origins in Inuit language, is also an Atwoodian play on words and hints at higher education's ostensible purpose of truth seeking, though the rhetoric of the academy is steeped in a certain ironic, dislocated tone that undercuts that purpose.

Atwood's *The Handmaid's Tale* alone would secure her place in the canon, but she continues to write with vigor and a maturity of craft that was recognized by the awarding of the prestigious Booker Prize for her 2000 novel *The Blind Assassin*. Her latest novel, *Oryx and Crake* (2003), ventures into an apocalyptic future of environmental disaster.

References and Suggested Readings

Atwood, Margaret. *The Handmaid's Tale*. New York: Fawcett Crest, 1985.

————. Inteview with Eleanor Wachtel. "Margaret Atwood." *Writers and Company: In Conversation with Eleanor Wachtel*. San Diego: Harcourt Brace, 1993. 190–203.

Stocks, Anthony G. "Atwood, Margaret (Eleanor)." *Contemporary Poets*. Ed. Tracy Chevalier. 5th ed. Chicago: St. James Press, 1991.

AUSTEN, JANE

With one of the most recognized and respected names in English literature, with six volumes still in print after nearly two hundred years, and not having to be recovered into the modern literary canon, Jane Austen presents an anomaly in the field of feminist literature. She was born in 1775, as the seventh of eight children, to the Reverend George and Cassandra Leigh Austen and lived a quiet life with her family. The Austen family enjoyed reading novels in a time when many scorned the genre as frivolous at best or immoral at worst. Jane's writing provided much entertainment in her family circle as her novels were passed around and read aloud within the group. Her brother Henry reports, "She read aloud with very great taste and effect. Her own works, probably, were never heard to so much advantage as from her own mouth; for she partook largely in all the best gifts of the comic muse" (259).

By chronology of production, Austen's six novels fall into two natural groupings: As Brian Southam notes, "*Sense and Sensibility*, *Pride and Prejudice*, and *Northanger Abbey* were begun in the 1790's and were rewritten and revised before their eventual publication; whereas the three later novels—*Mansfield Park*, *Emma*, and *Persuasion*—belong entirely to Jane Austen's years of maturity." The novels reveal a growing perfection of style and restraint, and had not Austen died at the early age of forty-one, doubtless her craft would have only continued to sharpen. What she has left us nonetheless is a body of work that reaches a level of perfection etched, as she says, on "the little bit (two Inches wide) of Ivory on which I work with so fine a Brush."

When her niece Anna writes to Jane Austen requesting suggestions for success in writing, Austen recommends that "3 or 4 Families in a Country Village is the very thing to work on." In another letter to her novel-writing nephew, Edward, Austen comments on the loss of two-and-a-half chapters of his work. She jokingly assures him that she has not "purloined" his work. She says, "What should I do with your strong, manly, spirited Sketches, full of Variety & Glow?" While perhaps she understates the vigor of her own writing, she likewise acknowledges that she has circumscribed a very small world in which she works.

Named in its early drafts *First Impressions*, *Pride and Prejudice* is a much revised work allowed to steep long in Austen's possession before this, her "own darling Child" was published in 1813. Perhaps Austen's most widely read and taught novel, it is greatly admired for its balance and symmetry. The novel opens with one of the most famous of all opening lines, "It is a truth universally acknowledged, that a single man in possession of a good fortune, must be in want of a wife" (3) and establishes at once the intelligent wit and irony of the author. In *Pride and Prejudice*, Austen follows the suggestion that she gives to her niece Anna. She writes of "3 or 4 Families in a Country Village" and centers on the Bennet family and their neighbors, the Lucas family, and visiting members of two other families, Mr. Bingley and his sisters, and Mr. Darcy. Austen sets the plot spinning with the machinations of Mrs. Bennet, who is eager to see her five daughters comfortably settled in the favorable economics of marriage. Both Mr. Bingley and Mr. Darcy are gentlemen of considerable means and are thus seen as viable prospects for marriage.

In most ways, the Bennet family is socially unacceptable to the upper class: Mr. Bennet has a modest income, his property is entailed to a distant male cousin, his wife lacks a measured sensibility, and he is the father of five daughters—all of whom must be provided for financially. Mrs. Bennet is an embarrassment to her husband and most of her children, though to her credit, however lacking in finesse, she *is* engaged in seeking a suitable arrangement for their futures. The eldest Bennet daughter, Jane, is quickly drawn to Mr. Bingley, and he is likewise attracted to her. Both have moderate and tractable personalities, and their initial romance is easily derailed by the interferences of Mr. Darcy. Mr. Darcy is universally disdained by the whole community for his appearance of inordinate pride. Even the sensible Elizabeth Bennet is swayed against him by her infatuation with Mr. Wickham.

As the intricacies of love and courtship would have it, Mr. Wickham and Mr. Darcy have a previous relationship that puts each at odds with the other. Wickham confides to Elizabeth the utter heartlessness of Mr. Darcy toward himself in spite of Darcy's father's will, which was to provide for him. When Wickham shows interest in Elizabeth Bennet and she returns his gaze, Mr. Darcy is determined to quiet all of his growing feelings for her. Meanwhile, Elizabeth has become the center of attention not only for Wickham and the reluctant Darcy but also for Mr. Collins, the distant cousin to whom the Bennet property is entailed, who enters the neighborhood determined to salve his conscience by offering himself in marriage to one of the Bennet girls. His overtures to Elizabeth are simultaneously obsequious and arrogant, and he refuses to accept her determined rejection of his proposals for marriage. Soon the fickle Wickham turns to other pleasures, and finally Mr. Collins shifts his attention from Elizabeth and within days secures a promise of engagement from Charlotte Lucas.

Charlotte presents a study of the times in that, though she has the good sense and active intelligence of Elizabeth, she does not have the strength of character to refuse a proposal of marriage that will pit her against a moral and intellectual unequal. She relinquishes all hopes of her own personal happiness and growth so that she can safely fulfill the only social role—short of spinsterhood—available for women of her day. For her, it is better to be with Mr. Collins in an assured income than to remain alone and independent, draining the circumstances of her parents' home.

By the time Mr. Bingley and his sisters and Mr. Darcy withdraw from the community and return to the city, neither Jane nor Elizabeth is closer to marriage than when their hopes were first raised. Jane goes to London for three months to visit her aunt and uncle and cherishes the thought that she might see Bingley, but her time there passes unnoticed by him. She despairs that the relationship, so warmly begun, has ended.

For the sake of her friendship with Charlotte Lucas Collins, Elizabeth agrees to visit at her new home with the insufferable Mr. Collins. While she is there, Mr. Darcy calls frequently and finally surprises Elizabeth with an ardent though officious offer of marriage. In her refusal, Elizabeth questions Darcy, "why with so evident a design of offending and insulting me, you chose to tell me that you like me against your will, against your reason, and even against your character?" and further berates him for "ruining . . . the happiness of a beloved sister" (126).

While the two elder Bennet sisters have been entangled in the circumlocutions of courtship, Lydia, the youngest Bennet sister, has encouraged all attentions from the visiting regiment of soldiers billeted nearby. Foolhardy and without the moral purity of Jane and the intelligent common sense of Elizabeth, she soon plunges into an ill-advised elopement with Mr. Wickham and sullies her reputation. Furthermore, her impropriety endangers the prospects of all her sisters. Always selfish and impervious to personal responsibility, she endangers the goodwill of her family by refusing to acknowledge her transgression. During their elopement, Lydia lives with Mr. Wickham for weeks without the sanction of marriage.

Mr. Darcy steps in and secretly brokers an agreement with Wickham that secures a marriage between him and Lydia. His actions are not because of his admiration for his childhood friend Wickham but because of his love for Elizabeth. That he secures Lydia's future and protects the reputation of the Bennet family is perhaps selfless, but it also protects his future insofar as he still seeks an alignment with Elizabeth.

Elizabeth has accompanied her aunt and uncle on a trip north, where they tour many estates. When they reach Pemberly, the ancestral Darcy estate, Elizabeth agrees to enter only on the assurance that Mr. Darcy is away. But of course, Mr. Darcy returns early and Elizabeth cannot escape him; thus, their relationship is once more forced into the foreground of the narrative. Mr. Darcy has likewise assured Mr. Bingley that he was in error in discouraging a match with Jane Bennet, and, soon after, Bingley and Jane announce their upcoming marriage.

When Lady Catherine De Bourgh, Darcy's aunt, visits Elizabeth and demands that she promise not to marry her nephew, it is certain that all previous miscommunications and misperceptions will soon be disentangled and these two will indeed marry as well. And so, both Darcy and Elizabeth transcend their *first impressions*, and the "3 or 4 Families in a Country Village" return to equilibrium.

References and Suggested Readings

Austen, Jane. "Letters." *Pride and Prejudice*. Ed. Donald Gray. New York: Norton, 2001.
————. *Pride and Prejudice*. 1813. Ed. Donald Gray. New York: Norton, 2001.

Austen, Henry. "Biographical Notice of the Author." *Pride and Prejudice*. Ed. Donald Gray. New York: Norton, 2001.

Southam, Brian. "Jane Austen." *British Writers, vol. 4*. 1981. *The Scribner's Writers Series*. CD-ROM. Nov. 1998.

See also Woolf, Virginia.

AUSTIN, MARY

Mary Hunter Austin was born in Carlinville, Illinois, in 1868 and graduated from Blackburn College in 1888. Her father and a sister both died while Mary was still young, and those deaths left an imprint on her that asserts itself in her ideology and fiction. After graduation from college, she left Illinois with her family to homestead in the Joaquin Valley of California. In 1891, she married Stafford Wallace Austin; they had a developmentally disabled daughter, Ruth. Their marriage ended in 1914. Austin's writing gained her modest success at home and abroad as a nature writer, playwright, and novelist. She became an advocate for the rights of Native Americans, and long before others were lamenting the lack of recognition of an aboriginal literary art, Austin was calling for its acknowledgment and respect.

The narrator of Austin's *A Woman of Genius* opens the novel by wondering what Pauline Mills, a childhood friend, will think of her life's story. The rhetorical move sets up the expectation that there will be a rupture between the two friends and that the narrator has moved beyond the provinciality of her friend. The narrator first clarifies what she means by *genius*; it is not a personal accomplishment but is rather a gift "[w]holly extraneous, derived, impersonal, flowing through and by" (4). She even goes so far as to describe genius as a kind of violence done to its recipient; it is a "seizure, a possession which overtook [her] unaware, like one of those insidious Oriental disorders which you may never die of, but can never be cured" (4). To be a "woman of genius" then, is to be thrust into a role that takes ownership of one's essential self, to become reconciled to "poverty and heartbreak as essen1tial accompaniments of [the] Gift" (5). What follows in Austin's novel is "the story of struggle between a Genius for Tragic Acting and the daughter of a County Clerk, with the social ideal of Taylorville, Ohianna, for the villain" (4).

Olivia Lattimore is the narrator of the novel; she was self-weaned from mother love early in her childhood, knowing that "the breast, the lap, and the brooding tenderness were the sole prerogative of babies" (12). Because her mother's youth was given over to the birthing, nurturing, and burying of many children, Olivia forever feels the absence of mothering. When she is but twelve, her father is struck and killed by loose scaffolding in a windstorm, and Olivia's notion of a God who gives and takes away capriciously is reinforced. As a woman grown, she feels the loss of a "man's point of view and the appreciable standards which grow out of his relation to the community" (27). Neither does she feel guided by her mother; she says, "though I have often heard my mother spoken of as one of the best women in the world, she was the last to have provided me with a definite pattern of behaviour" (27). Cut adrift from familial influence, suspicious of a god who fills her home with death, and burdened with a gift that is sure to estrange her from her unsophisticated community, Olivia is ripe for rebellion. When she is denied an allowance simply because she is a girl, she recoils with "a kind of horror of the destiny of women," which must "defer and adjust, to maintain the attitude of acquiescence toward opinions and capabilities that had nothing more to recommend them than merely that they were a man's" (44). In later years, when her brother, Forester, inherits a portion of his father's estate, Olivia wonders why she too cannot inherit her portion when she comes of age. Without training or education, Olivia is prepared for no life other than the one expected for her—marriage— even though she senses her lack of calling to the life. She delays marriage as long as possible until a social gaffe forces the issue. She is at a picnic with others of her age when she meets a stranger, Helmeth Garrett. They forge an immediate interest in each other that Helmeth seals with an impetuous kiss. The Taylorville code has been violated by Helmeth's advances, and well-meaning friends and family "repair" the social damage by forcing Olivia into a situation in which she marries the steady and reliable Tommy Bettersworth, even though she feels no strong attachment to him.

Olivia and Tommy Bettersworth move to Higgleston where he takes over as head of the sales department in a clothing store. When Olivia dares broach her mother on the issue of sex, her mother hesitates, "I can't help you. I don't know . . . I never knew myself" (75). With so little preparation and understanding of reproduction and pleasure, Olivia is doomed to a life controlled by her own body and by the desires of her husband. Soon she is pregnant, but after birth, her baby does not thrive, and she comes to know in a new way the sorrow that her own mother experienced in carrying and losing so many babies. An immediate second pregnancy follows, but it ends in miscarriage. Olivia wonders what "does Life care what it dos to the tender bodies of women" (77). In her maternity, she believes that she was "driven away from the usual, and I still believe the happier, destiny of women" (78).

Higgleston proves much the same as Taylorville in its lack of acceptance of women who feel they have a life outside the confines of the home and the devoted attention to their males. Still, Olivia recognizes an intrinsic longing in the inhabitants of Higgleston for something beyond their mundane lives; she says, "I thought of Higgleston as aching for life as I ached, and began to wonder if we mightn't help one another" (88). She offers her services to the annual theatricals of the Public School Library, to great success. Later, when an offer comes to join a dramatic production, Olivia takes the chance without any thought to what the community will view as an abandonment of her marriage duties. On the contrary, she asserts that "I didn't accept the Higglestonian reading of married obligations to mean that my whole time was to be taken up with just living for Tommy" (97). She longs for a "more spacious occupation" (97). Soon, Tommy does need more looking after, for his company closes their Higgleston store, and he is thrown into unemployment until he and a partner decide to buy the business and run it themselves. Now, as the wife of a local business owner, the community standards for Olivia's behavior are heightened, and her absences from home arouse even more suspicions.

Olivia's taste of freedom in her career is soon cut short by the news that her mother has had a stroke and she must return home. Although her mother serves as a negative foil to Olivia, her life becomes instructive for both Olivia and the reader. She is a woman who suffers a constant stream of pregnancies, the loss of several babies, and the loss of her husband at a young age. Though a young woman as she enters her widowhood, there is a tacit community expectation that she will not remarry; rather she must devote her life to her surviving children and to the reshaping of her son into the role of "man of the family," a role that emotionally cripples both of them. She is only fifty-two years old when her life is diminished by the stroke.

Throughout the novel, Austin places her narrator in the position of cultural adversary. Olivia questions why it is the wife's role to follow her husband's career and not the other way around; she questions why the prevailing wisdom of the day cautions a woman not to let her intelligence, vision, and drive eclipse that of her husband's. She wonders why a woman cannot have the usual privilege of a man—to have home, family, and career.

Back home in Higgleston, after her mother's illness called her from the theater, Olivia realizes once again that "the ordering of our four rooms over the store didn't appeal to me as a justification of existence" (126), and she longs for her art and occupation. When another opportunity presents itself, she jumps at the chance, though not without pleading with Tommy to accompany her. Forever cramped by ideas of small town success and propriety, Tommy cannot follow her. In Olivia's absence, Tommy becomes entangled in a romantic relationship with the seamstress in his clothing store, and he holds that it is nothing more than the natural outcome of her absence. Before the broken relationship is resolved, Tommy is drawn into a fight of honor with one of his club members, and his injuries lead to a fatal seizure.

Olivia is now free to follow her art in Chicago, but once there, she finds her abilities weakened by a "corroding poison at the bottom of [her] wound" (151). Though she struggles professionally, and is courted by poverty, Olivia initially finds some nurture in a renewed acquaintance with her childhood friend Pauline Mills. But Pauline's husband has made significant progress up the career ladder, enough to render Pauline increasingly morally smug and critical of Olivia. Their friendship begins to show the stresses of their conflicting social codes.

Olivia returns home at the death of mother, and once again her career is threatened by the social expectations that either she or her sister remain in the family home to be the companion and homemaker for their brother, Forester. "That a woman had any preferred employment beside cushioning life for the males of her family," she says, "had not impinged on the consciousness of Taylorville" (173). Olivia saves herself and her sister, Effie, from this fate by forcing Forester's long dalliance with Lily Jastrow into the marriage he had successfully avoided by reason of his obligations to his mother.

Olivia returns to Chicago where her career is foundering and where she finally asks Pauline Mills directly for financial support. Pauline responds with, "there's a kind of nobility in suffering for your art. It's what gives you your spiritual quality" (183). Brought to the very edges of her morality by the exigencies of food and shelter, Olivia is at the point of accepting alliance and protection from a down-on-his-luck actor when she casts her last hope on a great actor who once recognized her genius and pledged his support should she ever need it. Her desperate attempt pays off, and Olivia earns a profitable contract in New York where her career blossoms. Several highly successful years pass, and on a trip to Europe, Olivia meets once again Helmeth Garrett, the man who stole a kiss in their youth. An engineer with projects around the world, Garrett is a widower with two daughters; he and Olivia are drawn immediately into an emotionally charged relationship. They begin an affair so committed and natural that Olivia writes, "Whatever *you* may think, no god could have escaped the certainty of my being duly married" (240). Still, they plan to marry so that they can provide a home in which his children might be safe from public censure. Ultimately, however, Helmeth cannot reconcile Olivia's career in the theater, with its overtones of moral laxity, to her role as the mother of his children, and the idyllic affair comes to a fractured end.

The implicit ironies in the situation are lost on Helmeth, and the concomitant disappointment Olivia feels is compounded by her last frustrating conversation with her erstwhile friend, Pauline Mills, in which she spills forth her venomous critique of the social code that Pauline not only espouses but also insists all women live by. The novel ends with Olivia receiving a proposal of marriage from Jerry McDermott, her longtime friend and colleague in the theater. By leaving the proposal unanswered, Austin affirms marriage as an option for a woman who would be viewed as "fallen" by society; in the same rhetorical gesture, she suggests that a novel about a woman *can* end without marriage.

Nancy Porter notes that *A Woman of Genius* reveals two themes found in the larger body of her work: "The departure in the personal life from the social and sexual mores of the time and the prominence of work viewed both as self-realization and service to the community" (315). Austin's other fiction includes *The Basket Woman* (1904), *Isidro* (1905), *Santa Lucia* (1908), *Lost Borders* (1909), *The Ford* (1917), *No. 26 Jayne Street* (1920), and *Starry Adventure* (1931). Her nature essays include *The Land of Little Rain* (1903) and *The Flock* (1909).

References and Suggested Readings

Austin, Mary. *A Woman of Genius*. Old Westbury, NY: The Feminist Press, 1985.

Lanigan, Esther F. "Austin, Mary Hunter." *The Oxford Companion to Women's Writing in the United States*. Ed. Cathy N. Davidson and Linda Wagner-Martin. New York: Oxford University Press, 1995.

Porter, Nancy. Afterword. *A Woman of Genius*. By Mary Austin. Old Westbury, NY: The Feminist Press, 1985. 295–21.

AUTOBIOGRAPHY

Autobiography, or the writing of one's own story, springs from various motivations, among them travel, liberal individualism, quests for freedom, religious conversion, and oppositional self-representation. For women, autobiography has served as a necessary means of speaking for themselves against the grain of male-dominated societies that, both historically and even contemporarily, have been the mouthpiece for everyone. These women-authored texts have challenged male versions of history as well as the (male) literary canon that has traditionally devalued the "lower" forms of writing available to women, such as journals, letters, and diaries.

Initially, feminist scholarship explored the differences between men's and women's voices, asserting that "the" woman's voice was distinct and valuable. Authors Gilbert and Gubar, for example, contend that women have an identifiably female power and voice that must express itself either through or against patriarchal expression. As a result, they argue, this voice is not always obvious; it more often becomes a sort of textual undercurrent, so that what may seem on the surface to be a simplistic account of an individual life may also be a bold political assertion about the power of patriarchy.

Women's writing has, for these reasons and others, most often been evaluated separately from that of men by both male and female critics. In 1852, a male critic categorized women's writing as sentimental and observation-based; half a century later, another male critic suggested that women's writing was "self-conscious and didactic." And as recently as 1965, Elaine Showalter notes that men have commented on the "narrow focus" of women's work. In response to these criticisms, four basic justifications have emerged for distinguishing women's writing, according to Showalter: (1) biological, which relies simply on gender; (2) linguistic, which suggests that women have a unique and identifiable way of using language; (3) psychoanalytic, which argues that women write in response to their oppression, which in turn controls the text both consciously and unconsciously; and (4) cultural, which combines all of the other justifications and insists that women's socialization inevitably affects their writing.

Generally, then, women's writing has been discussed as more "fluid" or "spontaneous" than male linear traditions, thereby making it more comfortable in the self-telling genres such as autobiography. But autobiography roots itself in the Euro-American tradition, so when non-European women write autobiography, they are operating within a specific set of expectations that they must either fulfill or defy, and they do not necessarily write in the same way, though male critics have always assumed this to be the case. Generalizations about women's writing have been even further complicated by studies of the ways in which race, class, gender, and sexual orientation intersect to affect individual voices. In their study of autobiographies written by American Indian women, for instance, Bataille and Sands point out that the variable of race greatly affects voice, making it difficult to establish a consistent woman's voice. Unlike the European tradition, tribal traditions do not celebrate individualism:

Such concepts are not the material of autobiography in the Euro-American tradition with its celebration of individuality and originality. Paradoxically, it is the element of individualism in American Indian women's autobiography that is innovative. . . . When the Euro-American tradition is merged with indigenous elements, a unique form of expression results that gives the implicitly contradictory name American Indian autobiography. (4)

Women who write autobiographies bear in general, then, a more complex set of responsibilities: They are responsible to one another as a collective voice that represents female existence, and they are responsible to their individual heritages as well, so that the telling of the self is for women never really just about the self at all.

References and Suggested Readings

Bataille, Gretchen M., and Kathleen Mullen Sands. *American Indian Women Telling Their Lives*. Lincoln, NE: University of Nebraska Press, 1984.

Gilbert, Sandra M., and Susan Gubar. *The Madwoman in the Attic: The Woman Writer and the Nineteenth-Century Literary Imagination*. New Haven: Yale University Press, 1979.

Showalter, Elaine. *A Literature of Their Own: British Women Novelists from Brontë to Lessing*. 2nd ed. Princeton, NJ: Princeton University Press, 1977.

———, ed. *The New Feminist Criticism: Essays on Women, Literature, and Theory*. New York: Pantheon, 1985.

Lisa R. Williams

B

BARNES, DJUNA

Born in New York in 1892, Djuna Barnes, who also wrote under the name of Lydia Steptoe, is one of modernism's most intriguing figures. Her early education was conducted by her father, but she was also educated at the Pratt Institute and Art Student's League of New York. Barnes's unconventional family helped to shape her bohemian life and prepared her for the aesthetic of modernism with its fragmentation and disjunctions. Her parents divorced in 1912, and Djuna began a career in journalism to help support her mother and brothers. She married Courtenay Lemon in 1917 and divorced in 1919.

Barnes left New York in 1920 on assignment to *McCall's* magazine to cover the expatriate scene in Paris, and she lived there for the next twenty years. Contemporaneous with the giants of literary modernism, Barnes was friends with James Joyce, T. S. Eliot, Ezra Pound, and Gertrude Stein.

A novelist, short-story writer, essayist, playwright, and poet, Barnes is best known for her important novel *Nightwood*, though as Noël Riley Fitch suggests, she was "more revered than read." T. S. Eliot wrote the introduction for *Nightwood* and, along with his fellow modernists, values Barnes's fluidity and style and suggests her achievement is "very nearly related to that of Elizabethan tragedy" (xvi). As LeBlanc notes, the early responses to *Nightwood* focus on Barnes's stylistic achievement to the exclusion of its examination of a lesbian relationship.

In a 2000 Modern Library hardcover reissue of *Nightwood*, Dorothy Allison writes a new introduction that brings a feminist and lesbian focus to the novel. She says, "What I wanted when I first read *Nightwood* was a polemic, a manifesto, and a celebration of the lesbian in the demimonde," but she found that "trying to read *Nightwood* as a feminist text was profoundly awkward" (xi). Barnes herself rejected the label "lesbian," but Allison suggests that "*Nightwood* is a feminist novel in the best sense: complex, female-centered, and fearless" (xii).

The autobiographical *Nightwood* (1936) is based on Barnes's relationship with the American sculptor Thelma Wood, with whom she lived for many years. The title is a combination of the netherworld setting of the novel and perhaps the name Thelma Wood. Wood is the prototype for Robin Vote, the novel's main character.

Nightwood is a complicated story of Robin Vote and her several loves. She is "la somnambule," sleepwalking through life. She meets Baron Felix Volkbein, a man whose father stitched together his aristocratic heritage with old art reproductions and a desire for respectability. She marries Felix, accepting him as if her "life held no volition for refusal (43), but she often leaves him alone as she goes out into the night walking. He remains home in helpless concern. With Felix, she has a child, Guido, but she abandons him for Nora Flood.

Robin and Nora stay together for a while, traveling around Europe, so "'haunted' of each other that separation was impossible" (55). In this relationship too, Robin becomes a walker again, leaving Nora for stretches of time. They are together for years, but the rhythm of Robin's wanderings increase, and Robin leaves Nora. Jenny Petherbridge, a widow and survivor of four marriages, "[appropriates] the most passionate love she knows, Nora's for Robin. She was a 'squatter' by instinct" (68). Jenny and Robin sail for America, and Nora is left bereft.

Dr. Matthew O'Connor, a gynecologist of questionable qualifications, becomes a central character in the novel, engaging in lengthy monologues. Nora spends a long night of anguish in the company of Doctor O'Connor, who addresses her depression by endless monologues that whirl around her in the place between wisdom and nonsense. "Dr. Matthew-Mighty-grain-of-salt-Dante-O'Connor" (80) is the character around whom the others make sense of their lives.

The characters would be perfectly at home in the phantasmagoria of Eliot's *Wasteland*. Doctor O'Connor could be James Joyce's Buck Mulligan ratcheted up one more notch. One of his aphorisms is "You beat the liver out of a goose to get a pâté: you pound the muscles of a man's *cardia* to get a philosopher" (87).

The largely plotless novel is more a record of the lives touched and damaged by Robin Vote, the peripatetic lover. Felix decides to leave Paris for Vienna, certain that Robin will not come back to him. Nora knows that she has lost Robin to Jenny when she sees a doll in Jenny's home. Robin has once given her a doll too; she recalls, "when a woman gives [a doll] to a woman, it is the life they cannot have, it is their child, sacred and profane" (142). In America with Jenny, Robin begins wandering again. She finally goes to the area where Nora now lives. This final section of the novel is called "The Possessed," and the name captures Robin's condition. The novel ends with Robin on all fours in a deserted chapel snarling at Nora's dog.

Other works by Barnes include *Ladies Almanack* (1928), *Ryder* (1928), *A Night among the Horses* (1929), and *The Antiphon: A Play* (1958).

References and Suggested Readings

Barnes, Djuna. *Nightwood*. New York: New Directions Books, 1961.

Eliot, T. S. Introduction. *Nightwood*. By Djuna Barnes. New York: New Directions Books, 1961. xi–xvi.

Fitch, Noel Riley. "Djuna Barnes." *The Scribner's Writers Series*. CD-ROM. 1991 ed. New York: Charles Scribner's Sons, 1991. 31–46.

Herring, Phillip. "Barnes, Djuna." *American National Biography*. Ed. John A. Garraty and Mark C. Carnes. Vol. 2. New York: Oxford University Press, 1999.

Le Blanc, Ondine E. "Barnes, Djuna." *Gay and Lesbian Literature*. Ed. Sharon Malinowski. Detroit: St. James Press, 1994.

See also Allison, Dorothy.

BEHN, APHRA

The first professional woman writer in England, Aphra Behn was a member of the middle class, a widow who turned to writing out of financial necessity when other female writers were aristocrats. The facts of her early life are uncertain. Born in 1640 in Kent, Behn spent time in the West Indies during her youth, traveling there with her family when her father was appointed Lieutenant Governor of Surinam. In 1664, she returned to England and was married briefly to a London merchant named Behn, of either Dutch or German background. When her husband died shortly thereafter, probably in the Great Plague of 1665, Behn was thrown upon her own devices. She entered the intelligence service of King Charles II but was never sufficiently paid for her work. In 1668, she was committed to debtors' prison.

This experience led Behn to take an unprecedented step for a woman: She began to write for money. The English theater had reopened in 1660, with women permitted to perform on stage for the first time. Behn created strong, autonomous roles for women, presenting them as complex characters rather than as flat creatures. In 1670, her first play, *The Forc'd Marriage*, was produced on the London stage, launching her on an enormously prolific career as a professional playwright in the 1670s and 1680s. Her plays include *The Rover* (1677), a protofeminist comedy still performed in repertory today, *Sir Patient Fancy* (1678), *The Roundheads* (1681), and *The City Heiress* (1682).

In addition to plays, Behn also composed poetry, some of a frankly erotic nature. In Restoration literary circles, the moral license afforded male writers did not extend to women, and Behn's subject matters created a scandal. Attacked by contemporaries for her literary and sexual daring, she defended herself in the preface to her play *The Lucky Chance* (1686):

> All I ask, is the priviledge for my masculine part the poet in me . . . to tread those successful paths my predecessors have so long thriv'd in, to take those measures that both the ancient and modern writers have set me. . . . If I must not, because of my sex, have this freedom, but that you will usurp all to yourselves: I lay down my quill, and you shall hear no more of me.

As the market for plays dried up, the ever-resourceful Behn turned to prose fiction, publishing *Love Letters between a Nobleman and His Sister* (1684–1686), *The Fair Jilt* (1688), *Agnes de Castro* (1688), and *Oroonoko* (1688). Her best known and most widely read work today, *Oroonoko*, is a passionate protest against the institution of slavery, loosely based on Behn's personal experiences in Surinam. Written some thirty years before what has been regarded widely as the first British novel, Daniel Defoe's *Robinson Crusoe*, Behn's prose fictions helped pioneer the new novel genre, now recognized by many feminist critics as the form in which women finally established a literary voice of their own.

Within a year after the publication of *Oroonoko*, Behn died in poverty and was buried, surprisingly but fittingly, in Westminster Abbey. Although her reputation was obscured and tarnished for centuries, contemporary feminists have heeded Virginia Woolf's eloquent tribute to Behn in *A Room of One's Own*: "All women together ought to let flowers fall upon the tomb of Aphra Behn . . . for it was she who earned them the right to speak their minds."

The Rover remains the best known of Aphra Behn's plays. This Restoration "comedy of intrigue," still performed in repertory today, was first produced for the London stage in 1677. A witty and incisive exploration of seventeenth-century sexual politics, the play's themes are love, sex, marriage, and money—and the relationships among them. Set in Spanish-ruled Naples during Carnival, the play explores the double standard that granted sexual license to men, while women were cast as virgins or whores. Unlike many contemporaneous works, *The Rover* includes a range of strong female characters who act as sexual agents despite these constraints.

As the play opens, the aristocratic and virtuous Florinda and her sister, Hellena, are engaged in an impassioned discussion of love. Florinda is enamored of the English Colonel Belvile, but her father wishes her to marry the "rich old" suitor, Don Vincentio. Florinda vows she will not compromise her soul and obey her father's "unjust commands." The feisty and rebellious Hellena admires her sister's disobedience and reveals her own desire to defy the family's intention that she become a nun. Determined to find a man for herself, she vows: "I'm resolv'd to provide my self this Carnival, if there be e'er a handsom Fellow of my Humour above Ground, tho I ask first." Florinda appeals to her brother, Don Pedro, to intercede with her father to prevent the marriage to Don Vincentio, urging him not to "follow the ill Customs of our Country, and make a Slave of his Sister." Hellena adds: "Is't not enough you make a Nun of me, but you must cast my Sister away too, exposing her to a worse confinement than a religious Life?" Pedro urges Florinda to take advantage of their father's absence by marrying his good friend Don Antonio the next day, thus freeing herself from the onerous marriage to Vincentio. Dissatisfied with Pedro's solution, the sisters decide to outwit their brother and prepare to join the Carnival masquerade (I.i).

Amid the Carnival celebrations, the English cavaliers, or soldiers of fortune, Belvile and Frederick and their friend Ned Blunt, a country gull, meet up with Willmore, the philandering Rover of the play's title. Willmore engages in sexual banter with Hellena, who is disguised as a gypsy for the masquerade, while Florinda passes a letter to Belvile, seeking his help in escaping the forced marriage to Antonio arranged by her brother. As the Carnival revels continue, Ned Blunt is lured away by the prostitute Lucetta, and the other men learn that the famed courtesan Angelica Bianca has arrived in town, offering herself to a lucky man who can pay her price of one thousand crowns a month (I.ii).

As Act II begins, the men argue over the beautiful Angelica, who has placed a portrait of herself outside her house to advertise her availability. Pedro and Antonio propose to resolve their differences in a duel. Antonio then fights Willmore, who desires Angelica although he cannot afford her asking price (II.i). When Angelica emerges from within, Willmore gains entry to her chamber and succeeds in seducing her: "His words go thro me to the very Soul." Angelica asks Willmore if he will pay "the Price I ask," which she explains is "but thy love for mine." Seeing that her mistress is giving away what she had intended to sell, Angelica's serving woman Moretta rails against the "fate of most Whores" (II.ii).

Meanwhile Hellena has fallen madly in love with Willmore, much to the enjoyment of Florinda and their cousin Valeria. Valeria jokes: "thou wilt love this wandring Inconstant till thou find'st thy self hanged about his Neck, and then be as mad to get free again." Florinda wonders how her sister "learnt to love so easily" and compares her own more considered love for Belvile with her sister's rash love at first sight. When Willmore emerges from Angelica's house, he renews his courtship of Hellena, who declares herself "as inconstant as you." Angelica witnesses their banter in a jealous passion. Florinda, still disguised, tests Belvile's faithfulness, and he proves himself constant (III.i).

The country gull Blunt has been lured to Lucetta's house by her pimp Sancho. Together with Lucetta's lover Philippo, they fleece Blunt of all his clothes and possessions (III.ii). Intending to elope, Florinda is awaiting the arrival of Belvile in the garden of her house, when she is assaulted by a drunken Willmore who threatens to rape her—a disturbing eruption of the incipient sexual violence just beneath the play's comic surface. The arrival of Belvile and Frederick interrupts the deed, and the ensuing commotion foils the lovers' plan to escape together (III.iii). Belvile berates Willmore, calling him a "Beast," a "brute," a "senseless Swine," and Willmore protests that he did not recognize Florinda. As Antonio prepares to enter Angelica's house, having paid her asking price to the serving woman Moretta, Willmore challenges and wounds his rival. However, it is Belvile who is arrested (III.iv).

The wounded Antonio arranges Belvile's release from prison so that Belvile can fight the duel against Pedro on his behalf (IV.i). The next scene involves much confusion and intrigue involving disguised identities. Pedro hands Florinda over to Belvile thinking he is Antonio and then takes her back again when he realizes Belvile's true identity. Angelica laments the loss of her "virgin heart" to the false Willmore. Disguised as a man, Hellena finds Willmore with Angelica and, far from being distressed, claims his "unconstant Humour makes me love him." She determines to embarrass Willmore in front of Angelica and together they egg him. After both Willmore and Hellena depart, Angelica feels "this Ague of My Soul/The shivering Fit return" and resolves "to think on a Revenge/on him that sooth'd me thus to my undoing" (IV.ii).

Escaping from her brother, who has confined her to her chamber, Florinda is detained by Ned Blunt, who has resolved to revenge himself on womankind for his humiliation by the prostitute Lucetta. Blunt, soon joined by Frederick, threatens to rape Florinda, again exposing a latent undercurrent of sexual violence in the play. She averts the rape by appealing to Blunt in Belvile's name and offering him a diamond ring. Suspecting her nobility, Frederick states: "'twou'd anger us vilely to be truss'd up for a Rape upon a Maid of Quality, when we only believe we ruffle a Harlot." They lock her away (IV.iii).

In the final act, Don Pedro and the Englishmen arrive and learn of the imprisoned woman. Unaware of her identity, they draw lots to see who will have her. Pedro wins, and the masked Florinda is now pursued by her own brother. Saved by Valeria's arrival, Florinda is finally reunited with Belvile. The marriages of Belvile and Florinda and Frederick and Valeria are hastily arranged. Angelica arrives, brandishing a pistol, and declares her hatred for Willmore, whose inconstancy has destroyed her "fancy'd Power"—her illusion of sexual power over men: "Had I remain'd in innocent Security,/I shou'd have thought all Men were born my Slaves;/and worn my Pow'r like Lightning in my Eyes." Since her "richest Treasure," her "Honour," has already been lost, Angelica is indeed a tragic figure at this moment. Even Willmore seems moved by her fate: "I admire thee strangely/ I wish I were that dull, that constant thing,/Which thou woud'st have, and Nature never meant me." Antonio arrives and disarms Angelica, expressing his adoration for her. Seeing Antonio and Angelica together, Don Pedro is finally reconciled to Florinda and Belvile's marriage, granting his permission after the fact. Willmore invites Hellena to his bed, declaring: "Marriage is as certain a Bane to Love, as lending Money is to Friendship." Not wanting "A Cradle full of Noise and Mischief, with a Pack of Repentance at my Back," Hellena is savvy enough to demand a legal marriage, even though she enters it with open eyes, declaring Willmore and herself to be "of one Humour." Together, the two "inconstant" lovers declare their intention to venture "the Storms o'th' Marriage-Bed." As the play concludes with the resolution of the various marriage plots, Willmore's and Hellena's skepticism about marriage overshadows the more conventional union of the chaste and constant lovers Florinda and Belvile (V.i).

References and Suggested Readings

Behn, Aphra. *The Rover*. 1677. London: Methuen Drama, 1993.

Gilbert, Sandra M., and Susan Gubar, eds. *The Norton Anthology of Literature by Women: The Traditions in English*. 2nd ed. New York: Norton, 1996.

Kester-Shelton, Pamela, ed. *Feminist Writers*. Detroit: St. James, 1996.

Naismith, Bill. "Commentary." *The Rover*. By Aphra Behn. London: Methuen Drama, 1993.

Woolf, Virginia. *A Room of One's Own*. 1929. New York: Harcourt, 1957.

BLIXEN, KAREN

See Dinesen, Isak.

BRONTË, CHARLOTTE

Charlotte Brontë was born on April 21, 1816, in Thornton, Yorkshire, and died in 1855, just one month short of her fortieth birthday. In the space of that time, she suffered the deaths of her four sisters and one brother, all of consumption. Her father was a clergyman in the Church of England and sent his two eldest daughters, Maria and Elizabeth, to the Clergy Daughter's School at Cowan Bridge. Charlotte joined them there later, but both sisters fell ill and returned home to die. Thereafter, Mr. Brontë decided to educate his remaining children at home. In the close-knit remaining family, Charlotte, her two sisters Emily and Anne, and her brother, Branwell, flourished creatively and invented imaginary kingdoms (Angria and Gondal) about which they wrote histories and adventures.

In their adulthood, Charlotte and her two sisters Emily and Anne self-published a volume of poems that did not do well. They used male pseudonyms "to preserve secrecy and to avoid the patronizing treatment they believed critics accorded women." The book sold only two copies.

The sisters each began a novel, and Charlotte's *Jane Eyre* was the first completed and published, to great success. Again the sisters wrote under male pseudonyms. After the success of *Jane Eyre*, Charlotte also wrote *Shirley* (1849) and *Villette* (1853). An earlier novel, *The Professor*, was not published until 1857.

Charlotte Brontë married her father's curate in 1854, but her happiness was cut short when complications of her pregnancy aggravated her condition already weakened by consumption. She died just ten months after her marriage.

Jane Eyre (1847) is Charlotte Brontë's best known work and represents for many the classic Victorian love story, replete with a Byronic hero, a Gothic tale of treachery and attempted murder, and the enduring devotion of a plain but pure governess. But of course, *Jane Eyre* is more than that; it is a novel that simultaneously reflects and subverts the patriarchal paradigm of Victorian England. The novel opens with the stock character of nineteenth-century fiction—the orphan—in place. Young Jane Eyre lives with her Aunt Reed and tyrannical cousins in Gateshead. With all the entitlement of primogeniture, her cousin John Reed denies her use of the books in their library and throws a book at her when she dares defy him. Jane is punished by being locked in the red room, last used for the viewing of her dead uncle's body. Jane is so frightened by the ghost that she sees that the family is compelled to call an apothecary. It is he, Mr. Lloyd, who sets into action the plan that removes Jane from the disagreeable situation of being the dependent and unwanted relative in the Reed household.

Jane is sent to Lowood Institution, partly a charity school, for the education of clergy daughters. The director of the school, Mr. Brocklehurst, is Dickensian in his treatment of the girls and apparently unaware of any Christian discontinuity in his own sumptuous lifestyle. To her new community, he introduces Jane as deceitful and a liar. To her new-found friend, Helen Burns, Jane cries out, "When we are struck at without a reason, we should strike back again very hard; I am sure we should—so hard as to teach the person who struck us never to do it again" (50). The patient, enduring Helen advises Jane to suffer quietly the wrongs against her. But Helen's influence on Jane is short-lived; she dies of consumption shortly thereafter. Helen's character is modeled on Charlotte's sister Maria, to whom she was very close.

Jane continues at Lowood for another eight years—six as a pupil and two more as a teacher. When her only friend and companion, Miss Temple, marries and leaves Lowood, Jane comes to a turning point and recognizes her old self stirring anew now that the quieting influences of Miss Temple are gone. She longs for liberty, or "at least a new servitude," and advertises in the paper that she is looking for employment in a private home teaching children under the age of fourteen (74). Her only response is from a Mrs. Fairfax of Thornfield in Millcote, and Jane accepts a position as governess there.

Jane learns very little of Thornfield, save that its master is most often absent and the house is run by one of his dependent relations, Mrs. Fairfax. Her student is a young French girl, Miss Adela Varens, whose origins are obscure, but who is reportedly the illegitimate daughter of the master, Mr. Rochester.

Early in her stay at Thornfield, Jane hears a maniacal laugh coming from a passageway on the third story of the house. Mrs. Fairfax explains that the noise comes from Grace Poole, a servant. The laugh is "tragic" and "preternatural" as any Jane has ever heard, and when Grace exits, she hardly looks like anyone capable of such a sound.

Though the mysteries of Thornfield do not unravel themselves before Jane, she, now free from the conformity of Lowood, is coming into her own powers of recognition again. In a moment of intense reflection, Jane formulates her personal manifesto on gender:

Women are supposed to be very calm generally: but women feel just as men feel; they need exercise for their faculties and a field for their efforts as much as their brothers do; they suffer from too rigid a restraint, too absolute a stagnation, precisely as men would suffer; and it is narrow-minded in their more privileged fellow-creatures to say that they ought to confine themselves to making puddings and knitting stockings, to playing on the piano and embroidering bags. It is thoughtless to condemn them, or laugh at them, if they seek to do more or learn more than custom has pronounced necessary for their sex. (96)

Some months after Jane arrives at Thornfield, Rochester finally makes an appearance there and begins an unprecedented social life in the community. One night, Jane hears a demonic laugh, smells smoke, and goes to Rochester's room to find his bed engulfed in flames. Rochester blames the fire on Grace Poole, but Jane begins to puzzle out any number of scenarios that might account for such behavior on Grace's part. It is only then that she realizes that she herself has a growing affection for Rochester and that Grace's behavior might be the result of jealousy.

Meanwhile, Rochester goes to a house party and begins an ostensible romance with Blanche Ingram. When the party comes to Thornfield for an extended visit, the apparent relationship blooms into an unannounced engagement. Rochester does everything possible to lead Jane to believe that he will marry Miss Ingram. As Jane's love for Rochester increases, so does her torment. The party is interrupted by the appearance of a Mr. Mason from the West Indies. Rochester is visibly upset by Mason's arrival, and one night, Jane is drawn further into the mystery of the strange sounds emanating from the third story. Rochester calls Jane to help attend to Mason, who has suffered wounds from both a knife and from biting. Mason reports, "She sucked the blood: she said she'd drain my heart" (187). Still, for Jane, the mystery is only further obfuscated and not solved.

Soon after, Jane is beckoned by her Aunt Reed to come to her deathbed. John Reed has gambled away most of the family fortune and has committed suicide. The sisters are now without any dowry, and their marriageability has dramatically diminished. Jane goes to her once haughty relatives, even though, as a child, she shouted to her aunt, "I will never call you aunt again as long as I live. I will never come to see you when I am grown up" (31). Mrs. Reed tells Jane more of her family history—that she (Jane) is to become heir to the fortune of her uncle John Eyre of Madeira. Before Aunt Reed dies, Jane asks her forgiveness.

Once she returns to Thornfield, Jane watches Rochester make plans for his marriage to Miss Ingram. Aware that she can no longer stay in a home that will now have a mother for her young charge, Adele, and where she is painfully assailed by her own feelings for Rochester, Jane announces her intentions to leave Thornfield. It is only then that Rochester asks her to marry him. He reveals that Miss Ingram has only wanted the match with him for his money, and once he spread the rumor that his wealth was diminished, she showed her true colors. Jane and Rochester decide to marry within weeks, and Rochester looks forward to the day when he will "claim [Jane]—[her] thoughts, conversation, and company—for life" (234). Jane, however, insists that she will continue as Adele's governess and will earn her "board and lodging, and thirty pounds a year beside" (237).

One night, before the wedding, while Jane is sleeping, she is awakened by someone in her room. She explains, "It was a discoloured face—it was a savage face. I wish I could forget the roll of the red eyes and the fearful blackened inflation of the lineaments . . . the lips were swelled and dark; the brow furrowed; the black eyebrows widely raised over the bloodshot eyes" (249). Though Rochester tries to convince her that a mere ghost has visited her, Jane displays the veil of the wedding dress, torn in half.

It is not until her wedding day that Jane finally learns the truth about the singular presence in the house. Mr. Briggs, a solicitor from London, interrupts their wedding ceremony when he "declare[s] the existence of an impediment" (254). He claims that Mr. Rochester "has a wife now living" (255) and shows a copy of the wedding certificate. Mr. Mason steps in to witness that the wife, his sister, is still alive. As if to nullify his legal marriage by exhibiting the state of his wife, Rochester takes the wedding party to the third story of his home. There, "What it was, whether beast or human being, one could not, at first sight, tell: it groveled, seemingly, on all fours; it snatched and growled like some strange wild animal: but it was covered with clothing; and a quantity of dark, grizzled hair, wild as a mane, hid its head and face" (258).

Surprisingly, it was Jane's uncle in Madeira who set the wheels turning to prevent Jane from a false marriage. And now, with marriage no longer a possibility, Rochester asks Jane to accompany him to the South of France where they may live as a married couple without public censure. Rochester offers the history of his life as defense for his behaviors. As a second son, he would inherit nothing, and all his future depended on an advantageous match. His father and brother found a match for him in Jamaica that would bring thirty thousand pounds in dowry. They quickly orchestrated the marriage before Rochester could learn that his wife's mother was in a lunatic asylum and that her brother was a "complete dumb idiot" (269). Though he lived with his wife for four years, Rochester cannot stand her and "continued outbreaks of her violent and unreasonable temper" (269). The local doctors declared her mad, and she was shut up. Rochester then took her to England and disposed of her in the third story of Thornfield while he traveled through Europe leading a life of dissolution. He had a series of mistresses—one French, with whom he fathered Adele, one Italian, and one German.

Horrified at his suggestion that they live in bigamy, Jane quickly leaves Thornfield. Without friends or resources, she wanders destitute and alone. She sleeps outside, barters her personal effects for food, begs for work, and even eats food meant for the pigs before she is drawn by a warm light to a cottage at Marsh End. She can go no further and sinks on the doorstep where the local minister saves her. Through a series of coincidences, Jane arrives at the home of her cousins, St. John, Diana, and Mary Rivers. Though Jane gives a pseudonym of Jane Elliott, the truth soon enough emerges. Their common uncle, John Eyre, dies and leaves all his fortune to Jane, which she promptly divides equally among the four cousins. Meanwhile, St. John is preparing for a life as a missionary in India, and he determines that Jane is an appropriate helper for him. St. John proposes marriage, but Jane cannot accept the self-avowed "cold, hard man" (330). Her refusal only encourages him to assert his will upon her; his powerful presence imprisons her and takes away her "liberty of mind" (350). She grows daily more subject to total erasure by him. He tells Jane, "you are formed for labour, not for love. A missionary's wife you must—shall be. You shall be mine: I claim you—not for my pleasure, but for my Sovereign's service" (354).

Still, she resists his pressures but announces that she will accompany him as a sister and not as a wife. "I am ready to go to India, if I may go free" (356). St. John explains that the ties between brother and sister are too "loose"; instead he insists, "I want a wife: the sole helpmeet I can influence efficiently in life and retain absolutely till death" (357). Jane understands St. John to be a man of "hardness and despotism" (358). She realizes that, as his wife, she would be "at his side always, and always restrained, and always checked—forced to keep the fire of [her] nature continually low, to compel it to burn inwardly and never utter a cry" would be "unendurable" (359). When Jane refuses him, St. John treats her so coldly that she realizes "what severe punishment a good yet stern, a conscientious, yet implacable man can inflict on one who has offended him" (361). Jane realizes that if she were to marry him, "this good man, pure as the deep sunless source, could soon kill me: without drawing from my veins a single drop of blood, or receiving on his own crystal conscience the faintest stain of crime" (362). When she tells St. John this, he reprimands her with "Your words are such as ought not to be used: violent, unfeminine, and untrue" (363). Still, Jane is tempted to give into the logic of St. John. Just at that moment, she hears the voice of Rochester cry out to her, "Jane! Jane! Jane!" (369). She breaks away from St. John and affirms, "It was *my* time to assume ascendancy. My powers were in play, and in force" (370). With this affirmation of her own self and her will, Jane breaks free of St. John's despotic grasp.

She leaves Moor House on a journey back to Thornfield and finds upon arrival a blackened ruin. She learns the story of how, after she left, Rochester grew "quite savage on his disappointment" (376) and sent Mrs. Fairfax away with an annuity for life, sent Adele to boarding school, and shut himself up in the house. The lunatic wife set the house on fire and fled to the rooftop where she jumped to her death below. Rochester, hurt in the fire, is now stone-blind and has had a crushed hand amputated. He has gone to Ferndean, a manor house on the property, and lives there in seclusion with the faithful servant Old John and his wife.

Jane goes to him there and perceives in him a humbled man. He has begun to "experience remorse, repentance; the wish for reconcilement to [his] Maker" (393). Their love is rekindled and they marry. Jane goes to the school where Adele is kept and takes her from its repressive environment and places her in a more suitable school. After two years of marriage, Rochester gains some vision back in his one eye—enough to recognize the resemblance of their firstborn to himself.

Elaine Showalter suggests that the characters Helen Burns and Bertha Mason represent extremes of Jane's personality and must be done away with. Helen is "the perfect victim and the representation of the feminine spirit in its most disembodied form" (118). Bertha Mason, she suggests is "the incarnation of the flesh, of female sexuality in its most irredeemably bestial and terrifying form" (118). Both must be "sacrificed to make way for Jane's fuller freedom" (118).

In their signal reference *The Madwoman in the Attic*, Gilbert and Gubar call for a foregrounding of Bertha Rochester in the text, suggesting that she is "Jane's truest and darkest double" (360). Such an interpretative strategy will also challenge the long-held patriarchal reading of the text that suggests Rochester is acting within appropriate social and cultural boundaries when he imprisons his wife in an attic for countless years.

References and Suggested Readings

Alexander, Lynn M. "Elizabeth Gaskell." *An Encyclopedia of British Women Writers*. Ed. Paul Schlueter and June Schlueter. Revised and Expanded ed. New Brunswick, NJ: Rutgers University Press, 1998.

Brontë, Charlotte. *Jane Eyre*. 1947. New York: W. W. Norton, 1987.

Gilbert, Sandra M., and Susan Gubar. *The Madwoman in the Attic: The Woman Writer and the Nineteenth-Century Literary Imagination*. New Haven: Yale University Press, 1979.

Showalter, Elaine. *A Literature of Their Own: British Women Novelists from Brontë to Lessing*. Princeton: Princeton University Press, 1977.

See also Brontë, Emily.

BRONTË, EMILY

Emily Brontë was born in July 1818, the fifth child of Patrick and Maria Branwell Brontë. Brontë was well acquainted with grief and loss early in her life; her mother died when Emily was only three, and her two older sisters, Maria and Elizabeth, both died of tuberculosis in 1825. Brontë's childhood was largely shaped by the imaginative worlds that she and her remaining siblings created. Charlotte and her only brother, Branwell, created a fantasy world—Angria—peopled by characters with distinctive personalities and made manifest with a set of wooden soldiers given to Branwell by their father. When Charlotte left home for Roe Head School, Emily and the youngest, Anne, created their own world, Gondal. The imaginative richness of their mythic world was sufficient to hold their interest for years to come and was the seedbed of Emily's body of poetry. The Gondal poems are intimately connected to the work that was to become *Wuthering Heights* (1847), Brontë's only novel.

Brontë's poetry came to light through the midwifery of her own sister Charlotte. In 1845, Charlotte accidentally found a volume of Emily's verse and encouraged her to seek publication. Charlotte describes the poems as "condensed and terse, vigorous and genuine" and with a "peculiar music—wild, melancholy, and elevating" (315). In time, the three Brontë sisters published their poetry under the "positively masculine" names of Currer, Ellis, and Acton Bell. Charlotte explains, "we had a vague impression that authoresses are liable to be looked on with prejudice; we had noticed how critics sometimes use for their chastisement the weapon of personality, and for their reward, a flattery, which is not true praise" (315). Though the volume of poetry garnered favorable reviews, it sold only two copies. Each of the three sisters next offered the publishing world a novel; Charlotte's *The Professor* was declined, but Anne's *Agnes Grey* and Emily's *Wuthering Heights* were published in 1847.

By 1848, their brother Branwell, wasted by a life of dissolution and addiction, died in the Brontë home of consumption. Emily nursed him until the end but soon after his death became ill herself and within two months was dead on December 19, 1848.

As Stevie Davis points out, the date 1801 opens the novel *Wuthering Heights* (104). Davis notes that "the will to order, whether in the practicalities of housework or the making of a poem or novel, was uniquely strong" in Brontë (49). The "will to order" is easily recognizable in the chronology of the novel and the particular attention to atmospheric conditions of the moors. Considerable scholarly attention has been given to Brontë's precision in these matters.

In opening the novel, Brontë employs the use of an outsider narrator, Mr. Lockwood, who comes to the moors to escape his own troubles only to enter into a saga rich with mysterious origins, complicated relationships, and inexplicable behaviors. The use of Lockwood as narrator places the reader at a double advantage, for she is both instructed through his questionings and is able to decry his arrogance and intrusive actions. Lockwood comes to the area seeking a place to stay and a place to hide from his previous indiscretions. Mr. Lockwood immediately imposes himself upon his landlord, Heathcliff, and insinuates himself into Heathcliff's reluctant hospitality at Wuthering Heights when a snowstorm makes his return home too difficult to attempt. He spends the night at Wuthering Heights in the enclosed chamber bed that had previously belonged to Catherine Earnshaw. Lockwood is immediately drawn to the windowsill where he finds three names—Catherine Earnshaw, Catherine Heathcliff, and Catherine Linton—carved into the wood and a collection of books that have served as the diary for the young Catherine Earnshaw. Lockwood falls asleep and succumbs to a frightening dream of the "waif" Catherine Linton clinging to him and begging for admittance to the room. His own screams awaken him, and Heathcliff rushes to the room in anticipation that Catherine has returned. When Lockwood returns home, he questions the housekeeper, Mrs. Dean, about the inhabitants of the Heights, and she is willing to relate the story of the Earnshaw family.

Of Catherine she says: "She was much too fond of Heathcliff. The greatest punishment we could invent for her was to keep her separate from him" (Brontë 33).

While on a trip to Liverpool, Mr. Earnshaw encounters a "dirty, ragged, black-haired child" (29) whom he brings home to become a sibling to Catherine and her elder brother Hindley. The child is called "Heathcliff," in memory of an earlier Earnshaw child who died young. Over a course of years, both Mr. and Mrs. Earnshaw die, leaving the children orphans. Hindley returns home for his father's funeral with a wife. Heathcliff and Cathy have the run of the moors, become as wild children, ever increasing the passions of Hindley against them. They visit the neighboring Thrushcross Grange one evening to spy on the Linton children, Isabella and Edgar. A dog seizes hold of Cathy's ankle, and she stays there for her recovery, only to return with "manners much improved" (40).

Heathcliff is a dark, gypsylike child and is aware of the favor bestowed on the fairer Edgar Linton, "I wish I had light hair and a fair skin, and was dressed and behaved as well, and had a chance of being as rich as he will be!" (44). Animosity between the two boys, cut of such different cloth, only grows and festers as Cathy takes Edgar's side in a disagreement. When Hindley's wife dies soon after the birth of their child, Hareton, and Hindley descends into a surly and solitary mourning, the rudderless household is ripe for discord and disorder. Hindley lets his pain and anger fall on the usurping sibling, Heathcliff.

As the principal characters move toward young adulthood, pragmatic Catherine imagines that a marriage to Edgar Linton will secure her position and will enable her to maintain her intense friendship with Heathcliff. She asserts, "if I marry Linton, I can aid Heathcliff to rise, and place him out of my brother's power" (63). Heathcliff overhears just enough of Catherine's plan to believe that she is rejecting him thoroughly, and he leaves in the midst of a stormy night. He does not return, and the splitting of a tree during the storm indicates the violent rupture in his relationship with Catherine.

Catherine is so anguished by Heathcliff's disappearance that she falls dangerously ill; the Lintons come to her aid in her convalescence, but both parents "took the fever, and died within a few days of each other" (69). As is a pattern in the novel, once again, parents die quickly, leaving their tender and inexperienced offspring without the maturity and emotional resources to chart the treacherous course of adulthood.

Though Ellen (Nelly) Dean counsels Catherine against her headstrong plan to marry Linton, she nonetheless marries him and moves from the Heights to Thrushcross Grange to become mistress of that household. Ellen is forced to accompany her and to leave the now five-year-old Hareton in the care of his increasingly dissolute father. The joining of the Earnshaw and Linton households enjoys a static calm during its first year until Heathcliff returns from his lengthy absence.

The Heathcliff's return sets into motion the next wave of narrative events. Catherine remains emotionally connected to him, Linton grows increasingly jealous of him, and Isabella falls in love with him. Heathcliff soon comes into possession of Wuthering Heights when he wins it in a card game from the profligate Hindley. Though Edgar and Heathcliff become mortal enemies and Catherine objects strenuously to Isabella's infatuation, Isabella persists in lavishing her love on the scornful Heathcliff. Not even when Heathcliff hangs Isabella's dog, clearly indicating his violence and lack of compassion, does she relent in her passion toward him. Isabella and Heathcliff elope, and after six weeks, Edgar receives a note announcing their marriage and revealing that Isabella immediately recognized her mistake in aligning herself with Heathcliff. When Heathcliff and Isabella return to the Heights, Edgar refuses to see them, and Heathcliff treats Isabella with unmerciful disdain. Meanwhile, tended by the solicitous Edgar, Catherine languishes in poor health and in the effects of her pregnancy.

When Catherine gives birth to the second Catherine and dies two hours later, Heathcliff's reaction is one of great emotional violence. He challenges her to haunt him, to "Be with me always—take any form—drive me mad! Only *do* not leave me in this abyss, where I cannot find you! . . . I *cannot* live without my life! I *cannot* live without my soul!" (129). Catherine, too, has sworn that she will not rest in death until Heathcliff is with her.

Isabella visits Ellen Dean, and in a display of her unhappiness, she casts her wedding ring from her into the fire. She exclaims, "I've recovered from my first desire to be killed by him. I'd rather he'd kill himself! He has extinguished my love effectually, and so I'm at my ease" (133). Isabella flees Wuthering Heights and makes a new home in London where she delivers an "ailing, peevish creature" a few months after her escape. She never again returns to the Heights but dies in London when her son Linton is twelve years old. When she breaks with the abusive Heathcliff and takes up independent residence in London, Isabella also breaks from the mold of Victorian expectations.

Just six months after the death of his sister, Hindley dies of dissipation when he is only twenty-seven years old, and the whole of the property now belongs to Heathcliff. Hareton is reduced to a "state of complete dependence on his father's inveterate enemy" (145).

As the second Catherine grows, she develops a growing interest in what lies beyond Thrushcross Grange, and it is inevitable that she meets up with Heathcliff on one of her ramblings. She is sixteen, and in her, Heathcliff sees one more opportunity to seal his fortunes by arranging a marriage between her and his son. Though Catherine is forbidden to see Linton, they arrange a correspondence through the servants. Heathcliff finally uses the stratagem of imprisonment to secure Catherine's acceptance of Linton as her husband. Ellen Dean too is kidnapped and held for five days to keep Heathcliff's machinations free from interference. Upon her release, Ellen learns that Linton and Catherine have married and that Linton is treating her unkindly. As these events have transpired, Edgar Linton lies dangerously near death. With considerable effort, Catherine manages to leave Wuthering Heights and make her way to her father's deathbed. With the death of Edgar Linton, Heathcliff secures two of his consuming wishes: to place himself in the position of sole inheritor of all the Linton estate in the event of his own son's death and to achieve access to the grave of Catherine Earnshaw Linton.

When Edgar Linton's grave is being dug, Heathcliff bribes the sexton to open Catherine's coffin so that he might look upon her once again. He also has one side of her coffin opened so that when he himself dies, he will be placed next to her.

For Heathcliff's purposes, Edgar Linton dies none too soon. His own son, Linton Heathcliff, stands to inherit all of the Linton property if only he can outlive his father-in-law. Always weak and ill of health, Linton Heathcliff dies shortly after Edgar Linton. Catherine says, "He's safe, and I'm free" (223). However, her legal position is far more precarious because Linton was "threatened, or coaxed" into bequeathing "the whole of his, and what had been her, moveable property to his father" (223).

When Nelly Dean finishes the whole of her narrative, Lockwood visits Wuthering Heights for a final visit before leaving the country. Some months later, he happens to be once again in the neighborhood and drops by to settle arrangements with his landlord. What he finds is a remarkable change from his last visit. Catherine and Hareton are engaging in delightful play as she teaches him to read. Lockwood is surprised by both the presence there of Nelly Dean and her news of Heathcliff's death, hastened by his maniacal longing for the first Catherine.

Hareton and Catherine make plans to marry, now that they are free of the oppressive hold on their lands and very persons. Though neighborhood rumors suggest that Heathcliff and a woman travel the moors, Lockwood visits the three
graves on the hillside and imagines quiet "slumbers for the sleepers in that quiet
earth" (256).

References and Suggested Readings

Alexander, Lynn M. "Emily Brontë." *An Encyclopedia of British Women Writers*. Ed. Paul
        Schlueter and June Schlueter. Revised and Expanded ed. New Brunswick, NJ:
        Rutgers University Press, 1998.
Brontë, Charlotte. "Biographical Notice of Ellis and Acton Bell." 1850. *Wuthering Heights*.
        Ed. William M. Sale, Jr. and Richard J. Dunn. New York: W. W. Norton, 1990.
Brontë, Emily. *Wuthering Heights*. 1847. New York: W. W. Norton, 1990.
Davies, Stevie. *Emily Brontë, The Artist as a Free Woman*. Manchester: Carcenet, 1983.

See also Brontë, Charlotte; Woolf, Virginia.

BROWN, RITA MAE

Born in 1944 in rural Pennsylvania, Rita Mae Brown was adopted by working-
class parents, Ralph and Julia Ellen Brown. The family moved to Fort Lauderdale
when Rita Mae was just eleven, and in Florida, Brown excelled as a student and
earned a scholarship to the University of Florida. Brown's involvement in the Civil
Rights movement gained her enemies at the University of Florida; as Ladd notes,
an altercation with the dean of women ended with Brown accused of "seducing
the president of the Tri Delts and numerous other female women, as well as sleeping with black men *and* black women" (69). Brown soon left Florida for New York
where she enrolled at New York University and received a BA degree in 1968;
she earned a PhD degree in political science at the Institute for Policy Studies in
1973. Brown's early works include a volume of poetry, *The Hand That Cradles the
Rock* (1971), and a volume of political essays, *A Plain Brown Wrapper* (1976). It
is her 1973 novel *Rubyfruit Jungle*, however, that has secured her a continuing
critical and popular attention. Initially published by a small feminist house, Daughters Press, the novel was reissued by Bantam Books in 1977 and has obtained a
significant following. The success of this unapologetically lesbian novel has labeled Brown as a lesbian writer, a category she rejects as narrow and fraught with
an insidious sexism. She says, "Next time anybody calls me a lesbian writer I'm
going to knock their teeth in. I'm a writer and I'm a woman and I'm from the
South and I'm alive, and that is that."

Rita Mae Brown's largely autobiographical *Rubyfruit Jungle* (1973) is the com-
ing-of-age story of young Molly Bolt, who embodies the suggestion in her last name
and does bolt from both the expectations placed on her gender and from her in-
tolerant mother. Carrie Bolt, her mother, embodies yet another meaning of the
word *bolt*, for she carries a "bolt" that she hurls at Molly time and again—the
weapon is that Molly is illegitimate. When Molly is only seven, her mother first

taunts her with the information that she is "Ruby Drollinger's bastard" (7). Molly responds with her characteristic spunk, "I don't care. It makes no difference where I came from. I'm here, ain't?" (7). The attitude reveals Molly's continuing approach to life; her past, with all its shadows, will not overcome her present and future or the expectations that she places on them.

Brown divides the novel into four sections; Part I is devoted to the formation of Molly's identity and her growing awareness of the confining roles of gender. When playing doctor with a neighbor girl, Cheryl Spiegelglass, Molly wants to be the doctor. Cheryl echoes the community-held values when she replies, "Only boys can be doctors. It doesn't matter about brains, brains don't count. What counts is whether you're a boy or a girl" (31). Her cousin Leroy also warns Molly of the dangers of wishing for too much: "You're headin' for a hard life. You say you're gonna be a doctor or something great. Then you say you ain't gettin' married. You have to do some of the things everybody does or people don't like you" (36).

Though Molly's father insists that she should get a college education, Carrie Bolt holds tight to traditional gender roles and complains, "[Molly] don't want to learn none of the things she has to know to get a husband. Smart as she is, a woman can't get on in this world without a husband. We can't be sending no girl to school as it is" (39).

Not only is Molly learning of the confining roles placed on women in her culture, she is increasingly aware that she differs from the pattern in more significant ways. In sixth grade, Molly falls in love with Leota B. Bisland and wonders if a girl can marry a girl. They begin to visit the woods after school where they can kiss one another in privacy. About the time the physical relationship starts to be filled with more yearning and questionings, Molly is told by her family that they will move to Florida. She spends the night at Leota's house before going, and the two move beyond kissing to a fully sexual experience. Molly's first lesbian experience confirms what she has already intuitively known about her sexual orientation.

In the second section of the novel, Molly is introduced to yet another social pathology that she dares to question. On the drive south from Pennsylvania to Florida, Molly inadvertently enters a "colored" restroom. Carrie scolds her, "My God! if you ain't enough trouble now you want to go be a nigger," and warns her not to mix with "the wrong kind" (55). Molly responds to her mother's reproach with, "I ain't staying away from people because they look different" (59).

Once Molly enters school in Florida, she also begins to learn about class divisions and is aware that "[b]ack in the Hollow we were all the same. Maybe Cheryl Spiegelglass had a little more, but the gap didn't seem so wide. Here it was a distance line drawn between two camps" (61). Molly is determined to survive in the situation and recognizes that intelligence is an equalizer of sorts. She works on her grammar, abandons the dialect of her home language, buys fewer but better clothes, and develops a sense of humor to win friends.

Meanwhile, by eighth grade, her cousin Leroy, with whom she has always been close, says, "You know, I think you're a queer" (63). His accusation, though intuitively correct, is born of his own confusion about his sexual orientation. His definition of gender is contingent on differences in cultural roles, and he questions the tomboyish Molly, "I mean how do I know how to act if you act the same way?" (63). He confesses that he has been in a sexual relationship with Craig, an older guy at the filling station. Though Molly is frustrated with Leroy because of his need to "label everything" (76), she consents to have sex with him to see if he can gather any enthusiasm for a real sexual experience with a girl, his only other experience having been with a prostitute. The cousins grow apart emotionally through their high school years but continue to have occasional sex until Leroy gets a girlfriend and becomes "very righteous in his heterosexuality" (72).

Molly is elected student council president and belongs to the inside clique of school stars. She and her two best friends, Carolyn and Connie, all date football players but view them simply as "a convenience, something you had to wear when you went to school functions, like a bra" (99). Their friendship is complicated when Molly and Carolyn become lovers and Connie becomes jealous of the time they spend together. Though Molly's relationship with Carolyn cannot endure the stress, Molly recognizes in Carolyn and Connie two types of women she will encounter again and again. Carolyn, even though she has another woman lover and makes love to Molly, cannot abide the thought that she may be a lesbian. Certain that "[l]esbians look like men and are ugly," Carolyn insists that she and Molly "just love each other, that's all" (104). Connie recognizes but cannot move past her prejudice, and so ends her friendship with Molly. She explains, "I'll think about it every time I see you. I'll be nervous and wonder if you're going to rape me or something" (108).

Disgusted with the petty politics of high school, Molly chafes to move on but correctly imagines that college will only offer the same kind of experience. She accepts a full scholarship to the University of Florida but soon encounters the same prejudices and narrow-mindedness there that she experienced in high school. She and her roommate, Faye, become lovers but are soon shunned by the other women on their floor and by Faye's sorority sisters. Their behavior is treated as a discipline problem, and Molly is sent to the dean of women who sends her to the university hospital for psychiatric treatment. She plays the game with them until she is released, but she soon learns that her scholarships have been revoked on moral grounds, and she leaves the campus and her "last scrap of innocence" behind (131).

In Part III of the novel, Molly returns home to find that her mother is no more sympathetic than before; she is disgusted by Molly's sexual orientation and throws her out of the house. Molly leaves Florida for New York, where "there are so many queers . . . one more wouldn't rock the boat" (136). Still, she enters the city with a certain naïveté; when she is approached at a lesbian bar and asked if she is butch or femme, Molly is at first clueless and then astonished, "What's the point of being a lesbian if a woman is going to look and act like an imitation man?" (147).

After a few days of homelessness, Molly gets a job at a restaurant and meets Holly, a black middle-class woman from Illinois and the kept woman of an older actress. Holly's connections open up a similar possibility for Molly. Though enticed by the offer of living expenses and her NYU film school tuition, Molly rejects the offer, and in doing so realizes the influence of her mother, Carrie, who, though poor, is too proud to accept "welfare or anything, not even from the church" (168). Energized by her principled stand, Molly goes to NYU and wins a tuition scholarship. Holly cannot understand Molly's determination and, in fact, feels accused by Molly's decision. Part III of the novel ends with the breakup of their friendship.

The final section of the novel finds Molly working for Silver Publishing Company where she moves up from the typist pool to become an editor's assistant. Her advancement generates animosity in the office and, as is not unusual, Molly has trouble establishing relationships with women unless they are sexual. Her behaviors toward Rhea, another office worker, mirror the pranks she pulled against her adversaries in elementary school.

Molly does begin another relationship, this time with an author on whose book she is working. Polina Bellantoni is forty-one, a married art historian with a sixteen-year-old daughter. Before long, Molly and Polina are lovers, though Molly is disturbed by Polina's need to fantasize about men in public restrooms while they make love. Molly comes to an understanding of Polina's fantasy when she seduces Polina's male lover, Paul, and finds he fantasizes in a similar way. Meanwhile, Molly and Polina's daughter, Alice, become lovers, and the friendships begin to feel the strain of multiple deceits. Once all parties are aware of the web of relationships, Polina curtly dismisses Molly from the family.

To gain some perspective, Molly takes a trip back to the Pennsylvania town where she grew up. She looks up Leota B. Bisland, her first love, and finds her aged and haggard with "two brats hanging on her like possums" (216). It is clear from their short and strained visit that Leota has succumbed to the expectations of her community; she marries right out of high school, has two kids, and has avocado wall-to-wall carpeting. She urges Molly to marry and settle down and grows defensive when Molly says she will never marry. When she suggests that Molly is a "sickie" for her sexual preference, Molly decides that it is time to leave and go back to New York where she can be "more than a breeder of the next generation" (221).

Back in New York, Molly enters her senior year and begins her senior film project at NYU. As the only woman in the class, she struggles to get equipment time from a class of men who resent her presence. She finally "kidnaps" the equipment and takes a bus to Florida where she wants to capture "a twenty-minute documentary of one woman's life" (222). The time she spends with her mother in filming finally yields an initial but incomplete resolution to their lifelong animosity. Carrie reveals the secrets of her past that shaped her into the hardened woman Molly knew. Molly learns that Carrie had a first marriage and divorced her husband because of abuse. She then married Carl, who though loving, cheated on her and contracted syphilis. As a result they could never have children, and they adopted Molly to ease some of the pain of their relationship. Carrie never forgives Molly for not being her own birth child, however, and takes her pain out on the child. Now as an old woman, widowed and alone, she pleads with Molly, "Don't hate me, honey, don't hate me" (241). Molly comes away with a clarifying vision of who her mother is and loves her in spite of it. She acknowledges, "Even when I hated her, I loved her" (242).

Molly returns to New York with her film, a new understanding of her mother, and even information about her natural father. She graduates from film school *summa cum laude* and Phi Beta Kappa but still doesn't get a job in the film industry. The barriers of class and gender bar her from employment but not from her determination, "One way or another I'll make those movies and I don't feel like having to fight until I'm fifty. But if it does take that long then watch out world because I'm going to be the hottest fifty-year-old this side of the Mississippi" (246).

References and Suggested Readings

Boyle, Sharon D. "Rita Mae Brown (1944–)." *Contemporary Lesbian Writers of the United States.* Ed. Sandra Pollack and Denise D. Knight. Westport, CT: Greenwood Press, 1993.

Brown, Rita Mae. *Rubyfruit Jungle.* 1973. New York: Bantam, 1977.

Holt, Patricia. "*Publishers Weekly* Interviews Rita Mae Brown." *Publishers Weekly* (October 2, 1987): 16–17.

Ladd, Barbara. "Rita Mae Brown (1944–)." *Contemporary Fiction Writers of the South: A Biobibliographical Sourcebook.* Ed. Joseph M. Flora and Robert Bain. Westport, CT: Greenwood Press, 1993.

BURDEKIN, KATHARINE

Katharine Burdekin was born in Derbyshire, England, in 1896 to an upper-middle-class family. In 1915, she married Beaufort Burdekin, an Australian barrister, and the marriage lasted until 1922, at which time she left Australia and returned to England from Sydney with their two daughters. She began a lifelong companion-ship with another woman, and they lived together raising their respective children until Burdekin died in 1963. Burdekin often wrote under the pseudonym Murray Constantine. Her books include *Quiet Ways* (1930); *Proud Man* (1934); *Swastika Night,* her most widely read novel (1937); and *The End of This Day's Business,* written in the 1930s but published in 1989.

The End of This Day's Business opens on May Day of "the year 6250, Old Style," and features the characters twenty-four-year-old Neil Carlason and his aunt/ mother Grania. In this utopian novel, women are viewed as the natural leaders, thinkers, and rational beings; men are subordinate, emotional, and weak in all ways except physical. The world of 6250 reveals a society that, in many ways, is the reverse image of the world from which Burdekin wrote. The cultural ethos of their world says that women are "in all but physical strength, naturally superior" (6). Men are "naturally modest, and would not bare more than their arms, legs and heads in a public place" (7). Neil hates his body and he hates himself. He is beginning to feel objectified when women look at him and his physical beauty. In this world, "Women were not emotional except in a purely physical sense; they very rarely expressed surprise or grief or anxiety in their tones of voice or the look on their faces" (9).

Girls go through an initiation at age seventeen "in the utterly mysterious and forbidden hearts of the Women's Houses" (5). Boys get no such initiation. Men are kept on the outside of information; women talk to each other but never to men or boys. Men take lovers, but the women simply use them, expecting no attachments or promises. Sex is a biological function separated from emotional commitment.

For his life's work, Neil is has chosen to be a laborer in the gardens that are run by the women of the community. His mother is an engineer at the power station; his eccentric aunt Grania is an artist.

As the May Day celebration on the plain of Salisbury nears, Neil has been having an "incomprehensible vague discontent" for the last year, and he hopes the celebrations will "cure him forever of his strange glooms" (1). The night before May Day, Neil went up to Old Sarum and "had thrown himself face downwards on the short sweet down-grass, and had astonishingly wept" (3). He is so confused by his riot of thoughts that he puts aside his work and goes to see old Andreas, hoping that he will find Grania there too. Recently returned from Russia, his aunt Grania is the "ugliest, most unattractive woman probably in the world" (10). But she is attractive in her spirit, and Neil suddenly realizes that he likes her better than he does his own mother, her sister.

Neil feels close to Andreas too and recognizes in him a behavior contrary to the norm: "Andreas was the sole man of his acquaintance who would dare to argue with a woman about anything" (12). Both Andreas and Grania greet Neil, and he confesses his anxiety and emotional discomfort to Grania, "What I want to know is, can a person be miserable *inside* for a long time and not know it, and it all come bursting up?" (14). He says that when women look at him, he feels like "so much live *meat*" (15).

Though the society in which they live is distinctly and prejudiciously matriarchal, Grania recognizes the dignity of both women and men. When Neil asks if he will ever feel better, Grania tells him no, that "the embryo of the dignity of a human being cannot be aborted" (16). Having started the journey of feeling and questioning, there will be no turning back for Neil.

Grania is now in a critical position: Now that Neil has gone beyond the culturally prescribed world of male obsequiousness, she must decide if she will tell him of his origins and of the new world order that she envisions. The decision is no small matter, for there is a "psychic disturbance of a titanic conflict that was going on in Grania's mind. It was the last of a long series; whatever won this one was the final victor, for there would be no more battles" (16).

The title of the book comes from a line in Shakespeare that Grania remembers, "*Oh, that a man might know the end of this day's business ere it come. But it sufficeth that the end will come, and then the end is known*" (29). The business that

Grania proposes to herself is to violate her vows as a woman and to tell Neil of the time when men were viewed as capable, intelligent beings and when they weren't held in scorn and oppression.

Grania also decides that she must tell him that she is his biological mother and that Andreas is his biological father. Neil wants them to be his "think-Mother" and "think-Father" (19) since he feels emotionally tied to the woman he has always believed to be his mother, and "[n]o one could ever *feel* a father, anyway" (19).

Neil and Grania and Andreas go to the May Day festivities together, and Neil promises to give Andreas a place to sleep that night. Because Neil can have any woman he wants on the night of the festivities, he is torn between his impulses and his promise to host Andreas. When he honors his commitment to Andreas, Grania is pleased to see that he has the strength of will to counter all of his training and acculturation.

Grania undertakes a deliberate reeducation of Neil and decides to do life studies of him. Neil is reluctant to take off his shirt; he says, "I don't think men ought to go stripping off their clothes before women" (40). Grania says men are "starved with sex shame and so uneducated" that they "can't contemplate doing anything that's more than semi-skilled or undertaking anything at all that entails responsibility" (44). Grania explains what has happened to make women superior to men by using a parable of kittens: "Supposing you fed the she well and gave the tom only *just* enough food so that it could *just* live and *just* crawl about, the she would grow the biggest and strongest" (41). It has been nearly five thousand years since the time when men were in power, and Neil cannot comprehend that the world order in which he lives is constructed and not natural.

Neither can he believe that the world was riddled with wars and disease when men were in power, that people "caught their mental diseases" of "patriotism and fascism and death-hysteria" (65). Under the female hegemony, the population has remained constant, the economy stable, and there have been no wars. Grania is quick to tell Neil that, though men have fared better under the female rule than women did under male rule, the subjugation of men was "a cold, logical and slow process, passed from Mother to daughter" over a period of 250 years (91). The novel is not free from the intruding voice of Burdekin as she uses Grania as a mouthpiece for extended proclamations about Communism and Fascism that detract from its narrative integrity. Daphne Patai notes that Burdekin "makes ample use of explanatory dialogue, historical disquisitions, and didactic discourse" (169), certainly this is true in *The End of This Day's Business* to the detriment of the novel's fictional structure.

Slowly, Neil starts to internalize what Grania has been teaching him, and his behaviors change; he refuses to fight other men, not because he won't win but because fighting is an aggressive behavior. Now that Neil has exhibited two behaviors contrary to his presumed nature as a man—control over his sex desire and the refusal to fight—Grania sees hope for him.

Still, he remains credulous about the abilities of men; when Grania shows him a painting done long ago by a man, he cannot imagine that a man could be an artist. She replies, "Any human being can be an artist so long as its psyche is sufficiently developed to split into the bisexual psyche necessary to the artist" (56).

As Neil grows, he wants to tell his friend Magnus about the new information he is learning, but Grania restrains him. By telling Neil these parts of women's history, she is committing treason, a crime punishable by death; by listening, Neil is implicated and subject to the death penalty as well. Still, as Neil learns more, both he and Grania grow a little less careful in their enthusiasm. Grania takes pictures from the Women's House to show Neil the kinds of structural and human destruction that were done in the past by wars, and he invites a group of his friends to Grania's studio.

Before long, Grania is taken by a group of women to the Women's Council where she is called to account for breaking her oath of women's silence. She is sent to Munich where the General Secretary of the Women's Council will mete out her punishment. The General Secretary is Anna Karenstochter, an old friend of Grania's, and though Anna must legislate against Grania, she is nonetheless influenced by Grania's message. Grania says to Anna, "It's not right to hold a grudge for four thousand years, and from that grudge and that cowardice to deprive half the human race of its human right to grow. We call ourselves mature, and we say that in the race's maturity women must rule. But no race can ever be mature while one sex is infantile" (143).

Grania knows now that her influence will continue through Anna. Both she and Neil are sentenced to death, but Grania knows that Anna will continue the work. She and Neil drink their poison and die.

Daphne Patai is the scholar who has recovered much of Burdekin's work and was responsible for pulling the manuscript of *The End of This Day's Business* from a trunkful of material and seeing it to publication. Though Burdekin is adamant in her presentation of the misogyny of her times, Patai suggests that "[m]isandry is absent from Burdekin's writing, as is a tone of bitterness and despair" (175). Both are remarkable accomplishments in such a vocal polemic.

References and Suggested Readings

Burdekin, Katharine. *The End of This Day's Business*. New York: The Feminist Press, 1989.

Patai, Daphne. Afterword. *The End of This Day's Business*. By Katharine Burdekin. New York: The Feminist Press, 1989. 159–90.

Stec, Loretta. "Katharine Penelope Burdekin." *An Encyclopedia of British Women Writers*. Ed. Paul Schlueter and June Schlueter. Revised and Expanded ed. New Brunswick, NJ: Rutgers University Press, 1998.

CASTILLO, ANA

Ana Castillo, born in Chicago, Illinois, in 1953, earned a BA degree from Northern Illinois University in 1975, an MA degree from the University of Chicago in 1979, and a PhD degree from the University of Bremen in 1991. She writes both poetry and fiction, and her 1986 *The Mixquiahuala Letters* won the American Book Award. Her early volumes of poetry include *Zero Makes Me Hungry* (1975), *I close my eyes (to see)* (1976), *Otro canto* (1977), and *My Father Was a Toltec: Poems* (1988), republished in 1995 as *My Father was a Toltec and Selected Poems 1973–1988*. In addition to *The Mixquiahuala Letters*, Castillo's novels include *Sapogonia: An Anti-Romance in 3/8 Meter* (1990) and *So Far from God* (1993). *Massacre of the Dreamers: Essays on Xicanisma* (1994) is a nonfiction volume that served as her PhD dissertation. In the introduction to that volume, she describes herself, "I am a brown woman, from the Mexican side of town—torn between the Chicago obrero [working class] roots of my upbringing and my egocentric tendency toward creative expressions. Characteristically, as a poet, I am opinionated and rely on my hunches" (1).

Her creativity and her hunches have led her to a place of respect in literary circles, especially as she advocates for the voices and perspectives of Mexic Amerindian women from whom she descends. In *Massacre of the Dreamers*, Castillo notes that "the Mexic Amerindian woman had been gagged for hundreds of years," subject to a "double sexism, being females and indigenous." She has chosen the term *Mexic Amerindian* carefully, preferring it to *Chicana*, which she sees as "an outdated expression weighed down by the particular radicalism of the seventies" (10), and uses it interchangeably with the term *mestiza*. Castillo introduces the word *Xicanisma* to rename the concept of Chicana feminism and envisions reclaiming it from the "theoretical abstractions" of academia and moving it to the "work place, social gatherings, kitchens, bedrooms, and society in general" (11).

The ten essays in *Massacre of the Dreamers* address issues that are vital to a mestiza political activism: the role of patriarchal institutions, such as the Catholic Church, Socialism, and machismo, in repressing women's spirituality and human sexuality; the use of language that "[perpetuates] learned concepts of who we are and how we should live" (15); and the denigration of "mother" in society.

The Mixquiahuala Letters opens with a note to the reader: "It is the author's duty to alert the reader that this is not a book to be read in the usual sequence. All letters are numbered to aid in following any one of the author's proposed options." What follows thereafter are three reading agendas labeled "For the Conformist," "For the Cynic," and "For the Quixotic." Castillo also suggests that each letter can be read as a "separate entity" for those "committed to nothing but short fiction." The reader is immediately aware that she has entered the world of postmodern textual instability, that the "truth" of fiction is being assaulted by the playful author. But the text does not devolve into postmodern inanities; the narrative menus serve fair warning that this is a serious text confronting the serious identities that women write for themselves. Each reader is complicit in the text that she "writes" as the distance between the author and reader is collapsed. Rather than offering a single narrative closure, Castillo opens the interpretative possibilities. Norma Alarcón suggests that "[i]nsofar as each suggested reading by Castillo presents us with a resolution, we are handed an ideological nexus that forces us to reconstruct the meaning of Teresa's letters as always and already leading in that direction" (105). The several directions in which we (and Teresa) are led, however, complicate any desire to provide Teresa with an integrated self. Alarcón wonders if Teresa is "the vampish one, the docile one, the clever one, the fearful one, the liberated one, or the oppressed one?" (105). In the end, she proposes that Teresa is "all of them, and more" (105).

Just as Castillo blurs the function of the writer and the reader, so does she blur the lines between genres in this text. The volume is a collection of forty letters written by a young mestiza woman, Teresa, to her friend, Alicia, recounting ten years of friendship. Within the epistolary format is a mixture of poetry, story, myth, and travelogue as well. Castillo challenges yet another narrative convention when she abandons the construct of the first-person narrative "I" by using a lower case "i" to indicate that hers is a "collective identity" (My *Father Was a Toltec* xviii).

Teresa and Alicia, the main characters of *The Mixquiahuala Letters* meet as students when "[e]nrolled at a North American institution in Mexico City for a summer to study its culture and language" (24). The highlight of their largely disappointing scholarly experience is a weekend trip to Mixquiahuala, "a Pre-Conquest village of obscurity, neglectful of progress, electricity notwithstanding" (25). Their adventures there cement their friendship, and soon they share the stories of their loves and the all important gift of their laughter. Alicia, the artist, is light-skinned, long-limbed, "partially white/raised moderately comfortable/spoiled by mommy and grandma if not by daddy" and is sometimes the object of resentment by the mestiza poet Teresa who "ate/meals with tortillas and fingers, a peona by birthright comfort-/able without chair or table but squatted" (50). Teresa, with a fuller figure and an unpracticed sensuousness, attracts both the attention of men and the resentment of Alicia.

Both women journey to Mexico with tenuous attachments to men back home. By the end of the six-week term, Teresa acknowledges, "It was apparent I was no longer prepared to face a mundane life of need and resentment, accept monogamous commitments and honor patriarchal traditions, and wanted to be rid of my husband's guiding hand" (28–29). Alicia is in a long-term relationship with her lover, Rodney, "a poor, misdirected, deprived black man from/the ghetto" and must bear both his inattention and cheating as well as the scorn of her bigoted father. Both relationships end before the women take a second extended trip to Mexico. Finally, Teresa can no longer accept her husband's, Libra, disregard, and she leaves him. Alicia is warned in a dream of Rodney's infidelity and returns home to find the warning accurate. Throughout their personal disappointments, however, the two women remain friends with an intensity that leads Teresa to remark, "When I say ours was a love affair, it is an expression of nostalgia and melancholy for the depth of our empathy" (45). Yarbro-Bejarano notes that, while the relationship is not "devoid of homoerotic attraction, other barriers rise up in the borderlands of race, culture and class and combine with those related to gender and sexuality to prevent the establishment of real intimacy between the two women" (67).

Newly released from binding relationships and buoyed by mutual support, the two women journey again to Mexico to visit the ruins of civilizations past, hoping to reinvigorate their creativity. No longer under the aegis of a summer study program, the two women appear "in Mexico as two snags in its pattern" (65). "What was our greatest transgression?" asks Teresa. "We traveled alone. (The assumption here is that neither served as a legitimate companion for the other.)" (66). The two women traveling alone in the rigid patriarchy of Mexico unwillingly invite "ridicule, abuse, disrespect," and more than once, Teresa and Alicia are in danger (65). Twice Teresa saves Alicia with the power of her words. In the first instance, Alicia is dancing at a party, and several men grab at her in an attempt to pull her backstage to rape her; Teresa throws herself at the men and breaks their frenzied spell with language, "LEAVE HER BE! SON OF A BITCH! LEAVE HER ALONE OR . . ." (84).

In another incident, the two women are staying in a platonic arrangement with a group of engineers. One night, in a Ouija board séance, the message predicts that Alicia will not live to see the next day. She goes on to bed unperturbed, but Teresa is wary. In the middle of the night, their room is entered by a spirit, "no body, no feet, but a massive rolling of energy blacker than the darkness in the room" (88). Teresa remembers her grandmother's advice that "only fear could harm one," and she holds Alicia next to her and begins reciting the Lord's Prayer (88). The presence continues toward them, "rumbling, wanting, calling silently, pulling at our mortality" but is finally repelled by "Thy will be done . . . On earth as it is in heaven" (89). Though no longer a practicing Catholic (she ran out of the confession box when, as an eighteen-year-old virgin, she was badgered by a prurient priest to confess "titillating" details), Teresa has an awareness of and respect for the supernatural that Alicia, never having "been indoctrinated into an institutionalized religion" or never having heard "eerie folktales from the old ones," does not have (88). Teresa's power over the supernatural confirms her role as a poet, a priestess of language.

The texts recount and remember many other adventures of the two women, both in Mexico and in the United States, including the traumatic story of Teresa's abortion, of Alicia's abortion and subsequent sterilization, of the suicide of Alicia's lover, and of the birth of Teresa's son, Vittorio. Depending on which route through the text the reader takes, Yarbro-Bejarano suggests that the ending will resolve in "confirmation of maternal and cultural dictates," "the confirmation of women's betrayal of women," or with "quixotic preparations for yet another trip to Mexico" (68).

Whatever journey the reader takes, it remains clear that, for Teresa especially, the pull of the homeland is strong, "Mexico. Melancholy, profoundly right and wrong, it embraces as it strangulates" (*Letters* 65).

In her 1993 novel, *So Far from God*, Castillo employs magical realism to spin the tale of a strong woman and her four extraordinary daughters. Though Castillo has been faulted for overreaching her narrative gift in this novel, her achievement is nonetheless significant in that she leads the reader to a world of spiritualism, political activism, and humor in the garment of a parodic *telenovela*. The adventures of the five women may strain the tissue of verisimilitude, but their values ring true.

In a scene reminiscent of Isabel Allende's character Clara, from her novel *The House of the Spirits*, the youngest daughter dies when she is only three but comes to life in her coffin just before her funeral mass. She sits bolt upright and then flies to the top of the church and instructs the priest, "Don't touch me!" thus beginning her "life's phobia of people." When the priest wonders if the child is the "devil's messenger or a winged angel," the child's mother rises in defiance and charges the priest not to suggest a connection to the devil: "Don't you dare start this about *my* baby!" (23). Thus begins the second life of La Loca, as she comes to be called. When the priest suggests that he will pray for the child, she admonishes him, "Remember, it is *I* who am here to pray for *you*" (24). The local doctor offers the explanation that she is probably an epileptic, but the child is soon known as "La Loca Santa," and people come to seek miracles from her.

Caridad, Sofi's second daughter, shares spiritual attributes with La Loca, though she comes to her spirituality far later in life. Caridad is breathtakingly beautiful but is unable to ground herself. By the time she is out of high school, she is pregnant, married, has aborted the baby, and gotten an annulment. She has two more abortions, each performed by her sister La Loca. She tries college for a year only to dropout. Her life is marred by bad decisions about the wrong men, and soon she leads a life of indiscriminate sex and "shots of Royal Crown with beer chasers after work at the hospital where she was an orderly" (27). Her profligate lifestyle ends, however, after she is attacked and nearly killed by a *malogra*, an evil spirit/animal that mutilates her nearly beyond recognition. Her recovery is effected by La Loca and is simultaneous with that of her sister Fe's.

The third sister, Fe, at twenty-four has a stable life. She has a steady job at the bank and a long-term fiancé, Tom. They plan to marry, though just before the wedding, he breaks their engagement. Fe crumbles into a yearlong despair that is marked by "a loud continuous scream that could have woken the dead" (30). Sofi and her daughters care for Fe, feeding and dressing her. La Loca prays for her and for Tom, knowing that he suffers "from the inability to open his heart" (32). Meanwhile, Fe continues to grieve through her piercing scream that is relieved only by sleep. After the beating, stabbing, and mutilation of Caridad, Fe's problems move to the background of family concern.

It is the miraculous intercession of La Loca that heals both sisters. One evening, Esperanza, the oldest daughter, sees Caridad walk into the room wearing Fe's wedding dress. It is not the damaged and mutilated Caridad, however; she is "whole and once again beautiful" (37). La Loca reveals that she has prayed for Caridad; not only is Caridad healed, but Fe too is healed. Esperanza finds Fe holding Caridad, comforting her and realizes only later that Fe is calm and no longer locked in her shrill scream of grief and abandonment. From that moment on, Caridad no longer courts danger with her former recklessness, and Fe has no memory of her yearlong screaming.

Esperanza is the oldest of the sisters and the only one to graduate from college. She earns a BA in Chicano Studies and goes on to earn a master's degree in communications and becomes a TV news anchor and reporter. Her college lover, Rubén, dumps her just as they are ready to graduate; that she is thrown over for a wealthy white woman does nothing to assuage her pain. Just as her career is blossoming, Rubén enters her life again and they reestablish their relationship. Esperanza turns down an opportunity to anchor a news show at the Houston affiliate station so that she might devote her energies once again to Rubén. She follows him all over the Southwest, joining in with his recent involvement in the Native American Church. She attends prayer meetings and sweat lodges at the pueblos. Rubén's commitment to the relationship does not equal Esperanza's though, and he is soon leaving her for unaccountable periods of time. It takes the dramatic healing of her two sisters to snap Esperanza into good sense, and she then leaves Rubén to take a job in Washington. So, in fact, La Loca has healed all three sisters.

The torrent of events continues to spill into the narrative: Sofi's husband returns after nearly twenty years of unexplained absence; Caridad moves out of the family home and becomes an apprentice to an ancient curandera, doña Felicia; Esperanza is sent on assignment to Saudi Arabia during the Gulf War and is killed there and, though her body is never found, she returns to visit the family in an ectoplasmic state; and Caridad disappears for one year on a pilgrimage. But for all the apparent narrative clutter and even the interpolated passages, particularly that of Helena and Maria, the story is moving in a firm direction.

The lessons that Esperanza has always taught about social justice and political activism take root. Sofi decides to run for mayor of Tome, even though no such position exists. She says, "I have been living in Tome all my life and I have only seen it get worse and worse off and it's about time somebody goes out and tries to do something about it!" (137–38). When her friend accuses her of perhaps having too much imagination, Sofi retorts that her friend has always been a conformist, a person "who just didn't give a damn about nothing!" (139). The two women join forces, however, and set about on a campaign to improve Tome and put the town on a path to economic self-sufficiency. They start a successful "sheep-grazing wool-weaving enterprise, 'Los Ganados y Lano Cooperative'" (146). The skills that the community members learn operating their co-op translate into earned college credit and associate's degrees in an arrangement with the local junior college. Their market expands to the sale of hormone-free meat, and soon Sofi sells her Carne Buena Meat Market in shares and starts a food co-op. She is granted the honorific title Mayor of Tome out of gratitude for all she has done to make the community thrive.

Both Fe and La Loca become political activists as well. Fe has finally gotten over her lost love, Tom, and fallen in love with her cousin Casey. They marry, and Fe leaves her bank job to earn more money at Acme International, a chemical plant. She is assigned the handling of toxic materials without proper protection and soon develops cancer. Before she dies, she gathers damning information on Acme and blows the whistle on their operation.

The disregard for workers that ended in Fe's death moves La Loca to protest a blue jeans company that is unfair to its workers by ripping the back pocket and label off of her jeans. Sofi reminds La Loca that no one ever sees her since she does not leave the house, and therefore her protest is in vain. La Loca reminds Sofi that she has seen the torn pocket and asked. La Loca sensitizes her mother to the social injustice, and Sofi has soon alerted the whole community to the boycott. Her action keeps alive the spirit of La Loca who will soon die of an unexplained case of AIDS.

In addition to demonstrating a heightened social awareness in her main characters, Castillo is moving the story to spiritual closure in the character of Caridad. Since her miraculous healing, Caridad has exhibited supernatural powers. From her spiritual mentor, doña Felicia, she learns that "[a] curandera not only had the health of her patient in her own hands but the spirit as well" and that "[e]verything we need for healing is found in our natural surroundings" (62). Felicia takes Caridad on her first pilgrimage to Chimayo during Holy Week. While there, Caridad sees "the most beautiful woman she had ever seen sitting on the adobe wall that surrounds the sanctuary" and falls immediately in love (75). Her heart is "renewed, moved by another human being" for the first time in years (79). Caridad becomes obsessed by the woman, Esmeralda, and though they never come together in a physical relationship, they do join spiritually. They travel one day to Acoma Pueblo to visit Esmeralda's family, and while there, they hear the voice of Tsichtinako, "the Invisible One who had nourished the first two humans, who

were also both female" (211). Following the voice, the two women run over the
edge of the cliff and fall "deep within the soft, moist dark earth where Esmeralda
and Caridad would be safe and live forever" (211). In leaping over the cliff, the
lovers leap into eternity and into mythic status.

By the end of the novel, Sofi has lost all four of her beautiful and odd daughters, and if it were not for Castillo's use of magical realism and a wonderful ironic
humor, the tragedies would overwhelm the reader. Castillo ends the novel in a
comic triumph, however, as Sofi becomes the "founder and la first presidenta of
what would later be known worldwide as the very prestigious (if not a little elitist)
organization M.O.M.A.S., Mothers of Martyrs and Saints" (247).

About her own art, Castillo has said, "All I can do, in the most convincing
and powerful way that I know how, is to write from what is true to me." Certainly
her two greatest works, *The Mixquiahuala Letters* and *So Far from God*, sound the
ring of truth.

References and Suggested Readings

Alarcón, Norma. "The Sardonic Powers of the Erotic in the Work of Ana Castillo." *Break-
ing Boundaries: Latina Writing and Critical Readings*. Ed. Asunción Horno-Delgado,
et al. Amherst: The University of Massachusetts Press, 1989. 94–107.
Bennett, Tanya Long. "No Country to Call Home: A Study of Castillo's *Mixquiahuala
Letters*." *Style* 30 (1996): 462–78.
Carr, Irene Campos. Rev. of *So Far from God*, by Ana Castillo. *Belles Lettres* (Fall 1993):
52–53.
"Castillo, Ana." *Contemporary Authors: New Revision Series*, Vol. 51. Detroit: Gale
Research, 1996.
Castillo, Ana. *Massacre of the Dreamers: Essays on Xicanisma*. 1994. New York: Plume-
Dutton Signet, 1995.
———. *The Mixquiahuala Letters*. 1986. New York: Anchor-Doubleday, 1992.
———. *My Father Was a Toltec and Selected Poems*. New York: Norton, 1995.
———. *So Far from God*. 1993. New York: Plume-Dutton Signet, 1994.
Gonzalez, Ray. Rev. of *So Far from God* by Ana Castillo. *Nation* 7 June 1993: 772–73.
Saeta, Elsa. "A *MELUS* Interview: Ana Castillo." *MELUS* 22 (1997): 6 Jan. 1999
<http://www.ref.oclc.org:/FUNC/FTOP...Assessionid+1206593:29:/fstxt29.hmt>.
Yarbro-Bejarano, Yvonne. "The Multiple Subject in the Writing of Ana Castillo." *The
Americas Review* 20 (1992): 65–72.

See also Allende, Isabel.

CHOPIN, KATE

Neither an avowed feminist nor a suffragist, Kate Chopin nevertheless boldly
explored the feminist themes of the inequity of traditional marriage and of the
female desire for personal autonomy and sexual freedom, particularly in her best-
known novel *The Awakening* (1899). Born Katherine O'Flaherty in St. Louis in
1851, Kate led a life of well-bred privilege. Her father, an Irish immigrant, was a
successful merchant who had married into an aristocratic family of French origin.

Her upbringing, steeped in French language and culture, included a traditional convent education and the rounds of society balls.

After her marriage in 1870 to Oscar Chopin, a cotton trader from a prominent Louisiana Creole family, Kate moved to New Orleans and later to a rural plantation owned by her husband's family. A conscientious mother and a dutiful wife, Kate bore six children during her twelve years of marriage. After her husband died suddenly of swamp fever in 1883, she returned to St. Louis with her children, where she began writing seriously after the death of her mother in 1885. The deaths of these two important people apparently allowed her the space to develop as a writer. A decade later, she wrote in her diary:

> If it were possible for my husband and my mother to come back to earth, I feel that I would unhesitatingly give up every thing that has come into my life since they left it and join my existence again with theirs. To do that, I would have to forget the past ten years of my growth—my real growth. But I would take back a little wisdom with me; it would be the spirit of perfect acquiescence.

Her first two collections of stories, *Bayou Folk* (1894) and *A Night in Acadie* (1897), were received as delightful "local color" sketches and met with critical acceptance. However, Chopin's work was far more radical than it initially appeared, and she revealed in her chosen themes a more rebellious side to her personality that had not found expression in the roles of society belle and dutiful wife.

Chopin's defiant streak would find its fullest expression in *The Awakening* (1899), a novel about a woman's quest for erotic fulfillment and personal freedom outside of the prescribed roles of wife and mother. The scandalous subject matter caused a critical uproar; the novel was banned from libraries in Chopin's hometown of St. Louis, and Chopin herself was shunned by genteel society. Between the publication of *The Awakening* and her death five years later in 1904, Chopin, no doubt discouraged by her best work's negative reception, published very little.

The Awakening fell into obscurity and was not recognized as an American classic until the 1960s. Its frank treatment of the heroine Edna Pontellier's sexual and emotional awakening outside of her marriage created a scandal and led Chopin to issue a tongue-in-cheek "retraction": "I never dreamed of Mrs. Pontellier making such a mess of things and working out her own damnation as she did. . . . But when I found out what she was up to, the play was half over and it was then too late." More recently, Chopin's daring and unconventional representation of a woman's ultimately thwarted quest for autonomy and self-actualization outside the traditional roles of wife and mother has been the subject of much feminist critical attention and debate.

Set at a Grand Isle summer resort frequented by New Orleans Creole society, *The Awakening* opens with the image of a parrot in a cage, foreshadowing the theme of a woman's quest for freedom. Just as the parrot is the property of Madame Lebrun, proprietor of the resort, the twenty-eight-year-old Edna Pontellier is the property of her husband, Léonce, a man of forty, who looks at his sunburned wife "as one looks at a valuable piece of personal property which has suffered some damage" (40). While Mr. Pontellier occupies himself with business, Mrs. Pontellier's attention is taken up by the proprietor's son, Robert Lebrun, who is two years her junior. Although she has married into French Catholic Creole society, Edna is an outsider, a Kentucky Presbyterian, "an American woman, with a small infusion of French which seemed to have been lost in dilution" (6). Mr. Pontellier is a generous husband, lavish with material gifts to his wife, but the marriage is a vaguely unsatisfactory one. Pontellier finds his wife negligent in her duty toward their two young sons, Raoul and Etienne. In response to his criticisms, Mrs. Pontellier feels an "indescribable oppression . . . like a shadow . . . across her soul's summer day" (8).

Whereas the other matrons on Grand Isle are "women who idolized their children, worshiped [sic] their husbands, and esteemed it a holy privilege to efface themselves as individuals and grow wings as ministering angels" (10), Mrs. Pontellier is not a "mother-woman" (10). In particular, her closest friend, Adèle Ratignolle, represents this type to perfection, a "faultless Madonna" (12), wholly devoted to her husband and children. Under the influence of Adèle's Creole charm, Edna begins "to loosen a little the mantle of reserve that had always enveloped her" (15). Seated by the sea with Adèle, she recalls wading waist-deep in a Kentucky meadow in her childhood, "idly, aimlessly, unthinking and unguided" (18). Her childhood reverie leads her to recall her youthful infatuations before her marriage to Léonce, which was "purely an accident," not the result of a great passion. Meanwhile Adèle warns Robert about his attentions to Edna. Because Edna is not Creole, Adèle worries that she "might make the unfortunate blunder of taking [his attention] seriously" (21).

Edna is deeply moved by a performance of Chopin by Mademoiselle Reisz, another of the guests, "a disagreeable little woman, no longer young," whose "self-assertive" temper makes her quarrelsome (26). Following the concert, the guests go for a moonlight swim, and Edna masters the ability to swim for the first time. "Intoxicated with her newly conquered power," she swims far out to sea, "reaching for the unlimited in which to lose herself" (29). Temporarily, she panics, visited by a "quick vision of death" (29), before returning to shore. Accompanied home by Robert, she waits for her husband's return in a hammock outside their cottage. When her husband arrives, she defies his request that she go inside; "her will had blazed up, stubborn and resistant" (32).

The following morning, Edna uncharacteristically sends for Robert, proposing a boat trip to a neighboring island. On the boat, Edna feels "as if she were being borne away from some anchorage which had held her fast . . . leaving her free to drift whithersoever she chose to set her sails" (35). She spends the entire day with Robert, returning after dark. When Robert suddenly leaves for Mexico shortly thereafter, she feels tormented by the feeling that "she had been denied that which her impassioned, newly awakened being demanded" (46).

Upon returning to New Orleans, Edna begins to defy the social conventions of her circle, snubbing callers much to her husband's chagrin. After her husband criticizes her, she flings her wedding ring on the floor and tries, unsuccessfully, to crush it with her heel. Under the spell of her infatuation with Robert, she begins to abandon her duties as a wife, "casting aside that fictitious self which we assume like a garment with which to appear before the world" (57). She begins to paint in her *atelier* and rekindles her summer friendship with Mademoiselle Reisz. When she informs the pianist of her desire to be an artist, Mademoiselle Reisz tells her she needs not only the gift but also the courage to succeed, "the soul that dares and defies" (63). Mademoiselle Reisz also shares a letter she has received from Robert that reveals his continued feeling for Mrs. Pontellier. Meanwhile, Mr. Pontellier seeks the advice of the family physician, Dr. Mandelet, regarding his wife's odd behavior. Troubled by her notions about the "eternal rights of women" (65), he complains of her refusal to attend her sister's upcoming marriage on the grounds that "a wedding is one of the most lamentable spectacles on earth" (66). When the doctor sees Edna, however, he sees "no trace of that morbid condition which her husband had reported" (69); rather, she "reminded him of some beautiful, sleek animal waking up in the sun" (70).

While Mr. Pontellier goes on an extended business trip to New York, his mother takes their sons for an extended visit, leaving Edna alone at home with a sense of "radiant peace" (72). She begins to receive the attentions of Alcée Arobin, who is known in Creole society as a womanizer. Arobin draws out her "awakening sensuousness" (76), and Edna feels betrayed into infidelity, not to her husband, who "seemed to her now like a person whom she had married without love as an excuse" (77), but to Robert Lebrun. Enjoying her new found freedom and independence, Edna conceives of the audacious plan of moving into a small cottage, dubbed the "pigeon-house" (84), around the corner from her home and writes to her husband informing him of her plan. She reports to Arobin that Mademoiselle Reisz has warned her that "the bird that would soar above the level plain of tradition and prejudice must have strong wings" (82)—a pronouncement that foreshadows the novel's tragic end. Following a passionate kiss from Arobin, Edna feels both an "overwhelming feeling of irresponsibility" and a "dull pang of regret because it was not the kiss of love which had inflamed her" (83). Edna throws a dinner party on the eve of her move to the pigeon-house, after which she succumbs to Arobin's "gentle, seductive entreaties" (92).

Mr. Pontellier expresses his strong disapproval at his wife's change of residence and arranges to save appearances by ordering an extensive renovation of their house while he is in New York. Madame Ratignolle warns Edna that Arobin's attentions "are considered enough to ruin a woman's name" (95). Seeking refuge at Mademoiselle Reisz's, Edna comes unexpectedly upon Robert, who has returned from Mexico. Yet the reality of their encounter betrays her fantasies and makes her doubt if he really loves her. She reflects that "he had seemed nearer to her . . . in Mexico" (102) than at Mademoiselle Reisz's apartment. When she encounters Robert by chance at a garden restaurant, he accompanies her home. Her passionate kiss leads him to confess his love for her, his anguish that she belongs to another man, and his fantasy that Léonce Pontellier might "set her free" so that he could marry her. Robert is shocked by Edna's response: "I am no longer one of Mr. Pontellier's possessions to dispose of or not. I give myself where I choose. If he were to say, 'Here Robert, take her and be happy; she is yours,' I should laugh at you both" (106–7). Edna assures him of her love, telling him "it was you who awoke me last summer out of a life-long, stupid dream" (107). Yet, she departs abruptly, over Robert's protests, to attend the birth of Madame Ratignolle's child, begging him to wait for her.

At Adèle Ratignolle's bedside, Edna is "seized with a vague dread" (108). She witnesses the birth of the new baby with "an inward agony, with a flaming, out-spoken revolt against the ways of Nature" (109). As she leaves, Adèle calls after her to "think of the children." When she returns home, she finds Robert's note: "I love you. Good-by—because I love you" (111).

In the final chapter, Edna returns abruptly to Madame Lebrun's resort on Grand Isle, which is closed for the winter season. She asks Madame Lebrun's son Victor, the winter caretaker, for a room and announces her intention to go for a swim despite the coldness of the water. On the beach, she reflects: "To-day it is Arobin; tomorrow it will be someone else. It makes no difference to me, it doesn't matter about Léonce Pontellier—but Raoul and Etienne!" (113). She now understands what she meant long ago when she told Adèle "that she would give up the un-essential, but she would never sacrifice herself for her children" (113). On the beach, Edna sees a bird with a broken wing, an image that recalls Mademoiselle Reisz's earlier pronouncement. Shedding her clothes, she stands naked in the open air for the first time in her life, "like some new-born creature" (113). She swims far out to sea until exhaustion begins to overpower her. Briefly, she feels terror, followed by childhood memories that float into her mind: "There was the hum of bees, and the musky odor of pinks filled the air" (114).

Critics have debated whether Edna's dream of total personal freedom is a lib-erating feminist goal or an irresponsible escapist fantasy. Nevertheless, Edna's sui-cide suggests Chopin's ultimate pessimism about the possibility of a wife and mother realizing erotic freedom and personal independence in this particular cul-tural and historical moment.

References and Suggested Readings

Ammons, Elizabeth. *Conflicting Stories: American Women Writers at the Turn into the Twentieth Century*. New York: Oxford University Press, 1991.

Chopin, Kate. *The Awakening*. 1899. New York: Norton, 1976.

Gilbert, Sandra M., and Susan Gubar. *No Man's Land: The Place of the Woman Writer in the Twentieth Century, Vol. 2, Sex Changes*. New Haven: Yale University Press, 1989.

———, ed. *The Norton Anthology of Literature by Women: The Traditions in English*. 2nd ed. New York: Norton, 1996.

McQuade, Donald, ed. *The Harper American Literature*. New York: Harper, 1987.

CISNEROS, SANDRA

Born in Chicago in 1954, the Chicano feminist writer Sandra Cisneros established her reputation with her novel *The House on Mango Street*, a series of first-person vignettes told in the voice of a young working-class Latina girl struggling against sexism, racism, and classism to find self-definition.

Cisneros began writing *The House on Mango Street* when she was a twenty-two-year-old graduate student in Iowa City, Iowa, far from the multicultural, working-class community in which she had grown up in Chicago. Her subject reveals her desire to depart from an asthetic that reflected the middle- and upper-class backgrounds of her fellow classmates. She says, "That's precisely what I chose to write: about third-floor flats, and fear of rats, and drunk husbands sending rocks through windows, anything as far from the poetic as possible. And this is when I discovered the voice I'd been suppressing all along without realizing it" (qtd. in Olivares 145) Begun as a memoir, *Mango Street* transformed into a novel comprising a series of interlinked vignettes. Cisneros says of vignettes: "I said once that I wrote *Mango Street* naively, that they were 'lazy poems.' In other words, for me each of the stories could've been developed into poems, but there were not poems. They were stories, albeit hovering in that grey area between two genres" (qtd. in Olivares 145).

First published in 1984 by Arte Publico Press, the semiautobiographical novel won the Before Columbus Foundation Book Award in 1985. Revised and reissued in 1989 in a Vintage Books edition, the novel brought Cisneros to the attention of a wider feminist audience. Beloved by readers of all ages, the book is found as typically on junior high school as on university reading lists. In a second collection of short stories, *Woman Hollering Creek* (1991), Cisneros employs girl children narrators, as in the story "Eleven," but also develops a mature narrative voice, as in the title story, which concerns the domestic abuse suffered by a young Mexican bride newly arrived in the United States. Cisneros has also published several volumes of poems, including *My Wicked, Wicked Ways* (1987) and *Loose Women* (1994). *Caramelo* (2002) marks her return to the genre of novel and is her longest sustained work. She lives in San Antonio, Texas.

In *Mango Street,* Cisneros has created a young working-class Latina narrator, Esperanza Cordera, on the brink of adolescence who struggles in the face of sexism, poverty, and racial prejudice to find a sense of self-empowerment. Determined to escape the domestic drudgery and abuse that is the unhappy fate of so many of the women characters who populate Mango Street, Esperanza strives to adopt a different model of womanhood that includes autonomy and financial independence, as well as sense of community and loyalty to others.

In the opening vignette, "The House on Mango Street," Esperanza reveals her shame and disappointment about her family's new home, describing the disjunction between the dream house—"like the houses on T.V."—she longs for and the run-down house they can afford. In "My Name," she thinks about her namesake, a great-grandmother whose wild spirit is broken by marriage, who "looked out the window her whole life, the way so many women sit their sadness on an elbow." Esperanza has "inherited her name" (4) but refuses "to inherit her place by the window" (11).

"Marin" describes an older girl in the neighborhood, who longs for escape from the domestic drudgery of caring for her younger cousins; she stands in the doorway in her short skirts "waiting for a car to stop, a star to fall, someone to change her life" (27). A university student, Alicia chooses a different route of escape from the domestic responsibilities she has inherited since her mother's death; however, she must contend with a father who says "a woman's place is sleeping so she can wake up early with the tortilla star" (31) to prepare the lunchbox tortillas ("Alicia Who Sees Mice"). In "The Family of Little Feet," Esperanza and her friends approach the treacherous transition from childhood to adolescence, negotiating their budding sexuality as they play a childhood game of dress-up with high-heeled shoes.

In "Four Skinny Trees," Esperanza describes her affinity with the "four raggedy excuses planted by the city" (74) in front of her house. Like the "four who grew despite concrete," "four who reach and do not forget to reach," Esperanza longs to transcend the harsh environment in which she finds herself, "a tiny thing against so many bricks" (75). Most of the women in Esperanza's neighborhood have not escaped the fate of Esperanza's great-grandmother Rafaela, "who is still young but getting old from leaning out the window so much, gets locked indoors because her husband is afraid Rafaela will run away since she is too beautiful to look at" ("Rafaela Who Drinks Coconut and Papaya Juice on Tuesdays" 79); Minerva "is only a little bit older than me but already she has two kids and a husband who left" ("Minerva Writes Poems" 84); Sally marries far too young to escape from an abusive father and winds up trapped, staring at the four walls of her husband's house, observing "how neatly their corners meet, the linoleum roses on the floor, the ceiling smooth as wedding cake" ("Sally," "What Sally Said," "Linoleum Roses" 102). In contrast, Esperanza resolves not "to grow up tame like the others who lay their necks on the threshold waiting for the ball and chain. . . . I am one who leaves the table like a man, without putting back the chair or picking up the plate" ("Beautiful and Cruel" 88–89).

In "The Three Sisters," three mysterious, witchlike women predict that Esperanza will "go very far" and warn her: "When you leave you must remember to come back for the others. . . . You will always be Mango Street. You can't erase what you know. You can't forget who you are" (105). Esperanza continues to long for a home of her own: "Not a flat. Not an apartment in back. Not a man's house. Not a daddy's. . . . Only a house quiet as snow, a space for myself to go, clean as paper before the poem" ("A House of My Own" 108). In the final vignette, "Mango Says Goodbye Sometimes," Esperanza confronts the paradox of staying and leaving, belonging and refusing to belong, remembering and escaping Mango Street: "One day I will pack my bags of books and paper. One day I will say goodbye to Mango. I am too strong for her to keep me here forever. . . . Friends and neighbors will say, What happened to that Esperanza? . . . They will not know I have gone away to come back. For the ones I left behind. For the ones who cannot out" (110).

References and Suggested Readings

Cisneros, Sandra. *The House on Mango Street*. 1984. New York: Vintage, 1989.

———. *Woman Hollering Creek*. New York: Random House, 1991.

Kester-Shelton, Pamela, ed. *Feminist Writers*. Detroit: St. James, 1996.

Olivares, Julián. "Sandra Cisneros' *The House on Mango Street* and the Poetics of Space." *Contemporary Literary Criticism*, vol. 69. Detroit: Gale Research, 1992.

COFER, JUDITH ORTIZ

Judith Ortiz Cofer was born in Hormigueros, Puerto Rico, in 1952 and immigrated to the United States in 1956. She received a BA degree from Augusta College in 1974 and an MA degree from Florida Atlantic in 1977. Cofer is married to John Cofer, and they have one daughter; Ortiz Cofer teaches at the University of Georgia. Her works include *The Line of the Sun* (1989), nominated for the Pulitzer Prize in 1990; *Silent Dancing: A Partial Remembrance of a Puerto Rican Childhood* (1990); *The Latin Deli* (1993); *An Island Like You: Stories of the Barrio* (1995); and *The Year of Our Revolution: New and Selected Stories and Poems* (1998). Cofer reveals her teacherly instincts when, in the introduction to *Silent Dancing*, she wonders about "the genesis of ideas: How does a poem begin? Can the process be triggered at will? What compels some of us to examine and re-examine our lives in poems, stories, novels, memoirs?" (12). She agrees with Virginia Woolf in that "the very act of reclaiming her memories could provide a writer with confidence in the power of art to discover meaning and truth in ordinary events" (13).

Ortiz Cofer describes her grandmother, the focus of her often anthologized essay, "More Room," as "a homemaker and a feminist in a time when those terms did not co-exist." In addition to her grandmother, Cofer sees Lillian Hellman as an important role model. Hellman was the subject of Cofer's MA thesis and "represented the power of women who were determined to be in a field that was male-dominated in her time. She was a necessary part of my liberation." Virginia Woolf is another important model for Cofer, both as a feminist and as writer. Cofer credits Woolf with releasing her "from the limitations" of historical truth and allowing her art to reveal "poetic truth."

Cofer's formative life is chronicled in her memoir *Silent Dancing: A Partial Remembrance of a Puerto Rican Childhood* (1990). Her parents married when her mother was fourteen and her father eighteen. He joined the US Navy, and the lives of the young family shifted every time he was sent to sea. While he was stationed at the Brooklyn Naval Yard, the family lived in Paterson, New Jersey; when he went to sea, the family moved to Puerto Rico to live with their maternal grandmother in her sprawling house. *Silent Dancing* is a collection of essays on topics from her youth, each followed by a poem on the same topic. The primary struggle of the young Ortiz Cofer is the negotiating of two cultures, exacerbated by the frequent movement back and forth from New Jersey to Puerto Rico. Each community has different standards of behavior, different expectations for social adjustments, and different languages. Judith's mother was determined to create another Puerto Rico in the New Jersey high-rise they lived in and refused to learn English or establish friendships. It fell to the bilingual Judith to make the necessary business and social transactions while her father was out of the country.

In the fine essay "More Room," Ortiz Cofer tells the sad but amusing story of her grandmother's quest for autonomy and a life of her own. In Catholic Puerto Rico, the only control from pregnancy is abstinence, and Ortiz Cofer's grand-mother sacrifices her sexual relationship with her grandfather so that she would have the "right to own and control her body, so that she might live to meet her grandchildren" (28).

There in grandmother's house, amid her mother, her aunts, and female cous-ins, Ortiz Cofer hears the stories that entertain and instruct her; she rests under the sprawling umbrella of matriarchy that will shape and influence her for a life-time. When her grandmother held court under a mango tree, Ortiz Cofer first "began to feel the power of words" (76). She hears the story of María Sabida, the "prevailing woman" whose "main virtue was that she was always alert and never a victim" (76). In New Jersey, where young Puerto Rican girls were sometimes separated from the shelter of the matriarchy, Ortiz Cofer meets Vida, who falls prey to the lure of men who promise more than they are willing to give. Watch-ing the women in her high-rise apartment, young Ortiz Cofer learns that "a woman's body, with its capabilities to produce new lives, is a trump card in the balance of human relationships" (113). She learns that the options for women are very narrow in the Puerto Rican culture: "If you did not get married, you be-came a nun, or you entered 'la vida' as a prostitute" (141). It is through the strength of her grandmother and her stories that Ortiz Cofer can imagine another life for herself—a life as a storyteller.

In her mixed-genre collection *The Latin Deli: Telling the Lives of Barrio Women* (1993), once again Ortiz Cofer uses the voices of the women around whom she grew up to reveal the strong roots of a female community.

References and Suggested Readings

Cofer, Judith Ortiz. Inteview with Rafael Ocasion. "The Infinite Variety of the Puerto Rican Reality: An Interview with Judith Ortiz Cofer." *Callaloo* 17.3 (1994): 730–42.

———. Inteview with Rafael Ocasion. "Puerto Rican Literature in Georgia? An Inter-view with Judith Ortiz Cofer." *The Kenyon Review* 14.4 (1992): 43–50.

———. *Silent Dancing: A Partial Remembrance of a Puerto Rican Childhood*. Houston: Arte Publico Press, 1990.

See also Woolf, Virginia.

COMMUNITY

The definition of *community* has shifted throughout history. Initially, according to the *Oxford English Dictionary*, the word constituted "a body of individuals" or "the common people," with emphasis being on members living together and "hold-ing goods in common." Often, then, community relied on ownership rather than on political or even utopian visions. For feminist scholars, however, the history of this term has unfolded in a different manner, as emphasis on ownership often excluded women; as a result, community in its feminist sense can be said to have grown up in opposition to community in its traditional sense.

As scholars become more willing to acknowledge the various intersections of identity, the definition of community becomes ever more elusive. On the one hand, community denotes an inclusive environment based on commonalties; on the other, it necessarily excludes those not sharing the basic characteristics on which the community centers. Individual members' identities muddy this already complicated term in that they create space for people to be simultaneously inside and outside of their communities. This issue is addressed explicitly in Gloria Anzaldua's work on *la communidad*. Anzaldua wrote,

> Because I, a mestiza,
> continually walk out of one culture
> and into another,
> because I am all cultures at the same time,
> *alma entre dos mundos, tres, cuatro,*
> me zumba la cabeza con lo contradictorio.
> *Estoy norteada por todas las voces que me hablan simultaneamente.*

This highlights the difficulties inherent in structuring a community around "an" identity.

Forming a single feminist community obviously poses problems, and many feminist writers of color have criticized mainstream feminism for its tendency to dismiss difference. bell hooks wrote of this very problem, noting that feminists need to redefine their senses of what constitutes a communal identity:

> Women do not need to eradicate difference to feel solidarity. We do not need to share common oppression to fight equally to end oppression. We do not need anti-male sentiments to bond us together, so great is the wealth of experience, culture, and ideas we have to share with one another. (65)

Community does not necessarily hinge on shared characteristics such as race, gender, or sexual orientation. Rather, it emerges as a much more complicated term that suggests commonalties that fuse along the various lines of individual identities.

References and Suggested Readings

Anzaldua, Gloria. "La Conciencia de la Mestiza: Towards a New Consciousness." *Feminist Theory: A Reader*. Ed. Wendy Kolmar and Frances Bartkowski. London: Mayfield, 2000. 398–403.

Brown, Lesley, ed. *The New Shorter Oxford English Dictionary*. Vol. 1–2. Oxford: Clarendon Press, 1993.

hooks, bell. *Feminist Theory from Margin to Center*. Boston: South End Press, 1984.

See also hooks, bell.

Lisa R. Williams

DAVIS, REBECCA HARDING

Rescued from a century of critical neglect by the twentieth-century working-class feminist writer Tillie Olsen, Rebecca Harding Davis is recognized today as an important literary precursor to late nineteenth-century American naturalists, such as Stephen Crane and Theodore Dreiser, and to twentieth-century feminists like Olsen. Her reputation rests primarily on *Life in the Iron Mills* (1861), a novella that unflinchingly chronicles the harsh life of mill workers under industrial capitalism. Born in Washington County, Pennsylvania, in 1831, the eldest of five children of Richard W. Harding and Rachel Leet Wilson Harding, Rebecca Harding Davis moved with her family to Wheeling, Virginia (now West Virginia), in 1836. This booming steel town presumably served as the setting for *Life in the Iron Mills*, an extraordinarily realistic portrayal of working-class men and women who lived well outside the sphere inhabited by (in Tillie Olsen's words) a "housebound, class-bound, sex-bound" middle-class woman such as Davis herself.

Unconnected with literary circles of any kind, Davis's life changed dramatically after the acceptance of her first work by the prestigious *Atlantic Monthly*, which published *Life in the Iron Mills* anonymously in its April 1861 issue. Since the gender of the narrator was ambiguous, many assumed the novella's author was a man. The work met with instant acclaim, leading to a long-lasting friendship with Annie Fields, the wife of *Atlantic* editor James T. Fields, as well as briefer acquaintances with such notable literary figures as Hawthorne and Emerson. Following publication of the piece, Davis also began a correspondence with a reader-admirer, Lemuel Clarke Davis, several years her junior, whom she married in 1863. Davis moved to Philadelphia, where her husband was studying for the bar and working as a journalist.

Although a serialized novel, *Margaret Howth* (1862) and several shorter pieces about the Civil War appeared subsequently in the *Atlantic*, and Davis gradually moved away from her literary aspirations and began writing for magazines that could offer better pay. In addition to raising two sons and a daughter and supporting her husband's successful journalistic career, she continued to write prolifically and to publish extensively. In her fiction, she retained her commitment to confronting subjects related to the broader social and economic issues of the day; however, her subsequent work never matched the quality of her first publication. When she died at age seventy-nine, she was primarily remembered as the mother of the well-known reporter Richard Harding Davis rather than for her own literary achievements. Like the thwarted artistry she embodied so painfully in her protagonist Hugh Wolfe, Davis's own life is representative of the social limitations that restricted the artistic aspirations of so many women writers. Rescued from obscurity by Tillie Olsen and other feminists, her masterful novella now occupies its rightful place in American literary history. Davis died in 1910.

Rebecca Harding Davis was an unknown thirty-year-old unmarried woman, unconnected with any literary circles, when she published her novella *Life in the Iron Mills* anonymously in the prestigious *Atlantic Monthly* in April 1861. Its grim portrait of American working-class lives under the brutal conditions of mid-nineteenth-century industrialization anticipated the "naturalistic" novels of Émile Zola in France and Stephen Crane, Theodore Dreiser, and Frank Norris in the United States. The novella won her instant acclaim and was recognized as a literary landmark by such noteworthies as Nathaniel Hawthorne, Louisa May Alcott, and Ralph Waldo Emerson. Despite this initial reception and a subsequent prolific writing career, the work and its author eventually fell into obscurity. Tillie Olsen rediscovered *Life in the Iron Mills* and was instrumental in bringing about the novella's reissue by the Feminist Press in 1972, thus securing its place in the feminist literary canon. In her Afterword to that edition, Olsen draws an important analogy between the thwarted life and frustrated artistry of Davis's working-class male protagonist and the limitations "however differently embodied" Davis herself faced as "a daughter of the privileged class" (69).

Life in the Iron Mills is set in a town of iron-works thick with industrial smoke and "fog and mud and foul effluvia" (13). The narrator, who observes the brutalized lives of the working classes from her window, tells the story of Hugh Wolfe, a furnace-tender in one of the mills, and his cousin Deborah, a hunchback who harbors an unrequited love for Hugh. Although Hugh treats Deborah with kindness, she knows that "down under all the vileness and coarseness of his life, there was a groping passion for whatever was beautiful and pure,—that his soul sickened with disgust at her deformity, even when his words were kindest" (22–23). Hugh's "passion" is expressed in the "hideous, fantastic . . . strangely beautiful" (24) figures that he carves out of korl—the metal refuse from the iron-works.

One night, Hugh encounters a group of upper-class visitors to the mill and becomes aware of "a great gulf never to be passed" (30) between them. The men are taken by one of Hugh's korl figures, "a nude woman's form, muscular, grown coarse with labor . . . the wild, eager face, like that of a starving wolf's" (32). The men question Hugh about the figure's expression, and he describes her hunger not for meat but for "summat [something] to make her live" (33). The men engage in a patronizing discussion of the upper class's responsibilities toward the poor, which culminates when one of the men, Dr. May, tells Hugh he has the talent to be a great sculptor: "Make yourself what you will. It is your right" (37). Yet, Dr. May's words are hollow. As Mitchell, another of the group, points out, only money matters: "Let them have a clear idea of the rights of the soul, and I'll venture next week they'll strike for higher wages" (38).

After the men have departed, Deborah (who has brought Hugh's dinner to the mill and remained nearby) reveals that she has stolen a great sum of money from Mitchell and urges Hugh to keep it as his "right" (45), echoing Dr. May's words. Longing for a life of "full development" (46); Hugh gives in to temptation, only to be arrested and imprisoned for theft. Rather than face his sentence of nineteen years, "half a lifetime" (51), Hugh commits suicide, slitting his wrists with a piece of sharpened tin. In death, he leaves behind the "figure of the mill-woman cut in korl . . . through which the spirit of the dead korl-cutter looks out, with its thwarted life, its mighty hunger, its unfinished work" (64). Ironically, driven by financial and domestic exigencies, Davis never again matched the artistry she achieved in her first published work; in this sense, her life strangely paralleled the fate of her protagonist.

References and Suggested Readings

Davidson, Cathy N., and Linda Wagner-Martin, eds. *The Oxford Book of Women's Writing in the United States*. New York: Oxford University Press, 1995.

Davis, Rebecca Harding. *Life in the Iron Mills*. 1861. Old Westbury, NY: Feminist, 1972.

———. *The Norton Anthology of Literature by Women: The Traditions in English*. 2nd ed. *Life in the Iron Mills*. Ed. Sandra Gilbert and Susan Gubar. New York: Norton, 1996.

Olsen, Tillie. "A Biographical Interpretation." *Life in the Iron Mills*. By Rebecca Harding Davis. Old Westbury, NY: Feminist, 1972.

See also Olsen, Tillie.

DE PIZAN, CHRISTINE

Born in Venice, Italy, around 1365, Christine de Pizan (alternatively de Pisan) was the first woman in Europe to earn a living as a writer. Her father was appointed to the court of French king Charles V, and Christine studied from his library, becoming a more accomplished student than women of her time were generally allowed to become. She married Étienne de Castel, a notary and secretary at the royal court, when she was fifteen. Their ten years together, before he died in an epidemic, produced three children (a son died in infancy) and a love match that endured beyond his death, as her poetry attests. Before the death of her husband, Christine's father also died and she was left with limited resources to support her family. The young widow turned to writing as her declared profession and wrote lyric poetry and devotional texts. Her early subjects were chivalry and courtly love, but she later came to decry the institutions that subjugated women and valued them as passive sexual objects. Christine challenged misogyny of the kind that she saw in *The Romance of the Rose* (1228–1270) by Guillaume de Lorris and Jean de Meun, a much-vaunted medieval text that included misogynistic passages, and responded to the text with a series of works that include *The Epistle to the God of Love* (1399), *The Tale of the Rose* (1401), *Epistles on "The Romance of the Rose"* (1401–1402), and *The Book of the City of Ladies* (1405). Her work placed her in the midst of debate and firmly established her feminist position.

Other noteworthy works by the prolific Christine include *Book of the Three Virtues* (1405–1406), *Christine's Vision* (1405), and *The Tale of Joan of Arc* (1429).

"These are my habits and the way I spend my life: studying literature," Christine asserts as she begins *The Book of the City of Ladies* (1405), her most widely studied work today. It is her reading of Matheolus that prompts her to wonder why so many men "say and write in their treatises so many evil and reproachful things about women and their behavior" (119). Initially lured by the mere authority of text, Christine nearly succumbs to the mind of Matheolus and his judgment of the feminine sex. She prays to God, "why did You not let me be born into this world as a man . . . and be of such perfection as man is said to be?" (120). As she bemoans her estate, she sees before her three "crowned ladies of great nobility" (121) who come to repair her misinformation. The ladies, Lady Reason, Lady Rectitude, and Lady Justice, confirm that Christine's own willingness to accept the ideas of Matheolus and other misogynist writers is the result of cultural indoctrination and does not reflect the intended condition of woman. They commission her to write a book that chronicles the value and contributions of women through the ages. After a discourse that reeducates Christine to the inherent value of women, the volume, largely derivative of Boccaccio (Blumenfeld-Kosinski 118), recounts the stories of multiple women. She ends the volume with an appeal to women to defend their honor and chastity through pure living and by understanding the evils surrounding them.

References and Suggested Readings

Blumenfeld-Kosinski, Renate. Introduction. *The Selected Works of Christine de Pizan*. Ed. Renate Blumenfeld-Kosinski. New York: Norton, 1997.

de Pizan, Christine. *"The Book of the City of Ladies." The Selected Writing of Christine de Pizan*. Trans. Renate Blumenfeld-Kosinski and Kevin Brownlee. Ed. Renate Blumenfeld-Kosinski. New York: Norton, 1997. 116–55.

Strandness, Jean T. "Christine de Pizan." *MagillOnAuthors*. Dominican University, Rebecca Crown Lib. 4 September 2003 <http://www.dom.edu/>.

DINESEN, ISAK

Best known today for her memoir *Out of Africa* (1937) and for several critically acclaimed short story volumes, Isak Dinesen spent her early years painting and managing a coffee plantation in Africa, only beginning to write seriously in middle age. Born Karen Christentze Dinesen in 1885 in Rungstedlund, Denmark, Tanne (as she was nicknamed) was the second of five children of Ingeborg (Westenholz) and Wilhelm Dinesen. Tanne idolized her father, who committed suicide in 1895 when she was nine years old. Educated at home with her sisters while her brothers were sent to boarding school, Dinesen accompanied her mother and sisters to Switzerland in 1899, where she began to paint. Over family objections, Dinesen went to Copenhagen to study art and spent five semesters in the Royal Academy of Fine Arts. During this period, she also toyed with fiction writing, publishing several short stories in the Danish journal *Tilskueren* under the pseudonym Osceola, after a rebellious Seminole Indian leader.

After returning home from Copenhagen, Dinesen fell in love with a distant cousin, Hans Blixen-Finecke, who did not return her affections. Instead, she married his twin brother, the Baron Bror Blixen-Finecke. With the financial backing of Dinesen's family, Bror purchased several hundred acres of land near Nairobi, Kenya, intending to plant coffee. When they left for British East Africa in 1913, neither Dinesen nor her husband realized their acreage was inappropriate to sustain a successful coffee plantation, although Dinesen remained in Kenya until 1931, managing the plantation alone for ten years after her divorce from her husband.

In *Out of Africa*, Dinesen describes her experiences in colonial Africa but remains circumspect about the details of her personal life during this period. She was plagued by syphilis, which she contracted from her husband. Although she did not wish to separate from Bror, Dinesen fell in love with the British aristocrat Denys Finch-Hatton, who became her lover and frequently stayed in her home while her husband was away. After Bror began an affair with a woman whom he would eventually marry, Dinesen finally agreed to divorce him in 1921, continuing to manage the plantation alone in the face of natural disasters and poor harvests. In 1931, just before Dinesen's permanent return to Denmark, Finch-Hatton died in a plane crash.

During her years on the plantation, Dinesen's writing was confined mainly to letters. Published posthumously as *Letters from Africa*, many of these expressed interest in feminism, which she described in a 1926 letter as the "most significant movement of the nineteenth century." Dinesen also composed an essay during this period titled "On Modern Marriage and Other Considerations," which argued that partners in an ideal marriage should jointly commit themselves to family, kinship, or divinity, rather than to each other. After returning to Denmark, Dinesen took up writing in earnest, publishing her first volumes of stories, *Seven Gothic Tales*, in 1934 when she was forty-eight years old. Writing in English, the language of her deceased lover, rather than Danish, Dinesen also used the pseudonym "Isak," which means "one who laughs." The publication of her autobiographical *Out of Africa* in 1937 was followed by another critically acclaimed story collection, *Winter's Tales* (1942). Dinesen's only novel, the thriller *The Angelic Avengers* (1946), appeared under the pseudonym Pierre Andrezel. Of late, feminist critical attention has focused on a later volume of short stories, *Last Tales* (1957), and particularly on a story called "The Blank Page," which feminist critic Susan Gubar has read as a parable about female creativity in the face of societal constraints.

In her later years, Dinesen suffered greatly from untreatable syphilis. However, she continued to write and to travel, visiting the United States in 1959, where her books were widely admired, Following operations on her spinal cord and stomach, Dinesen's weight dropped to eighty-five pounds. She died of malnutrition in 1962.

Dinesen's story "The Blank Page," included in her collection *Last Tales* (1957), has been a particular focus of recent feminist critical attention. In this brief but intricate tale, written in her adopted English tongue, Dinesen develops a number of classic and intertwined feminist themes, among them the power of the female storyteller, the matrilineal oral storytelling tradition, the female body as a medium for women's creative expression, the domestic constraints placed on women, and the themes of silence and absence as, simultaneously, signs of oppression and resistance.

"The Blank Page" is a tale told by an "old coffee-brown, black-veiled woman who made her living by telling stories" (99), an art she has learned from her mother's mother, who in turn learned it from her mother's mother. From this matrilineal oral tradition, the old storyteller has been taught the following paradox: "Who then . . . tells a finer tale than any of us? Silence does. And where does one read a deeper tale than upon the most perfectly printed page of the most precious book? Upon the blank page" (100).

With this prologue pronounced, the old woman tells the following tale, which concerns an order of Carmelite nuns who "grow the finest flax and manufacture the most exquisite linen of Portugal" (101). The linen is so fine that it is used for the bridal sheets for the princesses of the neighboring royal houses. On the morning after the wedding, the sheet is displayed publicly to attest to the virginity of the princess, and the central piece of the blood-stained sheet, which "bore witness to the honor of a royal bride" (103), is framed and hung in a gallery in the convent, with the princess's name engraved on a gold plate underneath. Female pilgrims come to the gallery to read "the faded markings of the canvases" (103), each of which tells a version of the same story. The blood-stained sheets represent the bride's acquiescence to the ritual of marriage, in which virgins are passed from father to husband for the purpose of producing a male heir. There is, however, one exception to this script, one deviation from the norm: "In the midst of the long row there hangs a canvas which differs from the others. . . . on this one plate no name is inscribed, and the linen within the frame is snow-white from corner to corner, a blank page" (104).

Unlike the infinite variety of the stains on the others canvases, all of which tell the same story, the blank canvas's meaning is mysterious and impenetrable. But whether the nameless princess refused to consummate her marriage or chose some illicit sexual experience, it is this canvas above all that commands the attention of the visiting princesses, "worldly wise, dutiful, long-suffering queens, wives and mothers" (105). Likewise, "it is in front of the blank page that old and young nuns, with the Mother Abbess herself, sink into deepest thought" (105).

References and Suggested Readings

Dinesen, Isak. "The Blank Page." *Last Tales*. New York: Random House, 1957.
Gilbert, Sandra, and Susan Gubar, eds. *The Norton Anthology of Literature by Women: The Traditions in English*. 2nd ed. New York: Norton, 1996.
Gubar, Susan. "'The Blank Page' and the Issues of Female Creativity." *Writing and Sexual Difference*. Ed. Elizabeth Abel. Chicago: University of Chicago Press, 1982. 73–93.
Kester-Shelton, Pamela, ed. *Feminist Writers*. Detroit: St. James, 1996.

DOMESTICITY

Historically, women have been associated with the domestic sphere of work, which encompasses household and family-related tasks, while men have been praised for their "breadwinning" work outside of the home. Feminist scholars have pointed not only to the historical continuity of this division but also to its political ramifications: Men have been able to access the public arenas that grant power, while women have been limited to interaction on the home front. Therefore, the association of women with domestic work has contributed to their silence and invisibility.

Men have often praised women for their ability to "keep the home fires burning," but such acknowledgment has done little to alter the imbalance of power enforced by the division of labor. In her 1911 text addressing this issue, Olive Schreiner noted that although men praised woman for their childbearing capacity, the men's actions rarely communicated such a message:

> Through all the ages of the past, when, with heavy womb and hard labor-worn hands, we physically toiled beside man, bearing up by the labor of our bodies the world about us, it was never suggested to us, "You, the child-bearers of the race, have in that one function a labor that equals all others combined; therefore, toil no more in other directions, we pray of you. Neither plant, nor build, nor bend over the grindstone, nor far into the night, while we sleep, sit weaving the clothing we and our children are to wear! Leave it to us . . . Work no more; every man of the race will work for you!" (109)

Other women take much the same position as Schreiner, and contemporary scholars point to the continued existence of divided labor as an area of feminist concern even though nearly one century has elapsed since Schreiner addressed this issue.

The terms of the debate broaden when variables such as race are considered, for when compared cross-culturally, women's roles are hardly parallel. African

American women, for example, must confront not only oppression due to sex but also oppression due to race. As Anna Julia Cooper observed about nineteenth-century Southern women, "The colored woman of to-day occupies . . . a unique position in this country. . . . She is confronted by both a woman question and a race problem, and is as yet an unknown or unacknowledged factor in both" (92–93). Discussion of the imposition of domesticity, then, often assumed that women shared a common cause, when many women actually faced multiple oppressions that went ignored by these overarching concerns.

Some cultures, too, have elevated the work of women in ways that are less subject to criticism than those of Euro-American society. In many Native North American cultures, for example, women often assumed what European scholars saw as men's work while the men took on traditionally "feminine" tasks. Domestic work undertaken by women was often not seen as oppressive, for women's contributions were part of a larger system of power balance in which they knowingly participated. Nonetheless, ethnographers have often described Native women as beasts of burden, and early feminist scholarship sometimes took up this cause without understanding fully the dynamics of the society being discussed. Indian women's autobiographies, though, make evident the inaccuracy of such glossing descriptions of women's spheres: "Traditionally, Indian men have been expected to indulge in the pursuit of glory and the release of emotion, while Indian women have been repositories of tradition and concern for spiritual ideals, upholding the stability of the tribe through both spiritual and generative power," as Bataille and Sands note (18). In other words, Indian women, while also held to certain types of work, were known by both themselves and the men to be central to tribal survival, so that debates over the domestic are less relevant to some cultural traditions.

The domestic sphere, now clearly definable, does not necessarily coincide with oppression. While scholarship on the division of labor has done much to unearth the ways in which women have been held to certain types of work in order to further patriarchy, it has done little to consider the ways in which women themselves have had agency within domestic positions.

References and Suggested Readings

Bataille, Gretchen M., and Kathleen Mullen Sands. *American Indian Women Telling Their Lives*. Lincoln, NE: University of Nebraska Press, 1984.

Cooper, Anna Julia. "From a Voice of the South: By a Black Woman of the South." *Feminist Theory: A Reader*. London: Mayfield, 2000. 91–95.

Medicine, Beatrice. "Gender." *Encyclopedia of North American Indians*. Ed. Frederick E. Hoxie. Boston: Houghton, 1996. 216–18.

Schreiner, Olive. "From Women and Labor." *Feminist Theory: A Reader*. Ed. Wendy Kolmar and Frances Bartkowski. London: Mayfield, 2000. 108–10.

See also Schriener, Olive.

Lisa R. Williams

E

ERDRICH, LOUISE

Born in 1954 to an Ojibway-French mother and a German-American father, Louise Erdrich is an enrolled member of the Turtle Mountain band. From her parents, both teachers at a Bureau of Indian Affairs boarding school, she received early encouragement in her literary gift. Both sides of her family were rich with storytellers, and the confluence of her Ojibway and Euro-American heritages provides a double vision that informs her work. She entered Dartmouth University in 1972, the first year the school admitted women. It was in that same year that Dartmouth, whose original mission was to provide education to Indians, began their Native American Studies Program. The first director of the program was Michael Dorris, who later became Erdrich's husband and collaborative partner. After graduation in 1976, Erdrich completed a master's degree from Johns Hopkins University. By 1984, her literary career was off to an auspicious start with the publication of both a volume of poetry, *Jacklight*, and a novel, *Love Medicine*. Since that beginning, she has continued to publish regularly and has a growing body of respected work.

Erdrich's early recognition rests on her North Dakota tetralogy: *Love Medicine*, *The Beet Queen* (1986), *Tracks* (1988), and *The Bingo Palace* (1994). These novels reveal the energies and exploits of a group of characters, both native and non-native, who dwell in and around Argus, North Dakota. Erdrich's 2002 novel *The Last Report on the Miracles at Little No Horse* returns to the area and features a startling revelation concerning the androgynous Father Damien in *Tracks*.

Erdrich's work is characterized not only by the complicated webs of relationships across generations of the same families but also by the fluency of her narrative style, which features an admixture of literary and oral traditions and her luminous prose.

Though Erdrich's characters dwell at the fringes of society—single mothers, angry and abandoned children, displaced Indians, homosexuals, neurotic nuns, wise fools, and tricksters—they all demonstrate strength and the ability to survive. Though her stories are rich in pathos, her characters are never pathetic. Since the early Argus novels, Erdrich has written *Tales of Burning Love* (1996), *The Antelope Wife* (1998), and *The Master Butchers Singing Club* (2003). In addition to *Jacklight*, her first volume of poetry, she has also written *Baptism of Desire* (1989) and *Original Fire: Selected and New Poems* (2003). Her books for children include *Grandmother's Pigeon* (1996), *The Birchbark House* (1999), and *The Range Eternal* (2002). Her 1995 *The Blue Jay's Dance* received favorable reviews as her first nonfiction work, a memoir on birth and the writing process. She has also written a travel memoir, *Books and Islands in Ojibwe Country* (2003).

Early in her career, Erdrich and her husband, Michael Dorris, worked in a creative partnership that included narrative conception and close editing of each other's work. Since their divorce in 1995 and his death in 1997, Erdrich has returned to her earlier methods of writing alone, and her recent outpouring of creativity suggests that she will continue to spin her narrative web across the Great Plains.

Erdrich now lives in Minneapolis, Minnesota, and writes, raises her daughters, and runs a nonprofit independent bookstore, Birchbark Books.

Erdrich's *Love Medicine* is perhaps her most often taught novel, and it introduces the Lamartine and Kashpaw families who people many of her other novels. *Love Medicine*, a looping achronological collection of related stories that Erdrich expanded and republished in 1993, features three generations of characters; the central characters of the first generation are Lulu Lamartine, Marie Kashpaw, and the man they both love—Nector Kashpaw. The second generation focuses on Gerry Nanapush, Lulu's son, and June Morrissey, the adoptive daughter of Marie and Nector. In large part, the narrative impulse of the story belongs to Lipsha Morrissey, June's abandoned son, and the quest for his paternity and his right to belong to the community.

In the process of Lipsha's search, the story untangles to reveal that he is thoroughly grounded in the community and that he has as his two grandmothers the strongest and most important women on the reservation, Lulu and Marie. The satellite stories of June and Gerry, of Albertine Johnson and Henry and Lyman Lamartine, of Gordie Kashpaw, and of the evil nun Sister Leopolda all contribute to the densely woven texture of this rich first novel.

References and Suggested Readings

Erdrich, Louise. *Love Medicine: New and Expanded Version*. New York: Henry Holt, 1993.
Whitson, Kathy J. "Love Medicine." *Native American Literatures: An Encyclopedia of Works, Characters, Authors, and Themes*. Santa Barbara, CA: ABC-CLIO, 1999.

See also Motherhood; Tan, Amy.

FAUSET, JESSIE REDMON

Jessie Redmon Fauset was born in 1882 in Snow Hill Center Township, New Jersey. She received a scholarship to Cornell University and became the first black woman to graduate from that institution. She earned her MA degree from the University of Pennsylvania. Fauset taught French in public high schools and later used her language skills to translate works of French West Indian writing. In her capacity as literary editor of *Crisis*, the journal of the National Association for the Advancement of Colored People, from 1919 until 1927, she was at the heart of the Harlem Renaissance and published such writers as Claude McKay, Jean Toomer, Anne Spencer, and Langston Hughes.

Fauset wrote four novels, *There Is Confusion* (1924), *Plum Bun* (1928), *The Chinaberry Tree: A Novel of American Life* (1931), and *Comedy, American Style* (1933). When her literary output ceased, she returned to teaching in the public schools. At age forty-seven, Fauset married Herbert E. Harris, an insurance executive. She died in 1961 from heart failure.

Fauset's best novel, *Plum Bun*, is divided into five sections that illustrate and parallel the epigraphic nursery rhyme "To Market, to Market/To buy a Plum Bun;/ Home again, Home again,/Market is done." It is the story of Angela Murray, a young middle-class black who is able to "pass" as her mother has done before her. The difference in their "passing" is that the mother practices passing as a habit of occasional indulgence; she does not deny her black blood, and she is firmly rooted in the black community of Philadelphia. She passes from time to time to enjoy the privileges that are denied her as a black woman: having tea in a nice hotel, shopping in the nicer stores of Philadelphia. Angela's experience with "passing" will prove disastrous to her closest relationships.

Angela is fair like Mattie, her mother, but her sister Virginia is dark like their father, Junius. One day Mattie and Angela are shopping downtown and they see Junius and Virginia and they don't speak. Later, Mattie confesses to her husband that she had not spoken to him, and he replies that as long as "no principle was involved" he thinks nothing of the game of passing that she plays. The action has a profound influence on Angela though, who doesn't know that her mother and father have this agreement of sorts about passing.

Angela goes through school passing as white and forms a friendship with the most popular schoolgirl, Mary Hastings, who has recently moved to the community and does not know that Angela, though she is one of the only black girls in high school, was one of a group of black students in grammar school. She is "outed" by another schoolmate and Mary accuses her, "Coloured! Angela, you never told me that you were coloured!" (38). Angela replies (and it becomes a refrain later in life), "Why of course I never told you that I was coloured! Why should I?" (38). This betrayal by Mary is a signal and painful moment in Angela's life. Mary refuses to take Angela on as assistant on the school magazine editorial staff then for fear that Angela, a "coloured" person, would commit malfeasance with the funds.

Angela comes to the conclusion that color is "a curious business. . . . It was the one god apparently to whom you could sacrifice everything. On account of it, her mother had neglected to greet her own husband on the street. Mary Hastings could let it come between her and her friend" (44).

After high school, both Angela and Jinny take positions as schoolteachers, but both want to move beyond that profession. Angela wants to take art classes and enrolls at the Philadelphia Academy of Fine Arts (49) and Jinny studies music. They are surrounded by a group of young friends who discuss the race issues of the day. When Seymour Porter accuses Angela of speaking "as though colour itself were a deformity," she responds, "I don't think being coloured in America is a beautiful thing. I think it's nothing short of a curse" (53).

Angela voices another strong opinion when the young people in the group call for blacks to establish a higher standard of behavior so that whites may come to a different set of opinions. She says, "I'm sick of this business of always being below or above a certain norm. Doesn't anyone think that we have a right to be happy simply, naturally?" (54).

Both the parents die and leave the two young women, with their opposing natures, to make their own ways. The death of the parents clears the way for the philosophical rift between the two daughters to widen. They are without ties or grounding or censure, and they are free to move into a world of situations that they would never have experienced as single schoolteachers living in their parents' home. Virginia has always had an inchoate awareness that Angela will one day leave her, and race will prove to be the dividing factor.

At the art academy, Angela begins a close relationship with her instructor and his wife, but it too is disrupted when a model from Angela's past "outs" her and she is questioned as to why she did not reveal that she was black.

Meanwhile, Jinny maintains that the individual colored person must make sacrifices for the good of the whole race. Angela cannot agree, but begins to wonder, "Was there something inherently wrong in 'passing'?" (73). She recognizes
that "all the good things" lay with the whites, not because they were white, "but
because for the present they had power and the badge of that power was whiteness" (73). Just as Jinny has feared, Angela decides to leave Philadelphia and go
to New York where race might not shape her destiny.

Angela is idle at first in New York, just gazing about the city and taking it all
in. She realizes that she is neglecting her "Art" and enrolls in an art class in
Cooper Union, hoping to both study art and meet some people. She alters her
name to Angèle Mory, while "some troubling sense of loyalty to her father and
mother had made it impossible for her to do away with it altogether" (95).

In art class, Angela meets Anthony Cross, Rachel Powell, Martha Burden, and
Paulette Lister. With some help from Paulette, Angela moves from the hotel she
was living in to an apartment on Jayne Street. She is surprised to learn from
Paulette that all women do not save themselves for marriage and that Paulette
believes in free love, still a shocking idea for Angela. Paulette also models some
habits of mind that surprise Angela. She says, "There is a great deal of the man
about me. I've learned that a woman is a fool who lets her femininity stand in
the way of what she wants. . . . I employ the qualities of men, tenacity and ruth-
lessness to keep it" (105). Paulette has had lovers and wonders that Angela has
not.

Angela struggles with how a woman alone can achieve "position, power,
wealth," and suggests to herself, "I might marry—a white man. Marriage is the
easiest way for a woman to get those things, and white men have them" (111–
12). But she knows only one white man, Anthony Cross, and she is certain he
has no more access to those attributes than she does.

Through Martha Burden, Angela meets Roger Fielding, the son of a very
wealthy man. Roger does nothing for a living, exists only to spend his father's
money, but takes care not to misstep in his relationships, for his father is adamant
that Roger must marry within an acceptable circle. Angela is seduced by his power
and wealth but convinces herself that she would want his wealth only to improve
the efforts of her own people. On the night that she longs for Roger to propose,
everything is perfect until he leaves the table to ask the waiter to dismiss a group
of blacks who are dining nearby. His virulent reaction to the blacks sickens
Angela, but Roger is certain that her drained look confirms that she too "had no
time for darkies" (133). He continues his rant, proclaiming that he would send
all blacks back to Africa and would even be willing to finance the move. Angela
vows that she is through with Roger Fielding and does maintain a cold distance
for two weeks, but she misses his attentions, the elegant meals, and the reprieve
to her own bank account that his dinner dates give her.

In the meantime she sees Anthony Cross and is certain of his sincere affection for her. Anthony asks her if, "for the sake of love," she could "endure priva-
tion and hardship and misunderstanding," and thinking of her mother's sacrifices,

how on wash days, her mother's hands had "a white, boiled appearance" (142) she tells Anthony that she could not. He crumbles at the confession and says, "I almost touched happiness" (142).

Angela is now determined to "win Roger around to helping coloured people," but she does not know how to get Roger to propose to her (144). She asks her friend Martha, who is set back by the frankness of the question. Martha admits that it is a difficult social "game" that women must play, always offering a part of themselves as bait but taking care not to offer too much. She counsels, "If we give too much we lose ourselves. Oh, Angèle, God doesn't like women" (145). Angela begins seeing Roger again, holding him at some reserve, playing him for what she can, and being seduced all over again. But she now has some power over him; "She herself was power" (151).

Roger must leave town but promises that when he returns he has something of importance to say to her. Meanwhile she gets a note from Jinny who announces her arrival in New York and wonders if Angela might pick her up at the train station. Roger shows up unexpectedly, and Angela spurns her dark-skinned sister to save face with Roger. The resulting fracture in the relationship between sisters is repaired only after much grief.

What Angela imagines will be a proposal of marriage from Roger turns out to be something far less; he says, "I'm asking you to live in my house, to live for me; to be my girl; to keep a love-nest where I and only I may come" (182). Angela holds off for three months but continues to see Roger for conversation, and they develop a kind of daily intimacy. Roger continues to urge her, and finally Angela falls to the desires of her flesh, though she must continually rationalize her behaviors by insisting that she will only use the benefits that come from the relationship for the good, for furthering her race. At the time, "Hers was a curious mixture of materialism and hedonism, and at this moment the latter quality was uppermost in her life" (207). When Roger breaks off their relationship, Angela wonders, "God, isn't there any place where man's responsibility to woman begins?" (233).

She realizes that she is near poverty and takes a design job for a fashion journal. Having formed only loosely connected friendships without rootedness and depth, Angela is now alone in New York. Jinny, on the other hand, has found many friends and intimacies in New York and is flourishing. Finally, ashamed of her alliance with Roger, Angela decides to humble herself and go to Jinny. She finds Jinny in celebration over her engagement. Angela is certain that Jinny is engaged to Matthew Henson, a friend from home whom Jinny has always loved. The ensuing confusions are worthy of a Shakespearean plot. Though Jinny loves Matthew, Matthew loves Angela. Anthony Cross has also loved Angela, but has been rebuffed by her when she was in love with Roger. She resigns herself to a life of loneliness until she comes upon an idea: "She had thought of [marriage] once before as a source of relief from poverty, as a final barrier between herself and the wolves of prejudice; why not now as a means of avoiding loneliness?" (262). She then remembers Anthony Cross's former devotion to her and seeks him out. He reveals that he has been passing and had given up all hope that he could be with a white woman, so he has become engaged.

Finally Angela reveals that she too has been passing. Of course, it is to Jinny that Anthony is engaged. He has settled for her rather than Angela, and she has settled for him in the absence of her beloved Matthew. Roger reenters the picture and asks Angela to marry him.

A depressed Angela throws herself back into her artwork and wins the John T. Steward Prize while her black classmate Miss Powell wins another prize. Both win a time of study in France, but Miss Powell's award is retracted because she is black. Martha Burden and several others at the art school intercede on her behalf, but she finally asks them to abandon their efforts. Martha has a terrible outburst, "I wonder if couloured people aren't natural born quitters. Somethimes I think I'll never raise another finger for them" (338). Anthony takes up for Miss Powell, asserting that sometimes "they have to stop their fight for the trimmings of life in order to hang on to the essentials" (338). Then he reveals that he too is black. The climate becomes so antagonistic that Angela is finally moved to reveal her background. In the moral pivot of the book, she refuses her prize in solidarity with Miss Powell. When the incident is reported in the papers the next work day, Angela is fired for "deceit."

Angela decides to study in Paris for six months anyway, but before she goes, she has dinner with Matthew Henson and learns that he has grown to love Jinny. On Christmas Eve, Angela opens the door to the knock of Anthony, sent to her with the love of Jinny and Matthew. "Market is Done."

References and Suggested Readings

Fauset, Jessie Redmon. *Plum Bun*. 1928. Boston: Beacon Press, 1990.

McDowell, Deborah E. "Jessie Fauset." *Modern American Women Writers*. Ed. Lea Baechler and General A. Walton Litz. New York: Scribner's, 1991.

Wagner, Wendy. "Fauset, Jessie Redmon." *The Oxford Companion to Women's Writing*. Ed. Cathy N. Davidson and Linda Wagner-Martin. New York: Oxford University Press, 1995.

FERN, FANNY

Fanny Fern was born in 1811 as Sara Payson Willis in Portland, Maine, into a family involved in journalism and periodical literature for three generations. Her father, Nathaniel Willis, founded the *Boston Recorder*, "the first religious newspaper in America" and established the first periodical for children, the *Youth's Companion*, in 1827. Raised in Boston, Fern attended Catherine Beecher's Hartford Female Seminary and achieved the best education then available to women. She married Charles Harrington Eldredge in 1837 and over the coming years gave birth to three daughters. Their first daughter died in 1845, just a year after the death of Fern's mother. When Eldredge died of typhoid fever in 1846, Fern was left in a precarious financial position, but the series of blows was not ended. The young widowed mother received only the barest financial support from her family. Her seamstress skills could not garner Fern enough money to support her family, and her attempts to find a teaching job were unsuccessful. Finally, she reluctantly entered a marriage of convenience to Samuel P. Farrington. The alliance was a terrible mistake, and in a move counter to all social custom, Fern left the marriage and was divorced two years later by Farrington on charges of desertion. Once again, Fern was cast into financial jeopardy. She landed on the idea of writing for periodicals, having had some success in writing while a student, but when she appealed to her brother, Nathaniel P. Willis, Jr., the prominent editor of the *Home Journal*, he rejected her appeal out of hand. Without his help, Fern nonetheless began a slow ascent to national prominence and financial independence as she authored the first column written by a woman in the United States. Her experiences, first as a widow and later as a divorcée, tragically confirmed her earlier notions that a woman must have economic independence to have any measure of personal freedom.

In 1856, Fern married again, this time to James Parton, a man eleven years her junior. Fern insisted on a prenuptial agreement to protect her now considerable earnings and to provide for her children. Fern died in 1872.

Fern's journalistic successes were matched by her foray into fiction when she published *Ruth Hall: A Domestic Tale of the Present Time* in 1855 and *Rose Clark* in 1856. *Ruth Hall*, Fern's strongly autobiographical novel, has become her most studied work.

In *Ruth Hall*, Fern's main character, Ruth Ellet, has not had a happy childhood, growing up after the early death of her mother and with the chilling indifference of her Calvinist father. Though in her childhood Ruth adores her older brother Hyacinth, he is vaguely detached from her but quite willing to tell her that she is "plain" and "awkward" (4). After her mother's death, Ruth is sent to a boarding school where she does not quite fit in with the other girls. As she grows beyond her girlhood, however, she begins attracting attention and realizes that "she had found out her power!" and that she "could inspire love!" (6). She longs for the time when she can find her "twin-soul" so that she can "make somebody's heart glad" (6). Ruth continues her studies, though her friends wonder at her hard work, assuring her that it is "quite unnecessary for a pretty woman to be clever" (7). Her own father advises her "either to get married or teach school" (7), thus revealing the limited options for a woman of her social standing in the nineteenth century. When she is still a very young woman, Ruth does marry. On the eve of her wedding, Ruth remembers her parents' relationship—her father's petty demands and her mother's suppression of her own will to placate her husband. She wonders if the footfall that now makes her "heart leap" will ever "sound in her ear like a death-knell" (3). Ruth's marriage to Harry Hall yields a match that far exceeds her cautious expectations, however. She takes a very un-Victorian delight in her intimacy with Harry and loves the look of his toiletries and clothing lying next to hers in "unrebuked proximity" (11).

Ruth and Harry begin their marriage living in an apartment of his parents' home. Harry's father, a self-trained country "doctor," is as strongly opinionated as his wife, and only their strict Calvinism keeps them at peace with one another. They dote on Harry and believe he has never made a mistake since his birth, save to marry Ruth. The elder Halls are disapproving of Ruth's every move, and Ruth's newfound sense of freedom is quickly eroded by the dominance and economic enslavement of her mother-in-law. Mrs. Hall insists that Ruth hand over to her any pin money that Harry might give her and cautions her not to read "novels and such trash" (14). Ruth longs to confide in Harry but decides not to put him in a position where he must choose between his wife and his mother. He is, however, aware of the tension in the home and plans to move them to a home of their own.

Their union is soon blessed by the birth of a daughter, Daisy, "another outlet for [Ruth's] womanly heart; a mirror, in which [her] smiles and tears shall be reflected back" (19). Ruth and Harry finally get a home of their own only to have the elder Halls move near them. Still, the idyllic existence in the country with Daisy and Harry is enough to fulfill all her longings until tragedy strikes. Daisy develops a cough, and though Ruth and Harry send for Doctor Hall, he refuses to come. The child dies, and Doctor Hall views the death as a necessary affliction sent to humble Ruth. Ruth and Harry move away, trying to leave the bitter memories behind. Though they have two more daughters, the pain over Daisy's loss is never fully assuaged.

In their new home, Ruth meets Mary Leon, a woman who has married a cold and rigid man of wealth, a man cut from the same cloth as the Duke in Browning's "My Last Duchess." The story of Mrs. Leon offers yet another example of the bondage women are subject to in a society where they have no opportunities for employment and economic independence. Mrs. Leon warns Ruth to never let her daughters enter a loveless marriage, even for wealth. She says, "The chain is not the less galling, because its links are golden" (57). Years later, Ruth learns that Mary Leon has been placed in an insane asylum by her husband. Ruth visits the asylum and is horrified by the conditions of the women; some are chained and whipped, others are emotionally crushed by the law that takes their children from them. Her visit is too late for Mary though, who has died leaving her a note, "I am not crazy, Ruth, no, no—but I shall be; the air of this place stifles me; I grow weaker—weaker. I cannot die here; for the love of heaven, dear Ruth, come and take me away" (141).

In a social order where marriage is the only secure financial arrangement for women, the hazards are many, as Ruth learns all too well after the death of her husband. Harry Hall contracts typhus fever and dies after lingering for two months. He prays that God will spare him lest there is no one to care for Ruth. His fears prove true, for neither his parents nor Ruth's family want to help her from the financial insolvency in which Harry leaves her. Only the fear of public disapproval finally pressures both sets of parents to grudgingly offer scant support. Ruth and her children move into a seedy boarding house in an effort to curb expenses enough to keep the family intact, for the elder Halls are threatening to seize the children.

Ruth experiences another level of the social order in the boarding house. As a widow without the protection of a man, she is subject to the unsolicited attentions of the men who live there. When she seeks work as a seamstress in the shop of one of Harry's friends, she is turned down because women who "had seen better days" knew the "value of their labor" and could not be so easily exploited as the poor (98).

Ruth's friends and family will not visit her in the tenement for fear of "los[ing] caste" now that she is in reduced circumstances (100). Fern does not miss the opportunity to expose the hypocrisies of race and class. The black servants in Ruth's cousin's household are scandalized at how Ruth is forced to scrape by in poverty while her father, brother, and cousins flaunt their excess. One servant remarks, "white folks *is* stony-hearted" (101). While her wealthy relatives refuse to perform even the most obligatory act of Christian charity toward Ruth, it is Johnny Galt, a common ploughboy and former employee of Harry, who brings her apples and flowers in an act of human sympathy.

Ruth continues to struggle, and the longer she is in dire straits, the more sympathetic she becomes to those in like circumstances. Though always a woman who lived out the Christian imperative of loving one's neighbor, Ruth is acutely aware now of just who her neighbor is. One day she looks out her tenement window to see the "gray-haired men, business men, substantial-looking family men, and foppish-looking young men" visiting a brothel down the street. At the window she sees faces of women "young and fair" and "wan and haggard" (112). In an epiphanic moment, Ruth "knew now how it could be, when every door of hope seemed shut" (112). She too has experienced the hypocritical piety of those who "wrap themselves in morality" and "cry with closed purses and averted faces, 'Be ye warmed, and filled'" (112). Ruth blesses "Bethlehem's guiding star," which has saved her from a similar fate (113).

Once more Ruth tries to gain employment, hoping to start a school, but she has no references and cannot obtain any from her cool and distant family. She hears of a job at a primary school but is voted against by two men who know her qualifications and her need; both vote against her to curry favor with the most important man on the committee.

Fern moves the narrative back to the boarding house to provide another gritty slice of life in the story of Mr. and Mrs. Skiddy. With consummate skill, Fern successfully draws a sympathetic portrait of both unsavory characters. Mrs. Skiddy, who runs the boarding house where Ruth lives, takes her two older children and leaves Mr. Skiddy with a nursing baby. Only in her absence does the helpless Skiddy come to realize "how *many* irons Mrs. Skiddy had daily in the fire" (117).

After a time, Mrs. Skiddy returns, much to the disappointment of Skiddy who has learned to manage without her and her constant scolding. Mrs. Skiddy confides in Ruth she has learned that a married woman "must make up her mind either to manage or be managed" (135) and that she prefers to manage. Soon after

Mrs. Skiddy returns, Mr. Skiddy leaves the family to seek his freedom and fortune in California. Freed at last from the necessity to "manage or be managed," Mrs. Skiddy turns her boarding house into a lodging—offering no meals—and makes a success of her business. A year later, the failed Mr. Skiddy writes home asking for return passage from California, and Mrs. Skiddy responds with a hiss "like ten thousand serpents, the word 'N—e—v—e—r!'" (137). The insertion of the Skiddy story serves to show the bondage of a bad marriage and how it diminishes members of both genders. Mrs. Skiddy is to be applauded for her unwillingness to be "managed," but in the process of resisting oppression, she becomes the oppressor.

Perhaps buoyed by Mrs. Skiddy's financial success, Ruth develops another plan for independence; she sends writing samples to her brother Hyacinth, "now the prosperous editor of the *Irving Magazine*" (146). She doesn't hear back from him for a long while and then only to be discouraged by his callous response, "you have no talent [in writing]" (146).

Meanwhile, the elder Halls are scheming once again to get Ruth's children from her. They take Katy for a two-week visit but have no intentions of returning her and announce to their friends that Ruth has given her up. Ruth is so upset by their duplicity that she comes to doubt the good in people and wonders if religion is "only a fable" (152). She redoubles her efforts to earn a living through periodical writing. One editor dismisses her on the basis of her gender, another on account of her religion. Just when she is at the very edge of despair, she hears the comforting words of Scripture, "there remaineth, therefore, a rest for the people of God" (156). She finally gets an article placed in *The Standard*, though for a mere pittance. Slowly, however, she is gaining a readership and much public interest in the identity of "Floy," her *nom de plume*. With little success, she appeals to her editor for a raise. Her fortunes turn when a fan suggests that she gather her articles into a book and when she meets Mr. John Walter and begins to write solely for his paper. Finally, she is earning pay commensurate to her worth. Now that she has gathered a near-cult national following, her brother Hyacinth tries to claim that she has achieved her merit only through her connection to him.

Ruth's successes as "Floy" set up a series of satisfying closures to the novel. She is able to rescue Katy from the clutches of her abusive grandparents. Old Mrs. Hall has admiringly read Floy's book, only to be shocked and embarrassed when she learns who Floy is; all those in her family who refused to help her now must deal with the public humiliation that their relative labored in poverty without the benefit of familial assistance. The novel ends with the promise that "life has much of harmony yet in store" for Ruth Hall (272). Furthermore, it ends with "its heroine neither on the altar nor beside the hearth" (Huf 20), a distinct reversal of nineteenth-century formula fiction.

The immediate and continuing success of *Ruth Hall* controverts the opinion of one critic who wrote to the character Ruth Hall that "the *female* mind is incapable of producing anything which may be strictly termed *literature*" (Fern 214). As Joyce W. Warren notes, "because Fern was able to write in defiance of the restrictions that conventional nineteenth-century American society imposed upon women writers," *Ruth Hall* is "both a significant literary achievement and a valuable social document."

References and Suggested Readings

Fern, Fanny. *Ruth Hall*. 1855. New York: Penguin, 1997.

Huf, Linda. *A Portrait of the Artist as a Young Woman: The Writer as Heroine in American Literature*. New York: Ungar, 1983.

Smith, Susan Belasco. Introduction. *Ruth Hall*. By Fanny Fern. 1855. New York: Penguin, 1997. xv–xiv.

Warren, Joyce W. *Ruth Hall and Other Writings*. New Brunswick: Rutgers University Press, 1986.

———. "Text and Context in Fanny Fern's *Ruth Hall*: From Widowhood to Independence." *Joinings and Disjoinings: The Significance of Marital Status in Literature*. Ed. JoAnna Stephens Mink and Janet Doubler Ward. Bowling Green, OH: Popular, 1991. 67–76.

FOSTER, HANNAH WEBSTER

Hannah Foster was born in 1758 in Salisbury, Massachusetts, to Grant Webster and Hannah Wainwright Webster. Her education included a time at boarding school after the death of her mother. In 1785, she married the Reverend John Foster and moved to Brighton where he served as a minister. The Fosters had six children, the first of whom died soon after birth. Two of their daughters, Elizabeth Lanesford Cushing and Harriet Vaughan Cheney, went on to some success as writers. Though Foster wrote a second novel, *The Boarding School; or Lessons of a Preceptress to Her Pupils* (1798), she is best known for her first and superior novel, *The Coquette; or The History of Eliza Wharton; A Novel; Founded on Fact* (1797). Foster died in 1840 in Montreal.

Foster's novel is loosely based on the story of Elizabeth Whitman, "the daughter of a highly respected minister, the Reverend Elnathan Whitman." By the time Foster wrote of Whitman's tragic life—seduction, pregnancy, death in a roadside tavern—the story had already been sensationalized in the *Salem Mercury*. As Davidson notes, because of her violation of socially enforced morals, "Elizabeth Whitman had to become The Fallen Woman. . . . All that needed to be said about her character was that she had lost it" (ix).

The Coquette follows an epistolary format and, as such, offers the first person accounts of several characters: Eliza Wharton, Lucy Freeman Sumner, Mr. Boyer, Major Sanford, Mrs. Wharton, Mr. Selby, Mrs. Richman, and Julia Granby. Eliza Wharton's voice predominates at the beginning, and Davidson suggests that as she "sinks into physical infirmity and mental instability," she "becomes less present in the text."

When the novel opens, Eliza reports the death of a Mr. Haly, "a man of worth; a man of real and substantial merit" to her friend Lucy Freeman (Foster 5). Eliza was engaged to Mr. Haly but, beyond parental expectation and her admiration for his goodness, nothing bound Eliza to him. Though she helped nurse him in his final illness, she feels more exultation than grief at his death, for having played the dutiful daughter, she now can seek pleasures of her own. She is on an extended visit at the home of her friends, the Richmans, and is enjoying the first freedom from her mother's care. The voice in her letters betrays a certain innocent shallowness and blind willfulness. In the second letter, Foster already introduces Eliza's coquetry and her avowal to abandon any hint of it, though she insists, in a counter justification, that her behaviors are the "effusions of a youthful, and cheerful mind" (7). Eliza's tone borders on flippancy and certainly reflects a naïveté that portends a narrative disaster.

Once situated at the Richmans', Eliza becomes the focus of two suitors, Mr. Boyer and Major Sanford, characters of opposite dispositions. Boyer is a minister and is staid and agreeable but uninteresting to Eliza. She recognizes that to be the wife of a minister would be stultifying for her; she writes, "But his situation in life! I dare not enter it. My disposition is not calculated for that sphere" (39). Still, she is enamored of the game of love enough to keep Boyer in the mix. She is "loath to give up either; being doubtful which will conduce most to [her] felicity" (53).

When Eliza's friends caution her against Major Sanford and urge her toward the reputable, if predictable, Boyer, she begs freedom and extrication "from those shackles, which parental authority had imposed on [her] mind" (13). Sanford is forthright in his representation of his own motives as he writes a friend: "I fancy this young lady is a coquette; and if so, I shall avenge my sex, by retaliating the mischiefs, she mediates against us. . . . And let her beware of the consequences" (18). Still, he is fond of Eliza but finds her unsuitable for marriage because of her lack of a fortune.

Meanwhile, Eliza is losing her own companions to marriage. Mrs. Richman is married and now pregnant; Lucy Freeman is engaged to be married, and Eliza laments, "Marriage is the tomb of friendship. . . . The tenderest ties between friends are weakened, or dissolved" (24). As she writes to her friends of her love interests, she receives much admonition but little genuine friendship. Having secured themselves in their expected roles, they strongly advise Eliza to follow their example. Their concern for her reveals how few options there are and how many perils there are for women at that time: A woman who spends the capital of her youth without making an alliance is in danger of a life of financial dependency at best or debauchery at worst.

As the novel progresses, the warnings of her friends against Major Sanford and her own coquetry take on greater portent. Lucy Freeman warns, "Remember that you are acting for life; and that your happiness in this world, perhaps in the next, depends on your present choice!" (59).

Meanwhile, Sanford increases his attentions toward Eliza, all the while boasting of his wicked intentions; he writes to a friend, "Though I cannot possess her wholly myself, I will not tamely see her the property of another" (35). He does, however, buy an estate near her family's home so that he can be near her. As profligate in financial matters as he is in affairs of the heart, Sanford falls into debt and must marry an heiress to maintain his lifestyle.

Boyer finds Eliza to be a "young lady whose elegant person, accomplished mind, and polished manners have been much celebrated" (10). He is much devoted to her and presses her for an unofficial engagement, but Eliza is loath to commit herself to one suitor or the other. As she continues to accept engagements with both Boyer and Sanford, Boyer cannot bear the indignity of her coquetry. He grows increasingly impatient and finally breaks off all relationships with her but not before warning her a final time against Sanford. Sanford leaves the country, trying to escape his debts and for a year does not contact Eliza. She is distraught, having lost both of her suitors. In a moment of contrition, she writes Boyer and offers her heart "once prized" and her hand "once solicited" (102) only to learn that he will soon marry another.

When she learns that Sanford too has married, Eliza falls into a depression and is looked after by her mother and her friend Julia Granby. Sanford moves back to his estate near Eliza's home and begins his seduction of her once again, this time under the pretext of having her make friends with his wife. Depressed and without any hope for future happiness, Eliza succumbs to Sanford and is soon pregnant. Only at this point does Eliza come to an awareness of his true character. She writes to her friend Lucy, "But not long did I continue in the delusive dream of sensual gratification. I soon awoke to a most poignant sense of his baseness, and of my own crime and misery" (145). Eliza leaves her home in order to complete her pregnancy away from the eyes of her friends and family. Sanford makes arrangements for her at a roadside tavern some distance away and confesses to his friend that if his wife were to sue for divorce, he would marry Eliza. It would be a reluctant marriage though, for as he says, "It would hurt even my delicacy, little as you may think me to possess, to have a wife whom I know to be seducible" (157).

Sanford's morality of the double standard need not be vexed however, for Eliza dies after delivering a stillborn child. To the credit of her friends, Lucy Freeman Sumner and Julia Granby mark Eliza's grave with an inscription that throws "a veil over her frailties" and celebrates her virtues (169).

The power of Eliza's story—and that of her historical antecedent's—is attested to by the best-seller status of *The Coquette*, which West notes "appeared in at least thirteen editions" and was "dramatized as *The New England Coquette*."

References and Suggested Readings

Davidson, Cathy N. "Chronology of Hannah Webster Foster." *The Coquette*. By Hannah W. Foster. New York: Oxford University Press, 1986. xxiv.

———. Introduction. *The Coquette*. By Hannah W. Foster. New York: Oxford University Press, 1986. vii–xx.

Foster, Hannah W. *The Coquette; or The History of Eliza Wharton; A Novel; Founded on Fact*. 1797. Edited with an introduction by Cathy N. Davidson. New York: Oxford University Press, 1986.

West, Kathryn. "Foster, Hannah Webster." *The Oxford Companion to Women's Writing in the United States*. Ed. Cathy N. Davidson and Linda Wagner-Martin. New York: Oxford University Press, 1995.

FRIENDSHIP

Sigmund Freud's assessment of "normal" sexual development routinized opposite-sex relationships as the climax of that development. In part, because of this, the intensity of same-sex friendships, particularly among women, has long been noted and, prior to the twentieth century, accepted without question or concern. Women shared some of their most intimate experiences with one another, and often many expressed their inability to relate to men on the same level.

Carroll Smith-Rosenberg studied nineteenth-century women in order to look at how their friendships with other women affected their lives, and her research helped to extract them from their Freudian context—that is, their context within the spectrum of development that assumes any romantic attachment between two women to evidence a lack of sexual evolution. "These female friendships," writes Smith-Rosenberg, "served a number of emotional functions. Within this secure and empathetic world women could share sorrows, anxieties, and joys, confident that other women had experienced similar emotions." She went on to quote an excerpt of a letter one woman wrote to her dear friend: "To have such a friend as thyself to look to and sympathize with her—and enter into all her little needs and in whose bosom she could with freedom pour forth her joys and sorrows—such a friend would very much relieve the tedium of many a wearisome hour" (40). Using many similar excerpts from letters written by women to women, Smith-Rosenberg contends that it matters not whether such relationships involved sexual expression; instead, such friendships should "be related to the structure of the American family and to the nature sex-role divisions and of male-female relations both within the family and in society generally" (29).

The "American family" has hardly been a stable concept, and the role of friendship has, therefore, also shifted. Women in the eighteenth and nineteenth centuries relied on one another for support during schooling, courtship, childbirth, miscarriage, and even honeymoons; they were often more available to one another than women of today because of rigid gender roles that insisted they all belonged at home while their husbands worked. Even so, women of the twenty-first century still function within a society unable to accept relationships that could be interpreted as homosexual (whether or not they are actually physical). Because women are now no longer relegated strictly to the domestic sphere, they find that society sometimes imagines a close friendship to be a homosexual relationship, whether or not that is actually the case.

This shift in emphasis no doubt has to do with the emergence of queer theory, which has recovered many historical "friendships" and claimed them as evidence of a historical queer existence. Homosexual relations have not, after all, come into existence only recently; rather, they have simply become a more acceptable topic for discussion. The historical silence surrounding the complexities of "friendship" has to do with medical experts' views of same-sex inclination or activity as evidence of maladjustment. The medicalization of these connections left "friendship" as the only socially acceptable template for same-sex relations. But as Jonathan

Katz has pointed out, the evolution of the connotative power of friendship "is but one aspect of the changing social forms of love and hate, the social history of emotion, the sociology of sensibility—the study of the quality of human lives at a particular time, in a particular society" (452).

References and Suggested Readings

Katz, Jonathan. *Gay American History: Lesbians and Gay Men in the U.S.A.* New York: Harper, 1976.

Smith-Rosenberg, Carroll. "The Female World of Love and Ritual: Relations Between Women in Nineteenth-Century America." *The Signs Reader.* Chicago: University of Chicago Press, 1975. 27–55.

Lisa R. Williams

GASKELL, ELIZABETH

Elizabeth Gaskell was born in London in 1810, the daughter of a Unitarian minister, civil servant, and journalist. Her mother died when Elizabeth was young, and she was raised by an aunt. In 1832, she married a Unitarian minister, William Gaskell, and shared in his ministry. Together they had six children, two of whom did not survive infancy. Though she had been writing for some time, Gaskell's first novel, *May Barton*, was not published until 1848. She wrote several short pieces for *Howitt's Journal* and *Household Words* and continued writing novels. Both *Ruth* and *Cranford* were published in 1853; *North and South* was published in 1855.

Gaskell met many of England's literary giants, including Dickens, Wordsworth, and Charlotte Brontë. After her death in 1855, Brontë's father asked Gaskell to write a biography of her life. Gaskell's *Life of Charlotte Brontë* (1857) is still admired today. Other works by Gaskell include *Lizzie Leigh: A Domestic Tale* (1850), *The Moorland Cottage* (1850), *Lizzie Leigh and Other Tales* (1855), *My Lady Ludlow* (1858), *Right at Last and Other Tales* (1860), *Lois the Witch and Other Tales* (1860), *Sylvia's Lovers* (1863), *A Dark Night's Work* (1863), *Cousin Phillis: A Tale* (1864), *The Grey Woman and Other Tales* (1865), and *Wives and Daughter: An Every-Day Story* (1866). Gaskell died suddenly in 1865.

Elizabeth Gaskell's *Ruth* (1853) is the story of Ruth Hilton, a poor orphan girl who works in a dressmaker's shop; she is without family or friends. Her mother, the "daughter of a poor curate in Norfolk" (36), dies when Ruth is only twelve, and her father, an unsuccessful farmer, dies three years later. Her father unwisely set her future in place when he set up a legal guardianship at her birth that placed her in the care of the most prominent man he knew, but a man who had never even met Ruth. Her guardian's disinterest in Ruth is quickly made obvious when he settles the estate and immediately sets her into an apprenticeship with a dress-

maker. There she has no advocate other than a friend, Jenny, who too soon falls
ill and leaves Ruth once more alone. Not quite sixteen, orphaned, and friendless,
the beautiful but naïve Ruth is easy prey for handsome and wealthy Mr.
Bellingham. Mrs. Mason, the dressmaker, shares in the complicity of Ruth's downfall, for she treats Ruth as a commodity to improve her own business. Not only
are Ruth and the other seamstresses forced into intolerable working conditions
and used roughly, but Mrs. Mason insists on putting the most beautiful girls on
display at the shire-hall ball. There Ruth first meets the self-serving Bellingham,
and when Mrs. Mason later sees Ruth in the company of Bellingham, she turns
Ruth out of her service.

Gaskell sets the plot in the first pages of the novel when the narrator declares,
"The daily life into which people are born, and into which they are absorbed before they are well aware, forms chains which only one in a hundred has moral
strength enough to despise, and to break when the right times comes" (2). *Ruth*
depicts the moral development of the titular character as she breaks the chains that
have bound her. Alan Shelston notes that the novel "was explicitly conceived as a
social-problem novel" (vii), and clearly Gaskell is protesting against the limited freedoms of women, including their lack of meaningful and compensated work, their
limited legal rights, and the double standards imposed on their sexuality.

Ruth's lack of experience with men causes her to "fanc[y] that Mr. Bellingham
looked as if he could understand the feelings of those removed from him by circumstance and station" (Gaskell 17), but she misreads his character. Ruth, with
her "union of the grace and loveliness of womanhood with the *naïveté*, simplicity, and innocence of an intelligent child" (33) is no match for the worldly
Bellingham, and she initially succumbs to his offer to go with him to London. But
almost as quickly, she senses that such a move would only compound her problems, and even though she refuses Bellingham's offer, he abducts her nonetheless.

Ruth's social fall is complete, and she is eyed with scorn and disapproval wherever they travel. Her relationship with Bellingham further undermines her ability to see a solution to her situation, for he has grown tired of her and calls her
"stupid, not so good as a dummy" (66). Ruth comes to believe his assessment
and wishes she "had the gift of being amusing" (66) so that he would not feel
bored with her; she longs for the ability to interest him but feels unequal to the
task.

On a trip to Wales with Bellingham, the wheel of fortune turns finally in Ruth's
favor, though not without first throwing her into a most painful situation. The
townspeople subject her to verbal abuse because she is not married; Mr.
Bellingham falls ill with brain fever, and the innkeeper sends for his mother.
Though Ruth is willing to nurse Bellingham, she is pushed aside as morally lep-
rous, and his mother whisks off Bellingham. Ruth is once again left friendless and
alone. It is only the intercession of the vacationing Dissenter minister, Mr. Benson,
that saves Ruth from suicide. Benson quickly assesses the situation and sends for
his sister, Faith. Together they remove Ruth from Wales and take her to their
home where a new chapter of life begins for Ruth.

Before arriving home, the Bensons and Ruth enter the pact that her history will be rewritten to save the pregnant and abandoned Ruth from social ostracism and her unborn child from the stigmatization of illegitimacy. Ruth will go by the name Mrs. Denbigh and will be announced as a distant relation of the Bensons. With the loving care and spiritual nurture of the Bensons, Ruth repents her actions and begins a life of piety and devotion. By the time her son is born, Ruth has become an integral part of the Benson household. As her son, Leonard, grows, so too does Ruth whose "mind was uncultivated, her reading scant" (177). Mr. Benson begins her formal education, and soon Ruth "delighted in the exercise of her intellectual powers, and liked the idea of the infinite amount of which she was ignorant; for it was a grand pleasure to learn—to crave, and be satisfied" (191).

In Mr. Benson's parish is the stern and unbending Mr. Bradshaw, who takes a paternal interest in Ruth and offers her the role of nursery governess to watch over his two younger daughters. The potential job opens up a moral dilemma for Ruth and the Bensons; should they reveal the secret of Ruth's past to Mr. Bradshaw? In the end, they decide against it, but the choice to continue in an act of deceit in order to secure a positive outcome haunts Mr. Benson and will ultimately demand its due.

The Bradshaw family provides a window into the gender roles and marriage customs of the time. Mr. Bradshaw is the unequivocal ruler of the household, and his wife is "sweet and gentle-looking, but as if she was thoroughly broken into submission" (153). She is mute in his presence and cautions her children into "the attitude or action most pleasing to their father" (211). Bradshaw prides himself that his wife carefully reports all that takes place in his absence and that he has "trained her to habits of accuracy very unusual in a woman" (222). Their oldest daughter, Jemima, inwardly rebels against the strictures of her father, but her older brother has already patterned himself after their father and warns her that "many things are right for men which are not for girls" (213). Mr. Bradshaw chooses a marriage partner for Jemima based on the financial gain for himself and the opportunity to keep her under his watchful eye. Jemima finds it "degrading" to "alter herself to gain the love of any human creature" (219), and her strong will sets her up for a miserable existence with her father. Though she later marries Mr. Farquhar, a man less rigid and conventional than her father, even he looks forward to "the control which he should have a right to exercise over her actions" (375).

The novel moves to a new degree of complication when Bellingham, now known as Mr. Donne, enters the story again. Mr. Bradshaw is now wealthy and influential enough to put forth a candidate for Member of Parliament, the wealthy but dissolute Mr. Donne. Ruth's respectability and the well-intentioned lie of the Bensons unravel as Ruth and Donne inevitably meet and he learns of his son. Ruth is inwardly torn as she recognizes, "Oh, my God! I do believe Leonard's father is a bad man, and yet, oh! pitiful God, I love him; I cannot forget—I cannot!" (274). Even more troubling, Ruth fears that Donne will take Leonard from her, for "a child, whether legitimate or not, belonged of legal right to the father" (290).

Donne presses Ruth to enter once again into relationship with him, and even proposes marriage to legitimize Leonard's status, but Ruth holds firm against the alliance, knowing that any social gain would be offset by her own unhappiness with the dissipated Donne and her fear that he would lead Leonard into a similar path. To his credit, Donne does not pursue Ruth any further, but the wheels of her discovery are set into motion.

Bradshaw learns of Ruth's history and turns her out from his employment, breaks with the Bensons, and refuses to worship in Benson's church any longer. Ruth tells Leonard of his birth, and he is ashamed of her and angry at the taunts he faces from the community. No longer able to work as a governess, Ruth finally finds employment as a sick nurse to the parish surgeon where "[a]t first her work lay exclusively among the paupers" (390). While Ruth slowly builds her respectability once again, the Bradshaws are in a trajectory of moral ruin. Bradshaw's son and junior partner, Richard, has defrauded some clients, including Benson, of their life savings, and Bradshaw disowns him. Mrs. Bradshaw finally speaks out against the cruelty of her husband and vows she will choose her son over her husband unless he repents of his hard line against Richard. Mr. Benson intercedes and is able to restore the family and his friendship with Bradshaw to some equilibrium.

Time passes, and Ruth finds fulfillment in her work with the sick, though Leonard is still skittish around outsiders. When typhus fever rages across the countryside, Ruth volunteers to enter the pestilent hospital chambers to nurse the ill and comfort the dying. For three weeks, Leonard and the Bensons wait and pray for her survival. One evening, Leonard goes to the hospital and waits outside with the crowds of other anxious family members; he hears them speaking of his mother in tones of respect and approbation for the work she has done for their loved ones. He is "overwhelmed now to hear of the love and the reverence with which the poor and outcast had surrounded her" (429). Leonard gains a new appreciation of his mother and no longer is ashamed of her.

Ruth continues to minister to the ill through the height of the crisis and returns home only when the typhus is largely under control. She is given a public letter of commendation by the rector of the village, and it seems her reputation is now restored. Just as she is preparing for a seaside rest, she learns that Mr. Donne is ill with typhus, and nothing will hold her back from going to nurse him to health. The strain of nursing him on the heels of the three weeks in the typhus wards, however, takes its toll and Ruth falls ill, lingers, and dies. Donne offers to provide for Leonard, but the Bensons refuse; the doctor with whom Ruth has worked has already made provisions for Leonard to train with him and inherit his practice. Bradshaw buys a tombstone for Ruth's grave and seeks fellowship once more with Benson as friend and pastor.

References and Suggested Readings

Alexander, Lynn M. "Elizabeth Gaskell." *An Encyclopedia of British Women Writers.* Ed. Paul Schlueter and June Schlueter. Revised and Expanded ed. New Brunswick, NJ: Rutgers University Press, 1998.

Gaskell, Elizabeth. *Ruth*. 1853. Oxford: Oxford University Press, 1998.

Shelston, Alan. Introduction. *Ruth*. By Elizabeth Gaskell. Ed. Alan Shelston. Oxford: Oxford University Press, 1998. vii–xx.

See also Brontë, Charlotte.

GILMAN, CHARLOTTE PERKINS

Best known today for her short story "The Yellow Wallpaper" (1892) and her utopian novel *Herland* (1915), works revived in the 1970s by feminist critics, Gilman never considered herself a writer of fiction. When the well-known nineteenth-century man of letters William Dean Howells requested permission to reprint "The Yellow Wallpaper" in *Great Modern American Stories* (1920), Gilman reports in her autobiography: "I was more than willing, but assured him that it was no more 'literature' than my other stuff, being definitely written 'with a purpose.'" Indeed, Gilman's fictional works are often burdened by a tendency toward didacticism, because she consciously used them as vehicles to explore imaginatively the sociological ideas she discussed in her nonfiction works—the primary basis of her international reputation as a major feminist social critic at the beginning of the twentieth century.

Born in 1860 in Hartford, Connecticut, Charlotte Perkins was related on her father's side to the famous Beecher family. (Harriet Beecher Stowe was her great-aunt.) Charlotte's father, Frederick Beecher Perkins, left the family shortly after his daughter's birth, leaving his wife, Mary, to raise two children alone. Charlotte's financially strained childhood was marked by frequent moves. Largely self-educated, Charlotte went to the Rhode Island School of Design at age eighteen, where she studied painting and illustration. At the age of twenty-four, after much vacillation, she married Charles Walter Stetson, an artist.

After the birth of her daughter, Katharine, the following year in 1885, Charlotte sank into a deep depression. At the urging of her husband, she consulted S. Weir Mitchell, a prominent Philadelphia neurologist who specialized in the treatment of female nervous disorders. Dr. Mitchell's prescription of complete rest and abstention from intellectual stimulation nearly drove Charlotte insane, an experience that inspired "The Yellow Wallpaper." She wrote in her autobiography: "The real purpose of the story was to reach Dr. S. Weir Mitchell, and convince him of the error of his ways." Unlike the narrator of her fictional story, however, Charlotte did not go mad; instead, she left her husband and moved to California with her daughter, where she supported herself on her meager earnings as a writer, lecturer, and proprietor of a boarding house. Following their divorce, Walter remarried Grace Channing, who had been and remained a close friend of Charlotte. By mutual agreement, Katharine was sent to live with her father and his new wife—a decision that led the press to criticize Charlotte as an "unnatural mother."

Having rejected the conventional role of wife and mother, Charlotte embarked on a highly successful career as a lecturer and writer. Her most famous book, *Women and Economics*, appeared in 1898, establishing her international reputation. In 1900, she was married again to her first cousin George Houghton Gilman, another descendent of the Beecher family. The marriage was apparently a happy one, and it did not prevent Gilman from continuing her work as a feminist critic and lecturer. Among her nonfiction works are *Concerning Children* (1900), *The Home: Its Work and Influence* (1903), *Human Work* (1904), *The Man-Made World; or Our Androcentric Culture* (1911), and *His Religion and Hers: A Study of the Faith of Our Fathers and the Work of Our Mothers* (1923). Gilman also wrote a magazine called *The Forerunner* between 1909 and 1916, in which much of her fiction, including *Herland*, was published. In *The Forerunner*, Gilman advocated for the rights of women and sought to demonstrate the interdependence of feminist and Socialist ideas. Praised today for her progressivism and feminism, she has also been criticized by contemporary feminists for betraying racist, anti-Semitic, and xenophobic attitudes typical of her era in her writings.

After her second husband's death in 1934, two years after she learned she had inoperable cancer, Gilman returned to California from the east coast and lived briefly with Grace Channing, now also a widow, near her daughter's home in Pasadena. On August 17, 1935, Charlotte Perkins Gilman took her own life rather than face the ravages of cancer. The letter she left her family appears in the final chapter of her autobiography *The Living of Charlotte Perkins Gilman*, published posthumously in 1935. It reads in part: "No grief, pain, misfortune or 'broken heart' is excuse for cutting off one's life while any power of service remains. But when all usefulness is over, when one is assured of unavoidable and imminent death, it is the simplest of human rights to choose a quick and easy death in place of a slow and horrible one. . . . I have preferred chloroform to cancer."

Herland is the most playful and entertaining of the three feminist utopian novels written by Charlotte Perkins Gilman and was serialized in her monthly magazine *The Forerunner. Herland* was preceded by *Moving the Mountain* (1911) and followed by a sequel entitled *With Her in Ourland* (1916). Gilman chose the literary genre of the utopian novel, popularized in the nineteenth century by Edward Bellamy (whose utopian fantasy *Looking Backward* influenced Gilman) in order to explore imaginatively the feminist and Socialist ideas she espoused in her nonfiction writing. Long forgotten, *Herland* was rediscovered and published for the first time as a novel in 1979, when it was recognized as a precursor to such second-wave feminist utopian novels as Marge Piercy's *Woman on the Edge of Time* (1976) and Ursula Le Guin's *The Dispossessed* (1974).

Herland chronicles the experiences of three American male explorers who accidentally stumble upon an all-female society cut off from the rest of the world for two thousand years. In her characterization of the three main characters, Gilman satirizes a range of turn-of-the-century male attitudes toward women: Jeff Margrave "idealized women in the best Southern style" (11); Terry O. Nicholson thought "pretty women were just so much game and homely ones not worth considering" (11); and the narrator, Vandyke Jennings, "held a middle ground, highly scientific, of course, and used to argue learnedly about the physiological limitations of the sex" (11).

The men's beliefs and prejudices about women are gradually challenged as they learn more about the utopian society of *Herland*, which is remarkably free of the poverty, crime, violence, and disease that plague the world the men have left. They learn that reproduction occurs by parthenogenesis or "virgin birth" (47) and that motherhood, the most sacred function in this all-female society, is shared collectively. The narrator notes that the Herlanders are "strikingly deficient in what we call 'femininity'" (60), leading him to the conviction that "those 'feminine charms' we are so fond of are not feminine at all, but mere reflected masculinity—developed to please us because they had to please us" (60).

Eventually the three men fall in love with three young women and begin a courtship, the prologue to the reestablishment of a "bi-sexual state" (89). The reintegration of men into *Herland* proves tricky, however. Although Celis, Alima, and Ellador fall in love with Jeff, Terry, and Van, respectively, their expectations for marriage are very different from those of the men. In the course of two thousand years without men, they have lost their "sex-feeling" (93). In addition, the concept of "home" is alien to the Herlanders, who have a sense of individual privacy and cooperative community but "not the faintest idea of that solitude à deux we are so fond of" (124–25).

After their marriages, the "three modern American men" (121) react differently to this unusual state of affairs: Jeff, used to placing women on a pedestal, adjusts too easily and uncritically; Van strives with difficulty to learn to value Ellador's comradeship; and Terry, accustomed to mastering women, rashly attempts to force Alima to have sex with him—an action that leads to his expulsion from Herland. As the novel concludes, Van and Ellador prepare to return to the world with Terry, while Jeff is "so thoroughly Herlandized" (134) he decides to stay behind with his pregnant bride, Celis. As a result of their year-long stay, Van reflects on the profound change in consciousness they have gone through: "We were now well used to seeing women not as females but as people; people of all sorts, doing every kind of work" (138). Having made a promise not to disclose the existence of Herland until Ellador returns with her report of the outside world, the three set out—the story of Van and Ellador's tour of our world to be continued in Gilman's sequel *With Her in Ourland.*

"The Yellow Wallpaper," the classic short story by the feminist intellectual Charlotte Perkins Gilman, first published in 1892 in *The New England Magazine*, is a chilling, autobiographically inspired tale of a woman's descent into madness. Discouraged from doing intellectual work after the birth of her daughter, Gilman was nearly driven mad by her physician's "cure." She wrote "The Yellow Wallpaper," her finest work of fiction, as an indictment of Mitchell, the Philadelphia neurologist who treated her and who is specifically named in the story. At the time of its publication, "The Yellow Wallpaper" was read as a Poe-esque horror story. More recently, it has been rediscovered and acclaimed for its frank exploration of nineteenth-century sexual politics.

As the story begins, the narrator and her physician husband, John, have taken up summer residence in a large old mansion, which she playfully alludes to as a "haunted house" (165). Suffering from what her husband diagnoses as "nervous depression—a slight hysterical tendency" (165), the narrator is "absolutely forbidden to 'work' until I am well again" (165). Convinced that "congenial work, with excitement and change, would do me good" (166), she writes on the sly, whenever she can avoid the watchful eyes of her husband and his sister, "a perfect and enthusiastic housekeeper" (166). Yet, she admits, the necessity for subterfuge "does exhaust me a good deal" (170).

Although the narrator wishes to move into one of the downstairs bedrooms, her husband insists that they occupy the nursery, a large room with windows "barred for little children" (167) and a "great immovable bed" that is "nailed down" (171). The narrator is infantilized by her well-meaning but patronizing husband, who calls her "little girl" and "blessed little goose" (168). Confined to the nursery, she becomes increasingly obsessed with the hideous yellow wallpaper, whose sprawling pattern eludes her attempts to find a recurring design. She notices, "when you follow the lame uncertain curves for a little distance they suddenly commit suicide—plunge off at outrageous angles, destroy themselves in unheard of contradictions" (167).

Gradually, the narrator begins to see a "sub-pattern" (174) behind the "outside pattern" (174) of the wallpaper: the shape of a "woman stooping down and creeping about" (172). She imagines the yellow wallpaper pattern as prison bars behind which the woman is confined, much as the narrator is confined in the nursery under the care of her husband. As the narrator's hallucinations grow more and more vivid, she imagines the woman shaking the front pattern in an attempt to escape the stranglehold of the wallpaper. The woman multiplies into many women, and eventually she sees the women outside the wallpaper as well, creeping about the property by daylight. Gradually, we realize the narrator has been gnawing on the bedstead, as well as peeling the wallpaper off the walls in great long yards, in her attempt to free her counterpart from her imprisonment. Paradoxically, she also intends to use a rope she has on hand to tie the woman up if she attempts to escape. Through these various images, the narrator symbolically explores women's painfully restricted role in the culture of her day.

In the final scene, the narrator locks herself in her room and throws the key out the window. When her husband finally recovers the key and enters the nursery, he is aghast to find her creeping around the baseboards of the room on all fours like a caged animal. The narrator proclaims: "I've got out at last. . . . And I've pulled off most of the paper, so you can't put me back!" (180). Although Gilman herself survived her breakdown to become an extremely successful author and lecturer, the narrator of "The Yellow Wallpaper" meets a more depressing fate—her only escape is into madness. The story ends ironically with the narrator's naive words: "Now why should that man have fainted? But he did, and right across my path by the wall, so that I had to creep over him every time" (180).

References and Suggested Readings

Ammons, Elizabeth. *Conflicting Stories: American Women Writers at the Turn into the Twentieth Century*. New York: Oxford University Press, 1991.

Hedges, Elaine R. Afterword. *The Yellow Wallpaper*. By Charlotte Perkins Gilman. New York: Feminist, 1973. 37–63.

Lane, Ann J. *To Herland and Beyond: The Life and Work of Charlotte Perkins Gilman*. New York: Pantheon, 1990.

———. Introduction. *Herland*. By Charlotte Perkins Gilman. New York: Pantheon, 1979.

McQuade, Donald, ed. *The Harper American Literature*. New York: Harper, 1987.

Schwartz, Lynne Sharon. "Introduction." *The Yellow Wallpaper and Other Writings*. By Charlotte Perkins Gilman. New York: Bantam, 1989. vii–xxvii.

Solomon, Barbara H., ed. *Herland and Selected Stories by Charlotte Perkins Gilman*. New York: Signet Classic, 1992.

See also Stowe, Harriet Beecher.

GOTHIC

In the traditional romantic canon, *gothic* typically describes fiction that has a medieval setting, often complete with ghosts, castles, unexplainable happenings, and a hero or heroine. The term derives from the Goths, a Germanic tribe that invaded Eastern and Western empires, and has developed a connotation as barbaric, uncivilized, in bad taste, and reflecting the lower-class status accorded to gothic texts. Within feminist criticism, however, the term has come to reflect an entirely different problem: It is, according to many feminist critics, indicative of the sexism inherent in the canonization of literary texts.

Michael Crews Gamer notes that when gothic fiction rose to popularity in the 1780s and 1790s, British reviewers spoke of it as "modern romance" or a grouping of "historical novels," both of which were seen as "female" categories in spite of large male readerships (183). As a result, Gamer explains, the gothic novel began to decline in status; after all, with male cultural institutions such as the government criticizing such work, it had little chance of survival. By the 1820s, gothic works were relegated to chapbooks (184). In response to this process, feminist critics, such as Eve Kosofsky Sedgwick and Kate Ferguson Ellis, have assumed the task of showing the literary and social merit of gothic fiction, arguing that the texts within this genre reflect the social position of women forced to counter an all-powerful male society.

Not surprisingly, in gothic texts, the heroine often ends up "trapped," be it in a castle or a dark forest. The plot hinges on some sort of mystery that the reader must unravel, but, as Tracy Brown notes, it also typically involves a wedding ceremony that "restores the narrative to the rational from the supernatural" so that the domestic sphere is reinscribed as central to female existence. Ann Radcliffe and Mary Shelley provide two examples of this gothic tradition, which, according to some feminists, provided a supernatural space for women to contest sexism that they could not address in more realistic writing. American women writers in particular seem to have utilized the tradition of the "ghost story" to protest their subordinate status. Contemporary authors, too, "gothicize" their texts. Such is the case in Toni Morrison's *Beloved*, where the haunting bears a profound political message about the effects of slavery.

References and Suggested Readings

Brown, Tracy E. "Gothic Fiction." *The Oxford Companion to Women's Writing in the United States*. Ed. Cathy N. Davidson and Linda Wagner-Martin. New York: Oxford University Press, 1995. 360–61.

Gamer, Michael Crews. "Gothic." *Encyclopedia of Feminist Literary Theory*. Ed. Elizabeth Kowaleski-Wallace. New York: Garland, 1997. 183–84.

See also Morrison, Toni; Shelley, Mary.

Lisa R. Williams

H

HALL, RADCLYFFE

Radclyffe Hall was born in England in 1886 to Radclyffe Radclyffe-Hall and Mary Jane Diehl Radclyffe-Hall. She was raised by her mother and an Italian stepfather. She started writing quite early and produced several volumes of poetry and a number of novels including 'Twixt Earth and Stars (1906), A Sheaf of Verses (1908), Poems of the Past and Present (1910), Songs of Three Counties, and Other Poems (1913), The Forgotten Island (1915), The Forge (1924), The Unlit Lamp (1924), A Saturday Life (1925), Adam's Breed (1926), The Well of Loneliness (1928), The Master of the House (1932), Miss Ogilvy Finds Herself (1934), and The Sixth Beatitude (1936).

Her 1928 The Well of Loneliness is a frank account of the situation of the "invert" or homosexual in the early decades of the twentieth century. The book garnered popularity and notoriety when it was the subject of an obscenity trial. The book has always had an uneasy welcome, however, even in the feminist canon when it was reclaimed in the early 1970s. As Esther Newton suggests, "Heterosexual conservatives condemn The Well for defending the lesbian's right to exist. Lesbian feminists condemn it for presenting lesbians as different from women in general" (282).

The book opens with the arrival at Morton Hall of Lady Anna Gordon as a young bride. She and her husband, Sir Philip, have an affectionate relationship that does not bear children for ten years. They so longed for a son that they named their infant daughter Stephen Mary Olivia Gertrude. Lady Gordon has a distaste for her own daughter and is afraid to be affectionate with her; she "hated the way Stephen moved or stood still, hated a certain largeness about her, a certain crude lack of grace in her movements, a certain unconscious defiance" (16). At seven, Stephen is aware of her own differences and develops a crush on the servant girl,

Collins. When she learns that Collins has housemaid's knees, Stephen prays to Jesus that she may bear the pain of the housemaid's knee and that Collins be spared. She loves to dress up as Lord Nelson and spends much time with her father learning about the natural world. She says to her father, "Do you think that I *could* be a man, supposing I thought very hard—or prayed, Father?" (26). Always a sensitive child, Stephen has a sort of spiritual crisis when Jesus does not hear her prayers.

Stephen grows up under the careful tutelage of Sir Philip who takes her to the hunt and lets her ride astride her horse rather than sidesaddle, as was the custom of the women of the time. Stephen's father is at first dimly aware, and then increasingly so, that Stephen is different from other children. He longs to discuss this difference with Lady Anna but is afraid that the articulated knowledge of Stephen's lesbianism will drive a wedge in the relationship of mother and daughter. In neglecting to speak with Lady Anna, Philip believes he commits "the first cowardly action of his life. . . . In his infinite pity for Stephen's mother, he sinned very deeply and gravely against Stephen, by withholding from that mother his own conviction that her child was not as other children" (54).

While growing up, Stephen sometimes plays with a neighbor child, Roger Antrim. At ten years old, Roger is "already full to the neck of male arrogance," and Stephen envies him "his right to be perfectly natural; above all she envied his splendid conviction that being a boy constituted a privilege in life" (46, 47).

The young Stephen finds solace in her friendship with her pony and later a fine hunting horse named Raftery. Her teenage years are marked by an awkwardness in her physical being and her dress. She greatly prefers the unrestrictive clothing of the hunt to the bothersome dresses of a genteel society. She takes fencing lessons and wants to cut her hair, all of which earns the disapproval of her mother.

Stephen has two governesses, Mademoiselle Duphot, who has little control over the headstrong and willful Stephen, and Miss Puddleton (later affectionately known as Puddle). For all her other weaknesses in controlling Stephen, Mademoiselle Duphot does succeed in teaching her French. Miss Puddleton is brought in to exercise greater firmness and discipline with Stephen's education. Indeed, she does have an immediate way with the young girl, and Stephen is able to give herself devotedly over to her studies. Much later, we learn that Puddleton too is an "invert," though one who has denied any expression to her sexual orientation. She has instead submerged her life in study and teaching. She dearly hopes that Stephen will use her gifts of intellect and writing to fight the cultural prejudices of the time. She reminds Stephen that the only weapon she has is her writing.

When she is a young woman, Stephen meets Martin Hallam, an arborist from British Columbia. He and Stephen develop a lovely friendship until Martin finds that he has fallen in love with Stephen and asks her to marry him. Stephen is appalled and realizes for certain that she has no attraction for men, that what she has longed for with Martin is simple friendship, manly comradeship of the kind that she has with her father. Stephen goes to her father and asks, "Is there anything strange about me, Father, that I should have felt as I did about Martin?"

(105). Still trapped by his own fears about her sexuality, Sir Philip assures her that she is not different from others. Still, Stephen realizes that when she does not marry Martin, she chooses not to take the road that the other women in the community take to become a "breeder of children, an upholder of home, a careful and diligent steward of pastures" (108). She does not hold her friend Violet Antrim's opinion that "no woman was ever complete without marriage" (110).

When Stephen is nineteen, her father dies from injuries sustained while tending a snow-laden tree. On his deathbed, he regrets never having told his wife of Stephen's condition and makes a final effort to do so, though it is too late. At the very time when he can no longer serve as the buffer between them, he misses his last opportunity to ease the relationship between Stephen and Lady Anna.

When Stephen turns twenty-one, she comes into considerable money from her father's estate and becomes both wealthy and independent. She meets and falls in love with Angela Crossby of The Grange. Angela is married to a mean-spirited man, Ralph Crossby, who saved her from a life of poverty (and a failed career on the New York stage) and who expects at least simple gratitude and an absence of humiliation. Angela is bored with Ralph and takes up with Stephen, not truly out of love but out of her boredom and curiosity. Stephen genuinely falls in love with Angela, and their relationship progresses to an affair that soon arouses the suspicions of Ralph and the whole community. Meanwhile, Angela has also formed an attachment to the now grown Roger Antrim and begins a simultaneous affair with him. The uneven and disastrous affair between Stephen and Angela comes to a painful conclusion when Angela is caught with Roger by Stephen. Stephen writes a final letter to Angela, proclaiming her love; Ralph has come to suspect Angela of the second affair (with Roger) as well. With Stephen's letter, Angela sees an opportunity to rid herself of Stephen and to drive all suspicions from Ralph's mind. She gives the letter to Ralph and uses the urgent confessions of Stephen's love as the reason why she has been spending time with Roger. She betrays Stephen in her attempt to keep her affair with Roger a secret from Ralph. Ralph sends a copy of Stephen's letter to her mother and asks that Stephen never visit The Grange again. Lady Anna calls Stephen in and tells her that they cannot live under the same roof and that she must leave her beloved Morton Hall. The breach with her mother is final.

Stephen now knows a loneliness even deeper than the one she experienced at the death of her father. She is forever cut off from her mother, from her home, and has suffered the anger of people such as Ralph Crossby who calls her a "freak" and who advocates "that sort of thing [lesbianism] wants putting down at birth, I'd like to institute state lethal chambers!" (151).

Stephen goes to London in exile from Morton Hall; her mother is glad to be free of her but insists that she comes back twice a year to keep up appearances and keep gossip from running rampant about a break in their family. Stephen's beloved governess, Puddle, goes with her, and they make a comfortable if lonely life. There, Stephen writes and Puddle manages the house. Puddle tells Stephen that she indeed does know what Stephen is experiencing, for she too is an "invert," though she never acted upon it in her youth and is now an aging woman.

Freed at last from the "conspiracy of silence," Puddle consoles Stephen and encourages her to embrace her life's work:

> You've got work to do—come and do it! Why, just because you are what you are, you may actually find you've got an advantage. You may write with a curious double insight—write both men and women from a personal knowledge. . . . For the sake of all the others who are like you, but less strong and less gifted perhaps, many of them, it's up to you to have the courage to make good, and I'm here to help you to do it, Stephen. (205)

When Stephen returns home for a visit, she learns that, to his credit, Ralph Crossby has not made the knowledge of his wife's affair with Stephen public. They soon moved away from The Grange and scandal was snuffed. Her mother is able to congratulate her on the success of her first book. After the success of her first book, *The Furrow*, Puddle spurs her on, warning her against being a "one-book author" (213). Stephen's second novel is less successful.

But the visits back to Morton are a strain on Stephen, and when she goes back to London, she is unable to eat or sleep. She writes her mother a harsh letter announcing that she is going abroad and that Puddle will accompany her. Stephen maintains a social life in Paris but resents that her life is one of "perpetual subterfuge, of guarded opinions and guarded actions, of lies of omission if not of speech, of becoming an accomplice in the world's injustice by maintaining at all times a judicious silence" (243).

In the spring of 1914, when the war starts, Stephen returns to London and joins the London Ambulance Column, and Puddle gets a job in a government department. They find that many inverts are being used during the war effort. Stephen notes the irony that "bombs do not trouble the nerves of the invert," but rather they are hurt by the "terrible silent bombardment from the batteries of God's good people" (271).

Stephen is sent to France with the French Army Ambulance Corps and there meets Mary Llewellyn who becomes her driving partner and who will return home with her after the war. Stephen learns of the death of Roger Antrim who was "shot down while winning his V.C. through saving the life of a wounded captain" (290–91). Stephen realizes that she "wished him well, that his courage had wiped one great bitterness out of her heart and her life for ever" (291).

Stephen herself is wounded, hit by a "splinter of shell, and her right cheek cut open rather badly." She is awarded the Croix de Guerre, and as the attending surgeon said, she "will carry an honourable scar as a mark of her courage" (293). Stephen's injury causes Mary to confess her love and beg that they won't be separated after the war. The end of the war causes some anxiety among the women of the Ambulance Corps, for during the war, their covert lesbianism has been tolerated out of the need for their service, but "none could know what the future might hold of trivial days filled with trivial actions" (295).

The two return to Stephen's house in France and there have a difficult time adjusting to their relationship. Stephen is unwilling to consummate her passion with Mary for fear of leading Mary astray, of taking her to a dark region that Mary may regret. Perhaps Stephen's reluctance is understandable given her own past experience with social shunning and with Puddle's model of lifelong celibacy. It takes Stephen some time to realize that

> [t]here was many another exactly like her in this very city, in every city; and they did not all live out crucified lives, denying their bodies, stultifying their brains, becoming the victims of their own frustrations. On the contrary, they lived natural lives—lives that to them were perfectly natural. They had their passions like everyone else, and why not? (299)

Puddle returns to Morton Hall so that Stephen can forge a life of her own with Mary. Though they settle into a compatible relationship, soon Stephen is working too much and pushing Mary to the fringes of her life and treats her as an emotionally absent husband might treat a wife. Stephen does not invite Mary to Morton Hall when she goes for a visit, and her mother will not tolerate the sound of Mary's name. When Stephen returns from Morton Hall, their "halcyon days are over" (338).

Martin Hallam comes back into Stephen's circle of awareness and visits her and Mary in their Paris home. Stephen appreciates their intellectual relationship but is blind to Martin's attraction to Mary. When he confesses his love for Mary, Stephen finally decides to sacrifice her love for Mary in the hopes that Martin can provide her with a happier life. She fabricates a story that she has cheated on Mary with another woman, and the novel ends with Mary leaving Stephen for Martin. The unhappy ending has aroused a negative response from many feminists who see the reinforcement of a patriarchal paradigm in Stephen's behavior and the enforced morality of Mary's "inversion" conversion to heterosexuality. Still, the text is valued for its early discussion of lesbianism.

References and Suggested Readings

Hall, Radclyffe. *The Well of Loneliness.* 1928. New York: Anchor, 1990.

Newton, Esther. "The Mythic Mannish Lesbian: Radclyffe Hall and the New Woman." *Hidden from History: Reclaiming the Gay and Lesbian Past.* Ed. Martin Bauml Duberman et al. New York: New American Library, 1989. 281–93.

Parascandola, Louis. "Radclyffe Hall." *An Encyclopedia of British Women Writers.* Ed. Paul Schlueter and June Schlueter. Revised and Expanded ed. New Brunswick, NJ: Rutgers University Press, 1998.

HOOKS, BELL

Born in Hopkinsville, Kentucky, in 1952 as Gloria Watkins, bell hooks is a feminist writer and theorist. She writes with a pseudonym of "bell hooks" to give her emotional distance from her work but also to honor her great-grandmother, whose name she uses. She relates, "Old folds used to always address me as you must be kin to bell hooks, look like her and talk like her. Talking like her meant that I spoke my mind—clearly and decisively" (158).

hooks graduated from Stanford University in 1973, earned an MA degree from the University of Wisconsin, and a PhD degree from the University of California, Santa Cruz, in 1983. She wrote her doctoral dissertation on the early works of Toni Morrison.

hooks has been a prolific writer and sustained voice in the service of the fight against oppression since her first book, *Ain't I a Woman: Black Women and Feminism*, was published in 1981. She was an early voice in calling feminists to understand that, for women of color, feminism was not the starting place in the fight for justice. For hooks, the tentacles of class, race, and gender are all enmeshed in the web of oppression, and all must be addressed. She says in *Wounds of Passion*, "I keep saying there is no world where just gender matters. . . . We always have to think about the ways race matters, sometimes more than gender, sometimes the same as gender, but always in convergence and collusion" (206).

In *Wounds of Passion*, hooks addresses the writing life. She notes, "After all our feminist victory, there is still a grave silence about the issue of whether women can be in love relationships with men and truly develop as writers" (210). hooks is also concerned about the pulls of her activist feminism on her own poetry and confesses the difficulty of maintaining the integrity of both callings.

The memoir traces the author's salvific love of poetry, the way in which poetry compensated for the violence of her home and ultimately led her to transcendence. It was through poetry that she met her partner of twelve years and with whom she struggled against the questions of love and power, submission and dominance, the viability of two poets living and working together, the need for silences in creation, the possibilities of an open relationship, and the social constructs that still allow men freedoms that are denied to women.

hooks has held positions at several universities including, Southwestern University, the City College of New York, Oberlin College, and Yale University.

Her works on feminism and theory include *Ain't I a Woman: Black Women and Feminism* (1981), *Feminist Theory: From Margin to Center* (1984), *Talking Back: Thinking Feminist, Thinking Black* (1989), *Yearning: Race, Class and Cultural Politics* (1990), *Black Looks: Race and Representation* (1992), *Sisters of the Yam: Black Women and Self-recovery* (1993), *Teaching to Trangress: Education as the Practice of Freedom* (1994), *Outlaw Culture: Resisting Representation* (1994), *Killing Rage: Ending Racism* (1995), *Art On My Mind: Visual Politics* (1995), *Remembered Rapture: The Writer at Work* (1999), *Feminism Is for Everybody* (2000), *All About Love: New Visions* (2000), *Salvation: Black People and Love* (2001), and *Communion: The Female Search for Love* (2002).

References and Suggested Readings

hooks, bell. *Wounds of Passion: A Writing Life*. New York: Henry Holt, 1997.
See also Morrison, Toni.

HULME, KERI

Born in 1947, Keri Hulme grew up in Christchurch and Noeraki, New Zealand, and achieved acclaim with her first novel, *The Bone People* (1983). Hulme is one-eighth Maori and identifies more with that side of her heritage than the European or *pakeha* side. In an interview with Elizabeth Alley, she says, "That's where I draw my strength from, that's where I learnt about words first and that's the side I learnt to tell stories from" (143). In keeping with the Maori beliefs, Hulme acknowledges the importance of ancestors in her life and work. "I realized it was absolutely true—you are a continuum and your ancestors look through your eyes and you hear with their ears" (143). Hulme further suggests that her work is informed by

> [a] kind of ancestors' memory, or a collective unconscious, whatever you like to call it, but you can tap on it, you can draw on it and it's both good and a responsibility . . . perhaps I'm merely a sounding box and these things are being fed through. (145)

For all the richness that her Maori ancestry brings to her work, Hulme notes that being of mixed heritage has some pain: "You never truly belong to one side or the other—as a person who is intrinsically a mongrel you can never be fully committed to one way alone." But "the advantage and the joy is being able to be on both sides of the fence (and there is one), to have more than one set of ears, to have more than one set of eyes."

Hulme's work is also informed by other foundational experiences. Covi notes that she is "sexually an androgyne" (227), and Hulme suggests that though she has been "very public" about her "gender neuter status": "People find that hard to handle. They still want to see a man around." In reporting her spiritual history, she says, "I converted to Catholicism when I was eighteen and I was a very, very devout Catholic for a number of years till my logic ran full-tilt into the idea of Hell, which seems to me completely ludicrous now and I'm un-converted." Perhaps in the same way that her mixed heritage provides Hulme with "more than one set of eyes," her androgyny and bifurcated spiritual experience also doubles her vision.

Hulme's first novel, *The Bone People* (1983), won several prizes including the New Zealand Book Award for Fiction, the Mobile Corporation Pegasus Prize for Literature, and Britain's prestigious Booker Prize. The book is a mosaic of postmodernist techniques and at times a riot of language that is nearly Joycean.

As Covi notes, the title of the book encodes "a Maori pun meaning both ancestors and progenitors" (225). This circularity, the folding forward and backward of structure and meaning, is characteristic of Hulme's work. The book begins with the ending, as is announced by Hulme's "Prologue" titled "The End at the Beginning," and ends with a possibility of both ending and beginning, signified by the Maori phrase "Te mutunga—ranei te take," which translates "the end—or the beginning" (425). This circularity reflects a Maori ideology that does not see time with the rigid linearity of the Western view.

Covi takes the argument of structural circularity a step further and suggests that "*The Bone People*'s structure is actually that of the double spiral" (223). According to Bruce King, the double spiral is "a Maori symbol of life as interwoven continuity and of rebirth" (xlvi), and certainly the meaning of the symbol is born out by the novel's story.

The Bone People is the story of three people, each trapped in a harrowing private prison: Simon, the six-year-old mute boy who washes in from the sea, the sole survivor of a boat wreck; Joe, a Maori man who has lost both his wife and son to death and who cannot escape a pattern of violence and desperate love for the boy Simon; and Kerewin Holmes, a quasi-autobiographical character who lives in a tower in physical and emotional isolation. The intersection of the three lives constitutes the narrative line of the novel. Hulme suggests that the novel has six main characters, "not just Joe and Simon and Kerewin and the kaumatua (Tiaki Mira), but also the land and the sea."

The "Prologue" opens with a poem about each of the three main characters and then adds a comment on those characters: "They were nothing more than people, by themselves. . . . Together, all together, they are the instruments of change" (4). With this statement, Hulme does provide the end in the beginning, for the long journey of the novel is to bring the characters to the place where, together, they do become "instruments of change." The "Prologue" continues with a glimpse into the history and consciousness of Simon, Joe, and Kerewin that reveals each to be in psychic deterioration.

The three lives are joined one day when Kerewin comes home from the local bar and finds a mute child, Simon P. Gillayley, in her towerlike house. She takes a splinter from his foot, gives him his sandal she found on the beach, and bids him go. He will not leave, so she grudgingly fixes him a meal. From their early interactions, it is evident that she is accustomed to living alone in a gruff and crusty existence. His presence makes her regret "the gulf between her and her family" (22). Simon spends the first evening with her, and Kerewin learns from the phone operator that Simon has a pattern of running away from home twice a week, that he has a "touchpaper temper," a penchant for "sneakthievery and petty vandalism," is "emotionally disturbed or something" (34). The chance encounter sets in action a continuing and complex relationship between Simon and Kerewin and Simon's stepfather, Joe Gillayley. Gillayley, a Maori factory worker, arranges for Simon to be collected from Kerewin's tower and asks if he can drop by for a visit to convey his gratitude in person. He explains that Simon, the only survivor of a boat wreck, washed ashore badly broken in many places and with evidence of previous breaks and injuries. Joe and his wife, Hana, took Simon in while the authorities decided what to do with the child.

Joe and Kerewin are in an emotionally fragile condition as well. Joe has recently lost his wife and ten-month-old son to illness and was left alone to deal with the challenge of raising Simon, and Kerewin is estranged from her family of origin. In their dislocations, both feel separated from their Maori heritage; Kerewin says, "Now it feels like the best part of me has got lost in the way I live" (62).

Kerewin is financially independent and lives in a self-designed tower, surrounded by books, fine food and drink, her art, and her music. She is a self-sufficient loner, seeking out casual company only when she chooses. But she is emotionally hollow and her art is frozen; she can no longer paint. Even she does not know why she is so mistrustful of relationships; she says, "nobody's stomped on my heart except for family, so why am I so mistrustful of people?" (69). So it comes as a surprise to herself that she offers her family beach home to Joe and Simon for a holiday.

Joe's grief and sense of dislocation is more dangerous, for it leads him to drink and then to beating the recalcitrant Simon. When Simon shows up at the tower bruised and swollen one day, Kerewin suspects that Joe has beaten him, but he denies it. Simon does have trouble with other kids at school and is a general ruffian in the neighborhood, so Kerewin is willing to trust Joe for the time. It becomes clear that Joe is the culprit just before he and Simon are to leave for their vacation, and Kerewin impulsively joins them to guard Simon from Joe. The three weeks they spend together are difficult but ultimately redemptive as they confront areas of their inner darkness and experience some measure of health. Joe admits that he is sick; Kerewin has a positive experience in a chance meeting with one of her brothers, and they learn that, though he still does not talk, Simon can sing. Though Kerewin has no sexual interest in Joe, she comes to a greater understanding of and sympathy for him. The three begin forming their relationship as *whanau*, or extended family group.

The delicate equilibrium the three have reached is soon upset. In his truant wanderings, Simon finds a dead man, bloated and covered in flies. Shocked and inarticulate, Simon finds his way to Kerewin's tower, but not recognizing his need, she confronts him about a knife of hers that he has stolen. Frustrated, Simon lashes out and destroys Kerewin's most valued guitar; on impulse, Kerewin hits him and roughly dismisses him from her tower. He flees back to town and breaks the plate glass windows in all the shops on the street. A constable captures Simon and returns him to Joe who later responds to the incident by giving Simon the worst beating he has ever administered. While Simon hovers between life and death, Joe is arrested and charged with assault.

The embryonic "family" is shattered by the events in which they are all complicit. Kerewin dismantles much of her tower and leaves it in ruins. Before she leaves, she creates a sculpture that joins the faces of her and Simon and Joe. She builds a fire with the wood she pulls from the walls of her tower and fires the piece. She wanders about for a year, flirting with death by suicide attempt and with an untreated cancer of the stomach. She has lost all will to live. When Kerewin is at her very worst, she is visited by "a thin wiry person of indeterminate age. Of indeterminate sex. Of indeterminate race" (424). This person feeds her a "sour brew" and restores her to health. Kerewin is aware that "the thing that had blocked her gut and sucked vitality is gone" (425). The healer only asks that Kerewin record the visit with her art, "So paint me down, write me down. That'll mean something" (425). Restored, Kerewin begins the long journey back to the tower. Once she returns, she spends time rebuilding her home, not as a tower but as a round shell house that will "hold them all in its spiralling [sic] embrace" (442), and trying to unravel the mystery of Simon's past. She commissions a deep-sea diver to bring up the wreck of the boat from which Simon came and finds that it held a thirty million dollar cargo of heroin.

Before going to jail for a year, Joe sells his home and breaks his ties with the area. Upon release, he has no home to return to, and in the grip of despair, he throws himself off a cliff. Though he suffers a broken arm and some cuts, Joe survives the fall. He is found by a kaumatua, an elder, who says he has waited all of his life for the arrival of the "broken man" and that his life's work is not done until he restores him to health. The kaumatua is the guardian of "a stone that was brought on one of the great canoes" (363), and he asks Joe to take over his role upon his imminent death. The old man wills his property to Joe and dies. This interaction with Tiaki Mira, the elder, brings Joe to a renewed place of purpose and health. Not only does Tiaki Mira usher Joe into health, but he also provides a piece of the puzzle of Simon's history. In his small house, Tiaki Mira has a picture of a man, Timon Padraic MacDonnagh, who died as a heroin addict near his home. This evidence, coupled with that which Kerewin has found, confirms Simon's identity.

In the long year of their separation, Simon recovers beyond all expectations, though he does lose most of his hearing. After months of hospitalization, he is sent to a home as a ward of the state, but he escapes from it and makes his way back to Kerewin's tower. There he finds the sculpture she made right before she left, and he treasures this sign of their relationship. Both Kerewin and Joe also return to the tower, and the three have a reunion that includes both Joe's family and Kerewin's.

Critics have been dismissive of Hulme's "happily-ever-after" ending; Giovanna Covi, for instance calls it a "sentimental happy solution" (223). A puzzled Bruce King offers that the ending, "with its mysterious intervention of a tribal elder and a strange healer, might be explained by the way novels by women often resolve conflict through transformation of character, by Maori myth, or by the magic realism currently found in Third World literature" (xlvii).

In an interview with Elizabeth Alley, Hulme responds to the criticism that the novel has "a sort of happy ending, a kind of fairy-tale ending" (149): "I emphatically don't think it has. You have got some very damaged people there who remain damaged, but they do have one enormous hope and I wouldn't call it strong than that. . . . A definity, a probability, no; but a chance, yes. That was the whole point of the story. There is no point in going through all the anguish if it was all for nothing" (149–50).

Hulme's vision for the novel and her ending reflect the spirit of Aikido, which her character, Kerewin, has studied in Japan: "It is not a technique to fight with . . . it is the way to reconcile the world, and make human beings one family. Winning means winning over the mind of discord in yourself" (199).

Other works by Hulme include *Lost Possessions* (1985), *Te Kaihua* (1987), and *Bait* (1999).

References and Suggested Readings

Covi, Giovanna. "Keri Hulme's *The Bone People*: A Critique of Gender." *Imagination and the Creative Impulse in the New Literatures in English*. Ed. M.T. Bindella and G.V. Davis. Amsterdam: Rodopi, 1993. 219–31.

Hulme, Keri. *The Bone People*. 1983. New York: Penguin, 1986.

———. "An Interview with Keri Hulme." Interview with Andrew Peek. *New Literatures Review* 20 (Winter 1990): 1–11.

———. "Keri Hulme." *In the Same Room: Conversations with New Zealand Writers*. Ed. Elizabeth Alley and Mark Williams. Auckland: Auckland University Press, 1992. 140–56.

———. "Keri Hulme." *Talking About Ourselves: Twelve New Zealand Poets in Conversation with Harry Ricketts*. Ed. Harry Ricketts. Wellington: Mallinson Rendel, 1986. 17–29.

———. "Keri Hulme." Interview with Janet Charman. *Broadsheet* 173 (Nov. 1989): 4–16.

King, Bruce. "Fiction from the World's Edge." Rev. of *The Bone People* by Keri Hulme. *Sewanee Review* 94 (1986): xlv–xlvii.

HURSTON, ZORA NEALE

Born in 1891 in Eatonville, Florida, the African American novelist and folklorist Zora Neale Hurston grew up in the first incorporated, self-governing, all-black town in the United States—an experience that left a profound mark on her sense of racial identity as well as on her fictional and nonfictional writings. Her father, John Hurston, was a Baptist preacher and served as the mayor of Eatonville for three terms. Her mother, Lucy, was a strong female role model who encouraged Zora's independent and creative spirit. After her mother died when she was only nine years old, Zora was rejected by her father and his new wife and took up a wanderer's existence. At age fourteen, she joined a Gilbert and Sullivan traveling dramatic troupe, working as a wardrobe girl and maid. After landing in Baltimore, she enrolled in Morgan Academy and then went on to attend Howard University in Washington, D.C.

In 1925, Hurston arrived in New York City, where she became involved with the circle of writers and artists associated with the Harlem Renaissance, a black arts movement of the 1920s. Hurston contributed a story to Alain Locke's influential collection *The New Negro* (1925) and helped edit the journal *Fire!!* founded by Langston Hughes and Wallace Thurman in 1926. Hughes and Hurston collaborated on a play called *Mule Bone*, an artistic endeavor that led to their subsequent falling out. Hughes later criticized Hurston for playing the "perfect 'darkie'" in order to obtain patronage from wealthy white individuals. Ironically, Hughes himself accepted support from the same elderly white patron, Mrs. R. Osgood Mason, who supported Hurston for several years.

During her early years in New York, Hurston enrolled at Barnard College, study-ing with the noted anthropologist Franz Boas. From 1928 to 1931, she collected folklore throughout the South and later published *Mules and Men* (1935), an anthropological study of "hoodoo" practices and stories among blacks in Louisi-ana and Florida. Two successive Guggenheim fellowships in 1937 and 1938 per-mitted Hurston to travel to Jamaica and Haiti to do more field research, resulting in a second volume of folklore entitled *Tell My Horse* (1938).

Hurston's love of African American oral storytelling traditions and folkloric culture infuses her most famous novel, *Their Eyes Were Watching God* (1937), set in the all-black town of Eatonville in which she was raised. This lyrical novel about a black woman's quest for self-realization and equality in marriage was writ-ten in seven weeks in Haiti at the conclusion of a failed love affair. (Hurston herself was married briefly twice, once in 1927 to Herbert Sheen and again in the late 1930s to Albert Price.) Widely acclaimed today, *Their Eyes* was largely dis-missed upon publication because it was out of step with the decade's penchant for proletarian realist fiction like Richard Wright's *Native Son*. Indeed, Wright wrote a scathing review of *Their Eyes* in the leftist magazine *New Masses*, criti-cizing Hurston for perpetuating "minstrel" stereotypes of African Americans.

Rather than emphasizing the oppression and victimization of black Americans as Wright did, Hurston chose to portray the positive side of African American life and culture in her anthropological and fictional writings. In a now-famous and controversial essay, "How It Feels to Be Colored Me" (1928), Hurston wrote:

> I am not tragically colored. . . . I do not belong to the sobbing school of Negrohood who hold that nature somehow has given them a lowdown dirty deal and whose feelings are all hurt about it. . . . No, I do not weep at the world—I am too busy sharpening my oyster knife.

While this characteristic attitude has earned Hurston much criticism, it has also fueled praise, including Alice Walker's admiration for Hurston's "racial health" and her "sense of black people as complete, complex, undiminished human beings.

Hurston was the most prolific African American woman writer in the United States from the 1920s to the 1950s. In addition to writing numerous short sto-ries, articles, and plays, she published seven books: her two anthropological works; four novels, including *Jonah's Gourd Vine* (1934), *Moses, Man of the Mountain* (1939), and *Seraph on the Suwanee* (1948); and her autobiography *Dust Tracks on a Road* (1942). Yet her career took a sharp downturn in the forties and fifties. In the 1940s, she suffered from health problems and faced a spurious child sexual abuse charge that was ultimately dismissed but that proved psychologically dev-astating. Hurston's politics, always controversial, moved increasingly to the right. She opposed the Supreme Court's 1954 desegregation decision, resenting what she viewed as its implication of black inferiority; she also published anti-Communist articles during the McCarthy era. In the 1950s, unable to make a living solely from her writing, Hurston found herself under severe financial pressures. She was forced to take a variety of jobs, even working briefly as a maid. After suffering a stroke in 1959, Hurston entered the St. Lucie County Welfare Home and died penniless the following year, her body buried in an unmarked grave.

In her 1975 essay, "Looking for Zora," Alice Walker movingly describes her trek to find and restore the unmarked grave of Hurston, an act of respect symbolic of efforts by Walker and other black feminist writers to recover a black female literary tradition, akin to the British female literary tradition Virginia Woolf went looking for in *A Room of One's Own*. Walker's essay, originally published in *Ms.* magazine, helped to launch a revival of Hurston's work that has continued unabated since that time. Relegated to virtual obscurity at the end of her own lifetime, Hurston has finally achieved the widespread recognition and readership she deserves.

The best-loved novel by Zora Neale Hurston remained out of print and unread for thirty years following its initial publication in 1937. Now acclaimed for its feminist sensibility, strong unconventional female heroine, and poetic celebration of African American folk traditions and dialects, the theme of a woman's search for self-realization was, quite simply, out of step with literary fashion in the 1930s and 1940s. In the late 1960s, black feminist writers and critics rescued the book from obscurity and secured its status as a black feminist classic. *Their Eyes* has influenced a subsequent generation of black feminist writers, including Alice Walker, who has written: "There is no book more important to me than this one."

Their Eyes uses a framing device and begins at the end of the story with the heroine, Janie Crawford, returning to her home in Eatonville, an all-black town in Florida that was modeled after the town where Hurston was born. As she walks through the town dressed in "overhalls," a "forty year ole 'oman . . . wid her hair swingin' down her back lak som young gal" (2), the women of the community pass harsh judgment on her unconventional dress and behavior. Janie's best friend, Phoeby Watson, separates herself from the other women, brings Janie some dinner, and settles down to hear her story, which comprises the main part of the novel.

Janie recalls her childhood growing up with her grandmother in "de white folks' back-yard" (9). At the age of sixteen, she experiences a sexual awakening under a blossoming pear tree, watching "a dust-bearing bee sink into the sanctum of a bloom" (10). The pear tree represents Janie's romantic idea of marriage. In contrast, Nanny sees marriage as a form of "protection" (14) in which financial security, not love, is important. We learn about Nanny's past as a slave and as the concubine of her master. On the eve of emancipation, she gives birth to his daughter. Hoping to secure a better future for her child, she places her in school; however, the daughter is raped by the schoolteacher and later runs away, leaving Nanny to raise Janie. These deeply painful experiences explain Nanny's theory that "de nigger woman is de mule uh de world" (14).

Nanny marries Janie to Logan Killicks, an older farmer with sixty acres, who she believes will provide Janie with respectability and security. However, Janie is desperately unhappy with Logan, who, ironically, treats her like a mule, the very role that Nanny hoped she might escape. After Nanny dies, Janie meets Joe Starks, an ambitious man who is headed to Eatonville, Florida, to help build "a town all outa colored folks" (27). Janie hesitates before running away with him, because "he did not represent sun-up and pollen and blossoming trees, but he spoke for far horizon" (28). Joe marries Janie, buys two hundred acres of land, and installs himself as the mayor of Eatonville and proprietor of the town's general store. His large, white house makes "the rest of the town [look] like servants' quarters surrounding the 'big house'" (44). Janie becomes another one of his possessions, a sign of his status, and something else to be envied by the other townspeople. Joe aims "tuh be uh big voice" (43), but he forbids Janie to participate in the rich oral culture of storytelling and gossiping that takes place on the porch of the store where Janie listens eagerly to "big picture talkers . . . using a side of the world for a canvas" (51). He jealously forces her to hide her beautiful hair in a headrag. Joe orders her around the store, telling her: "Somebody got to think for women and chillun and chickens and cows. I god, they sho don't think none theirselves" (67).

The marriage further deteriorates when Joe slaps Janie repeatedly over a ruined dinner. Janie feels "something [fall] off the shelf inside her" (67). Having lost its spirit, the marriage becomes something maintained for public show; Janie "had an inside and an outside now and suddenly she knew how not to mix them" (68). Janie also begins to assert herself more and to find her own voice—causing Joe to accuse her of being "too moufy" (71). Similarly, in chapter seven, Janie publicly talks back to Joe when he insults her. Again, Joe strikes her; nevertheless, Janie's retort has "robbed him of his illusion of irresistible maleness" (75) and humiliated him before the other men gathered at the store. As Janie gains her voice, Joe appears to age and to deteriorate. Suspicious of Janie, who he believes is trying to "fix" him, Joe seeks the help of "root-doctors." When Joe is on his deathbed, Janie speaks her mind, accusing Joe of being "too busy listening tuh yo' own big voice": "All dis bowin' down, all dis obedience under yo' voice—dat ain't whut Ah rushed off down de road tuh find out about you" (82). Joe's death immediately follows this confrontation.

Following Joe's death, Janie burns her headrags and lets her hair swing free in one long braid, a symbol of her new liberation. A rich and attractive widow, she is courted by men from all over South Florida, but, after six months of wearing black, "not one suitor had ever gained the house porch" (87). When Janie meets Vergible "Tea Cake" Woods, a good-natured and attractive man twelve years her junior who has a reputation as a poor man and a gambler, he courts her, teaches her to play checkers, takes her fishing, and takes her to the big Sunday School Picnic. The townspeople are disapproving and warn Janie that Tea Cake is just after her money, but Janie thinks he "could be a bee to a blossom—a pear tree in bloom" (101). She tells Phoeby: "Dis ain't no business proposition, and no race after property and titles. Dis is uh love game. Ah done lived Grandma's way, now Ah means tuh live mine" (108).

Janie sells the store and leaves Eatonville to meet Tea Cake in Jacksonville, where they are married. One morning, she wakes up and finds both Tea Cake and the two hundred dollars she has hidden from him for safekeeping gone. Janie is haunted by memories of Annie Tyler, a fifty-two-year-old widow seduced, robbed, and abandoned by a young man named Who Flung. Tea Cake finally returns early the next morning, and she learns that he has spent all of the money throwing a "big chicken and macaroni supper . . . free to all" (117). Having spied the money, more than he had ever seen before in his life, he decided to "see how it felt to be a millionaire" (117). Janie is angry, not because he spent the money but because he didn't include her, fearing that she would see the "railroad hands and dey womenfolks" (118–19) as beneath her. They agree that they will "partake wid everything" (119) together. An ace gambler, Tea Cake wins back Janie's money and then some. He tells her to put it away; he will support her himself by working "on de muck" as a picker in the Everglades. Janie feels "a self-crushing love" and her "soul crawled out from its hiding place" (122).

In the Everglades, Tea Cake and Janie join other migrant farmers who come to pick the bean crop. Tea Cake teaches Janie to shoot a rifle; she begins to wear overalls and joins in with the talking, playing, and gambling. Eventually, she begins to work in the fields alongside Tea Cake, and he helps her with supper afterward. Although she knows that the Eatonville community would think she had come down in the world, she prefers the life of pleasure and equality she now enjoys. Their relationship is not perfect, however. Janie feels jealousy when Tea Cake flirts with Nunkie, another picker, and tries to hit Tea Cake. Likewise, Tea Cake's jealousy is aroused when Janie is befriended by Mrs. Turner, a "milky sort of woman" (133) who believes "we oughta lighten up de race" (133). Admiring Janie's light complexion, Mrs. Tyler tries to come between Janie and Tea Cake by fixing Janie up with her brother. In response, Tea Cake whips Janie in order to relieve "that awful fear inside him" (140). He rationalizes, "Being able to whip her reassured him in possession. No brutal beating at all. He just slapped her around a bit to show he was boss" (140). Eventually, Mrs. Turner is punished for her internalized racism when Tea Cake and his friends deliberately incite an altercation in her restaurant.

A destructive hurricane brings an end to their routine life on the muck. Following the example of the white landowners rather than the Seminole Indians, the Bahaman workers, and the various wild animals who are fleeing to higher ground, Tea Cake and Janie stay on the muck until it is too late to escape. They are caught in the brunt of the flood when the enormous Lake Okechobee breaks out of its bed. They realize the time has passed for asking white folks for answers; "their eyes were watching God" (151). When Janie is swept off into the flood waters, she grabs onto the tail of a cow, which is swimming with a mad dog on its back. As the dog rushes to bite Janie, Tea Cake stabs it to death but not before he is himself bitten in the face.

In the wake of the flood, Janie and Tea Cake return safely to the muck, but Tea Cake has contracted rabies, which goes untreated until it is too late. Rather than have him tied up like a "mad dog," Janie cares for him herself. As his symptoms worsen, his jealousy is reawakened by the news that Mrs. Turner's brother has returned. When Tea Cake pulls a pistol on her and fires, Janie is forced to kill him in self-defense, shooting him with the very rifle that he had taught her to use so well. Janie is tried and found innocent of the murder of Tea Cake. Although her actions were clearly taken in self-defense, Tea Cake's friends express great anger at the trial, testifying against her. Later, they are reconciled to Janie and run Mrs. Turner's brother off the muck. Janie buries Tea Cake and grieves for him in her overalls: "She was too busy feeling grief to dress like grief" (180).

In the final chapter, Janie returns to Eatonville, where she still has a house and money in the bank. The frame story is completed, as Janie tells Phoeby she has "been tuh de horizon and back" (182). Phoeby responds, "Ah done growed ten feet higher from jus' listenin' tuh you. Ah ain't satisfied wid mahself no mo'" (182–83). In sharing her story with her friend, Janie has both found her voice and inspired her female listener—and her female reader—to embark on her own quest for self-realization. As the novel closes, Janie holds the memory of Tea Cake, who "could never be dead until she herself had finished feeling and thinking" (183). She "pulled in her horizon like a great fishnet. . . . So much of life in its meshes! She called in her soul to come and see" (184).

Critics have debated the extent to which Janie attains full independence and autonomy in the course of the novel; however, there is no doubt that Hurston's character represents a landmark turning point in American literature. Defying previous stereotypical representations of black women as "mammies," "jezebels," and "tragic mulattos," Hurston's Janie has inspired subsequent black feminist writers, including Alice Walker. "Condemned to a desert island for life, with an allotment of ten books to see me through," Walker writes, "I would choose, unhesitatingly . . . *Their Eyes Were Watching God*, because I would want to enjoy myself while identifying with the black heroine, Janie Crawford."

References and Suggested Readings

Awkward, Michael, ed. *New Essays on* Their Eyes Were Watching God. New York: Cambridge University Press, 1990.

Gates, Henry Louis, Jr. Afterword. *Their Eyes Were Watching God*. By Zora Neale Hurston. New York: Harper, 1990.

Gilbert, Sandra, and Susan Gubar, eds. *The Norton Anthology of Literature by Women: The Traditions in English*. 2nd ed. New York: Norton, 1996.

Hurston, Zora Neale. *Their Eyes Were Watching God*. 1937. New York: Harper, 1990.

McQuade, Donald, ed. *The Harper American Literature*. New York: Harper, 1987.

Walker, Alice. *In Search of Our Mothers' Gardens: Womanist Prose*. New York: Harcourt, 1983.

Washington, Mary Helen. Introduction. *I Love Myself When I Am Laughing . . . & Then Again When I Am Looking Mean and Impressive: A Zora Neale Hurston Reader*. Ed. Alice Walker. Old Westbury, NY: Feminist, 1979.

Wright, Richard. "Between Laughter and Tears." *New Masses*: October 5, 1937.

See also Walker, Alice; Woolf, Virginia.

HYSTERIA

The word *hysteros*, which in ancient Greek refers to the woman's womb, evidences the long-standing connection between women and diagnoses of hysteria. Contemporary feminists have responded to this connection by theorizing that oppression of women leads to "hysterical" symptoms that are not medical conditions but, rather, symptoms of patriarchal control. Such oppositional theory can be identified in texts like "The Yellow Wallpaper," in which the female protagonist ends up "creeping" along the walls of her bedroom because her husband and doctor smother her in an effort to control her "illness." Such a tale shows the displacement of the real issue: patriarchal control.

Nineteenth-century doctors diagnosed Charlotte Perkins Gilman, author of "The Yellow Wallpaper," with neurasthenia, which was the term used to describe women thought to be emotionally disturbed (though the "symptoms" were often as simple as fatigue and headache). Her personal experience with men's perceptions of women inform her writing, and her narrator in "The Yellow Wallpaper" undergoes a psychological transformation that blames patronizing treatment and an overreactive diagnosis for her insanity at the end of the text. As had been the case with Gilman herself when she was diagnosed, the narrator desired time and space to write, but her husband, John, instead enforced the "rest cure," which kept her away from activity of any kind. John keeps his wife locked in a room that obviously used to contain mental patients, and the wife sees ghosts of other women "creeping" through the hedges outside. Elaine Showalter argues that these ghosts are literary, that they are reminiscent of Bertha Mason, the infamous "madwoman in the attic."

Madwomen, Showalter seems to suggest, still exist, but only because they remain unaware of the true source of their madness. "Contemporary hysterical patients," she writes in *Hystories*, "blame external sources—a virus, sexual molestation, chemical warfare, satanic conspiracy, alien infiltration—for psychic problems. A century after Freud, many people still believe psychosomatic disorders are illegitimate and search for physical evidence that firmly places cause and cure outside the self" (4). Showalter's position, while certainly contested even within feminist circles (Camille Paglia has criticized Showalter as one of those "beaming Betty Crockers, hangdog dowdies, and parochial prudes" who disrupts real feminists' work), helps to strip Freud's work of some of its power.

According to Freud, children who were molested and who suppressed that experience were likely to experience hysteria as adults. Later, Freud revised this theory to suggest that hysteria was the reappearance of emotions attached to early sexual experiences; often, Freud argued, hysteria occurred because girls repressed their desires to sleep with their fathers and so merely fantasized that they had been seduced, making the hysterical symptoms false. Post-Freudean feminist scholars, such as Showalter, have revived the notion of hysteria in order to point out that hysterical reactions, rather than being overreactive or fantasy-based, are legitimate and, ultimately, feminist. Because patriarchal societies devalue emotional responses generally and female responses specifically, though, feminists have found that such arguments are not always well received, even by women. After all, when hysterics hear that their symptoms might not be under their control, that they are the result of social oppression, the likelihood of an immediate "cure" slips out of reach. Or, as Dianne Hunter phrases it, "so long as our social institutions are dominated by the idea that men are sturdy pillars of rationality and control, while women are idealized as loving mothers without the aggression, desire, or talent required for other achievements, hysteria will exist to give that idea the lie" (203). And feminist scholars, in the meantime, will continue to work at undermining the explanations for Freudian hysteria.

References and Suggested Readings

Gilman, Charlotte Perkins. "The Yellow Wallpaper." *The Heath Introduction to Literature*. Ed. Alice S. Landy. Lexington, MA: D.C. Heath, 1996. 121–33.

Hunter, Dianne. "Hysteria." *Encyclopedia of Feminist Literary Theory*. Ed. Elizabeth Kowaleski-Wallace. New York: Garland, 1997. 202–4.

Showalter, Elaine. *Hystories*. New York: Columbia University Press, 1997.

———. *A Literature of Their Own: British Women Novelists from Brontë to Lessing*. 2nd ed. Princeton, NJ: Princeton University Press, 1977.

See also Brontë, Charlotte; Gilman, Charlotte Perkins.

Lisa R. Williams

IRON, RALPH

See Schreiner, Olive.

JACOBS, HARRIET ANN

Born a slave in Edenton, North Carolina, around 1813, Harriet Ann Jacobs authored her 1861 autobiographical slave narrative, *Incidents in the Life of a Slave Girl,* under the pseudonym Linda Brent. Although subtitled "Written by Herself," the autobiography was long assumed to be fictitious or ghostwritten, perhaps authored by the well-known white feminist abolitionist Lydia Maria Child, who is named as editor on the book's original title page. In the 1980s, the feminist scholar Jean Fagan Yellin authenticated Jacobs's narrative and authorship, providing detailed documentation of the actual names of individuals and places Jacobs wrote about in *Incidents.*

In early childhood, Jacobs lived a relatively sheltered life under the protection of her father, a carpenter who hired his own time from his owner, and her maternal grandmother, a freed slave who operated a bakery in her home. At age six, following her mother's death, Jacobs went to live with her mistress, who bequeathed her to a niece. Jacobs was subjected to unrelenting sexual harassment at the hands of her young mistress's father, Dr. James Norcom. Rather than become his concubine, Jacobs entered into a willing sexual liaison with a white neighbor, Samuel Tredwell Sawyer, who was later elected to the U.S. Congress. Sawyer fathered Jacobs's two children, Joseph and Louisa Matilda.

Determined to secure freedom for herself and her children, Jacobs ran away in the hopes that her absence would induce Norcom to sell her children to Sawyer, which he did. For almost seven years, Jacobs hid in a crawl space above the storage room in her grandmother's house. In 1842, Jacobs escaped north and was reunited with her daughter, whom Sawyer had sent to live in Brooklyn. In New York, she found domestic work in the home of Nathaniel Parker Willis. She sent her son to Boston to live with her brother John S. Jacobs, an escaped slave and abolitionist lecturer. In 1849, Jacobs joined her brother in Rochester, New York, where she became part of a circle of antislavery feminists, among them Amy Post, who had attended the 1848 Women's Rights Convention in Seneca Falls. Post, who became a close friend, convinced Jacobs to write her life story as a weapon in the battle against slavery.

After the passage of the Fugitive Slave Law in 1850, Jacobs returned to the Willis home in New York. In 1852, Mrs. Willis bought Jacobs's freedom, an action that brought Harriet welcome relief from the continued pursuit of the Norcom family but that also inspired understandably mixed feelings. "To pay money to those who had so grievously oppressed me seemed like taking from my sufferings the glory of triumph" (225), she wrote in *Incidents*. Jacobs initially intended to involve Harriet Beecher Stowe, the author of the best-selling antislavery novel *Uncle Tom's Cabin*, in the writing of her story; however, Stowe's patronizing response alienated her, and she later undertook the project herself, completing it in 1858. In 1861, after her publisher went bankrupt, Jacobs self-published the work with an introduction by Lydia Maria Child. Intended to rally its audience of white northern women to the abolitionist cause, *Incidents in the Life of a Slave Girl* raises the veil on the sexual oppression of women under the institution of slavery, as well as chronicles a mother's valiant struggle to secure freedom and a home for herself and her children. Following publication of her slave narrative, Jacobs continued to be active in abolitionist and Quaker circles. She spent her last years in Boston and Washington, D.C., with her daughter. She died on March 7, 1897, in Washington, D.C., and is buried in Cambridge, Massachusetts.

In *Incidents in the Life of a Slave Girl, Written by Herself*, Jacobs employed the pseudonym Linda Brent for the autobiography's first-person narrator and changed the names of other individuals as well. A gripping and moving account of Jacobs's life in slavery and her struggle to secure freedom for herself and her two children, *Incidents* focuses on the particular experiences of oppression faced by women in slavery both as mothers and as objects of sexual exploitation. Recognized today as an important counterpart to Frederick Douglass's classic 1845 male slave narrative, *Incidents* is widely recognized as a foundational work in the canon of African American women's writing. Its dual critique of the interlinked institutions of racism and patriarchy looks ahead to works such as Frances E.W. Harper's *Iola Leroy* and Toni Morrison's *Beloved*, both of which powerfully explore women's sexual abuse under slavery.

Jacobs's pseudonymous narrator, Linda Brent, begins by assuring the reader that "this narrative is no fiction" (xvii), although she has "concealed the names of places, and given persons fictitious names" (xvii). Born a slave, Brent "was so fondly shielded that I never dreamed I was a piece of merchandise" (1). Her father was a carpenter who paid his mistress an annual fee for the privilege of hiring his own time, and her maternal grandmother was a baker, who had been freed from slavery in middle age. Following the death of her mistress, Brent is bequeathed to the five-year-old daughter of Dr. Flint (Dr. James Norcom), a respected physician in the white community who proves to be both a cruel and licentious master.

Similarly sadistic, Mrs. Flint (Mary Matilda Horniblow Norcom) "had not strength to superintend her household affairs; but her nerves were so strong, that she could sit in her easy chair and see a woman whipped, till the blood trickled from every stroke of the lash" (9).

Before long, Dr. Flint begins a persistent campaign of sexual harassment against Linda, who resolves not to give in to his seductions despite her powerless position in his household. She becomes the object of her mistress's jealousy and hatred rather than her protection. Brent falls in love with a free-born black man who wishes to marry her, but Dr. Flint is determined to break her will and refuses to allow her lover to buy her freedom. Rather than surrender to Dr. Flint's unwanted sexual advances, Brent willingly enters into a sexual liaison with Mr. Sands (Samuel Tredwell Sawyer), an unmarried white neighbor who later becomes a U.S. congressman. She says, "It seems less degrading to give one's self, than to submit to compulsion. There is something akin to freedom in having a lover who has no control over you, except that which he gains by kindness and attachment" (59). Jacobs's narrator expresses pain over her status as a "fallen woman" and her violation of nineteenth-century standards for feminine morality. Using the language of sentimental propriety typical of the popular women's fiction of the day, she asks her northern white female reading audience to "pity" and "pardon" her (60). However, she also makes a persuasive and cool-headed argument that "the slave woman ought not to be judged by the same standard as [free women]," since they are treated as property and "entirely unprotected by law and custom" (60).

Brent gives birth to a son and a daughter, fathered by Sands. Since the child follows the condition of the mother under the institution of slavery (a legal practice that, as Jacobs observed, encouraged the rape of slave women by their masters), her children become the property of Dr. Flint. Brent maintains her refusal to become Dr. Flint's concubine, preferring to be sent to away to work on a plantation. When she learns her children will be sent to join her, she resolves to run away in the hopes that her absence will induce Dr. Flint to sell them to their father. Although Sands does buy the children, he fails to keep his promise to Brent to emancipate them. Hidden by sympathetic white and black townspeople, Brent eventually conceals herself in a crawl space above the storeroom in her grandmother's house, a "loophole of retreat" (128), where she remains for nearly seven years. This garret hiding place becomes a paradoxical place of power from which she can spy unseen on Dr. Flint's fruitless efforts to locate her in the North.

Eventually, Brent escapes to the North, where she is reunited with her daughter, Ellen (Louisa Matilda Jacobs), whom Sands has sent to live in Brooklyn. She locates employment with Mrs. Bruce (Mary Stace Willis), an English woman with whom she develops a sympathetic bond. Placing her son, Benjamin (Joseph Jacobs), in the care of her brother William (John S. Jacobs) in Boston, Brent continues to suffer the insecurity of a fugitive slave and longs to obtain true freedom for herself and her children. After the death of Mrs. Bruce, Brent spends a year in Rochester living with the family of the abolitionists Isaac and Amy Post and finally returns to New York to work for Bruce (Nathaniel Parker Willis), who has remarried. However, the passage of the Fugitive Slave Law in 1850 has turned New York into an area just as fraught with the dangers of capture as was the South.

Brent's freedom is finally secured by the second Mrs. Bruce (Cornelia Grinnell Willis), who has resolved to "put an end to this persecution by buying my freedom" (225). Yet Jacobs's narrator admits "the idea was not so pleasant to me as might have been expected" (225). Her bill of sale is a testament to the painful fact that "women were articles of traffic in New York, late in the nineteenth century of the Christian religion" (225–26). In concluding, the narrator again reminds her reader of the distance between the privileged situation of free white women and her own experience of womanhood: "Reader, my story ends with freedom; not in the usual way, with marriage. I and my children are now free!" (227). Yet, she adds: "The dream of my life is not yet realized. I do not sit with my children in a home of my own" (227). By emphasizing the importance of home, Jacobs adds an important element to the quest for freedom and literacy that has been identified as the defining characteristic of the classic male slave narrative authored by Frederick Douglass. At the same time, by refusing the typical "marriage plot" ending and representing the quest for home as an elusive one, *Incidents* highlights the distance between black and white women's narratives in nineteenth-century American literature.

References and Suggested Readings

Carby, Hazel V. *Reconstructing Womanhood: The Emergence of the Afro-American Woman Novelist*. New York: Oxford University Press, 1987.

Jacobs, Harriet A. *Incidents in the Life of a Slave Girl*. 1861. New York: Signet-New American Library, 2000.

Lauter, Paul, ed. *The Heath Anthology of American Literature*. 2nd ed. Lexington, MA: Heath, 1994.

Yellin, Jean Fagan. Introduction. *Incidents in the Life of a Slave Girl*. By Harriet A. Jacobs. Cambridge, MA: Harvard University Press, 1987.

See also Morrison, Toni.

JONES, GAYL

Gayl Jones was born in Lexington, Kentucky, on November 23, 1949. She earned a BA degree in English from Connecticut College (1971), and both an MA degree and DA degree from Brown University in creative writing. Much of Jones's work focuses on the abusive relationships that exist between men and women. As a result of her content, Jones says, "I think I have an unfortunate public image, because of the published work. People imagine you're the person you've imagined." But critics, including Melvin Dixon, point out that Jones's "primary concern . . . is with the human capacity for redemption and regeneration" (247). Certainly the movement toward redemption and regeneration is the focus of Jones's *Corregidora*.

Jones's first novel, *Corregidora*, was published in 1975 and is an important voice in the telling of a slave story and the concomitant tragedies of sexual abuse and personal destruction. It is the story of a young woman, Ursa, and her journey toward health as she tries to understand and counter the psychological trauma imposed on generations of her family by a slaveholding white man named Corregidora, who fathered both her great-grandmother and grandmother. From her childhood on, Ursa's mother and grandmother issue the imperative that she "make generations" in an attempt to eradicate the family's painful history of sexual enslavement.

The story is primarily rendered in a first-person narrative that alternates with an italicized stream-of-conscious historical narrative. The italicized sections repeat some information several times, as if in an effort to burn the story into the mind of both the narrator and the reader. Ursa's voice opens the novel with "It was 1947 when Mutt and I was married" (3), and this relationship frames the novel. Ursa is a nightclub blues singer and attracts the unwanted attention of men in the clubs; Mutt is jealous of the attention other men pay Ursa and is threatened by her independence. Ursa says, "he said that's why he married me so he could support me. I said I didn't just sing to be supported. I said I sang because it was something I had to do" (3). Mutt's jealousy leads to violence, and Ursa suffers from a fall down the stairs. Her womb is removed, and she separates from Mutt. Tadpole McCormick owns the club where Ursa sings, and he insinuates himself into her life when she is recovering from her injuries. After Ursa is divorced from Mutt, she marries Tadpole, but that relationship too is ultimately doomed as a result of his infidelity.

Ursa's last name is from Corregidora, "the Portuguese slave breeder and whoremonger" (9), the father and lover of her grandmother. The women of her family form a solidarity of remembrance and storytelling because "when they did away with slavery down there they burned all the slavery papers so it would be like they never had it" (9). Each generation is bound to tell the story and to make new generations hear the story. Ursa's fall and subsequent barrenness frustrate her place in the stream of history. She tells her story through song, through the blues, and through the narration.

Like her foremothers before her, Ursa keeps a photograph of Corregidora so she will "know who to hate" (10). When Ursa shares the photograph with Tadpole, he responds with the story of his orphaned white grandmother who was taken in and later married by his black grandfather. In relating "One of the children came out black and the other one came out white. But she never did get crazy though" (13), Tadpole is suggesting that Ursa and her maternal ancestors take their hatred so seriously that it drives them crazy. Whether or not the Corregidora women are crazy, they are certainly caught in the psychic grip of their history. Ursa thinks back to Mutt's response when she doesn't change her name in marriage. He recriminates her, "Ain't even took my name. You Corregidora's, ain't you? Ain't even took my name. You ain't my woman" (61).

The one healthy way Ursa responds to her history is to sing the blues. She says her mother and grandmother *squeezed Corregidora into me, and I sung back in return"* (103). Her mother doesn't approve of her singing and says, "Songs are devils. It's your own destruction you're singing. The voice is a devil" (53). Instead, she says, the voice needs to be "raised up to the glory of God" (53). But when her mother asks where Ursa got the songs, Ursa replies, "I got them from you" (54). Indeed, Ursa's mantra of survival is, "*I am Ursa Corregidora. I have tears for eyes. I was made to touch my past at an early age. I found it on my mother's tiddies. In her milk. Let no one pollute my music. I will dig out their temples. I will pluck out their eyes*" (77).

Betrayed before birth by Corregidora and the history of sexual abuse in her family, betrayed by her first husband, Mutt, and her second husband, Tadpole, betrayed by her own body's inability to reproduce, Ursa reaches a place where she must find peace with herself and her history. Though her grandmother has always been forthcoming about her memories, Ursa's mother has not, and the gaps in their relationship make it difficult for Ursa to find a sense of wholeness. Ursa makes a trip to see her mother, hoping her mother will finally unfold the missing piece of her identity. She is rewarded with information that is both difficult and provocative. She learns the identity of her biological father and that he was abusive toward her mother. But she also learns the probing question that her father dared to ask her mother—the question that no one else would ask: "How much was hate for Corregidora and how much was love?" (131).

The question becomes a key in the puzzle that Ursa must unlock, and in time, she will be able to use the question to arrive at the truth of her history. Just as her litany of abuse is at the hands of the men she loves, so too is her journey toward healing. Another step toward healing occurs when Ursa accepts Mutt's wisdom concerning the story of Corregidora; he tells her, "Don't look like that, Ursa. Whichever way you look at it, we ain't them" (151). At the time Mutt tells her this, Ursa is only able to respond that "the way I'd been brought up, it was almost as if I was" (151). During her marriage to Mutt, Ursa is so bound by the story of Corregidora that she cannot stop telling and living it.

Twenty-two years after Ursa first marries Mutt, she sees him again in the club where she is singing. During the decades of their separation, Ursa has been making slow and painful sense of her tormented history. It is not until she and Mutt come together in sexual release that she finally understands the split-second admixture of love and hate that was integral to the complicated relationships of Corregidora and his women, to the relationship of her and Mutt, to her mother and father. She wonders, "was what Corregidora had done to [Great Gram], to *them*, any worse than what Mutt had done to me, than what we had done to each other?" (184). Together, she and Mutt move beyond the tangle of their histories to a new depth of love. Dixon suggests that Ursa's "reconciliation with Mutt is achieved through sex and a ritualized dialogue that assumes the rhythm, structure, and tone of a blues stanza" (240). The final passage of the novel,

"I don't want a kind of woman that hurt you," he said.
"Then you don't want me."
"I don't want a kind of woman that hurt you."

"Then you don't want me."
"I don't want a kind of woman that hurt you."
"Then you don't want me." (Jones 185)

does, as Dixon suggests, lead Ursa "from blues solo to the blues duet" (241). The song exchange between Mutt and Ursa ends with the resolution, "I don't want a kind of man that'll hurt me neither" (185). In this final line of the blues duet, Ursa acknowledges her entitlement for happiness and her departure from the bonds of victimization that were so tightly wrapped around her by the Corregidora story. She has moved to the place where she can finally see what Mutt has told her years before, "we ain't them."

Other works by Jones include *Eva's Man* (1976), *White Rat: Short Stories* (1977), *Song for Anninho* (1981), *The Hermit-Woman: Poems* (1983), and *Xarque and Other Poems* (1985). After a nearly fifteen-year silence, Jones returned to the literary world with *The Healing* (1998), which was a finalist for the National Book Award, and *Mosquito* (2000). Jones's long silence was broken in February 1998 when her husband, Bob (Higgins) Jones, committed suicide in the couple's Lexington, Kentucky, home. Jones herself was admitted to the psychiatric ward of the local hospital when she threatened suicide as well. Since her release, Jones continues to write prolifically.

References and Suggested Readings

Dixon, Melvin. "Singing a Deep Song: Language as Evidence in the Novels of Gayl Jones." *Black Women Writers 1950–1980: A Critical Evaluation.* Ed. Mari Evans. New York: Anchor-Doubleday, 1984.

Jones, Gayl. "About My Work." *Black Women Writers 1950–1980: A Critical Evaluation.* Ed. Mari Evans. New York: Anchor-Doubleday, 1984.

———. *Corregidora.* Boston: Beacon, 1975.

Manso, Peter. "Chronicle of a Tragedy Foretold." *New York Times* 19 Jul. 1998, final ed., sec. 6: 32+.

Patrick, Barbara. "Gayl Jones." *Contemporary Fiction Writers of the South.* Ed. Joseph M. Flora and Robert Bain. Westport, CT: Greenwood, 1993.

KELLEY, EDITH SUMMERS

Edith Summers Kelley was born in 1884 in Toronto, Canada, and died in 1956. She graduated from the University of Toronto in 1903 and then moved to New York where she met Upton Sinclair and became his secretary. She was familiar with Sinclair's circle at Helicon Hall, a Socialist commune inspired by the ideas of Charlotte Perkins Gilman. She married Allan Updegraff and had two children with him. After they separated, she became the common-law wife of the sculptor C. Fred Kelley. They later had a son, and Kelley wrote her first novel, *Weeds* (1923), between childcare and other household duties. Kelley also wrote *The Devil's Hand*, published posthumously in 1974. Both novels are about farm life.

Weeds is an aching tale of a young woman who is cosmically misplaced into a world of cultural expectations that will eventually demand the sacrifice of her will and artistic genius if she is to survive. Judith Pippinger is the preternaturally bright child of a man cast in the genial mode of Rip Van Winkle and of a mother who dies when she is only twelve. Surrounded by docile and intellectually sluggish siblings, Judith stands out with an "energy that craved constant outlet" (15). Judith is an artist who draws incessantly with "great vigor and clarity of vision," and she scandalizes her relatives with "her contempt for the decent and domestic" (25). She finds no encouragement for or understanding of her gifts and her predisposition to the life of the mind.

In Scott County, Kentucky, in the first decades of the twentieth century, a strong gender paradigm is in place. The free-spirited, tomboyish Judith talks like the boys, with obscenities and vulgarities, and is scolded by her sister for not acting like a girl should. Judith resists the categorization, "Well, anyway, I don't feel like one" (57). When their older brother Crawford brings gifts to the younger sisters, it is "for the pleasure of listening to their excited squeals of delight and feeling male and superior" (58). The "superiority" of males was acknowledged then, as now, in the area of wages. Judith hires out to a local family after she finishes her schooling. When she leaves the place some time later, Aunt Eppie, her employer, is sorry, knowing that "they would now have to pay a male hired man four times what they had been paying to Judith" (82).

While Judith works at Aunt Eppie's, she is attracted to a local young man she has known all her life, Jerry Blackford. The two begin a courtship that ends in marriage. The differences between her and Jerry are established in an early childhood scene where he tortures a cat and she flies to its defense. Always sensitive beyond her peers, Judy will not find a partner who can measure up to her natural inquisitiveness or her desire for art and conversation. Her closest soul mate is the elderly Jabez Moorhouse.

After an earnest courtship in which Judith playfully toys with Jerry, they marry. It is with some measure of pride that Jerry notes, "You're the on'y woman I know that's got a man's ways, Judy" (103). Their early married days are marked by idyllic happiness and connubial frolic. Judith enjoys the work around the farm far more than she enjoys the necessities of housekeeping. When it is time to lay in the first tobacco crop, Judith helps Jerry with the bone-wearying work as they race against the window of opportunity presented by the weather. Judith's hard work is seldom broken by a social life except an occasional visit to and from Hat Wolf, a neighboring farm wife. Coarse and shallow, Hat is an unsuitable companion for the bright Judy. Hat's untutored instincts are informed by a monthly magazine, *The Farm Wife's Friend*, that instructs her in home remedies, household hints, moralistic poems, and stories of romance. Hat's husband, Luke, is "a big, stupid looking lout" (131) who feels no compunction at stealing Jerry's precious tobacco sets or leering at Judy when they work together at the tobacco barn.

Judith's joys in her daily chores and in her warm relationship with Jerry are threatened when she becomes pregnant. For the first time in her life, she is revolted by the rich colors and smells around her. It is Hat who informs Judy that she is pregnant and cautions her, "Wimmin has troubles caows [cows] don't never even dream on. You'll find that out afore you're married long" (148).

In the community, women begin to take Judith into their circles of confidence and advise her on the intimate and mysterious world of women's things, and she is put off by their presumptions of ownership of her condition. After one such prolonged visit from a well-meaning neighbor, Jerry finds Judith "sitting slackly in the old rocking chair, her long hands hanging limp like dead things" (157). Once the baby comes, the dailyness of his care "[begins] to fret her like the tug of innumerable small restraining bands" (158). She becomes "irritated and harassed by the constant small cares that his presence demanded of her" (159). Judy begins to suffer "from starvation of spirit" (160).

Soon there are signs of strain on the relationship between Judy and Jerry. Judy wants to accompany Jerry to the monthly Court Day in Georgetown, but he has plans to go with Joe Barnaby, and he claims that the baby will interfere with her trip. Judy prevails and leaves the baby with Jerry's mother; it is her first separation from the baby since his birth eleven months ago. On their long wagon ride into town, Judith has a startling revelation: "She found herself wishing that it was Uncle Jabez who was sitting beside her instead of Jerry" (170). Since her childhood, Judith has shared an affinity for the beauty and wonder of the world with Uncle Jabez. The sudden flash across her mind makes her realize the dearth of intellectual kinship in her life with Jerry.

For Judy, the long-awaited holiday of Court Day brings one more cleavage in her relationship with Jerry. All day, she is aware of the leering looks and snickers of Jerry's friends as she walks around town. In exchanges over a bottle, Jerry has revealed to his friends that he and Judith had sexual relations before their marriage. Outraged by the knowing looks of Jerry's friends, Judith is even more hurt that Jerry would divulge their private lives to casual friends. Fueled by Judith's refusal to forgive Jerry in his moment of infrequent drunkenness, "a bitter feeling of estrangement and mutual distrust grew" between them (184).

No sooner is the first baby weaned than Judith is pregnant again. While she is irrevocably changed by the strains of pregnancy, childbirth, and motherhood, Jerry is unchanged. Even bad farm years do not touch him in the way she is marked by motherhood. Ill-equipped for the struggles of her role, Judith often slaps young Billy "savagely," more out of her frustration than her lack of parental love (208). Blithely unaware of Judith's need for an inner life and for the recovery of her own identity, Jerry thinks that if only the crops bring in enough money, he can solve whatever bothers her: "It never for a moment occurred to him that she could ever want anything which he could not supply if he were only given a decent chance" (209). The birth of her second child takes an enormous physical as well as psychic toll on Judy, and she is slow in recovering from the delivery.

Aware that her feelings for Jerry are growing numb and that she is not always a successful parent, Judy grows introspective and broods about her failures. She longs for the wide-eyed acceptance that she sees in her shallow sister, Lizzie May. She grows increasingly aware that she is not a "mother woman." More and more she "found herself longing ardently for a single day, even a single hour when she could be by herself, quite alone and free to do as she chose" (217). The bondage of motherhood depresses Judith, and she loses her spontaneity: "She never sang or romped any more. She could not rejoice and be glad with these things of nature" (252).

A ring of external events tighten the bands on Judy as well; Jerry's crop doesn't bring much money when the tobacco market crashes, Lizzie May's husband is killed in an accident, and, once again, Judith finds herself pregnant with their third child, Annie.

Deeply mired in depression and in a growing estrangement from Jerry, Judith becomes involved in an affair with a traveling evangelist from the local revival meeting. She feels no sense of moral transgression for the affair but is deeply grieved upon discovering that she is once again pregnant. Feeling repeatedly betrayed by her own biology and by "man's lust and nature's cunning," she attempts suicide but fails (299–300). She makes multiple attempts at abortion until she is successful.

Her relationship with Jerry grows ever more strained and culminates in physical violence. After the fight, in which both violently hit each other, Judith moves out of the marriage bed and sleeps separate from Jerry.

When Joe Barnaby's wife, Bessie Maud, is taken to the insane asylum after repeated bouts of destruction, including nearly throwing the baby into the fire, Judith has a greater understanding of her behavior and a keener sympathy for her. Judith imagines that "perhaps Bessie Maud had not been able to draw comfort out of the sunset and the late twitter of birds, and that was why life had gone so hard with her" (308). Judith's understanding of the causes of Bessie Maud's descent into madness confirms the danger she herself is in as she is no longer able to sing or romp or "rejoice and be glad with these things of nature" (252).

The strained relationship between Judith and Jerry culminates when she learns that Jerry and Hat have been having an affair. On the heels of this discovery, their little girl, Annie, gets sick and hovers at the edge of death for days. Both Judith and Jerry guard her carefully, and when she finally makes a turn for the better, they collapse in each other's arms, sobbing in an imperfect and silent reconciliation. She acknowledges the "strong ties" by which she is bound to Jerry and resigns herself to the life that stretches before her, realizing "the uselessness of struggle" (330).

Her surrender to a spiritless and lonely life is sealed when Uncle Jabez dies; with his death, Judith loses her only soul mate, companion of her thoughts and feelings. Her world is starkly empty. The novel ends with Judith answering the "inevitable summons" to her role as wife and mother as Jerry calls for dinner (333).

References and Suggested Readings

Blain, Virginia, Isobel Grundy, and Patricia Clements. "Kelley, Edith (Summers)." *The Feminist Companion to Literature in English.* New Haven: Yale University Press, 1990. 601–2.

Kelley, Edith Summers. *Weeds.* 1923. New York: The Feminist Press, 1996.

See also Gilman, Charlotte Perkins.

KINGSTON, MAXINE HONG

"I feel that it's a mission for me to invent a new autobiographical form that truly tells the inner life of women," Maxine Hong Kingston has said, "and I do think it's especially important for minority people, because we're always on the brink of disappearing." In her highly acclaimed book *The Woman Warrior: Memoirs of a Girlhood Among Ghosts* (1976), Kingston forges a unique combination of autobiography, fiction, myth, and history, drawing on American, Chinese, and Chinese American culture. Inspired by her Chinese immigrant mother's "talk-stories," which blurred the boundaries between truth and fiction, Kingston's autobiography blends fact and fiction to get at the underlying truth of her experience growing up as a Chinese American woman. In the process, she embraces a strongly feminist voice that defies stereotypical expectations about femininity across multiple cultures.

Kingston was born on October 27, 1940, to Chinese immigrant parents who operated a laundry in Stockton, California. After graduating from the University of California at Berkeley in 1962, she married the actor Earll Kingston. In 1967, Kingston settled with her husband and their son, Joseph, in Honolulu, where she taught English at the Mid-Pacific Institute, a private high school, and at the University of Hawaii. Her autobiographical work *The Woman Warrior* won the National Book Critics Circle Award for nonfiction in 1976 and was named by *Time* magazine as one of the ten best nonfiction books of the decade.

In 1980, she published a companion volume, *China Men*, which focuses on the experiences of Chinese men in America through the stories of her male family members. *China Men* won the National Book Award in 1981. Kingston has said that the two books, much of which were written at the same time, were once meant to be part of one larger book. In both *The Woman Warrior* and *China Men*, Kingston engages and challenges stereotypical representations of Chinese American men and women in ways that have been groundbreaking as well as controversial.

More recently, Kingston has returned to Berkeley to teach creative writing at the University of California. In 1989, she published her critically acclaimed and best-selling novel *Tripmaster Monkey: His Fake Book*, set in San Francisco in the 1960s, about a fifth-generation Chinese American named Whittman Ah Sing— a tribute to the American poet Walt Whitman. An admirer of Virginia Woolf's *Orlando* and William Carlos Williams's *In the American Grain*, Kingston has established a creative voice at once strongly feminist and insistently American. At the same time, she has been widely credited with inspiring the contemporary boom in Asian American writing through her trailblazing efforts to give literary voice to the Chinese American experience. Her latest work includes *To Be the Poet* (2002), based on her 2000 William E. Massey Lectures at Harvard, and *The Fifth Book of Peace* (2003).

Comprising five self-contained but interlinked chapters, *The Woman Warrior* begins with "No Name Woman," the most frequently anthologized of the book's chapters. "No Name Woman" tells the story of Kingston's father's sister who drowned herself in a well in China after becoming pregnant outside of marriage and bringing disgrace on her family. Kingston deliberately breaks the silence surrounding her disowned and dishonored aunt. In the book's opening sentence, she deliberately repeats and thus defies her mother's injunction to collude in this silence: "'You must not tell anyone,' my mother said, 'what I am about to tell you'" (3). Whereas Maxine's mother tells the story as a cautionary tale when Maxine begins to menstruate, Kingston's retelling explores more complex meanings of her aunt's story, inventing and imagining various scenarios (rape, romantic love, incestuous violation) that may have led to her aunt's pregnancy. Reclaiming the ghost of this disgraced female ancestor, Kingston refuses to continue to participate in her punishment.

In "White Tigers," Kingston radically alters and transforms the traditional Chinese ballad of Fa Mu Lan to create a Chinese American fantasy about the life of a woman warrior. Listening to her mother's bedtime "talk-stories," the young Maxine "learned that we failed if we grew up to be but wives or slaves. We could be heroines, swordswomen" (19). Weaving her own fantasy talk-story, Kingston describes the fifteen years she spends training to be a woman warrior, preparing to avenge her family and village against its enemies by taking her father's place in battle. Dressed as a man with words of revenge carved on her back, she leads her peasant army to victory against the feudal lords, defying the traditional Chinese sayings she hates: "Girls are maggots in the rice" and "It is more profitable to raise geese than daughters" (43). Returning from battle to reunite with her husband and son, parents-in-law and parents, Kingston is both a triumphant woman warrior and the embodiment of "perfect filiality" (45).

In contrast, she writes: "My American life has been such a disappointment" (45). Negotiating the contradictory expectations surrounding American and Chinese notions of proper femininity proves far more difficult in real life, as does identifying the enemy and even confronting the very notion of a woman warrior. "I dislike armies" (49), Kingston admits. Yet "the swordswoman and I are not so dissimilar" (53), she concludes. "What we have in common are the words at our backs. . . . And I have so many words—'chink' words and 'gook' words too—that they do not fit on my skin" (53).

The third chapter, "Shaman," focuses on Kingston's mother's Brave Orchid experiences as a medical student in Canton, before she left China to join her husband in the United States. The chapter juxtaposes modern science with ancient superstitions, describing how the young female medical students entertain themselves with "scare orgies" (65) about the ghosts who haunt the dormitory. Brave Orchid impresses the other students (and lives up to her name) by sitting up alone until midnight in the "ghost room" (66), where she confronts the "sitting ghost" (69) and survives. The chapter explores the cultural and generational gaps that separate mother and daughter, as the young Maxine, born in the United States during World War II, tries to make sense both of the ghosts from Brave Orchid's Chinese past and the alien white Americans—the "Taxi Ghosts, Bus Ghosts, Police Ghosts, Fire Ghosts, Meter Reader Ghosts, Tree Trimming Ghosts, Five-and-Dime Ghosts" (97) who populate her Chinese American childhood.

In chapter four, "At the Western Palace," Kingston switches from a first-person to a third-person narrator in order to tell the story of the sixty-eight-year-old Brave Orchid's reunion with her sister, Moon Orchid, whom she has brought to the United States from Hong Kong after a thirty-year separation. The use of the third-person enables Kingston to adopt her mother's generation's perspective, highlighting (with both seriousness and humor) the cultural and generational gaps among the newly immigrated Moon Orchid, the only partially acculturated Brave Orchid, and Brave Orchid's Americanized children. The chapter's central event occurs when the strong-willed Brave Orchid forcefully persuades the dainty and meek Moon Orchid to drive to Los Angeles to confront her ex-husband. Having remarried a younger Chinese American woman, he has created a new life as a doctor in the United States, sending only financial support to the first wife and daughter he left behind long ago in China. Of course, Brave Orchid's insistence that Moon Orchid demand her rightful place as "First Wife" in her husband's house is doomed to fail in the context of American law and culture. Caught between the old ways and the new, the fragile Moon Orchid never successfully acculturates to her new country, developing a paranoid fear of "Mexican ghosts." "Creeping along the baseboards and peeping out windows" (155), like the narrator in Charlotte Perkins Gilman's "The Yellow Wallpaper," Moon Orchid slips gradually into madness.

The final chapter, "A Song for Barbarian Reed Pipe," returns to the twinned themes of silence and voice with which the book opened. Beginning with the startling image of her mother cutting the frenum under her tongue so it "would be able to move in any language" (164), Kingston goes on to describe her silence in school and her struggle to find her voice. In an arresting scene, she also recounts her bullying confrontation with a fragile, quiet Chinese American girl who serves as a double for Maxine and a mirror for her self-hatred. In the book's penultimate scene, the young Maxine confronts her mother with a "list of over two hundred things that I had to tell my mother so that she would know the true things about me and to stop the pain in my throat" (197). Erupting into speech, Maxine accuses her mother: "You lie with stories. . . . I can't tell what's real and what you make up" (202). Her mother, in turn, accuses her of being a kind of ghost—perhaps because she was born on "Gold Mountain," the Chinese immigrants' name for America. Negotiating the confusing territory between cultures in her own blend of fiction and truth in *The Woman Warrior*, Kingston continues "to sort out what's just my childhood, just my imagination, just my family, just the village, just movies, just living."

Kingston ends *The Woman Warrior* with a version of the story of Ts'ai Yen, a Chinese poetess born in the second century A.D. Kidnapped during a raid by the Southern Hsiung-nu, enemies of the Han dynasty, Ts'ai Yen spent twelve years among the barbarians, giving birth to two children who did not speak Chinese. While there, she was taken by the music the barbarians played on their flutes, and she sang songs about China that matched the sounds of the reed pipes. Once ransomed and returned home, Ts'ai Yen "brought her songs back from the savage lands, and one of the three that has been passed down to us is 'Eighteen Stanzas for a Barbarian Reed Pipe,' a song that Chinese sing to their own instruments. It translated well" (209). Like Ts'ai Yen's song, *The Woman Warrior* attempts to translate across linguistic and cultural barriers in order to give voice to Chinese American women's experience.

References and Suggested Readings

Fishkin, Shelley Fisher. "Interview with Maxine Hong Kingston." *American Literary History* 3 (1991): 782–91.

Gilbert, Sandra M., and Susan Gubar, eds. *The Norton Anthology of Literature by Women: The Traditions in English*. 2nd ed. New York: Norton, 1996.

Kingston, Maxine Hong. *The Woman Warrior: Memoirs of a Girlhood Among Ghosts*. 1976. New York: Vintage, 1989.

Lim, Shirley Geok-lin, ed. *Approaches to Teaching the Woman Warrior*. New York: MLA, 1991.

McQuade, Donald, ed. *The Harper American Literature*. New York: Harper, 1987.

See also Woolf, Virginia.

L

LIM, SHIRLEY GEOK-LIN

Born in Malacca, Malaysia, as a Chinese and baptized at age eleven as a Catholic, Lim was named after a Hollywood icon (Shirley Temple). Lim explains that her mother's people were *peranakans*—"a distinctive Malayan-born people of Chinese descent assimilated into Malay and Western cultures," and her father was a Chinese Malayan whose family spoke the Hokkien dialect of China. She grew up speaking the home language of Malay, her mother's language, but became fluent in English once she started her British school education at age six. The confluence of Chinese, Malayan, and colonial British languages and cultures both enriched and confused the young Shirley. Her early years were spent in the extended family home of her paternal grandfather, surrounded by many Hokkien-speaking aunts and a shadowy Malay-speaking mother who was an outsider in her husband's father's home. When her father opened his own business and moved his young family away from the ancestral home, Shirley notes in *Among the White Moon Faces*, "It was as if I woke up from a dark and discordant infancy into a world of pleasure in which my mother was the major agent" (11–12).

Her mother was "funny, knowing, elegantly obscene," and young Shirley delighted in her mother's language, her humor, her smells. But when Shirley was eight, her mother abandoned the family, and Shirley recalls, "I was never certain that she loved her children till later in life, when she needed us" (14).

Both her parents were enchanted by Western culture and the celluloid world of Hollywood. The children loved the cinema too and would buy treats. "We could already taste the tropical treasures in our eager mouths together with the American imaginary—the luxurious orchestra sweep, panoramic scenes, close-ups of white male and female beauty—to be ingested in cool darkness and silence. We emerged from the cinema hall gorged with Western images" (22).

Lim was educated in Malaysia and then earned her PhD degree in English and American Literature in 1973 at Brandeis University in Waltham, Massachusetts. She won the Commonwealth Poetry Prize in 1980 for *Crossing the Penninsula* and the American Book Award in 1989 for *The Forbidden Stitch: An Asian American Women's Anthology* and again in 1996 for *Among the White Moon Faces*. In an interview with *Contemporary Authors* she says, "As a Chinese/Malaysian/American, the only constant in my life has been my relationship with this 'imperial' language, a language . . . which . . . now plainly belongs to the entire human species, like rice, cotton, or paper" (285–86).

Her other works include *Another Country and Other Stories* (1982), *No Man's Grove and Other Poems* (1985), *Modern Secrets: New and Selected Poems* (1989), and academic works such as *Approaches to Teaching Kingston's "The Woman Warrior* (editor, 1991), *Reading the Literatures of Asian American* (co-editor, 1992), *One World of Literature: An Anthology of Contemporary Global Literature* (co-editor, 1992), and *Nationalism and Literature: English-Language Writers form the Philippines and Singapore* (1993). Her most significant contribution is to the field of feminist and Asian/Asian American Studies. In her article "The Ambivalent American: Asian American Literature on the Cusp" she states, "Those on the margins or outside the circles of power will always be questioned on their credentials to participate in inner-circle conversations and will be made to wear identification tags to authenticate their authority to be present" (14).

Lim's memoir, *Among the White Moon Faces: An Asian-American Memoir of Homelands* (1996), won the American Book Award. The memoir is an attempt to extricate herself from the racial, linguistic, gender, and national ties that define her and forge her own identity.

As she suggests in *Among the White Moon Faces*, gender is an issue of paramount concern to her. Shirley grew up as the only daughter in a family of eight boys. When she was favored by her father because she was a girl, but scorned by her brothers for the same reason, Shirley decides her "brothers' acceptance was preferable to [her] father's favoritism," and thus she "rejected the identity of a girl" (25). Not a natural tomboy, Shirley finds her price of acceptance to be a difficult challenge; she explains, "It was my brothers' enmity that made me refuse to be a girl. To be a girl, as I saw through their mocking distance, was to be weak, useless, and worse, bored. It was to stay in one place and gossip for hours the way my mother sat gossiping with my aunts and grandaunts" (26).

By the time Shirley is six, all is not well with her parents' marriage. Her father goes to the hospital for an appendectomy and later continues a relationship with a nurse he met there. His "pursuit of women, his gambling, and his rages" finally drive Shirley's mother to leave him and the increasing burden of six children. Shirley begins a complicated life with her father, whom she loves but of whom she sometimes is ashamed. Though he beat Shirley in his rages, and though he began living with the daughter of their former household servant, Shirley has "kept faith with him" because he loved his children (31). She writes her memoir in part because "[h]is life has remained undocumented, unrecorded, and therefore unvalued and unsaved. I write to make my father's life useful" (32).

Lim's memoir recovers her parents' and grandparents' early years in an attempt to understand who they have come to be. Her parents married just before the outbreak of the war in the Pacific and suffered the deprivations of the Japanese Occupation of Malaya from 1941 until 1945. Shirley was born "toward the end of the bleakest period of the war" (37), and she suggests that "the absence of physical intimacy, the coldness I felt even as a very young child toward my mother, may be, in part, derived from the history of war-time maternity" (38).

By the time she was eight, Shirley's father was bankrupt, and the family lost almost everything they had, including her father's business, and the family had to move once again into the home of her grandfather. The pinch of poverty was alarming, and Shirley says, "After that evening I remained hungry for almost two years" (43). The family circumstances hasten the end of her parents' marriage; her father hits her mother and breaks two of her teeth. Shirley notes:

> Yet that moment was decisive for her. He had crossed the last boundary in marking her violently and in choosing a younger woman of an inadmissible class, the daughter of our servant. Breaking those taboos, he gave my mother permission to break that final social taboo for women, that of abandoning her children. (47)

From that time on, her mother was not spoken of. "She was forbidden, someone who was not dead and also not alive" (52). Once her father's lover moved in with them, Shirley's mother was an unspoken continent. Shirley is scandalized to have a stepmother, especially one who is only seven years older than herself, pregnant with her father's child, and the daughter of their former servant. Their relationship was a frozen one: "We barricaded ourselves behind our different languages. We lived together in the closest quarters as linguistic strangers, our mutual hostility remaining unexpressed and seemingly contained" (59).

Lim's text is also concerned with "Western ideological subversion, cultural colonialism, what ever we call those forces that have changed societies under forced political domination" (64). But rather than rail against the dominance of colonial culture, Lim "actively appropriat[ed] those aspects of it that I needed to escape that other familial/gender/native culture that violently hammered out only one shape for self" (65).

It is through education that Lim appropriates the skills she needs to break out of the poverty of her home and the chauvinism of Chinese male culture. In school, however, Lim daily learns that silence is the path to success and that to assert oneself—especially in defiance of a nun—is to court disaster and humiliation. Shirley begins her own regimen of reading that confirms that it is through language and literature that she can reconcile the two worlds she lives in—the world of Malacca and the world of imagination. She vows, "I knew I would someday write this world down, finding a language that would do justice to it" (75).

As Lim grows, she becomes aware of her own sexuality and the dangers it poses to her as a female in a male world. One of her mother's cousins abuses her and ushers her into the confusing dichotomy of pleasure and humiliation. But without a "clear model of womanhood" (91), Lim determines that "becoming a woman signified losing my virginity" (92). As a university student, she quickly dispenses with her last known boundary to the world of being a woman. But still,

> The problem that confused me for years . . . was what to do with my life as a woman: not simply, what kind of work I wanted, but how to grow up as a woman. That problem kept bringing together what are usually mandated as separate—sexuality and career, emotion and intellect, the personal and the professional. (101)

The men she is close to do not allow her the freedom to explore her intellect without the suspicion that her work is not her own. One university professor seduces her; her steady boyfriend is jealous and controlling, and finally Lim takes a bottle of tranquilizers. The suicide attempt is unsuccessful, and though Lim leaves the relationship with her boyfriend, she is soon engaged with another equally controlling man. It becomes clear that "merit was not the main criterion for professional status" and that in Malaysia, she "would always be of the wrong gender and the wrong race" (133). So Lim leaves Malaysia for Boston on a Fulbright Fellowship. In America, Lim flounders for a while in loneliness, isolation, and cultural estrangement until a friend takes her to the Crisis Intervention Center where she meets "the first of women strangers in the United States to help me learn what my mother never taught me" (151).

After living in a series of disastrous and sometimes dangerous alliances with other graduate students, Lim moves into a single room. In finding a "room of her own," Lim takes the "first step to entering the United States on [her] own terms" (155). She forms supportive relationships with other women and recognizes

> [a]lthough some feminist theorists have bracketed the concept of "sisterhood" as an anachronistic embarrassment, it is the only term I can find to suggest not only the necessity for coalition and the work of solidarity but also the sensibility of support that grows when social gender is recognized as a shared experience. (157)

Lim's life takes a more settled turn as she forges a network of friends, meets the man who will become her husband, and finishes working for her PhD degree. She must now decide where to follow her career—in America or return to Malaysia. Though she would be granted a university position in Malaysia, her husband would not, so Lim stays in America and teaches. She gains American citizenship, she and her husband have a son, and both have challenging careers.

Lim taught for many years in New York's community college system. Her contribution to the field of Asian American studies is undeniable, and she now teaches at the University of California, Santa Barbara.

As is true of most memoirs, the formative years hold more narrative tension and possibility for deeper reflection than do the years of one's present. But the unflinching truth in the end of Lim's memoir is that "home is the place where our stories are told. Had I more time to talk to Mother, perhaps I could have learned to forgive, listening to her stories. . . . Listening, and telling my own stories, I am moving home" (232).

References and Suggested Readings

Lim, Shirley Geok-Lin. "The Ambivalent American: Asian American Literature on the Cusp." *Reading the Literatures of Asian America*. Ed. Shirley Geok-Lin Lim and Amy Ling. Philadelphia: Temple University Press, 1992. 13–32.

———. *Among the White Moon Faces: An Asian-American Memoir of Homelands*. New York: The Feminist Press, 1996.

———. *Contemporary Authors*. Ed. Donna Olendorf. Vol. 140. Detroit: Gale Research, 1993.

LISPECTOR, CLARICE

Today viewed as an important novelist in Brazil, Clarice Lispector received little popular attention early in her career and was brought to international attention by the feminist theorist Hélène Cixous. Though there are some discrepancies concerning her birth year, 1925 is generally accepted as the year of Lispector's birth in Ukraine. Her Jewish parents immigrated to Brazil shortly after her birth, and Lispector was educated in and wrote in Portuguese. Lispector earned a degree in law, married another law student, and had two sons. After the dissolution of her marriage, Lispector lived in Rio de Janeiro until her death from cancer in 1977.

Lispector's first novel, *Near to the Wild Heart* (1944), was written when she was only nineteen, but it has retained an important place in her body of work and in the general modernist canon. She takes her title from a line in James Joyce's *A Portrait of the Artist as a Young Man*, and certainly her style shares many modernist conventions, such as stream of consciousness, internalized intellectualism, and narrative discontinuity. Lispector's main character, Joana, is a lonely and precocious child abandoned by her mother and largely ignored by her father. The first chapter ends with the question, "What's to become of Joana?" and establishes the narrative angst of the novel (15).

Part I of the novel opens with Joana's childhood experiences and moves to her marriage. As a child, Joana is aware of her own creativity, a "restrained force, ready to explode into violence," and she feels compelled to repress its power (16). An ongoing dialogue with herself centers on this urge to release the "animal" within (16) and the need to restrain it. The young Joana is hurt by her father's playfulness when he tells one of his friends, "She has told me that when she grows up she's going to be a hero" (24). Insofar as the novel has autobiographical roots, Joana's prophecy is not far from wrong.

After the early death of her father, Joana goes to live with her aunt and uncle in an environment without stimulation or understanding. The preternaturally sensitive Joana, who recognizes "the tranquility that came from the eyes of an ox, the tranquility that came from that sprawling expanse of sea, from the sea's deep womb, from the cat lying rigid on the pavement" (42), meets no sympathetic vibrations in her aunt's home. When she steals a book, Joana's aunt and uncle are all too eager to send her to boarding school so that the "strict discipline" "might help to tame her" (46).

As a young woman, Joana marries Otávio and loves him, after a fashion, but wonders, "how was she to tie herself to a man without permitting him to imprison her?" (29). Captivated herself by the power of language and thought, she is an unlikely match for a man so rooted in the practical. In response to a question such as "has it ever occurred to you that a dot, a single dot without dimensions is the maximum of solitude," Otávio can only comment on the weather or his appetite (31).

Otávio marries Joana after abandoning his fiancé, Lídia. Otávio's intentions toward Lídia are self-serving only: "He felt sorry for Lídia, he knew that even without any motive, even without knowing any other woman, even if she were the only woman, he would abandon her at some point" (82). And he does leave Lídia to marry Joana. But in doing so, his purposes once again serve only himself. He is aware that "[h]e wanted her not in order to make a life together, but so that she might allow him to live" (88). Lispector reveals Joana's ambivalence toward her marriage with the single sentence paragraph, "She got married" (90). Not surprisingly, a few months after her marriage, "Her life consisted of tiny, complete lives, of perfect circles, that became isolated from each other" (92).

Part II of the novel focuses on Joana's adulthood—her marriage, her predictable unhappiness, and ultimate divorce. Even early in her marriage, she is certain that she will "leave him one day" (103). Her early instincts about Otávio are confirmed when he begins an affair with Lídia, his former lover, and together, they have a child. But it is not the infidelity that precipitates Joana's departure from the marriage so much as "the knowledge that he existed robbed her of any freedom" (100).

Joana carries out an affair of her own, though she never really knows or cares about her vague and shadowy figure named only "The Man." She remains inviolate in her deepest core. As the novel ends, she is free of Otávio and feels her own powers surging within her. The novel of self-discovery ends with Joana's avowal, "I shall rise as strong and comely as a young colt" (186).

As Lispector's translator, Giovanni Pontiero notes, "Plot or intrigue in any conventional sense is disregarded. Any physical action is sparse. Her characters are much less interested in external reality than in their own inner responses to the people and objects around them" (190). Lispector's stylistic devices in this and her following novels share a strong affinity with the quintessentially modernist styles of Virginia Woolf and Djuna Barnes.

Other novels by Lispector include *O lustre* (*The Chandelier*), 1946; *A cidade sitiada* (The Besieged City), 1949; *A maçã no escuro* (*The Apple in the Dark*), 1961; *Uma aprendizagem: Ou, O livro dos prazeres* (*An Apprenticeship: Or, The Book of Delights*), 1969; and *Água viva* (*The Stream of Life*), 1973. *Laços de família* (*Family Ties*), 1960, is one of Lispector's most important volumes of short stories. A posthumous memoir, *Um sopro de vida* (*A Breath of Life*), 1978, is noted by Earl Fitz as "perhaps the most poignant—and the most revealing—of all her works."

References and Suggested Readings

Fitz, Earl E. "Clarice Lispector." *Dictionary of Literary Biography, Volume 113: Modern Latin-American Fiction Writers.* Ed. William Luis. 30 August 2003 <http://galenet.galegroup.com/>.

Lispector, Clarice. *Near to the Wild Heart.* 1944. Trans. Giovanni Pontiero. New York: New Directions, 1990.

See also Barnes, Djuna; Woolf, Virginia.

LORDE, AUDRE

A self-identified "black lesbian feminist warrior poet," the African American writer and activist Audre Lorde boldly explored her multiple identities as female, black, and gay in her writing. She used the term "sister-outsider" to describe her experience as a member of multiple, different, and often incompatible social groups. Lorde was accomplished in a variety of genres, including poetry, autobiography, and the political/personal essay. All of her writing combines a poet's lyricism with a strong sense of political consciousness. As she put it, "The question of social protest and art is inseparable for me."

Born in New York City on February 18, 1934, Lorde grew up in Harlem, the youngest of three daughters of West Indian parents from Grenada and Barbados. She received a BA degree from Hunter College and a master's degree in Library Science from Columbia University. After working as a librarian for the City University of New York for several years, she taught creative writing at Tougaloo College in Mississippi and at John Jay College and Hunter College in New York. In 1962, Lorde married lawyer Edwon Ashley Rollins, and they had a son and a daughter together. Following their divorce a decade later, Lorde began having long-term relationships with women.

Lorde published her first book of poetry, *The First Cities*, in 1968. Her second volume of poetry, *Cables to Rage* (1970), contains her first explicit representation of eroticism between women. Following the publication of two more volumes of poetry, Lorde finally gained a wider audience when the mainstream publishing house W. W. Norton brought out *Coal* (1976), a compilation that included poems from her first two, hard-to-find books and featured jacket copy by another Norton author, the white lesbian feminist poet Adrienne Rich. Lorde's finest volume of poetry is widely regarded: *The Black Unicorn* (1978), which explores her identity as a black woman and a lesbian, and draws on African themes and images. In 1980, she published *The Cancer Journals*, a courageous account of her struggle with the disease.

Her best-known prose work is *Zami: A New Spelling of My Name* (1982), a fictionalized chronicle of Lorde's coming of age as a lesbian and a poet. Lorde referred to *Zami* as "biomythography" rather than autobiography, emphasizing both the mythic and communal elements of her personal story. Lorde's essays and speeches on a variety of political and personal themes are collected in *Sister Out-*

sider (1984) and *A Burst of Light* (1988). A feminist classic widely taught in women's studies courses, *Sister Outsider* includes such well-known essays as "Poetry Is Not a Luxury," "Uses of the Erotic: The Erotic as Power," and "The Master's Tools Will Never Dismantle the Master's House," a powerful critique of racism and homophobia in white-dominated U.S. feminism. Among her later volumes of poetry are *Our Dead Behind Us* (1986) and *Undersong: Chosen Poems Old and New* (1992), a selection of previously published work.

In her life and her writing, Lorde gave voice to the voiceless, claiming, "When I say myself, I mean not only the Audre who inhabits my body but all those feisty, incorrigible, beautiful Black women who insist on standing up and saying I am and you can't wipe me out, no matter how irritating I am." After struggling with cancer for more than a dozen years, Lorde finally succumbed to the disease in 1992; however, in her work, she continues to speak out courageously, claiming a voice on behalf of the traditionally disempowered.

Audre Lorde preferred the term *biomythography* to autobiography in describing the genre of her 1982 prose work *Zami: A New Spelling of My Name*. A fictionalized account of Lorde's coming of age as a lesbian and a poet in New York City during the thirties, forties, and fifties, *Zami* is a synthesis of history, biography, and mythology that draws on the imagery and symbols of her Caribbean ancestry. *Zami* explores women's emotional as well as erotic connections in the context of American sexism, racism, and homophobia, affirming female bonding as an important source of power.

In the work's untitled opening section, Lorde pays tribute to the "images of women flaming like torches" (3) to whom she owes "the power of my voice, what strength I have become, yeasting up like sudden blood from under the bruised skin's blister" (3). In the "Prologue," she describes her desire to be both "man and woman," "to enter . . . and to be entered," and she substitutes the "age-old triangle of mother father and child" with the "elegantly strong triad of grandmother mother daughter" (7).

In chapter one, Lorde describes her West Indian roots, recounting how her parents immigrated to New York from Grenada and Barbados. Lorde, the youngest of their three daughters, grows up thinking of home as a far away place, "a place I had never been to but knew well out of my mother's mouth" (13). She establishes her connection to the tiny island of Carriacou off the coast of Grenada, where her mother and foremothers "built their women's houses . . . harvested the limes, wove their lives and the lives of their children together . . . survived the absence of their sea-faring men easily, because they came to love each other, past the men's returning" (14).

She grows up with her mother as a role model, a "powerful woman" (15) who shared in all the decision making with her husband. She experiences her mother as "different" from other women, explaining "to this day I believe that there have always been Black dykes around—in the sense of powerful and woman-oriented women—who would have rather died than use that name for themselves. And that includes my momma" (15). Lorde depicts incidents of racism and describes the ways her mother "took pains, I realize now, to hide from us as children the many instances of her powerlessness" (17). In a section titled "How I Became a Poet," Lorde recalls her early childhood memories of crawling into bed with her mother and of their sensual physical intimacy, provocatively linking her development as a lesbian and a poet with her mother's body.

As an adolescent, Audre attends Hunter High School and befriends a group of girls who write "obscure poetry" (82) and refer to themselves as "The Branded" (81). They were "the Lunatic Fringe, proud of our outrageousness and our madness, our bizarre-colored inks and quill pens." Her revolutionary political fervor, sparked when a white waitress refuses to serve her family vanilla ice cream in the nation's capital, flourishes. Audre meets Gennie, "the first person in my life that I was ever conscious of loving" (87), who tragically commits suicide, leaving Lorde with a lasting sense of loss. Audre's mother's disapproval of their friendship is just one sign of the growing discord between the two, which eventually leads Audre to move out of her parents' house two weeks after her high school graduation. She says, "shaky and determined, I began to fashion some different relationship to this country of our sojourn. I began to seek some more fruitful return than simple bitterness from this place of my mother's exile" (104). Finding herself pregnant by a boyfriend who leaves her, Lorde arranges an illegal abortion. Even this harrowing experience does not change her resolve to live on her own, despite the fact that "no nice girl left her mother's house before she was married, unless she had become a whore," which, in the eyes of a friend's mother, "was synonymous with being Black anyway" (120).

After a year at Hunter College, Audre leaves New York and goes to Stamford, Connecticut, where she takes a job as a factory worker, running quartz crystal through a commercial X-ray machine—a hazardous job that is one of the few open to women of color. Audre has her first lesbian love affair with Ginger, a divorced woman who is "secretly relieved" (147) when Lorde decides to return to New York. She saves up enough money to go to Cuernavaca, Mexico, where she joins a group of American expatriates, refugees from McCarthyism. In Mexico, she becomes lovers with an older lesbian, Eudora. She revels "in this land of color and dark people who said negro and meant something beautiful" (173), finally able to stop "feeling invisible" (173). Although Eudora eventually sends her away, she feels herself pass "beyond childhood, a woman connecting with other women in an intricate, complex, and ever-widening network of exchanging strengths" (175).

When she returns to New York, still not yet twenty, Audre gets caught up in the Greenwich Village "gay-girl" (177) scene of the fifties. Lorde describes the loneliness of being black and gay, naming her experience as an "exotic sister-outsider" (177) in her predominantly white Downtown lesbian circle, while acknowledging that "Uptown, meaning the land of Black people, seemed very far away and hostile territory" (177). Attempting to build sisterhood, "however imperfectly" (179), Lorde and other lesbians in the fifties anticipated the creation of female community, "which twenty years later was being discussed in the women's movement as a brand-new concept" (179). Lorde's straight, white room-mate Rhea, a fellow activist during the Rosenberg trial, moves out. Lorde later realizes it is because her association with a black homosexual is seen as damaging to the cause by her progressive political colleagues.

Lorde takes a new job as a clerk in the New York Public Library Children's Services and enters into her first serious committed relationship with a woman named Muriel, who reminds Lorde of "a chrysanthemum, always slightly bent over upon itself" (199) and whose mental illness ultimately dooms the relationship. During the trauma evoked by Muriel's numerous infidelities, Audre pours boiling water on her own hand, an act of self-mutilation that enacts pain and rage. Yet, she also experiences a sense of rebirth on a bus one day on Second Avenue. Hear-ing a chorus of an old spiritual swelling in her head, the bus slides away, and she finds herself "in the center of an unknown country, hearing the sky fill with a new spelling of my own name" (239).

One night in a Village bar, Lorde meets a black lesbian named Kitty, who says her name is short for "Afrekete" (243). They make love in Kitty's Harlem apart-ment, returning Lorde figuratively and literally to her West Indian roots and heal-ing her from the pain of her breakup with her white lover Muriel. After her abrupt departure, Lorde "never saw Afrekete again, but her print remains upon my life with the resonance and power of an emotional tattoo" (253).

In the epilogue, Lorde reiterates that "every woman I have ever loved has left her print upon me" (255) and explains that Zami is "a Carriacou name for women who work together as friends and lovers" (255). *Zami* ends as it begins with an invocation of Lorde's mother and her maternal roots: "Once home was a long way off, a place I had never been to but knew out of my mother's mouth. I only dis-covered its latitudes when Carriacou was no longer my home. There it is said that the desire to lie with other women is a drive from the mother's blood" (255).

References and Suggested Readings

Evans, Mari, ed. *Black Women Writers (1950–1980): A Critical Evaluation*. Garden City, NY: Anchor, 1984.

Gilbert, Sandra M., and Susan Gubar, eds. *The Norton Anthology of Literature by Women: The Traditions in English*. 2nd ed. New York: Norton, 1996.

Kester-Shelton, Pamela, ed. *Feminist Writers*. Detroit: St. James, 1996.

Lorde, Audre. *Zami: A New Spelling of My Name*. 1982. New York: Quality Paper Back Book Club, 1993.

Smith, Valerie, ed. *African American Writers*. New York: Scribner's, 1991.

Summers, Claude J., ed. *The Gay and Lesbian Literary Heritage*. New York: Henry Holt, 1995.

Tate, Claudia, ed. *Black Women Writers at Work*. New York: Continuum, 1983.

MARKHAM, BERYL

Beryl Markham was born in England in 1902 and grew up in Nairobi, British East Africa. Beryl thrived in Africa under the tutelage of her horse trainer father; her mother returned to England after only one year in Africa.

Markham's autobiography, *West with the Night*, is a fascinating account of her childhood and young adulthood in British East Africa. It is curiously absent of any mention of Markham's personal life, her three marriages (to Alexander Laidlow "Jock" Purvis, Mansfield Markham, and Raoul Schumacher), many affairs, or three children. Instead it focuses on her successful negotiation of the male world of hunting, horse training, and aviation. The book is the focus of an authorial controversy stemming from rumors circulating at the time of its initial publication. According to Robert Viking O'Brien, Markham's third husband, Raoul Schumacher, said in 1943, "Beryl did not write *West with the Night* or any of the short stories. Not one damned word of anything!" Mary S. Lovell's *Straight on Till Morning: The Biography of Beryl Markham* refutes those early suggestions that Markham was not the author of her autobiography and, for a time, seemed to have settled the issue. However, in *The Lives of Beryl Markham*, biographer Errol Trzebinski asserts that Schumacher is the true author of the book. Concerns of authorship aside, the book nonetheless offers a portrait of a woman who dared to live a life unconfined by traditional gender roles. The book is a paean to Africa as well.

West with the Night is divided into four sections. Book One opens with the question, "How is it possible to bring order out of memory?" (3). Using the model of a pilot's log to generate her remembrances, Markham opens her story with an account of flying to Nungwe in 1935 to deliver a cylinder of oxygen to a dying gold miner. Markham is a freelance pilot and the "only professional woman pilot in Africa at that time" (9), and her memories of flying dominate the first book. Her memories are forged while "swing[ing] suspended between the earth and the silent sky" (12), where she sees her beloved Africa from another perspective.

Markham's autobiography reveals a colonist's admiration for the vast and indefinable quality of the land and racist's condescension toward its inhabitants. At one point she muses,

> I couldn't help wondering what Africa would have been like if such physique as these Kavirondo had were coupled with equal intelligence—or perhaps I should say with cunning equal to that of their white brothers. (21)

She longs for the time when the "undeveloped and 'savage' country would be transformed from a wasteland to a paradise of suburban homes and quaint bathing cabanas and popular beaches, all redolent, on hot days, of the subtle aroma of European culture" (21).

Still, Africa was the "breath and life" (13) of Markham's childhood, and she learned to appreciate the land and its beauty with the eye of a naturalist. She notes, "There is a silence after a rainstorm, and before a rainstorm, and these are not the same" (48). She offers a keenly observant treatise on the zebra and the nature of the African twilight.

In Book Two, she recounts her childhood adventures as a barefoot hunter with the Murani when she learns how to track and hunt, is attacked by a lion, and participates in Nandi hunting rituals. Her playmates are not the village girls but the young boys. On her father's farm, she is free to roam at will; she loves all that is associated with his horse barns and even helps deliver a colt, which her father then gives to her. She names the colt after the winged horse Pegasus, presaging her love of flying.

In this section, Markham makes some changes in tense and point of view that increase the effectiveness of her narration. She begins the tale of a warthog hunt in past tense, but as the action intensifies, and her beloved dog, Buller, is wounded in the chase, she shifts to present tense. In another scene, she describes the arrival of an especially fine horse to her father's barns but then shifts to the horse's point of view. The horse's narration grows a bit precious as he stoically yields to Beryl's care, but the narrative experimentation itself is noteworthy.

In Book Three, Beryl's idyllic childhood is brought to an end by a drought in British East Africa that causes her father's financial ruin. He pays his debts, but leaves Africa for Peru, where he will continue to breed horses. Though he asks Beryl to come with him, she asserts that at seventeen, she is no longer a child and that she will stay in Africa and learn to train horses. She goes to the stables in Molo and earns her license by the time she is eighteen. One day a man comes to work for her; it is her childhood playmate Kibii, now grown to a man and called by his adult name Arab Ruta. The entrenched effects of colonialism erase their childhood equality; he becomes her servant and calls her Memsahib. She notes that "he will walk behind me now, when once, in the simplicity of our nonage, we walked together" (149).

With Arab Ruta helping in her stables, Markham continues to build her reputation for hard work and positive results as her horses become winners. But her passion for horses is challenged when she meets Tom Black, a flyer with a dream to build an aviation business in Africa.

In Book Four, Markham leaves horse training behind for the excitement of flying. Tom Black teaches her to fly, and she earns her "A" license and then her "B" license that allows her to carry passengers. She starts a business as a freelance pilot and enters another stage of her adventurous life where she is companion and cohort with the legendary White Hunters, Baron von Blixen and Denys Finch-Hatton. Of her quality of life, Markham reflects, "I have had responsibilities and work, dangers and pleasure, good friends, and a world without walls to live in" (239).

Still another challenge calls to her, and she accepts without reservation the suggestion that she attempt a transatlantic flight, flying east to west. She flies "west with the night" (284) from Abingdon, England, before landing nose down in a bog on Cape Breton Island, Nova Scotia. Her twenty-one-hour and twenty-five-minute nonstop flight earns her great acclaim on both sides of the Atlantic. Her rejoicing in the accomplishment is diminished by the news that Tom Black, her aviation mentor, has died in a plane crash.

When urged by friends to write about her experiences, Markham sets down to write her autobiography, "memory in ink" (293), and the result is *West with the Night*.

Other works by Markham include *The Splendid Outcast*, her collected short stories edited by M.S. Lovell in 1987, and *The Illustrated West with the Night* (1994). Markham died in Nairobi, Kenya, in 1986.

References and Suggested Readings

Kohl, Judith C. "Beryl Markham." *An Encyclopedia of British Women Writers*. Ed. Paul Schlueter and June Schlueter. Revised and Expanded ed. New Brunswick: Rutgers University Press, 1998.

Markham, Beryl. *West with the Night*. New York: North Point Press-Farrar, Straus and Giroux, 1983.

O'Brien, Robert Viking. "Author and Hero in *West with the Night*." *The Journal of African Travel-Writing* 1 (1996): 14–23. 28 January 2001 <http://www.unc.edu/~ottotwo/authorandhero.html>.

MARRIAGE

As a legal contract and social institution, marriage wields a great deal of power in society, both contemporarily and historically. Scholars have argued in recent years that, in spite of its benefits, marriage is often enforced and oppressive; such arguments have suggested that marriage normalizes and mandates heterosexuality, restricts women to the domestic sphere, and, generally, underpins male dominance. These kinds of arguments have fed the distinction between the public and private spheres of existence, with marriage most often assumed a component of the latter. Feminists argue that, on the contrary, no such division truly exists. The "personal is political," they suggest, and in the case of marriage, women's consistently lower social status results in always unequal partnerships between men and women who marry. Marriage also reinforces an imbalanced economic system that underprivileges domestic labor.

Many feminists of color, as well as gay, lesbian, and transgendered scholars, have criticized traditional critiques of marriage by noting that they tend to ignore intersections of race, class, and gender. Women's campaigns for control over the conditions of reproduction, for example, have often been assumed to originate in the issue of abortion, but, in reality, this battle has a long history: African American women subjected to slavery were constantly faced with slaveowners' insistence that they reproduce so as to enlarge the workforce.

Also, little work has been done demonstrating the effects of marriage on sexuality, a gap in scholarship that led Adrienne Rich to position marriage as a manifestation of "compulsory heterosexuality." And bell hooks notes that women of color (and working-class white women) have traditionally had to work outside of the home, a model not often accounted for in traditional criticisms of marriage.

As economic opportunities increase, women become less reliant on marriage as a means of survival. Nonetheless, marriage remains a powerful cultural force: It is equated with stability and commitment and therefore often idealized as the most stable environment for children. The traditional nuclear family—"nuclear" because of its supposedly solid, identifiable center, which is the wedded mother and father—has been touted by conservatives in general and religious groups in particular. Such groups romanticize marriage as a superior demonstration of love (while its material benefits, such as tax breaks and health insurance, are rarely discussed as incentives to marry). These same benefits are often withheld from nonmarried, nontraditional couples, which arguably uphold not only the institution of marriage but also its counterpart of heterosexuality. The traditional family, after all, teaches gender roles to its members by illustrating each family member's "place" in the overall structure.

Gwyn Kirk and Margo Okazawa-Rey observe that the United States workplace still centers on the assumption that "men are the breadwinners and women are the homemakers" even though more women than ever are participating in the workforce. Similarly, marriage has been upheld as the ideal in spite of the current divorce rate of 50 percent. Significantly, most of these divorces are initiated by women, suggesting that the myth of marriage as romantic pinnacle may not be entirely sound.

References and Suggested Readings

hooks, bell. *Feminist Theory from Margin to Center.* Boston: South End Press, 1984.
Kirk, Gwyn, and Margo Okazawa-Rey. *Women's Lives: Multicultural Perspectives.* 2nd ed. Mountain View, CA: Mayfield, 2001.

Rich, Adrienne. "Compulsory Heterosexuality and Lesbian Existence." *Blood, Bread, and Poetry*. New York: Norton, 1984.
See also hooks, bell.

Lisa R. Williams

MARSHALL, PAULE

Novelist and short story writer, Paule Marshall was born in Brooklyn, New York, in 1929 to recent immigrants from Barbados. Marshall graduated from Brooklyn College and was hired as a writer for the African American magazine *Our World*, where she grew in discipline as a writer. While working for the magazine, she spent her evenings writing what was to become her first novel, *Brown Girl, Brownstones* (1959). Her still-growing body of work includes *Souls Clap Hand and Sing* (1961), *The Chosen Place, the Timeless People* (1969), *Praisesong for the Widow* (1983), *Reena and Other Stories* (1983), *Daughters* (1991), and *The Fisher King* (2000).

Marshall is intentional about what she hopes to achieve in her writing and is guided by several goals. She wishes "to create a body of work that will offer young black women . . . a more truthful image of themselves in literature. . . . It gives us the sense of our right to 'be' in the world, and once you have that sense of your right to be in the world, all positive things follow from that." She also asks, "How do I as a woman—a black woman—and a writer continue to function and grow in a society that almost daily assaults my sense of self?" Furthermore, she places black women at the center of her works in order "to make up for the neglect, the disregard, the distortions, and untruths."

As Marshall began work on *Brown Girl, Brownstones*, she felt empowered by Gwendolyn Brooks's *Maud Martha* because, she says, "for the first time, you had the interior life of a black woman dealt with in great depth. It was really helpful to me in designing and creating the character Selina." What Marshall accomplished in *Brown Girl* is partially autobiographical text that reflects the longings of a young girl to make sense of her life's complicated cultural mosaic.

The book opens with a description of the brownstones that line the street in the neighborhood where Selina, a ten-year-old tomboy with an acute sensitivity, lives. That Marshall opens by focusing on both the brownstones and on Selina reinforces the titular intent of the novel. The brownstones take on near character status; certainly they are metonymic for the middle-class hopes of the Barbadian immigrants, most tragically portrayed in the person of Selina's mother, Silla. Silla and her husband, Deighton, could not be more unlike in their desires for a life in America. Silla is driven by the desire to become a property owner and to secure a better place for her family in a country that offers more opportunities than does Barbados, which is still in the clutches of British colonialism. Deighton is far more interested in "wearing" his new freedoms and opportunities. While Silla wants to save money and invest it in real estate, Deighton is content to spend their money so long as he cuts an impressive figure. He is a dreamer, but Silla is a doer, and their conflicting personalities constitute one of the poles around which their relationship turns. Another less-obvious one is the unresolved death of their second child, a boy with a weak heart whose death Silla believes was hastened by Deighton's irresponsibility.

Caught in the middle of the tempestuous relationship are Selina and her older sister, Ina. A less strongly defined character than either parent or Selina, Ina responds to the dreams of her parents with a studied disinterest. For Ina, survival is acquiescence to the role expected of a first generation American: she completes her education and marries a quiet Barbadian young man. But for Selina, the transition from childhood to adulthood and the negotiation of her relationship with each parent separately will not be so smooth a journey. Selina embodies her father's imagination and penchant for dreaming and her mother's stubbornness and manipulative drive for self-determination and success. That Selina must find her place in the family is intimated in the description of a family portrait in which she is present only in her mother's womb. When she views the portrait, Selina wants to "send up a loud importunate cry to declare herself, to bring someone running" (6). The heart of the novel is Selina's cry for self-definition.

Selina's emotional connections are to her father, but, even as a child, she realizes that it is her mother who is her real anchor and steady place. Nonetheless, several adults, all fringe characters in the community, primarily aid Selina in her journey to adulthood: Suggie Skeete, a woman with an insatiable sensual appetite and a refreshing point of view on the Barbadian (Bajan) community; Miss Mary, a white woman with a past that shames her; and Miss Thompson, an old Southern woman who bears a "life-sore," a tale of racism, on her body. Selina makes her rounds of the neighborhood, visiting these women who nurture and validate the wise child within her.

The event that triggers the conflict between Silla and Deighton is his inheritance of two acres of land from his sister back in Barbados. Silla wants to sell the land so that she can apply the money to buying their brownstone; Deighton dreams about the land, the home he will build on it, and its value in nullifying his demeaning memories of being an alien in his own home. The legacy of British colonialism is never far from Deighton's remembrances of home, and they all coalesce in the memory of dressing in his best British wool suit and seeking employment, only to be turned away from the store. Deighton was raised by his mother as a son of privilege; she sacrificed for him so that he was always dressed to perfection, that he had an education at Harrison College "so he could be a schoolmaster" (32), but the balloon of entitlement she created around him was punctured by the "white people in town" who would "chuck him out fast enough" when he would seek employment (33).

Silla cannot understand Deighton's longing for their island home. Her childhood in Barbados is marked by her experience as a member of the Third Class, "a set of little children picking grass in a cane field from the time God sun rise in his heaven till it set. With some woman called a Driver to wash yuh tail in licks if you dare look up" (45). She is unwilling to compromise her dream for a New York brownstone for Deighton's desire to return to the islands in a show of recovered dignity.

Selina's friend Beryl Challenor and her family offer the model of the immigrant family who has embraced the American Dream with a smug success; to Selina, Beryl's father, Percy, looks like "a pagan diety . . . too big to live among ordinary people" (54). In his pomposity, Percy Challenor scorns Deighton Boyce as "spree boy" and a "disgrace" for taking pride in his ownership of land but not handling the property in such a way as to make a profit from it. For Selina, "Percy Challenor had established irrevocably that her father was a disgrace" (55).

Silla determines that she will find a way to sell Deighton's inheritance and use the money for a down payment on their brownstone. She becomes monomaniacal in her quest and designs a successful scheme that includes deception and forged signatures. When the check arrives, however, it must be cashed by Deighton, and Silla's deception comes to a catastrophic conclusion; rather than bringing home the money, Deighton spends the day on Fifth Avenue buying extravagant gifts for Silla and the girls. The lavish shopping trip is simultaneously his passive-aggressive strike back at Silla and his impotent rejoinder to the British shopkeepers who turned him away as a young man in Barbados. Whatever sense of esteem Deighton gains from his public show of providing for his family, it is not shared by the Bajan community. When he arrives late at a wedding reception, the dancing is already in progress, and the community closes the circle and refuses to let Deighton in; they drive him away with the song, "Small Island, go back where you really come from!" (150).

Soon after the debacle at the wedding reception, Deighton is injured at his work, suffering a physical maiming that mirrors his injured status in his family and community. He pulls away from his family and joins the "kingdom" of Father Peace, a character closely based on the historical Father Divine. When Selina visits him at Father Peace's, she is undone by her father's diminishment; she thinks of the godlike Percy Challenor and wonders of her own father, why "was he the seduced follower and not the god?" (169). Deighton's separation from family culminates in a scene at the breakfast table when Selina casually requests, "Pass the butter, Daddy" (171). Deighton explodes in a tirade against familial relationships and in praise of Father Peace; he soons moves out of the family home and goes to live in the "kingdom" with Father Peace.

Now abandoned by Deighton, Silla exercises one last power play against him; he has entered the United States illegally, and she has him arrested and deported. Silla's actions create a visible rift in her relationship with Selina. Selina calls her mother "Hitler" and covers her with angry blows, all the while clinging to her mother. Silla rocks her to sleep, aware that "each caress declared that she was touching something which was finally hers alone" (185).

Deighton doesn't fully return to Barbados; according to the cable the family received, he "had either jumped or fallen overboard and drowned at a point within sight of the Barbados coast" (185).

Though Selina's first allegiance is to her father, she maintains an adversarial love for her mother and realizes that "she longed to understand the mother, for she knew, obscurely, that she would never really understand anything until she did" (145). Selina always refers to her mother as "the mother" and thus reveals her ambivalence toward Silla; Selina longs to distance herself from her mother, but she also recognizes the qualities in her mother that reflect an encompassing maternal presence.

Selina has an inchoate but growing awareness of her own artistic abilities and her desire to embrace life. She has witnessed her mother "hunched over the table all night" and her father "stretched on a cot" in a tomblike existence, and she fears that she will "never find a way out" but will move from "one death to another" (204). But even her ability to speak her inarticulate yearnings is a measure of her ultimate success:

> She knew what she wanted. It was not so much a thought as something deeply felt. To flow out of herself into life, to touch and know it fully and, in turn, to be touched by it. And then, sometime, to withdraw and be quiet within herself. . . . But how? How even to begin? She did not know. (204)

When Selina goes to college, she does find an outlet for her artistic soul in dance. She joins a campus dance club and begins to form relationships in the dance community. She is chosen for the solo dance at the final recital and dances the life cycle from birth to death. At a postperformance party, she visits the home of a white friend, and that mother grills Selina on her background. The woman then gives an accounting of her own lack of prejudice with such comments as "Oh, it's not their fault, of course, poor things! You can't help your color. It's just a lack of the proper training and education. I have to keep telling some of my friends that" (288). She goes on, "you don't even act colored. I mean, you speak so well and have such poise" (288). The woman reduces Selina to minstrelry when she ask, "Oh, please say something in that delightful West Indian accent for us!" (289). Selina, who has been largely shielded from racial prejudice in her Bajan community, realizes "with a sharp and shattering clarity—the full meaning of her black skin. And knowing was like dying" (289). The painful lesson provides Selina with a fresh understanding of her own mother and the trials she has surely faced as a black woman.

As Selina grows into her womanhood, she walks the precarious line between expressing her own essential self and having that self shaped by her mother's values. Her mother urges her to join the Barbadian Association, a group of homeowners who concentrate their growing financial clout on assailing the white establishment's stranglehold on property and business. Selina disagrees with the Association and tries to distance herself from it, but increasing pressure from her mother ends in a compromise visit to an Association meeting. There, Selina's instincts are confirmed, but she learns of a scholarship that the Association will provide for a worthy Barbadian student. She is enmeshed in an affair with Clive Springer, an enervated artist trapped in his mother's demands and his own lack of drive. Selina determines to win the scholarship so that she and Clive might start a new life together. She involves herself in Association activities and energizes the organization, though, all the while, she knows she is simply using the system to achieve what she wants.

Clive draws a picture of Selina, and she is shocked at the likeness to her mother, at the look of "someone ruthlessly seizing a way and using, then thrusting aside, others" (247). When she wins the scholarship, she realizes that she has used the same deceptive strategies that her mother used in selling her father's property. Rather than compromise her principles further, she refuses to accept the scholarship. She determines to go away alone to "the islands" (308) and takes strength from her mother's own example: "Everybody used to call me Deighton's child. Remember how you used to talk about how you left home and came here alone as a girl of eighteen and was your own woman? I used to love hearing that. And that's what I want. I want it!" (307).

As she walks through the city one night, Selina passes by blocks of brownstones being destroyed to make room for a new city project and sees a "carved oak stairway [leading] only to the night sky" (309). It is clear that the Bajan community in New York can no longer take Selina where she needs to go. She takes one of the two silver bangles on her arm—there since childhood—and throws it away into the city. In doing so, she leaves something of herself behind and thus acknowledges her connections to New York; but she keeps one bangle to carry home with her as she embraces a new life in the islands of her parents' origins. In going, she not only begins her own journey, but she ends the aborted journey of her father.

References and Suggested Readings

Marshall, Paule. *Brown Girl, Brownstones*. 1959. New York: The Feminst Press, 1981.
———. Inteview with Daryl Cumber Dance. "An Interview with Paule Marshall." *The Southern Review* Winter 1992: 1–20.
———. Inteview with Joyce Pettis. "A *MELUS* Interview: Paule Marshall." *MELUS* Winter 1991–1992: 117–29.
Washington, Mary Helen. Afterword. *Brown Girl, Brownstones*. By Marshall Paule. 1959. New York: The Feminist Press, 1981.

MCCULLERS, CARSON

Born Lula Carson Smith in Columbus, Georgia, in 1917, Carson McCullers is known for representation of "the grotesque" in her fiction that is all centered in the American South. Her first novel, *The Heart Is a Lonely Hunter* (1940), was published when she was just twenty-three; other works include *Reflections in a Golden Eye* (1941), *The Member of the Wedding* (1946), *The Ballad of the Sad Café* (1951), and *Clock without Hands* (1961). Bigelow notes that McCullers's works "explore the variety and the complexity of human isolation and expose the destructive repercussions of that alienation, especially when the separation of the individual from society is occasioned by racial and gender bigotry" (257–58).

McCullers herself suffered from "human isolation" and alienation by virtue of her precocious childhood, her bisexuality, her troubled marriage, and her many illnesses. In 1937, she married Reeves McCullers, but divorced him in 1940. They remarried in 1945, but their relationship was strained, in part because the success of her first novel cast her husband into shadow. Reeves McCullers killed himself in 1953 after a failed attempt to persuade Carson to join in a double suicide.

An accomplished pianist, the young Carson McCullers went to New York to study music at the Julliard School but was unable to pay the tuition; instead, she studied writing at Columbia and New York University. Throughout her life, she suffered a number of health problems, including rheumatic fever in her childhood, several strokes that left her with some paralysis, depression, a heart attack, and breast cancer late in her life. She died in New York in 1967 from complications resulting from a stroke.

A Member of the Wedding is the story of a twelve-year-old girl wrestling with the onset of puberty and her own struggle to understand her preternatural sensitivity in a town that she feels can only see her as a freak. The novel opens in the summer when Frankie Addams "had not been a member" (1), when she was afraid, when "she was sick and tired of being Frankie" (20). Frankie does lead a lonely existence: Her mother died at Frankie's birth, her father works at his jeweler's shop and comes home to collapse in emotional and physical lethargy, and her only company is her six-year-old cousin, John Henry, and Berenice, the black housekeeper. The unlikely trio of Frankie, John Henry, and Berenice forms the emotional center of the novel, and though Frankie's concerns are foregrounded, both Berenice and John Henry encounter tragedy by the end of the novel.

The Member of the Wedding is presented in three parts. Part One establishes the context for Frankie's melancholy. Although she is pleased that her brother Jarvis is getting married, she is pained that his upcoming union throws her own aloneness into relief. Her sense of isolation is heightened, and she begins to imagine that the cure for her loneliness is to move into the circle of intimacy drawn by the love of Jarvis and Janice. She notes the rightness of their marriage, signaled by the same two initial letters in their names. Frankie longs for a name that would draw her naturally into the circle and fashions a new name for herself: F. Jasmine Addams. Berenice warns her that it is against the law to change her name, but the change for Frankie not only allows her to reshape her identity, it encodes her ownership of Jarvis and Janice and the bond they represent. She calls her brother and his fiancée the "Jas," and her new name captures them: JAs=mine.

She determines that she must leave her hometown where she so recently has courted disaster by breaking the law; she has stolen a knife from Sears and Roebuck, has taken her father's pistol around town and shot cartridges "in a vacant lot," and she has committed a "queer sin" with Barney MacKean, "and how bad it was she did not know" (23). To follow her other JAs wherever they go offers a perfect solution, not only as an escape from the "law" but also as a correction to her loneliness. When Frankie tells Berenice of her plan to leave with Jarvis and Janice, Berenice declares that she has a "crush" on the wedding. But Frankie sees a place where she will finally fit in; "she was a member of the wedding. The three of them would go into the world and they would always be together. And finally, after the scared spring and the crazy summer, she was no more afraid" (43).

Part Two of the novel is centered on the day before the wedding of Frankie's brother, a day "not like any day that F. Jasmine had ever known" (44). On this day, F. Jasmine scorns the neighborhood children who are trying to dig a swimming pool in their yards; she knows that "though they would work and dig in various yards, not doubting to the very last the cool clear swimming pool of water, it would all end in a big wide ditch of shallow mud" (48–49). In much the same way that the swimming pool will never manifest more than a "ditch of shallow mud," neither will Frankie's dream of oneness with Jarvis and Janice come to anything. But that information is shielded from her on this day of expectation. She feels open to all possibilities, ready to make her destiny come true. She goes downtown to the Blue Moon, a seedy hotel, which, in the days of the old Frankie, she knew she had "no valid right to enter there" (53). But now as F. Jasmine, "the old laws she had known before meant nothing" (53). She enters the Blue Moon and meets a redheaded soldier who, taking her to be older than she is, asks her to join him on a date that night at nine o'clock. She drinks a beer with him in the hotel bar. Frankie spends the day roaming around the downtown, seeking people to tell her tale of the upcoming wedding and her imminent move. After she buys a dress for the wedding, Frankie goes home for what she imagines is the last dinner she will eat in the familiar kitchen with Berenice and John Henry. Fantasizing about her new life with the JAs, Frankie works herself into a frenzy. Berenice pulls her to her lap, and while they sit in the growing darkness, Berenice articulates what Frankie has been trying to express all day:

> I think I have a vague idea what you were driving at. We all of us somehow caught. We born this way or that way and we don't know why. But we caught anyhow. . . . Everybody is caught one way or another. But they done drawn completely extra bounds around all colored people. (113–14)

As Berenice, Frankie, and John Henry sit in the kitchen, they are caught in a rhapsodic moment where they all involuntarily start to cry. It is as if the weight of their lives presses upon them so that they have no choice; it is a moment of grief that soon passes but has an efficacy that will extend beyond the day.

As the moment passes, Frankie leaves the house once more to have her fortune told by Berenice's mother. Big Mama predicts a wedding, a sum of money, and a departure and a return. Frankie is disappointed by her fortune, but goes on to keep her date with the soldier nonetheless. They have a drink, and when he asks her to his room, Frankie "did not know how to refuse. It was like going into a fair booth, or fair ride, that once having entered you cannot leave until the exhibition or the ride is finished" (128). When the soldier makes sexual overtures toward her, Frankie cracks him over the head with a water pitcher and leaves by the fire escape. She reaches home safely, though a bit shaken, and goes to bed in preparation for the next day's wedding.

Part Three of the novel is the brief account of the wedding and Frankie's (now called Frances) disappointing return to her home. Just as Berenice predicted, Jarvis and Janice will not take Frankie with them, and she disgraces herself by "flinging herself down in the sizzling dust" and crying out, "Take me! Take me!" (135). Back home, she packs a bag, gathers her father's pistol and wallet, and runs away; before she can hop an outbound train, she is found by a policeman who returns her to her father.

After that night, "Frances was never once to speak about the wedding" (149). The fever of her twelfth summer passes, and all their lives change. Frankie and her father move from their home to live with Aunt Pet and Uncle Ustace in the suburbs; Berenice gives notice and marries her long-term beau, though he doesn't give her the shivers; her brother is arrested and sent to work on a chain gang; and John Henry dies a painful death from meningitis. Amid all the communal grief, Frankie moves beyond her private confusions, and on a last night in the old kitchen with Berenice, she once again feels "an instant shock of happiness" (153).

Though the novel records the coming of age of a young girl, the territory it covers in that journey reveals a more adult awareness. Cast over the conversations that Berenice, John Henry, and Frankie have are stories of transgendered persons, homosexuals, domestic abuse, murder, sexual abuse, and lost loves. All three characters give their version of the world that a more attentive God would have made. One aspect of Frankie's world would allow people to "instantly change back and forth from boys to girls, which ever way they felt like and wanted"; in John Henry's world "people ought to be half boy and half girl" (92). Berenice's comments focus on race and a world where "there would be no colored people and no white people to make the colored people feel cheap and sorry all through their lives. No colored people, but all human men and ladies and children as one loving family on the earth" (91). For her honest depictions of difficult subjects— race and gender in the South of the 1940s—and her lyric prose, Carson McCullers has well earned her continued readership.

References and Suggested Readings

Bigelow, Pamela. "McCullers, Carson." *Gay and Lesbian Literature*. Ed. Sharon Malinowski. Vol. 1. Detroit: St. James Press, 1994.

McCullers, Carson. *The Member of the Wedding*. 1946. New York: Bantam, 1973.

Torsney, Cheryl B. "Carson McCullers." *Modern American Women Writers*. Ed. Elaine Showalter et al. New York: Scribner's, 1991.

MORRISON, TONI

Winner of the 1993 Nobel Prize for literature (the first African American woman to be so honored), Toni Morrison has established herself as one of the most important novelists writing in America today. Although Morrison doesn't explicitly define herself as feminist in interviews, her angle of vision has consistently privileged and explored black women's experiences in ways that have resonated deeply with feminist perspectives. In characters such as Sula in *Sula* (1973) and Sethe in *Beloved* (1987), Morrison has created strong, independent, rebellious women who struggle to claim a sense of self, even at the cost of being cast out by their communities.

Born Chloe Anthony Wofford, Morrison grew up in Lorain, Ohio, during the Great Depression, the second of four children. Her father, George Wofford, was a steel mill worker who had left behind the racial oppression of his home state of Georgia. Her maternal grandparents had similarly left Alabama for Kentucky, later settling in Ohio as well. Her mother, Ramah Willis Wofford, sang jazz and opera, and her maternal grandfather played violin. Morrison's childhood was steeped in black music, folklore and culture; as a teenager, she also read widely in the European and English classics.

At Howard University, where she received a BA degree in English with a minor in Classics, Morrison picked up the nickname Toni. The first person in her family to attend college, she went on to receive a master's degree from Cornell University, writing her thesis on the theme of suicide in Faulkner and Woolf. She taught English at Texas Southern University before returning to a teaching position at Howard, where she wrote a short story that would later evolve into her first novel, *The Bluest Eye*.

In 1958, while at Howard, she married Harold Morrison, a Jamaican architect. They had two sons before the marriage ended in 1964. Morrison, who has never remarried, raised her children as a single mother, supporting her family through teaching and editing jobs. During this period following the breakup of her marriage, she began to write seriously, working on *The Bluest Eye*. After a stint as an editor in Random House's textbook division in Syracuse, New York, Morrison moved to New York City in 1968, where she became a senior editor at Random House. During her twenty-year publishing career, she was instrumental in bringing the works of such black writers as Angela Davis, Toni Cade Bambara, Henry Dumas, and Gayl Jones onto Random House's lists.

Following the publication of *The Bluest Eye* (1970) and *Sula* (1973), both novels that focus primarily on women's experiences, Morrison's career took off with *Song of Solomon* (1977). Her third novel, whose central character, Milkman Dead, is male rather than female, won the National Book Award and became a main selection in the Book-of-the-Month club, the first work by an African American to be thus featured since Richard Wright's *Native Son* (1940). *Song of Solomon* was followed by *Tar Baby* (1981), *Beloved* (1987), arguably her finest work and the winner of the Pulitzer Prize for Fiction in 1988, and most recently *Jazz* (1992), *Paradise* (1998), and *Love* (2003). In interviews, Morrison has described *Beloved* and *Jazz* as part of an intended trilogy of novels that focuses on the ways women's gift for nurturance can involve a disturbing surrender of the self. In a 1985 conversation with Gloria Naylor, she described her fascination with the phenomenon "peculiar to women," whereby "the best thing that is in us is also the thing that makes us sabotage ourselves."

In 1992, her book of essays, *Playing in the Dark: Whiteness and the Literary Imagination*, joined *Jazz* on the *New York Times* best-sellers list. An important contribution to American literary criticism, *Playing in the Dark* focuses on the "Africanist presence" in American literature, discussing the ways canonical white writers—including Poe, Cather, and Hemingway—have appropriated black lives and language in their work. More recently, Morrison has engaged herself in analyzing racial and gender dynamics in contemporary American culture, editing an essay collection on the Clarence Thomas–Anita Hill controversy and coediting a volume on the O.J. Simpson trial. Since 1984, when she left Random House, Morrison has held academic professorships at SUNY Albany and, currently, at Princeton University, where she has a joint appointment in African American studies and Creative Writing.

Morrison won the 1988 Pulitzer Prize for Fiction for her fifth novel, *Beloved* (1987), a brilliant and powerful treatment of the painful psychological and historical legacy of slavery, widely recognized as her best work to date. Based on the true story of Margaret Garner, an escaped slave who, in 1851, murdered her daughter rather than see her returned to bondage, *Beloved* revisits the psychic and physical trauma of slavery, focusing particularly on slave women's uniquely gendered experiences of sexual violation and the disruption of maternal bonds. The novel fictionally reworks the firsthand historical record of black women's oppression under slavery documented in such slave narratives as Harriet Jacobs's *Incidents in the Life of a Slave Girl* (1861). In interviews, Morrison has described her larger theme in *Beloved* as the exploration of women's tendency toward self-surrender. The violent disruptions of the bonds between mothers and children under the institution of slavery suggested to her an "ideal situation" to explore the way that women's extraordinary capacity for nurturance of others can also end up being a kind of self-murder or self-sabotage.

The narrative proceeds in a circular, nonlinear style that mimics the process of what Morrison calls "rememory," one of its central themes. Part One begins in 1873 in the house at 124 Bluestone Road, where Sethe and her daughter, Denver, live alone with the ghost of Sethe's dead baby daughter. Sethe's mother-in-law, Baby Suggs, has died nine years before, and Denver's brothers, Howard and Buglar, have fled the troubled house, haunted by the ghost of the baby whose mother cut its throat. While Sethe tries hard to forget her painful past, the appearance of Paul D, "the last of the Sweet Home men" (9), brings back memories of the ironically named Sweet Home plantation where they had both been slaves in Kentucky eighteen years before, together with Sethe's husband, Halle; Paul A; Paul F; and Sixo. Fragmentary recollections of the events of 1855—in particular the fateful day in which their joint escape attempt from Sweet Home ends in disarray and tragedy—are interspersed throughout the narrative. This includes Sethe's painful memories of her physical and sexual violation at the hands of the slavemaster, Schoolteacher, and his young protégés who beat her, leaving a mass of scars on her back in the shape of a chokecherry tree, and who "milk" her as if she is a barnyard animal.

Paul D moves in with Sethe and Denver, chasing the baby ghost from the house and taking them to a carnival, their first social outing in eighteen years. Briefly, it seems as if Paul D's presence will result in a reconstituted family and a return to the normalcy that has eluded the residents of 124 ever since the murder of the baby girl eighteen years before, after which the community shunned Sethe for what they viewed as her outrageous and prideful act. Upon their return from the outing, however, they find a stranger, a young woman about nineteen or twenty, who has materialized out of nowhere. She gives her name as Beloved, recalling to Sethe the words she had carved upon her dead baby's tombstone. Morrison describes Beloved's arrival through an extended metaphor of childbirth, and this unusual guest develops a greedy devotion to Sethe, much like a baby has for its mother. When Denver sees the scar on Beloved's throat, she realizes the visitor is her older sister, the resurrection of the ghost of the dead baby.

Sethe takes Denver and Beloved to the Clearing, where her mother-in-law, Baby Suggs, used to hold prayer meetings. When she summons the spirit of Baby Suggs, longing for her healing touch, she instead feels someone strangling her throat vengefully. Gradually, Beloved's greedy desire toward Sethe increases, and she begins to disrupt Paul D's relationship with Sethe, first moving him bit by bit out of the house and then seducing him. Paul D feels unmanned by the ghost, much as the experience of slavery had unmanned him at Sweet Home, making him feel like less of a man than even the barnyard rooster Mister, ironically called by the very title denied to male slaves.

Meanwhile, the events of eighteen years previously are delivered through a series of flashbacks from the point of view of various characters. Sethe learns from Paul D that her husband, Halle, had witnessed her sexual violation and that the experience had broken his mind, presumably followed by his death, together with that of Sixo, Paul A, and Paul F, during the aborted escape attempt. Paul D and Sethe are the only ones who successfully escape from Sweet Home, each following separate paths. With the assistance of a white runaway indentured servant named Amy Denver, Sethe births Denver en route to the house on Bluestone Road near Cincinnati, Ohio, where Baby Suggs has made a home after her son Halle bought her out of slavery with his Sunday labor. There, Sethe rejoins the children she had sent ahead and enjoys a brief period of freedom. However, twenty-eight days after her arrival at 124 Bluestone Road, the slavecatchers arrive to return them to Sweet Home. In response to this threat, Sethe attempts to murder all four of her children and succeeds in murdering Denver's older sister, cutting her throat in the woodshed with a saw.

Part One of the novel ends when Stamp Paid, the old family friend who helped ferry Sethe and the newborn Denver across the river to freedom and who witnessed Sethe's act, shows Paul D a newspaper clipping about the murder. When Paul D confronts Sethe with his new knowledge, she explains her intention to "put her babies where they'd be safe" (164). Paul D judges her love "too-thick" (164) and reminds her that she has "two feet . . . not four" (165), thus painfully reproducing the slaveowners' treatment and characterization of her as an animal. The first section of the novel ends with Paul D's abrupt departure from 124 Bluestone Road.

In Part Two, Stamp Paid, filled with regret about chasing Paul D away, decides to pay a call at the house on Bluestone Road. When he approaches the house, he is repelled by the sounds of mumbling voices from within. With Paul D gone, Sethe, Denver, and Beloved, whom Sethe now realizes is her dead baby restored to her, are left alone together, cut off from all contact with the community. The sounds Stamp Paid hears coming from the house are "the thoughts of the women of 124, unspeakable thoughts, unspoken" (199). At the center of Part Two are three monologues comprised of the interior thoughts of Sethe, Denver, and Beloved, respectively, followed by a poetic dialogue that includes their comingled voices. Beloved's monologue simultaneously describes the trauma of a baby girl dying at the hands of its mother and the trauma of a slave in the Middle Passage from Africa to America. Beloved thus functions on two levels: She is both the spirit of the dead baby and a representative of the "Sixty Million and more" slaves to whom Morrison dedicates the novel.

In Part Three, Sethe and Beloved are locked in a pathological dependency fueled by a mixture of love, revenge, and guilt over the trauma of the past. Beloved, now pregnant with Paul D's child, grows plumper and more demanding of Sethe by the day. Denver realizes that Beloved is slowly killing Sethe and that she will "have to leave the yard; step off the edge of the world . . . and go ask somebody for help" (239). Word spreads among the black women in the community that "Sethe's dead daughter, the one whose throat she cut, had come back to fix her" (255). Finally forgiving Sethe both for her crime and for her pride, they gather together to help exorcise the ghost that is destroying her. As they approach the house, they witness a white man, Denver's new employer, Edward Bodwin, approaching 124 in his cart to bring Denver to her new job. For Sethe, the scene reenacts the trauma of eighteen years ago: "He is coming into her yard and he is coming for her best thing" (262). She tries to stab Bodwin with an ice pick, redirecting the violence toward the white man rather than toward her daughter and simultaneously exorcising the ghost of Beloved, who disappears as suddenly as she came. Paul D returns to nurse Sethe back to health. When Sethe mourns the loss of Beloved ("She was my best thing") (272), Paul D replies: "You your best thing, Sethe. You are" (273). Her tentative reply—"Me? Me?" (272)—underscores both her newfound sense of selfhood and its fragility.

Viewing her children as an extension of herself, Sethe both makes a bold claim of independence from the tyranny of the slave institution and also performs a kind of self-sabotage, directing harm against herself rather than against her perpetrators. *Beloved* chronicles Sethe's lifelong struggle to reclaim the sense of self-possession that has been stolen from her in slavery. As Morrison puts it: "Freeing yourself was one thing; claiming ownership of that freed self was another." In interviews, Morrison has connected Sethe's struggle to reclaim her sense of self with contemporary black women's struggle to avoid the traditionally female self-abnegating role of mother and wife. In her struggle to find ways to nurture others without sabotaging or murdering her self, Sethe is a powerful feminist heroine and role model for contemporary women.

The novel ends with a lyrical evocation of Beloved, "disremembered and un-accounted for" (274), like the many anonymous and forgotten slaves of the novel's dedication. In the novel's final pages, the multiple meanings of the repeated injunction "This is not a story to pass on" (275), engages the paradox of mediating between the need to remember and the need to forget the historical trauma of slavery.

The second novel by Morrison, *Sula* (1973), has been of particular interest to feminists both for its depiction of the enduring friendship between its two black heroines, Nel Wright and Sula Mae Peace, and for its daring characterization of Sula as a woman who defies traditional stereotypes of feminine behavior. Child-hood friends, Nel and Sula take very different paths into womanhood. Raised to be "respectable," Nel remains within the tightly knit black community, pursuing a traditional self-abnegating role as wife and mother; in contrast, the unconventional Sula becomes an outlaw and a pariah, leaving home to lead a life of independence and sexual freedom. The novel unsettles easy assumptions not only about female gender roles but also about the nature of good and evil.

The novel proceeds in seemingly chronological fashion, using dates as chapter titles; however, *Sula's* narrative style is nonlinear, episodic, and fragmentary rather than realistic. A brief untitled chapter establishes the ironic setting for the story, the black section of the town of Medallion, Ohio, which is "called the Bottom in spite of the fact that it was up in the hills" (4) and that symbolically represents both the oppression and the resilience of the African American community. In "1919," we are introduced to Shadrack, a shell-shocked black World War I veteran, who institutes "National Suicide Day," because "he hit on the notion that if one day a year were devoted to [death and dying] . . . the rest of the year would be safe and free" (7). Like the Bottom, Shadrack's National Suicide Day paradoxically engages the reality of oppression for American blacks and the strategies for survival it engenders: "Easily, quietly, Suicide Day became a part of the fabric of life up in the Bottom of Medallion, Ohio" (16).

In "1920," we meet Helene Wright, whose name expresses her rigid upright-ness and unbending morality. The "daughter of a Creole whore," she is raised in New Orleans by a grandmother "constantly on guard for any sign of her mother's wild blood" (17). Married and settled in Medallion, Helene attends to her daughter Nel's upbringing with the same vigilance: "Any enthusiasms that little Nel showed were calmed by her mother until she drove her daughter's imagination underground" (18).

In contrast, Sula's home, presided over by her one-legged grandmother, Eva Peace, is as chaotic as Nel's is ordered. Abandoned by her husband BoyBoy, Eva has single-handedly raised her three children, Hannah, Eva (called Pearl), and Ralph (called Plum). Although the fate of Eva's missing leg is never revealed, the rumors that circulate suggest some supreme maternal sacrifice, perhaps an exchange for insurance money to keep her children alive. Eva runs her home as a boarding house, letting rooms and taking in stray motherless children, referred to collectively as the "Deweys."

In "1921," Eva's house is also home to a white drunk named Tar Baby; the widowed and promiscuous Hannah; Hannah's daughter Sula, who is marked by a rose-shaped birthmark over one eye; and Plum, who has returned from the war with a "sweet, sweet smile" (45) and a dope addiction. The chapter "1921" begins with recollections of Eva's heroic sacrifices to save her children in the face of their father's abandonment; it ends with her lighting the kerosene-soaked Plum on fire as he lies in a drugged stupor in his bed: "He opened his eyes and saw what he imagined was the great wing of an eagle pouring a wet lightness over him. Some kind of baptism, some kind of blessing, he thought" (47).

In "1922," the twelve-year-old Nel and Sula are brought together, joined by a "loneliness . . . so profound it intoxicated them" (51): "Because each had discovered years before they were neither white nor male, and that all freedom and triumph was forbidden to them, they had set about creating something else to be" (52). Their inseparable bond is further solidified when Sula accidentally drowns a boy named Chicken Little as Nel watches. The deranged and outcast Shadrack is the only potential witness to her crime, linking Sula to Shadrack and foreshadowing Sula's fate as a pariah in the community. At the funeral, Sula and Nel stand with hands clasped, keeping their terrible secret.

In "1923," Hannah confronts her mother Eva, demanding to know why she killed Plum. Eva explains: "he wanted to crawl back in my womb. . . . I birthed him once. I couldn't do it again" (71). A series of "strange" happenings culminates when Hannah accidentally lights herself on fire. Although Eva makes a heroic attempt to save her, hurling herself from a second-story window, Hannah dies on the way to the hospital, leaving Eva to "[muse] over the perfection of the judgment against her" (78). Eva is also disturbed by the recollection that Sula stood by and watched her mother burn "not because she was paralyzed, but because she was interested" (78).

The chapter "1927" brings the marriage of Nel to Jude Greene. Nel's "parents had succeeded in rubbing down to a dull glow any sparkle or splutter she had" (83), and her marriage to Jude promises to seal her fate: "The more [Jude] thought about marriage, the more attractive it became. Whatever his fortune, whatever the cut of his garment, there would always be the hem—the tuck and fold that hid his raveling edges; a someone sweet, industrious and loyal to shore him up. . . . The two of them together would make one Jude" (83). During the wedding reception, Nel catches a glimpse of Sula "gliding, with just a hint of a strut, down the path toward the road" (85).

Part II of the novel opens in "1937" with Sula's return after ten years of absence, accompanied by a plague of robins. Eva complains "ain't no woman got no business floatin' around without no man" (92). For Nel, Sula's return is "like getting the use of an eye back, having a cataract removed" (95). Their rekindled friendship is disrupted, however, when she finds Jude and Sula together in her bedroom. She laments: "That was too much. To lose Jude and not have Sula to talk to about it because it was Sula that he had left her for" (110).

By "1939," the town has become convinced of Sula's "evil." Sula becomes a "pariah" in a community where "[women] with husbands had folded themselves into starched coffins" (122) and "[women] without men were like sour-tipped needles featuring one constant empty eye" (122). In contrast, Nel now "belonged to the town and all its ways" (120). Sula's easy promiscuity earns her the censure of the community, but it does not really interrupt her profound solitude. Ajax, the son of a conjure woman, is drawn to Sula because of her difference from other women, but he leaves when she begins to feel the desire to possess him: "soon she would, like all of her sisters before her, put to him the death-knell question 'Where have you been?'" (133).

In "1941," Nel visits Sula on her deathbed. Nel tells her a "colored woman . . . can't act like a man" (142) and asks Sula to explain why she betrayed her with Jude. Sula responds "being good to somebody is just like being mean to somebody. Risky" (144–45). As Nel leaves, Sula questions which one of them was really "good": "I mean maybe it wasn't you. Maybe it was me" (146). Following Sula's death, the townspeople experience "general relief" followed by "restless irritability" (153), since they no longer have a scapegoat to blame their troubles on.

In the final chapter ("1965"), Nel visits Eva in a nursing home after a lapse of many years. Eva confronts her about her complicity in Chicken Little's death: "Tell me how you killed that little boy" (168). When Nel protests that it was Sula who threw him in the water, Eva responds: "You. Sula. What's the difference?" (168). Nel realizes that she had enjoyed watching him drown and that her calm response "was only the tranquillity that follows a joyful stimulation" (170). The oppositions of good/evil, virgin/whore collapse as Nel realizes that Sula is part of her. Eva's words prompt Nel to visit Sula's grave, where she finally experiences the loss of Sula after twenty-five years: "All that time . . . I thought I was missing Jude. . . . We was girls together. . . . O Lord Sula . . . girl, girl, girlgirlgirl" (174).

Sula Mae Peace has attracted much feminist critical attention because of the bold way her character resists the traditional feminine roles of wife and mother. In a community in which women were expected to subordinate their desires to the needs of others, Sula "lived out her days exploring her own thoughts and emotions, giving them full reign, feeling no obligation to please anybody unless their pleasure pleased her" (118).

In a 1989 essay, Morrison has described her character as a "new world black and new world woman extracting choice from choicelessness, responding inventively to found things. Improvisational. Daring, disruptive, imaginative, modern, out-of-the-house, outlawed, unpolicing, uncontained and uncontainable. And dangerously female."

References and Suggested Readings

Gilbert, Sandra M., and Susan Gubar, eds. *The Norton Anthology of Literature by Women: The Traditions in English.* 2nd ed. New York: Norton, 1996.

McKay, Nellie Y., ed. *Critical Essays on Toni Morrison*. Boston: G.K. Hall, 1988.

Morrison, Toni. *Beloved*. New York: Knopf, 1987.

———. *Sula*. New York: Knopf, 1973.

———. "Unspeakable Things Unspoken: The Afro-American Presence in American Literature." *Michigan Quarterly Review* 28 (Winter 1989): 1–34.

Taylor-Guthrie, Danille, ed. *Conversations with Toni Morrison*. Jackson: University Press of Mississippi, 1994.

See also Naylor, Gloria; Woolf, Virginia.

MOTHERHOOD

Bored with what she saw as the confines of femininity, Betty Friedan wrote in 1963 that the suburban wife "made the beds, shopped for groceries, matched slipcover material, ate peanut butter sandwiches with her children, chauffeured Cub Scouts and Brownies, [and] lay beside her husband at night" while secretly fearing "the silent question" of "Is this all?" And motherhood, the ultimate aim of traditional femininity, was for Friedan a primary component of that "problem that has no name." Today, while many women view motherhood as less central to their identities, the birth and upbringing of children still are viewed (particularly by men) as female responsibilities.

Men have long praised the reproductive capacity of women, but as feminists have observed, such praise sprang forth from enforced gender inequities. Women have long been aware of reproduction as a service to their societies, and some have even gone so far as to suggest that compensation from the government would be appropriate. Charlotte Perkins Gilman, taking up this idea, argues, "If this is so, if motherhood is an exchangeable commodity given by women in payment for clothes and food, then we must of course find some relation between the quantity or quality of the motherhood and the quantity and quality of the pay" (99). Modern feminist scholarship focuses not only on the economic ramifications of motherhood but also on the gender-based ones.

Audre Lorde, rather than positioning mothers as long-suffering victims, suggests that motherhood also can be viewed as an avenue to change and power. She suggests that women raising boys have agency in shaping definitions of manhood: "I wish to raise a Black man who will recognize that the legitimate objects of his hostility are not women, but the particulars of a structure that programs him to fear and despise women as well as his own Black self." She further suggested that "[t]he strongest lesson I can teach my son is the same lesson I teach my daughter: how to be who he wishes to be for himself." Alice Walker also writes of the value of motherhood in an essay entitled "A Writer Because of, Not in Spite of, Her Children." Walker describes her first encounter with the book *Second Class Citizen* as an eye-opener; the dedication page reads, "To my dear children/without whose sweet background noises/this book would never have been written." Walker marveled over this dedication, for she had spent many an hour of conversation grumbling about the difficulty of working after her daughter was born. She reached the conclusion, though, that the text "raises fundamental questions about how creative and prosaic life is to be lived and to what purpose, which is more than some books, written while one's children are banished from one's life, do."

Not all feminists agree with these assessments of the value of motherhood. More radical writings have pointed women away from marriage and motherhood altogether. Valerie Solanas's 1967 "SCUM Manifesto" advocated the complete destruction of men, in fact, arguing that "[t]o be male is to be deficient, emotionally limited; maleness is a deficiency disease and males are emotional cripples." Solanas predicted that "[m]any women will for awhile continue to think they dig men, but as they become accustomed to female society and become absorbed in their projects, they will eventually come to see the utter uselessness and banality of the male." Yet in spite of these revised interpretations of motherhood, many women still wrestle with the reality of being the only ones biologically equipped for childbirth. "We can pump gas, lift weights, head a corporation, lead nations, and tune pianos," writes Louise Erdrich, but "[s]till, our bodies are rounded vases of skin and bones and blood that seem impossibly engineered for birth." Erdrich describes her pregnancy in terms that better align with radical feminist ideas, however; for she writes that "I feel myself becoming less a person than a place, inhabited, a foreign land." This distance from the body, though here described as an experience not necessarily related to radical feminism, captures perfectly the sentiments supporting so many feminist theories about motherhood: The female body, having too often been used as a commodity within patriarchal systems, needs to be returned to the woman who owns it.

References and Suggested Readings

Erdrich, Louise. *The Blue Jay's Dance: A Birth Year*. New York: HarperCollins, 1995.

Friedan, Betty. "From *The Feminine Mystique*." *Feminist Theory: A Reader*. Ed. Wendy Kolmar and Frances Bartkowski. London: Mayfield, 2000. 164–69.

Gilman, Charlotte Perkins. "From *Women and Economics: A Study of the Economic Relation Between Men and Women as a Factor in Social Evolution*." *Feminist Theory: A Reader*. Ed. Wendy Kolmar and Frances Bartkowski. London: Mayfield, 2000. 97–99.

Lorde, Audre. *Sister Outsider*. Freedom, CA: The Crossing Press, 1996.

Solanas, Valerie. "From 'SCUM Manifesto.'" *Feminist Theory: A Reader*. Ed. Wendy Kolmar and Frances Bartkowski. London: Mayfield, 2000. 172–74.

Walker, Alice. *In Search of Our Mothers' Gardens: Womanist Prose*. San Diego: Harcourt Brace, 1984.

See also Erdrich, Louise; Gilman, Charlotte Perkins; Lorde, Audre; Walker, Alice.

Lisa R. Williams

MUKHERJEE, BHARATI

Bharati Mukherjee was born in Calcutta, India, in 1940 to a wealthy Brahmin family who valued education. Her father was a PhD-trained chemist who founded his own pharmaceutical company, and Mukherjee and her two sisters received private school education in India. Mukherjee earned a BA degree in English from the University of Calcutta and an MA degree in English and ancient Indian culture from the University of Baroda before traveling to America to earn an MFA degree in writing and a PhD degree in English and comparative literature from the University of Iowa, all before turning thirty. While at the Iowa Writer's Workshop, Mukherjee married Clark Blaise, a fellow student and Canadian writer, even though her parents were already selecting a proper Indian husband for her.

Both Mukherjee and Blaise held tenured professorships at McGill University until Mukherjee could no longer tolerate the racism she encountered in Canada. In 1980, they moved to New York and have lived in America since. Since 1972, Mukherjee has been writing novels and teaching in various university settings. She presently lives in California and teaches at the University of California at Berkeley.

Mukherjee's work includes *The Tiger's Daughter* (1972), *Wife* (1975), *Days and Nights in Calcutta* (written with Clark Blaise, 1977), *Darkness* (1985), *The Sorrow and the Terror* (also with Blaise, 1987), *The Middleman and Other Stories* (which won the National Book Critics Circle Award in 1988), *Jasmine* (1989), *The Holder of the World* (1993), *Leave It to Me* (1997), and *Desirable Daughters: A Novel* (2002).

Mukherjee says the purpose of her writing is to "make the familiar exotic; the exotic familiar." While she writes about much that would be considered "exotic" to the Euro-American reader, Mukherjee insists in her essay, "A Four-Hundred-Year-Old Woman," that she not be ghettoized as a hyphenated writer:

> I am an American. I am an American writer, in the American mainstream, trying to extend it. This is a vitally important statement for me—I am not an Indian writer, not an exile, not an expatriate. I am an immigrant; my investment is in the American reality, not the Indian. (34)

Mukherjee's *Wife* (1975) is an early novel that features an immigrant who can neither maintain her former cultural connections nor assimilate into her new context. The novel is divided into three sections in which we see the main character, Dimple Dasgupta, move from a girl in her father's home wishing for a fortuitous match in marriage to her married and immigrant state in New York City to her final state as the murderer of her husband.

The opening sentence of *Wife* establishes the essential tension of the novel: "Dimple Dasgupta had set her heart on marrying a neurosurgeon, but her father was looking for engineers in the matrimonial ads." Dimple is enmeshed in a set of cultural expectations that cannot be satisfied by the unavoidable outcomes demanded by that culture. She is willing to accept one aspect of the cultural dictates—that a woman is not complete until she is married. She looks forward to marriage, believing it will bring her "freedom, cocktail parties on carpeted lawns, fund-raising dinners for noble charities. Marriage would bring her love" (3). She cannot, however, accept the Indian patriarchal corollary to the necessity of marriage—that her father should select her mate.

Her confusion is understandable, given her Indian culture, which on one hand, valorizes the story of Sita, the mythical woman who lived to serve her husband, even walking through fire for him, and on the other hand is informed by an encroaching Westernization and its notions of female identity and autonomy.

Dimple is twenty years old and, although not unattractive, does not have the requisite light skin and stunning body that would make her marketable. In the nuptial negotiations, Dimple's father is only able to attract a consultant engineer with two dependents from a family who makes it clear that Dimple is "not their first choice" (15).

One of the first signs that Dimple's marriage will not be the storybook image she imagined is that her husband, Amit Basu, renames her "Nandini," insisting that "Dimple" will never do for a name for his wife. Stuck at home all day in a cramped apartment with a demanding mother-in-law, Dimple's first months of marriage are less than ideal. Amit will not allow her to use birth control, asserting that it's "for other people. . . . The world deserves our baby" (34). When she becomes pregnant, she is certain that her life is compromised, that she will never again be able to own her identity, so she aborts the baby through strenuous jump roping.

Part One of the novel ends with Amit's announcement that he has quit his job and that he and Dimple are going to America. Amit and Dimple arrive in New York and are greeted by Amit's old college roommate who takes them to live with his family until they are settled. While Amit looks for work, Dimple is offered a part-time job that she is not allowed to accept because of her husband's fear that she will become too independent and freethinking. The cultural pressure to maintain the standards of India are very strong, and Amit has confirmation for his behaviors in his friend Jyoti who says, "When a woman starts going wrong, it's usually because her husband didn't look after her enough" (68).

Dimple's life in New York is not unlike her confined life in India; she remains in the apartment all day with the wife and child of her host family and watches soap operas. Her previous life as a university student is far behind her, and she has no intellectual stimulation until she meets an American woman at a party. There her hunger for meaningful interaction is reawakened, but it will find no fulfillment in her relationship with Amit. Still, the longer he remains unemployed, the less able Amit is to project the unassailable image of the strong male and the more Dimple is tempted to construct a more realistic picture of him. She wonders if "minor irritations accumulated over decades could erupt into the kind of violence she read about in the papers" (88), and she even dares to talk back to her husband.

Amit does get a job, though it is one that he feels is beneath him. Finally, the Basus are able to move into their own apartment that they sublet from an Indian friend and his American wife. There Dimple again stays at home all day, and she falls into an engulfing depression. Her days are spent in front of the TV, and it grows "harder and harder to distinguish between what she had seen on TV and what she had imagined" (157). One winter day, she dresses in an amalgam of clothes and sits for six hours on a park bench outside their home, nearly freezing. Dimple finds it more and more difficult to disentangle reality from the world of imagination, dreams, and TV.

Amit tells her that she is suffering from culture shock, insisting that it is common among Indian wives in America. Indeed, she is suffering from culture shock, but it is only partially the shock of being immersed in American culture; Dimple is also suffering from the shock of seeing her culture of origin through new eyes. Dimple's recognition is not unlike a similar recognition Mukherjee herself makes when she sees India with American eyes: "It was only when I came to Iowa, to the writers [sic] workshop, that I realized the damage of colonialism."

Isolated from other Indian friends who live across town, isolated from her husband, and with her reality shaped by images of violence seen on TV, Dimple devises a list of nine ways to kill herself and chants the list when she is anxious. As she becomes more dislocated, Dimple engages in behaviors that violate her cultural taboos. She eats beef, enters a friendship with Milt Glasser, an American man, and finally sleeps with him. The novel abruptly ends with Dimple's murder of her critical husband who complains once too often. That Dimple has progressed so quickly from a woman whose "life had been devoted to pleasing others, not herself" (212) to a woman who commits adultery and murder is an indication of both her descent into madness and her inability to imagine a life other than the one designed for her by her culture.

In an interview with *The Iowa Review*, Mukherjee says of the ending of the novel:

> Dimple, if she had remained in Calcutta, would have gone into depression, and she would have found a very conventional way out of for unhappy Bengali wives—suicide. . . . But in the United States, she suddenly learns to ask herself "self"-oriented questions. Am I happy? Am I unhappy? And that, to me, is progress. So, instead of committing suicide, turning the society-mandated violence inward, she, in a misguided act, kills the enemy. So, of course, I'm not approving of murder. . . . It's meant to be a positive act. Self-assertive. (20)

Jasmine is Mukherjee's best known and most often taught work. The discontinuous narrative spans several incarnations of the main character. In her native Punjabi village of Hasnapur, she is Jyoti, a young girl whose fate has been predicted by the village astrologer. When told she will become a widow and an exile, the young Jyoti reacts strongly and falls, cutting her forehead. The cut leaves a star-shaped scar that she calls her "third eye," not unlike the "third eye" of the "holiest sages" who use the eye to see "invisible worlds" (5).

Jyoti comes from a culture where a daughter had to be "married off before she could enter heaven, and dowries beggared families for generations" (39). As the fifth daughter and seventh of nine children, Jyoti's birth is more a burden than joyous event. From the beginning, though, she is a survivor, outliving the attempted infanticide that leaves a "ruby-red choker of bruise" on her throat and "sapphire fingerprints" on her collarbone (40). When the young Jyoti reveals her aspirations to be a doctor and set up a clinic (51), she is proclaimed mad. Her paternal grandmother says, "Blame the mother. Insanity has to come from somewhere. It's the mother who is mad" (51).

At fourteen, however, Jyoti is married to Prakash Vijh, a friend of her brother. It is a love match unattended by ritual and traditional ceremony—a "no-dowry, no-guests Registry Office wedding" (75). Her best friend, Vimla, disapproves of the wedding, warning "once you let one tradition go, all the other traditions crumble" (75).

Prakash is a nontraditional man who encourages Jyoti to leave India's feudal past. He gives her a new name, Jasmine, and encourages her to become more urbanized and modern. He discourages the cultural expectation that she get pregnant immediately after marriage: "We aren't going to *spawn*! We aren't ignorant peasants!" (77). In her adjustment to the new life her marriage brings, she says, "Jyoti, Jasmine: I shuttled between identities" (77).

When Prakash receives an offer from a former professor to go to America to study, Jasmine starts to brush up on her English. The egalitarianism of their marriage flourishes, and Jasmine helps Prakash in his electronic repair business. He holds forth the dream that they will open their own store one day—"Vijh & Wife. Maybe even Vijh and Vijh" (89).

Prakash's countertraditional philosophies have not gone unnoticed by political traditionalists, and one day as he and Jasmine are shopping in preparation for their trip to America, he is killed by the bomb of a political terrorist. At seventeen, Jasmine is a widow, and thus half of her childhood prophecy is fulfilled.

She determines to go to America alone and stand on the campus of the university where Prakash was to study. There she plans to build a funeral pyre with the new suit he bought for the trip to America and to sacrifice herself in the ritual of sati. With illegal documents that she obtains at great cost, Jasmine sets out. The journey is not on the major airlines in a simple route but is a series of stops across three continents facilitated by those who work in the underbelly of human commerce.

Jasmine's final leg of the trip is guided by an unscrupulous man she calls Half-Face. Under the guise of giving her safe haven on her first night in America, Half-Face violently rapes Jasmine. Though her first impulse is to kill herself, to "balance [her] defilement with [her] death" (117), Jasmine instead kills Half-Face as he sleeps.

Jasmine meets up with Lillian Gordon, a Quaker humanitarian worker, who takes her in and urges her to "let the past make you wary, by all means. But do not let it deform you" (131). Lillian coaches Jasmine in the necessary skills to survive in America and sends her on to New York. There she stays for a time with her husband's former professor until she aches for an experience larger than the recreations of India in a circumscribed Queens apartment.

Through Lillian Gordon's daughter, she finds work as an *au pair* in the home of Taylor and Wylie Hayes. There she is reinvented again; Taylor calls her Jase, and she gives account of her lives in this way: "Jyoti was now a *sati*-goddess; she had burned herself in a trash-can funeral pyre behind a boarded-up motel in Florida. Jasmine lived for the future, for Vijh & Wife. Jase went to movies and lived for today" (176).

Soon Jase is tutoring for extra money and strengthening her English. Just as Jase is flourishing in the new environment, Wylie announces that she is leaving Taylor. Jase's friendship with Taylor grows, and she feels secure in her role, knowing that Taylor "didn't want to scour and sanitize the foreignness" (185). All is well until one day in the park, the man who killed her husband recognizes Jase, and she realizes she must flee to protect not only herself but Taylor and his daughter as well. She moves to Iowa, choosing it because it was the birth state of Duff, Taylor's adopted daughter.

Jasmine moves to Baden, Iowa, in the county where Duff was born and there is known as Jane, a de-exoticized American name to fit with solid middle-American farm values. In relation to her shifting identities, the character says, "Plain Jane is a role, like any other" (26).

She finds a job as a bank teller, and soon the bank owner, Bud Ripplemeyer, is attracted to her. He leaves his wife of many years, and he and Jane move in together. Though they don't marry, the conservative community is forgiving of their relationship because, soon after its beginning when Bud is shot and paralyzed by an angry farmer, Jane faithfully stays with him. When Jane becomes pregnant with their child, Bud urges her to marry him, but she is unwilling to test her fate of widowhood once again.

The new Ripplemeyer family is a diverse lot of people. Bud, a stalwart community leader who leaves his wife for Jane, an illegal Indian immigrant, has also adopted a teenage Vietnamese orphan, Du Thien. In the sea of blond Germans, Danes, and Swedes of Elsa County, Iowa, the patched together family is both a divergence from the norm and a harbinger of the multicultural mix that is drawing a new face on middle America. Jane recognizes though that the new multiculturalism is not on her terms. Bud does not want her to talk about her past in India, and he is most at ease with her when she is safely "Jane" and not Jasmine or Jyoti.

Though Jane says, "For me, experience must be forgotten, or else it will kill" (33), the denial of her identity is not an option that she can live with forever. Thus, when Taylor Hayes reestablishes their relationship through a series of postcards, she remembers and appreciates that he always accepted her in her cultural context. When Taylor and Duff come to Iowa with the invitation for Jasmine to join them in California, she is ready to reconcile with her own past and join them. She says, "It isn't guilt I feel, it's relief. I realize I have already stopped thinking of myself as Jane" (240).

The threads of the plot have all been pulled together to allow Jane to leave Iowa; Du has left home for California to see his last remaining sister; Karin, Bud's former wife, is still in love with him and will care for him. Jasmine embraces the courage to challenge her fate: "Watch me re-position the stars, I whisper to the astrologer who floats cross-legged above my kitchen stove" (240).

References and Suggested Readings

Alam, Fakrul. *Bharati Mukherjee*. New York: Twayne, 1996.

Mukherjee, Bharati. "Bharati Mukherjee: An Interview with Runar Vignisson." *SPAN: Journal of the South Pacific Association for Commonwealth Literature and Language Studies* 34–35 (1993): 25 July 2002.

———. "A Four-Hundred-Year-Old Woman." *The Writer on Her Work: Volume II*. Ed. Janet Sternburg. New York: Norton, 1991. 33–38.

———. Interview with Michael Connell, Jessie Grearson, and Tom Grimes. "An Interview with Bharati Mukherjee." *The Iowa Review* 20 (Fall 1990): 7–32.

———. *Jasmine*. New York: Grove, 1989.

———. *Wife*. New York: Fawcett Crest, 1975.

N

NAYLOR, GLORIA

Gloria Naylor was born in 1950 in New York City to parents who had just imigrated from Robinsonville, Mississippi, in order to provide their children with the opportunities denied them in the segregated South. She says in an interview with Charles Rowell, "My family came out of the Mississippi Delta where they were tenant farmers. And in one generation they saw me graduate from Yale University with a master's degree" (184). Naylor's journey to Yale University, though, was not by a direct route. After high school graduation, Naylor served for seven years in her newfound faith with the Jehovah's Witnesses before going to college. Disillusioned by the political process, she had turned to the Jehovah's Witnesses hoping to find a more efficacious system for change, but that system too brought disillusionment. She turned to education, first attending Medgar Evers College in Brooklyn, pursuing a nursing degree until she realized that she had little interest in medicine. She then transferred to Brooklyn College as an English major. Though she had been an introspective child, given to reading and writing, she did not imagine that becoming a writer was a realizable dream until she found the works of Toni Morrison, Zora Neale Hurston, and Ntozake Shange when she was a student at Brooklyn College in the late 1970s.

Naylor wrote the stories that eventually became *The Women of Brewster Place* in a creative writing class at Brooklyn College. When she sent her first story to *Essence* magazine, the editor asked to see more, and Naylor's career was launched. As has happened with many African American women writers, Naylor has been criticized for her negative portrayals of black men. Her rejoinder to that criticism is notable:

The underlying presumption has always been, until lately, that anything male should be central, and if males are not central, then it's jarring. And if something jars us we tend to think, Well, what is wrong with it? As opposed to, What is wrong with the way we have been programmed to think? I tended to explain all this in the beginning, but now I don't even bother. I'm getting old and cranky, and this country needs to grow up.

Gloria Naylor's *The Women of Brewster Place* is a fascinating look at one neighborhood and some of the women who live there. What is most important about the women is what has brought them to Brewster Place as well as what keeps them there.

Naylor announces that the book is a novel in seven stories and thus pushes the edges of both the short story and novel. The novel opens with a history of the street and couches it in the birth metaphor. The street was conceived in a "damp, smoke-filled room" (1) and born in the city legislature. The street had always been home to the lowest social demographics of the city, and when the story opens, the residents are primarily African Americans.

The first story features Mattie Michael, a woman who becomes a central unifying figure to both the neighborhood and the novel. Mattie grows up in the rural South, in the sugarcane of Tennessee. Her conservative and religious father protects her from the ways of the world with an iron fist, to the point of even choosing her friends. One day in her father's absence, she leaves the house to chop some sugarcane with the attractive and seductive Butch Fuller. For Mattie, the outcome of the one seductive afternoon is pregnancy and the wrath of her father. Her father insists that she marry Fred Harris, the only man he has allowed to court her. Mattie denies that the child is Fred's but will not confess her dalliance with Butch. The father flies into a fury and beats Mattie unmercifully. One week later, she is on a Greyhound bus headed to North Carolina where she is greeted by her friend Etta Johnson. Mattie stays with Etta until her son, Basil, is born, but then Etta leaves North Carolina for New York City where she hopes to find more action. Mattie struggles alone with her son until he is bitten by a rat, and she can no longer stay in her apartment for fear of his safety. She flees the apartment in an irrational moment and walks through the streets until she is exhausted and hopeless. A woman calls to her from her porch and invites her in. The hospitable but eccentric woman is Eva Turner, survivor of five husbands and dispenser of common wisdom. Miss Eva is raising her granddaughter, Lucielia, and she provides Mattie with the excuse that Basil will be a good playmate for Lucielia. The night of hospitality turns into thirty years of friendship, and Mattie has found a home for herself and her son.

Basil becomes the object of Mattie's overindulgence, and he grows up to be a demanding and irresponsible man who feels no compunction about using his mother. When he is thirty, he calls home one night to announce that he is in jail for killing someone, and he demands that she come get him out. Mattie cannot stand the thought that Basil must endure difficult conditions in jail for the two weeks before his trial, so she uses her house against his bail. When Basil jumps bail, Mattie loses everything. Mattie leaves her home and moves to Brewster Place, carrying with her a legacy of sorrow and a spirit of survival.

The second story focuses on Etta Mae Johnson, the woman who gave shelter to Mattie Michael over thirty years earlier when she was pregnant with Basil. Now the situation is reversed, and Etta Mae comes to Brewster Place to live with Mattie. Whereas Mattie has devoted her whole life to only her son and has never risked loving a man, Etta Mae has lived with rambunctious abandon. From her teenage years back in Tennessee, Etta "was not only unwilling to play by the rules, but . . . challenged the very right of the game to exist" (59). She learned to "hook herself to any promising rising black star, and when he burnt out, she found another" (60). Etta Mae's free spirit and enterprising ways have earned her the scorn of whites and the sanctimonious disdain of her own people. The life of independence and using others before she can be used has taken a toll on Etta Mae, and she comes into Brewster Place broken in spirit. She turns to Brewster Place and her lifelong friend, Mattie, for the unspoken "love and comfort that awaited her" (74).

Kiswana Browne is the third woman to whom we are introduced. Formerly Melanie Browne, Kiswana has changed her name to signify her allegiance with the social revolution of the times that she has fully embraced. She has moved from the black middle-class neighborhood of Linden Hills to Brewster Place so that she might live the conditions she is trying to change. Her family does not understand her calling and urge her to return to the material security of home; she claims they have "a terminal case of middle-class amnesia" (85). Unlike Kiswana, her brother Wilson did not spend his college years trying to reclaim his roots, and she scorns him as a sellout to the establishment. When her mother voices concern about her living, as she does, amid "these people," Kiswana takes offense.

The story centers around a visit Mrs. Browne makes to Brewster Place to convince Kiswana that she should return to Linden Hills. Kiswana explains her decision to drop out of college, saying, "Those bourgie schools were counter-revolutionary. My place was in the streets with my people, fighting for equality and a better community" (83).

When Kiswana confronts her mother, Mrs. Browne stands up and gives her a speech: "Black isn't beautiful and it isn't ugly—black is! It's not kinky hair and it's not straight hair—it just is" (86). Mrs. Browne continues, saying that she has used "everything I had and could ever get to see that my children were prepared to meet this world on its own terms . . . that's not being white or red or black—that's being a mother" (86). The visit yields reconciliation and an understanding between the women that is triggered by Kiswana's recognition that she and her mother have more in common than she had imagined. Mrs. Browne gives her tacit approval of Kiswana's choice of life when she leaves an envelope with seventy-five dollars in the couch. Kiswana looks at her mother and sees "the woman she had been and was to become," but she warns her mother, "I'll never be a Republican" (87–88).

The fourth story is about Lucielia Louise Turner, the granddaughter of Eva Turner, who took in Mattie Michael when she was a young mother with nowhere to turn. Now Ciel lives on Brewster Place and her friendship with Mattie has continued. Ciel's partner, Eugene, is the father of her child, Serena, but he cannot endure the strictures of family life for long stretches. After he returns to Brewster Place, he loses his job, Ciel is pregnant again, and Eugene is spoiling for a fight. Though she doesn't really want to, Ciel decides to have an abortion, hoping that there will be one less stress on the family. The abortion buys Ciel some peace in her family, but once again, Eugene is ready to leave the family in the quest of his next adventure. As they argue and Eugene packs his bag, the toddler Serena wanders into the kitchen and plays with the electrical outlet.

When Serena dies from the electrocution, Eugene once again absents himself from the family and doesn't even attend the funeral. Ciel is grieved beyond her ability to cope and simply shuts down. She doesn't cry, eat, drink water, or bathe. Mattie Michael finally realizes that Ciel is grieving to death, and she steps in and cares for her with the tenderness of an Ur mother, rocking Ciel until she can begin to cry a thin, piercing moan. She bathes Ciel and puts her to bed where she "lay down and cried. But Mattie knew the tears would end. And she would sleep. And morning would come" (105).

The next story features Cora Lee, a stereotypical incompetent mother. She loves babies, and loves to care for them with great tenderness, but once they grow past infancy, she is neglectful of them. She sits at home and rocks her latest infant and watches soap operas. She has suffered abuse from men, the "shadows" who drift into her life just long enough to leave her with one more baby. Though she means well, she has no control of her children, and they run freely throughout the apartments, eating from the garbage, disturbing the tenants, and getting into scrapes with other children.

It is not until Kiswana Browne knocks on her door one day, seeking her assistance in getting a tenant's association started, that Cora Lee's life begins to change. Kiswana invites Cora Lee and her children to an all black production of A Midsummer Night's Dream in the park; at first Cora Lee is offended, thinking Kiswana is critical of her parenting, but then she uses her anger as motivation. She scrubs the children and mends their clothes in preparation for the big event. At the park, Cora Lee is touched by the play, and something long dormant inside her is unlocked. Kiswana's desire to change her neighborhood takes its first root in the life of Cora Lee and her children.

The last women featured in the book are Theresa and Lorraine, lesbians who "seemed like such nice girls" at first (129). Soon, the rumor mill is oiled and in place, generating stories about the two women. Lorraine reacts with a characteristic submission, but Theresa responds to Lorraine's anxiety with a determination not to be forced out of one more neighborhood. Their circumstance highlights a growing fracture in their relationship: Theresa perceives a softness in Lorraine that she once believed to be tenderness but now sees as weakness.

Lorraine goes to the tenants' association meeting and volunteers to take notes, but the meeting devolves into accusations, and Lorraine leaves the meeting hurt. She is met by Ben the caretaker and invited into his apartment. There they begin to unburden their painful life stories and forge an unlikely friendship. As homophobic tensions in the neighborhood escalate, the troubles between Theresa and Lorraine also increase. Lorraine leaves one night after an argument, and on her return from the club she has visited, she is attacked and brutally raped by a local gang of young men. As she lingers in the alley, near death, old Ben finds her, but she is deranged by pain and attacks him with a brick, killing him.

The long-awaited block party planned by the tenants' association is preenacted by Mattie's dream of the event. Critic Michael Lynch suggests that "the widespread guilt surfacing in various women's dreams, is a sign of the 'phoenix' of this neighborhood rising from destruction and achieving solidarity in realistic hope for a better place to live" (188–89).

Of *The Women of Brewster Place*, Naylor says, "The book just drove itself in its own passion and innocence" (*Backtalk* 244). She continues to write with passion and the wise innocence of a now seasoned novelist. Her other novels are *Linden Hills* (1985), *Mama Day* (1988), *Bailey's Café* (1992), and *The Men of Brewster Place* (1998).

References and Suggested Readings

Lynch, Michael. F. "The Wall and the Mirror in the Promised Land: The City in the Novels of Gloria Naylor." *The City in African-American Literature*. Ed. Yoshinobu Hakutani and Robert Butler. Madison: Fairleigh Dickinson University Press, 1995. 181–95.

Naylor, Gloria. Interview. *Backtalk: Women Writers Speak Out*. By Donna Perry. New Brunswick, Rutgers University Press, 1993. 217–44.

———. "An Interview with Gloria Naylor by Charles H. Rowell." *Callaloo* 20.1 (1997): 179–92.

———. *The Women of Brewster Place*. 1982. New York: Penguin, 1983.

See also Hurston, Zora Neale; Morrison, Toni; Shange, Ntozake.

NEW WOMAN

The ideal of the New Woman represented a female revolution beginning roughly in 1890. Unlike the true woman of previous decades, who had been defined as the realization of "feminine" characteristics, such as piety and purity, the new woman was seen as independent, ambitious, educated, and a formidable consuming force. Olive Schreiner, one such new woman, described her priorities by positioning herself opposite the theorist who believes "woman should seek no fields of labor in the new world of social conditions that is arising around us, as she has her function as child-bearer . . . that woman should perform her sex functions only, allowing man or the state to support her, even when she is potentially a child-bearer and bears no children" (108). New Womanhood, then, represented a shift from emphasis on maternalism and the family and promoted instead women's pursuit of individual happiness.

In recent years, as explained by Sally Ledger in *The New Woman: Fiction and Feminism at the Fin de Siecle*, the new woman concept has been expanded so as to include literary models such as Ibsen's Nora, who in *A Doll's House* says to her husband that she "was simply transferred from Papa's hands to yours. You have arranged everything according to your own taste, and so I got the same tastes as you—or else I pretended to" (66). The concept did not have a name, however, until 1894, when Sarah Grand and Ouida coined it. Because the new woman bears the attributes so often associated with feminism, it becomes easy to assume a consistent representation in the texts that showcase her. But in reality, "The New Woman was an emphatically modern figure" whose representation did not always offer "a particularly attractive model for late twentieth-century feminism" because of her embeddedness in heterosexuality and imperialist discourse (Ledger 6).

References and Suggested Readings

Ibsen, Henrik. *A Doll's House. The Heath Introduction to Literature.* 5th ed. Ed. Alice S. Landy. Lexington, MA: D.C. Heath, 1996. 820–76.

Ledger, Sally. *The New Woman: Fiction and Feminism at the Fin de Siecle.* Manchester, UK: Manchester University Press, 1997.

Schreiner, Olive. "From *Women and Labor.*" *Feminist Theory: A Reader.* Ed. Wendy Kolmar and Frances Bartkowski. London: Mayfield, 2000. 108–10.

See also Schreiner, Olive.

Lisa R. Williams

NIGHTINGALE, FLORENCE

Born to a wealthy family in 1820, in Florence, Italy, Florence Nightingale was raised in England. Her family was formally Anglican because her mother felt that that religious affiliation was more fitting for their class, but they were more Unitarian in practice. Always spiritually sensitive, Florence felt an early call to service and considered nursing but was discouraged by her mother. Instead, Florence was expected to follow the pattern of the leisured upper-class Englishwoman and stay occupied with handwork, recreational reading, and social calls. Though she and her older sister, Parthenope, were given a classical education at home by their father—unusual for the time—she still railed against the enforced idleness and insubstantial engagement with life. During this time, though, Nightingale devoted her leisure to writing a response to the national crisis of faith developing as a result of the overcrowded tenements and onerous working conditions brought on by the Industrial Revolution. Poovey suggests that the text was "probably composed between 1850–1852" and grew into her religious treatise *Suggestions for Thought*, her "most sustained treatment of religious ideas." Her 1860 publication of the text earned the favorable attention of John Stuart Mill. Though *Suggestions* began as a religious meditation and call to faithful service, it transmuted into a treatise on a woman's right to have a profession.

By now, long past the common age for marriage and after several abortive attempts to gain parental approval for a life of service, Nightingale finally began work as the superintendent of the Harley Street Hospital for Gentlewomen in August of 1853, though her father provided her an annual allowance to save her from the indignity of earning a salary. In 1854, the Crimean War broke out, and Nightingale responded to the cry for medical care by organizing a group of nurses. By November 1854, they were in the field. After her return to England in 1856, Nightingale wrote *Notes on Matters Affecting the Health, Efficiency, and Hospital Administration of the British Army* (1858) and rallied support, as Poovey notes, for the "establishment of an Army Medical School and for the appointment of a Royal Commission on the health of the army" (xii). Nightingale's next book, *Notes on Nursing: What It Is, and What It Is Not* (1860), was her most popular and perhaps has had the greatest sustained impact. Nightingale's contribution to the embryonic field of professional nursing has continued to bear fruit, and in that field, she is still heralded today as a foremother, particularly in the areas of hospital administration and statistical data.

For the feminist, Nightingale's contribution to the question of women and work is invaluable. Though she is considering the women of the upper classes, Nightingale's arguments extend beyond those circumstances and theoretically have relevance in contemporary culture. She poses the two roles possible for women of her time: to marry—as often as not, a stranger—or to continue in the home of her parents as a dependent and finally the caretaker of relatives. For the daughter who marries, by law, all her inheritance now belongs to her husband. Likewise, the dependent "is penniless." Nightingale asserts that "[i]t is the hardest slavery, either to take the chance of a man whom she knows *so little*, or to vegetate at home, her life consumed by *ennui* as by a cancer" (66). For Nightingale, neither option constituted a profession or meaningful work. The married woman steps into a subservience that is cloaked by the illusion of some household authority, though she has no true control over her own kitchen or nursery; those duties are relegated to servants in order to prop up the notion that a successful man would be shamed by a wife who needed to work. For those women who don't marry, it is hoped "that if they don't marry, they will at least be quiet" (66). Particularly meaningful for Nightingale, who never married, is her assertion that

> daughters are now their mothers' slaves, just as much as before; they are considered their parents' property; they are to have no other pursuit, nor power, nor independent life, unless they marry; they are to be entirely dependent upon their parents—white slaves in the family, from which marriage alone can emancipate them. (139)

While men are allowed an inviolate day to accomplish their work, women are not allowed to devote their energies to art or science or any meaningful work in significant stretches of time. The prevailing wisdom that women can accomplish much in the "odd moments" of the day and that they need not have an occupation that is socially and culturally validated is a diminishment of the gifts of women and their impulses to service. The "odd moment" theory creates a host of women who have superficial apprehension of a number of subjects but who can never move beyond dabbling to mastery. They might acquire surface knowledge, "but if there is no digesting done, or if there is no time for digesting afterwards, the acquiring perhaps is not of much benefit" (72). Nightingale continues, "We shall think it curious, looking back, in a future state, to see that we have condemned people to do nothing, and called it a duty, a self-denial, a social virtue" (75).

For Nightingale, the predicament of women is tied inextricably to the attitudes of the Church of England. The Church of England has work and offices of service for men, but "She has for women—what? . . .They would give her their heads, their hearts, their hands. She will not have them" (88). Rather than do handwork and visit each other,

> a women longs for a profession—struggles to open to women the paths of the school, the hospital, the penitentiary, the care of the young, the sick, the bad—not as an amusement, to fill up odd times, to fancy they have done something when they have done nothing, to make a sham of visiting—but, systematically, as a reality, an occupation, a "profession." (132–33)

For all her dissatisfaction with the Church, Nightingale nonetheless remains devotedly interested in her spiritual life. On her fundamental belief, she says, "I believe that there is a Perfect Being, of whose thought the universe in eternity is the incarnation" (14). Far from orthodoxy, her religious thoughts included the idea that "[m]ay we all be Saviours in some way to humanity!" (79), and that "[t]he next Christ will perhaps be a female Christ" (230).

Florence Nightingale's life embodies her dream for all women—that they might be allowed to develop their intellect and that they might find meaningful work in service to their ideals.

References and Suggested Readings

McDonald, Lynn. "Florence Nightingale: Passionate Statistician." *Journal of Holistic Nursing* 16.2 (1998): 267–77.

Nightingale, Florence. *Cassandra and Other Selections from Suggestions for Thought*. Washington Square, NY: New York University Press, 1993.

Poovey, Mary. Introduction. *Cassandra and Other Selections from Suggestions for Thought*. By Florence Nightingale. Ed. Mary Poovey. Washington Square, NY: New York University Press, 1993. viii–xxix.

Sheets, Robin. "Florence Nightingale." *An Encyclopedia of British Women Writers*. Ed. Paul Schlueter and June Schlueter. Revised and Expanded ed. New Brunswick, NJ: Rutgers University Press, 1998.

NOVEL

The eighteenth-century novel provided an outlet to women who were still at that time denied access to higher education. Women read as well as wrote novels, and much of the scholarship on the novel points out its tendency to focus on day-to-day existence, which also suggests that its authors and consumers were, at least initially, predominantly female. As a result, most of these texts were dismissed by critics as "sentimental" in spite of their widely varying subjects, themes, and messages. In fact, the popularity of women's writing prompted Nathaniel Hawthorne to complain in 1855 that America was being overtaken by a "mob of scribbling women," the implication being that women were not writing anything of literary merit.

Elaine Showalter has revised this derogatory classification of women's writing by proposing four descriptors that can be used when talking about female-authored texts: biological, which relies simply on the gender of the author; linguistic, which assumes that women have a unique and distinguishable way of using language; psychoanalytic, which argues that women write in response to their oppression; and cultural, which combines all of these categories and argues that women's socialization guides their writing. She explains,

> Women writers should not be studied as a distinct group on the assumption that they all write alike, or even display stylistic resemblances distinctively feminine. But women do have a special history susceptible to analysis, which includes such complex considerations as the economics of their relation to the literary marketplace, the effects of social and political changes in women's status upon individuals, and the implication of stereotypes of the woman writer and restrictions of her artistic autonomy. (858–59)

Showalter has further divided the history of women's writing into three stages: feminine, feminist, and female. Feminine writing, she argues, is dominated by imitation of the male tradition, as demonstrated by the frequent adoption of male pseudonyms. The second stage, that of "feminist" writing, included protest literature such as that of Sarah Moore Grimke and Elizabeth Cady Stanton. And the final stage, female writing, showcases self-discovery through the search for a separate identity.

The inevitable political charge of women's writing makes matters even more complicated. Because women authors were being subjected to the same trials to which they subjected their heroines, their texts were often heavily autobiographical. This author-text relationship dictates a new definition of art: A female-authored text does not merely reflect experience; it also serves to undermine, however subtly, the existence of patriarchal values, so that any text penned by a woman is in some sense always already feminist. And so as with any form of "minority" literature, critics have struggled with learning to value the work for its own characteristics instead of attacking it for its lack of mainstream ones.

Unlike the "greats" of the literary canon, the novel has been consistently accessible to and revered by a variety of social classes. Cathy Davidson notes, for instance, that "[i]n a number of novels, classical allusions are actually defined in the text, again making the books accessible to readers who did not possess sophisticated literacy skills" and that "lending libraries in even the smallest frontier communities made novels available at prices that women could afford" (635). As a result, feminism owes much to the novel, for it provided an outlet in which women could communicate their hopes and desires, which surely helped to set the stage for women's assertion of their rights.

References and Suggested Readings

Davidson, Cathy N. "Beginnings of the Novel." *The Oxford Companion to Women's Writing in the United States*. Ed. Cathy N. Davidson and Linda Wagner-Martin. New York: Oxford University Press, 1995. 635–37.

Showalter, Elaine. "Women and the Literary Curriculum." *College English* 32 (1971): 855–62.

———. *A Literature of Their Own: British Women Novelists from Brontë to Lessing*. 2nd ed. Princeton, NJ: Princeton University Press, 1977.

———, ed. *The New Feminist Criticism: Essays on Women, Literature, and Theory*. New York: Pantheon, 1985.

Lisa R. Williams

OLSEN, TILLIE

Tillie Olsen's reputation as an important twentieth-century feminist writer rests on a relatively small but highly respected body of fictional and nonfictional work, which has been praised by Margaret Atwood, Adrienne Rich, Alice Walker, and Maxine Hong Kingston, among others. In the tradition of Virginia Woolf's *A Room of One's Own*, Olsen's nonfiction essay collection *Silences* (1978) explores the "relationship of circumstances—including class, color, sex; the times, climate into which one is born—to the creation of literature." Like Woolf's fantasy scenario about the limitations that Shakespeare's "gifted sister" Judith might have faced, Olsen's own literary career exemplifies the "unnatural thwarting of what struggles to come into being, but cannot" (n.p.), which she takes as her theme in *Silences*.

Born Tillie Lerner to Russian Jewish immigrant parents in Omaha, Nebraska, in 1912 or 1913, Tillie was raised in a Socialist, humanist, secular household. Her father, Samuel Lerner, left Russia after the failed 1905 revolution and fled to the United States where he married fellow Russian immigrant Ida Beber. Samuel Lerner eventually became secretary of the Nebraska Socialist Party, and Tillie became a political activist in her teens, joining the Young People's Socialist League and the Young Communist League. Her formal education ended in the eleventh grade, but she read widely and eclectically. During the early thirties, she was jailed for helping to organize a strike at a packing house in Kansas City.

At the age of nineteen, Tillie moved briefly to Minnesota to recover from tuberculosis. While there, she became pregnant and began working on a novel (later published as *Yonnondio*). She moved to California in 1933, continuing to work as a political activist and writer. The following year, she published a few poems and a short story titled "The Iron Throat" (later the first chapter of *Yonnondio*) in the *Partisan Review* and "Thousand-Dollar Vagrant" (an account of her arrest in the landmark San Francisco maritime strike) in *The New Republic*. She married fellow union activist Jack Olsen in 1936, and together they had three children.

Olsen spent the next two decades trying to write during "stolen moments" while raising four daughters and holding a variety of clerical and other jobs to support them, a lifestyle that effectively silenced her as an artist. "It is no accident," she wrote in *Silences*, "that the first work I considered publishable began: 'I stand here ironing, and what you asked me moves tormented back and forth with the iron'" (19). That story, written in 1953 and 1954, was published as "Help Her to Believe" in a small magazine called *The Pacific Spectator*. Retitled "I Stand Here Ironing," the story was included in Olsen's 1962 short-story collection *Tell Me a Riddle*, whose title story won the O. Henry Award for Best American Short Story in 1961. Although the 1950s saw Olsen's reawakening as a writer, this was also a difficult time for Olsen and her husband, who were blacklisted during the anti-Communist witch hunts of the period.

The silences imposed by the burdens of race, poverty, and gender are Olsen's greatest theme in both her fiction and nonfiction. In 1972, Olsen wrote the afterword for the Feminist Press reissue of Rebecca Harding Davis's *Life in the Iron Mills* (1861), which she first read at age fifteen in "one of three water-stained, coverless, bound volumes of the *Atlantic Monthly*, bought for ten cents each in an Omaha junkshop" (157). She credits *Life in the Iron Mills* with teaching her, "'Literature can be made out of the lives of despised people,' and 'You, too, must write'" (158). The afterword is also included in *Silences*—her eclectic and unconventional collection of nonfiction pieces concerned with how social circumstances silence people, especially women.

In the early 1970s, Olsen also rediscovered and reconstructed the fragments of the novel she had begun and abandoned in the 1930s. Finally published in 1974 as *Yonnondio: From the Thirties*, the novel bridges the "red decade" of the thirties and the social movements—especially the women's movement—of the sixties and seventies.

In recent years, Olsen, who lives in San Francisco, has received fellowships from the Guggenheim Foundation and the National Endowment for the Humanities, as well as several honorary degrees. Her lifelong efforts to reclaim forgotten women writers from obscurity and to give voice to the experiences of poor and marginalized women in her writings continue to be an important influence on the current generation of feminist writers.

Published in 1962, *Tell Me a Riddle* is a critically acclaimed collection of four short stories by Olsen. Originally conceived of as part of a novel, the stories chronicle moments in the lives of three generations of an extended working-class family in the postwar United States. The title story is an extended portrait of the deterioration of a nearly fifty-year marriage, which astutely analyzes the sharply different, gender-based feelings and perceptions of both husband and wife. Of the volume's three other stories, all written during the 1950s, "I Stand Here Ironing" and "O Yes," stories that insightfully portray the bonds between women, have been frequently anthologized.

"I Stand Here Ironing" is an extended monologue in which a mother ruminates about her relationship with her nineteen-year-old daughter. She recalls the deprivations of her daughter's childhood: "We were poor and could not afford for her the soil of easy growth" (12). Painfully acknowledging all of the circumstances that have thwarted her daughter's development, she ends with a fervent prayer for her daughter's will to transcend these environmental limitations: "So all that is in her will not bloom—but in how many does it? There is still enough left to live by. Only help her to know—help make it so there is cause for her to know—that she is more than this dress on the ironing board, helpless before the iron" (12).

In "Hey Sailor, What Ship?" Whitey, a sailor on shore leave, pays a visit to his old friends, Helen and Lennie, and their two children Jeannie and Carol. His alcoholism disrupts the family and highlights the distance between the present and the past, when the old friends had worked side by side as progressive union activists.

"O Yes" explores an adolescent female friendship between twelve-year-old Carol and her best friend, Parialee Phillips. Helen watches with sadness as her white daughter grows increasingly estranged from her black friend, as the inevitable process of "sorting" by race and class, which occurs in junior high school, intrudes on the less boundaried world of the friends' early childhood.

"Tell Me a Riddle" explores the painful end of the forty-seven-year marriage between Jeannie and Carol's Russian-Jewish immigrant grandparents, David and Eva. As the story begins, the couple is locked in a battle of wills over whether to sell their house and move to the Haven, a cooperative for the aging. While David longs for the companionship and freedom from financial worry the Haven represents, Eva is resolved to guard her solitude and swears "never again to be forced to move to the rhythms of others" (68). Having raised seven children in poverty and lived all her life "for people" (76), she can no longer live with people.

When Eva falls ill with cancer, David conceals the truth from her, taking her on extended visits to her daughter in Ohio and to her granddaughter Jeannie, a nurse in Los Angeles. As Eva's condition deteriorates, the roots of her bitterness are gradually revealed. We learn of her idealistic girlhood as a revolutionary in Czarist Russia and her passion for reading. In her dying delirium, she utters remembered fragments of songs and books from her youth—a youth that was betrayed by the realities of wifehood and motherhood, as well as by the events of the twentieth century, the Holocaust, World War II, and the atomic bomb. In dying, she discovers a special bond with her granddaughter, who reminds her of a comrade from her youth in Russia. David, too, finds the peace of reconciliation with his wife, awakening once again to the idealistic passion they once shared in their youth.

Olsen began writing her unfinished novel *Yonnondio* when she was nineteen years old and worked on it intermittently between 1932 and 1937. The novel's title, taken from a Walt Whitman poem, is a Native American word meaning "lament for the lost." Among other meanings, the title refers to the novel it-self, which was never completed. Set aside because of the exigencies of work and motherhood, the fragments of the manuscript in progress languished for-gotten for forty years before they were rediscovered by Olsen in the early sev-enties. As she recounts in "A Note About This Book," the mature Olsen reconstructed the novel as best she could "in arduous partnership" with her younger self. It was finally published in 1974. The novel has been acclaimed widely for its realistic and unflinching depiction of working-class lives. Unlike many works of 1930s social realism that focus exclusively on working men, Olsen's novel articulates a feminist as well as a Socialist perspective, giving voice to working-class women's unique experiences of poverty and oppression in the Depression-era United States.

The novel begins in a Wyoming mining town in the early 1920s, where the constant threat of death by gas explosion hangs over the workers. Jim Holbrook labors in the mine, while his wife Anna dreams of an "edjication" (3) for her children: Mazie, Will, Ben, and Jimmie. In chapter one, the six-and-half-year-old Mazie encounters Sheen McEvoy, the victim of a "gas explosion that had blown his face off and taken his mind" (10). McEvoy attempts to throw Mazie down a mine shaft, a sacrifice his unbalanced mind imagines will appease the mine's desire for more men. Mazie is rescued by a night watchman and returned to her father, who is drinking in a local saloon. Horrified, Jim and Anna vow to start life over as farmers in the spring, but Mazie's delirious and mocking laughter foreshadows the difficulties ahead.

In chapter two, the Holbrooks continue to battle "poverty's arithmetic" (16), saving for their new life. The dreaded whistle shrieks, signaling another mining accident, which seals many of the workers "in an open grave" (19) Jim is "brought up quiet and shaken five days later" (21). When April finally arrives, the Holbrooks set out for South Dakota, which represents the promise of a better life, full of green grass and fresh air. However, they soon learn the brutal economic reality of tenant farming; after a year of hard labor, they wind up in debt. For half a dollar, Jim sells the books Mazie receives from a kindly neighbor, "though Anna cursed him for it" (39). Anna's fifth pregnancy drains her energy; frustrated by her failure to keep up with the household chores, Jim grows violent and leaves home for ten days. Baby Bess is born, and the Holbrooks decide to move on again to find work in the slaughterhouse.

In chapter five, the Holbrooks arrive in a city (presumably Olsen's hometown Omaha, Nebraska). They find a place to live amid the "taverns and brothels and rheumy-eyed stores" (47) and must endure the sickening stench of the packing houses. Jim gets a job working in the sewers and comes home with "the smell of liquor on his breath" (58). Anna, worn out by childbearing and motherhood, moves about in dizziness and pain. Will, the oldest son, turns to the lure of the streets, and Mazie escapes into memories of the farm and brings home a failure report from school. After Jim forces Anna to have sex with him, she suffers a miscarriage. Repentant, Jim despairs that he cannot afford any of the things the clinic doctor recommends for her.

Seriously ill, Anna makes heroic attempts to care for her children and do the housework. Yet "she felt so worn, so helpless . . . it loomed gigantic beyond her, impossible ever to achieve . . . that task of making a better life for her children to which her being was bound" (88). Anna and Jim reconcile, and Jim strokes her hair, "silently making old vows again, vows that life will never let him keep" (90).

As the story continues, Anna feels suffocated by the house and longs to be "under a boundless sky" (93). She takes the children to gather dandelions, and Mazie experiences a difference in her mother, "as if she had forgotten them, as if she had become someone else, was not their mother any more" (100). Mazie feels "the strange happiness in her mother's body, happiness that had nought to do with them, with her; happiness and farness and selfness" (101). Mazie finds her own escape in "passionate absorbed activity, in rapt make-believe" (103) at a local dump where the despised children of packingtown gather to play with the city's outcast and discarded things. As the dog days of summer set in, the stench and heat grow unbearable. Jim labors under inhuman conditions in the packinghouse, where the bosses have ordered a speed-up despite the horrific heat, turning the plant into a hell. At home, Anna labors over her canning in equally hellish heat.

Despite the dehumanizing pressures of the Holbrooks' environment, however, Olsen ends the novel (only a fraction of the much more ambitious work she had originally intended) with a celebration of human agency. As the family gathers at the end of the brutally exhausting day, Baby Bess grabs a fruit jar lid and repeatedly bangs it on the table: "Centuries of human drive work in her; human ecstasy of achievement. . . . I can do, I use my powers; I! I!" (132). The unfinished novel ends with a momentary break in the heat wave, foreshadowing better times ahead, as Anna says, "The air's changin, Jim. . . . I see for it to end tomorrow, at least get tolerable" (132).

References and Suggested Readings

Coiner, Constance. *Better Red: The Writing and Resistance of Tillie Olsen and Meridel Le Sueur*. New York: Oxford University Press, 1995.

McQuade, Donald, ed. *The Harper American Literature*. New York: Harper, 1987.

Olsen, Tillie. "A Biographical Interpretation." *Life in the Iron Mills and Other Stories*. By Rebecca Harding Davis. New York: The Feminist Press, 1985.

———. *Silences*. New York: Delta, 1978.

———. *Tell Me a Riddle*. 1962. New York: Delta, 1989.

———. *Yonnondio: From the Thirties*. New York: Delta, 1974.

Rosenfelt, Deborah. "From the Thirties: Tillie Olsen and the Radical Tradition." *Feminist Criticism and Social Change: Sex, Class and Race in Literature and Culture*. Ed. Judith Newton and Deborah Rosenfelt. New York: Methuen, 1985.

———, ed. *Tell Me a Riddle*. By Tillie Olsen. New Brunswick, NJ: Rutgers University Press, 1995.

See also Atwood, Margaret; Davis, Rebecca Harding; Kingston, Maxine Hong; Walker, Alice; Woolf, Virginia.

PETRY, ANN

Ann Lane Petry was born into one of the few black families of Old Saybrook, Connecticut, where her father was the local druggist. Petry received her PhG degree in 1931 from the University of Connecticut and returned home to work in the family business from 1931 until 1938. From 1944 to 1946, she studied creative writing at Columbia University. She married George Petry in 1938, and the couple settled in Harlem, where Petry worked for *The Amsterdam News* writing advertising copy and as a reporter and editor for *The People's Voice*. Her short story "On Saturday, the Sirens at Noon" was published in *The Crisis*, a magazine of the NAACP, and led to her contract with Houghton-Mifflin to write *The Street*, which was both a commercial and critical success. Thomas calls *The Street* the "first major literary work" to focus on the streets of Harlem, made remarkable because Petry's "exposure to Harlem street culture had been limited to nine months working with an experimental after-school program on West 116th Street" (9). Petry's other novels are *Country Place* (1947) and *The Narrows* (1953), but neither achieved the success of *The Street*. She also wrote books for children and young adults; two of the best known are *Tituba of Salem Village* and *Harriet Tubman: Conductor on the Underground Railroad*. Her volume of short stories, *Legends of the Saints*, was published in 1970, and *The Street* was reissued as a paperback in 1992 (9).

Chapter one of *The Street* opens, as does nearly every other chapter, with a description of the street. This foregrounding of the setting gives the street character status and certainly establishes the primacy of the street in shaping the narrative. The street becomes a silent, but pervasive, agent of malignancy in the novel, and Lutie Johnson, the main character, views the street as an adversary second only to the film of racism that covers the black experience in America.

The narrative is not presented chronologically, and the novel opens when Lutie is in need of an apartment to rent and is the mother of an eight-year-old boy, Bub, so the threat of the street is palpable. For a single woman with a young son in the 1940s, apartment hunting is a bleak and dismal enterprise. Lutie finds an apartment in her price range on 116th Street, but it is a dark hovel whose first floor is given over to a house of prostitution and the apartment of the furtive and leering Super. The circumstances that have brought Lutie to this place of desperation are not unusual and that makes her situation all the more socially abhorrent and all the harder to counter.

In years past, Lutie lived with her husband, Jim, in a house they owned, but as an uneducated young black man, Jim was unable to find work. Lutie took a job in Connecticut as a domestic and was absent from her family for most of each month. In order to get the job, Lutie had to provide a reference, which she got from the neighborhood vegetable woman who offered this advice in addition to the letter: "It's best that the man do the work when the babies are young. And when the man is young. Not good for the woman to work when she's young. Not good for the man" (33). The woman's warning was all too prophetic. Lutie went to work taking care of a white family's home and child while Jim stayed home with their two-year-old son. His inability to get a job, the reversal of gender roles, and the attendant frustration lead to the disintegration of Jim's dignity and finally of their marriage. The money Lutie carefully earned, hoarded, and sent home for the mortgage payment and household expenses soon went to the upkeep of Jim's new lover.

Lutie begins a new chapter in her life when she takes her son and moves in with her father. The years are filled with struggle as Lutie takes a job in a steam laundry and goes to night school to study shorthand, typing, and filing. She takes the civil service exam, and after four years at the steam laundry, she finally gets a job as a file clerk. But all is not well at home where her father and his girlfriend, Lil, bootleg and keep a steady stream of unsavory characters through the flat. Lutie is determined to remove Bub from the potentially damaging situation by finding an apartment of her own. But in the end, Lutie only trades one set of dangers for another.

In the new apartment, Lutie has no childcare for Bub, and he shifts for himself after school. Lutie remembers the care of her Granny who brought her up and offered companionship, guidance, as well as a buffer of protection from the outside world. Now, neither she nor Bub has even the slimmest margin of protection from the dangers of the street. Lutie is under a constant, but silent, bombardment from the Super and Mrs. Hedges, who runs the brothel on the first floor of her building. In a culture only a few generations removed from the trafficking of human flesh in slavery, Lutie is still valued only for her body. William Jones, the Super, is driven to obsession by his sexual desire for Lutie, and Mrs. Hedges sees the commercial value Lutie would bring to her business. The commodifying of Lutie's body as a sexual object is just another manifestation of a culture that uses her physical strength to run a steam press or clean the houses of wealthy white people with no regard for her spirit.

The neighborhood into which Lutie has moved is a small planet that revolves around the sun of one man's power and influence. Mr. Junto is the white property owner who shapes the lives of the people of the neighborhood. He owns the bar into which Lutie goes one night for a break from the monotony and drudgery of her life. There, in an unmarked moment too insignificant to notice, Lutie's life shifts into a precarious position from which she will never recover. In the bar she meets Boots Smith, a flashy and well-heeled bandleader who is immediately attracted to her. He lures her into his web with the promise that she can earn a lot of money singing with his band. In Boots, Lutie sees the opportunity to escape from the threat of the street. But her plan to use Boots's band as an avenue out of her poverty is destined to be thwarted, just as is his scheme to gain her as a sexual object. Unknown to her, Mr. Junto has claimed Lutie as his private property, and he threatens Boots until he backs off from his pursuit of her. Lost in the tangle of motives and emotions is any real possibility that Lutie can make a career as a big band singer, though under Junto's direction, Boots continues to string her along. Once again, Lutie becomes nothing more than someone's depersonalized puppet. Her notion that, with the apartment and the chance for meaningful and remunerated work, she was "one step farther up on the ladder of success" and that "Bub would be standing a better chance" is nothing more than an illusion (26).

Meanwhile, the struggle for ownership of Lutie escalates. Jones, the Super of her building, attacks her one night and forces her into the furnace room; only the interference of Mrs. Hedges saves Lutie from desperate harm. Mrs. Hedges cannot save her from another of Jones's insidious plans, however. Realizing that he can never have Lutie except through violence or possibly blackmail, Jones involves Bub in a mail-tampering scheme. When Bub is caught by the police and sent overnight to the juvenile home, Lutie enters a vortex from which she will not escape. Afraid for Bub, she seeks the advice of a lawyer, who in his dishonesty and avariciousness, claims that Bub can be released only through the agency of a lawyer. The two hundred dollar fee he will charge is prohibitively beyond Lutie's capability to pay, so she appeals to Boots for the money. When she goes to his apartment to get the money, she unknowingly steps into a web of sinister connections and motives that extend far beyond her own hopeless situation.

Junto has applied pressure on Boots to use this opportunity when Lutie is broken and helpless to secure her for him as a sexual object. For Boots, the distance back to being a porter on a Pullman is dangerously short, and he knows that only Junto stands between him and the ignominy of "No Name, black my shoes. No Name, hold my coat. No Name, brush me off. No Name, take my bags. No Name. No Name" (264). Boots carries within himself the same rage against America's sometimes silent but institutionalized racism as Lutie does. He lashes out at the system and against the hold that Junto has on him in an act of rash desperation. He decides that he will take his pleasure with Lutie before he hands her over to

Junto. When she resists, he says, "Maybe after I beat the hell out of you a coupla times, you'll begin to like the idea of sleeping with me and with Junto" (429). Lutie grabs a candlestick and hits Boots in self-defense, but the knot of rage uncoils in her and she continues to beat Boots until he is bloodied and dead. Lutie has had an impending sense of doom, an intuitive fear that all opportunities will cease to exist for her and that she will be walled in for life. When she strikes out against Boots, "that one last brick was shoved in place" (423).

Standing before a dead body, and standing in only the remaining husk of a person, Lutie is afraid that Bub's life will only be worse if he is branded as the son of a murderer. She takes money from Boots's wallet and goes to Pennsylvania Station where she buys a one-way ticket to Chicago. Completely broken, Lutie can only think that it was the street that took her through the "twists and turns of fate" that "landed her on this train" (436).

Petry says of *The Street*:

> I hope I have created characters who are real, believable, alive. For I am of the opinion that most Americans regard Negroes as types—not quite human—who fit into a special category and I wanted to show them as people with the same capacity for love and hate, for tears and laughter, and the same instincts for survival possessed by all men. (71)

Certainly, Petry has achieved her goal in her body of work and in Lutie Johnson has created a fully human and alive character.

References and Suggested Readings

Petry, Ann. Interview with James W. Ivey. "Ann Petry Talks about First Novel." *Ann Petry: A Bio-Bibliography*. Ed. Hazel Arnett Ervin. New York: 1993. 69–71.
———. *The Street*. 1946. Boston: Mariner-Houghton Mifflin, 1974.
Rayson, Ann. "Ann Lane Petry." *American Women Writers: From Colonial Times to the Present*. Ed. Lina Mainiero and Langdon Lynne Faust. Vol. 3. New York: Frederick Ungar, 1981.
Thomas, Robert McG., Jr. "Ann Petry, 88, First to Write a Literary Portrait of Harlem." *New York Times* 30 Apr. 1997, Late ed., sec. B: 9.

PHELPS, ELIZABETH STUART

Elizabeth Stuart Phelps [Ward] was born in Andover, Massachusetts, in 1844; her mother was the writer Elizabeth Stuart Phelps, and her minister father was on the faculty of Andover's theological seminary. Her mother died when Elizabeth was only eight, and she assumed some responsibility in caring for her younger siblings. Though she was christened Mary Gray, the young girl took her mother's name after her death and was then known as Elizabeth. Phelps was a prolific essayist and novelist. Her novels include *The Story of Avis* (1877), Doctor *Zay* (1882), *The Silent Partner* (1891), *A Singular Life* (1895), and *Confessions of a Wife* (1902) under the pseudonym Mary Adams.

Phelps's *The Story of Avis* opens at a time when "young ladies had not begun to have 'opinions' upon the doctrine of evolution, and before feminine friendship and estrangements were founded on distinctions between protoplasm and bioplasm" (3). Avis Dobell has just returned to Harmouth from Europe where she has studied painting in Florence and Paris. Avis creates a sensation in her community for her desire to have a career as a painter, and even her reluctantly supportive father feels that she should follow the long-established social design for women.

Avis's father, Hegel Dobell, professor of Ethics and Intellectual Philosophy, married when he was thirty-five. Avis's mother wanted a life in the theater, but married Dobell instead and lost her opportunity, not without some regrets. When Avis is nine, her mother is ill, "It was quite certain that she had no disease, only the waxing and waning and wasting of a fine, feverish excitement, for which there seemed to be neither cause nor remedy" (25). Her death leaves Avis without an ally of artistic temperament. Hegel's sister Chloe, who has raised Avis since the early death of her mother, is constantly baffled by her lack of interest in and repulsion toward the chores of domesticity.

Avis strains against the sewing and domestic work that Aunt Chloe insists on. Though Hegel understands that he too would chafe against such work, he cannot bring himself past a weak understanding that it is "unquestionably proper for all women, certainly for all women belonging to him, to be versed in those domestic accomplishments to which the feminine nature was created to adjust itself happily at some cost" (28).

As a young girl, Avis finds refuge from the oppressiveness of domesticity in her excursions to her father's apple orchard. There she would climb to the "highest, airiest branch" of the trees and read Elizabeth Barrett Browning's *Aurora Leigh*. In the company of another artistic spirit, Avis feels a quickening of her understanding and a call to art. In the edenic setting of the apple orchard, Avis experiences her personal "fall" into knowledge. When she tells her father that she would like to be an artist, he calls it nonsense, the "womanish apings of a man's affairs, like a monkey playing tunes on a hand organ" (33). His disapproval shrinks her spirit, but only for a while.

When Avis is nineteen, she goes to Europe with family friends, the Hogarths, and her best friend, Coy Bishop, for a year. When the year is up, she asks to stay on so that she might study art. Her father reluctantly agrees. She spends two years unlearning bad habits and then goes to the famous artist Alta Mura for two years of instruction. She continues her studies in Paris for two final years.

Upon her return from Europe, Avis reestablishes her friendship with Coy but is keenly aware that they are more ideologically separated than ever before. Coy has no aspirations for education and believes "the University . . . existed for the glorification of men" (8). When the two enter Avis's home one evening after a visit with friends, Coy is amazed that Avis has a latchkey to her house. Avis's response is, "Why shouldn't a woman have a latch-key?" (15). Throughout the novel, Coy serves as the foil to Avis.

Avis arrives back in Harmouth just at the time that a new tutor, Philip Ostrander, is receiving the notice of the young women of the community and the professional approval of Avis's professor father. Coy urges Avis to attend a poetry reading so that she might meet Ostrander. Nearly thirty years old, Ostrander presents the picture of great learning and Renaissance accomplishment. He is a tutor in Latin and also teaches German and geology; he has a medical background as well.

At the poetry reading, Coy forces the point of showing Avis's latest picture illustrating Spenser's Una and her knight. All misunderstand the painting except the newcomer, Mr. Ostrander. Embedded in his interpretation is a prescient understanding of Avis herself: "Every nerve and muscle is tense for flight. She will turn and run before that clumsy knight gets up to her—if she can" (9).

Beyond her name, which associates her with birds, Avis is often described in reference to birds. At the poetry reading, Avis purposefully places herself against a bank of carmine drapes to complement her own coloring: "Avis went to it as straight as a bird to a lighthouse on a dark night. She would have beaten herself against that color, like those very birds against the glowing glass, and been happy, even if she had beaten her soul out with it as they did" (7). Ostrander is correct in sensing Avis's tendency toward flight.

Phelps gives us two strong warnings that a relationship between Ostrander and Avis is doomed to a sorrowful and bitter end in a scene she draws early in the novel. On a stormy April night, Ostrander is walking along the beach and sees a woman in some peril, trying to make it back across the reef before the rising tide cuts off her way. It is Avis, who has been out to the lighthouse rescuing birds brought in by the storm. Ostrander saves her, and because she is so chilled, he takes a baby blue jay she had brought back and puts it in the breast of his coat to warm it. As they make their way across the rocks, Avis wonders about the cleft in a large purple rock, and Ostrander, the aspiring geology professor, explains, "The two sides of that gorge are thrust apart by flood or fire. They were originally of one flesh. It was a perfect primeval marriage. The heart of the rock was simply broken" (46). When the two make it back to Avis's home, they find that the bird "upon his heart lay dead" (49).

In order to spend more time with Avis, Ostrander commissions a portrait of himself to give to his mother as a birthday gift. As she is painting Ostrander, they talk, and Avis reveals to him that she has had a solitary life; immediately she regrets the moment of vulnerability, "She felt a sudden sick emptiness of soul, as if an artery had been opened there, which no human power could ever bind" (58). In the course of the months of sitting for the portrait, Ostrander falls in love with Avis and boldly proclaims it to her. She is unnerved and denies that she loves him. Nonetheless, Ostrander persists, "When a man loves a woman as I love you, he expects to be loved; he has a right to be; he must be" (67). She continues, "Marriage is a profession to a woman. And I have my work; I have my work!" (71).

Ostrander leaves Harmouth to fight in the Civil War, "moved by a profound and intelligent hope that he might never come out of it" (91), but he is injured at the Battle of Bull Run and comes back to Harmouth to recover. There, he is in the care of Barbara Allen, another of Avis's childhood friends, and Ostrander responds to her interest in him with an unofficial engagement.

Avis is reluctant to visit the injured Ostrander and is shocked when she does see him in so ruined a state. Quite against her better judgment and own will, she is compelled to recognize her emotional response to Ostrander. She says, "If this be love, I am afraid I love you now" (101). She is immediately aware of the cost this yielding will have on her life and her art, but, being incapable of "either coquetry or cruelty," she cannot call back her words. Encouraged by her admission, Ostrander shifts his love interest from Barbara Allen back to Avis.

Now begins a "civil war" within Avis. She is certain that yielding to love will mean a certain death to her art and her own self. Ostrander cannot understand but promises that he will honor her essential self and its expressions. Avis longs to break the engagement to Ostrander. In a physical response to the emotional fettering that she feels, she tears her engagement ring from her finger.

However, they do marry, but with Avis still harboring a nagging feeling that her art will be the sacrifice. Ostrander sees her as an object to be mastered and controlled. He throws himself into his work and has colleagues over, placing domestic duties heavily on Avis; she is forced to deal with a steady stream of hired help that doesn't work out. She is unable give attention to her painting. Her new home doesn't even have a studio yet, and she must go back to her father's home to use her old studio. All her fears are being borne out.

Avis gets a new look at Ostrander when they journey to the deathbed of his mother. Avis begins to wonder if perhaps Phillip has neglected his mother; she also notices a young woman who seemed quite fond of his mother, yet Ostrander does not speak to her. She will later learn that this young woman is another woman to whom Ostrander implicitly promised marriage before abandoning her.

With a growing uneasiness about her decision to marry and about the character of her husband, Avis continues on in her role as wife and partner. A son is born to them, and she is somewhat disappointed that he is a boy. Avis is very aware that she doesn't have "maternal affection" for him and finds him to be "a great deal of trouble" (150–52). The strains of motherhood wear on Avis, and Ostrander quickly forgets his assurance that he did not marry a housekeeper.

Meanwhile, Coy has happily married John Rose and eagerly assists him in his lifework of ministry. Coy urges her husband to keep office hours for those who are sick in their souls, and his ministry increases tremendously. Soon he is involved in social ministry to those in all manner of need and invites Avis to make a ministerial visit to the "lower end of the town" (159). There she meets a woman who looks hauntingly familiar. Later, the woman comes to Avis's door at home and reveals a story that shakes Avis's faith in her husband. She tells Avis that she is moving to Texas: "My husband has come home, and taken the notion to go to Texas. The law compels me to go with him as if I were a horse or a cow. Women don't think of such things when they marry. I've had a hell of a life with my husband" (161). The woman, Susan Jessup, is Susan Wanamaker from Ostrander's hometown in New Hampshire. They once had a relationship, an understanding that they would marry, but Ostrander broke it off. Susan entered a marriage with an abusive husband, and her life has been terrible since. Avis loses respect for Ostrander, and even Ostrander himself realizes that he is less a man than he thought he was.

Avis gives birth to a second child, a girl. Ostrander is not performing well at work, and Professor Dobell comes to tell Avis that Philip will be dismissed if he doesn't improve. Ostrander has "shirked the drudgery of the class-room" and has "an extraordinary lack of intellectual constancy" (173, 174). Avis fleetingly regrets that she has given birth to a girl who will have to bear the burden of womanhood in a male-dominated social order. Ostrander crumples under the disapproval of his peers, and Avis wonders how "her soul had ever gone upon its knees before the nature of this man" (178). She realizes that now she has three children to care for, and "It seemed to her a kind of mortal sin that she should have bestowed upon her children a father whom she might not bid them kneel to worship" (178).

Avis becomes very ill and nearly dies until she determines that she will live for her children. Barbara Allen comes to live with them and take care of Avis and the children. Even while Avis is recovering, Ostrander flirts with the dangers of adultery in his friendship with Barbara Allen, and, one evening, Avis finds them in a compromising position at two in the morning. Avis tells Barbara, "It is so dangerous for a woman to commit an indecorum! Society does not excuse her as it does a man" (187). Yet the next day, Ostrander takes Barbara's umbrella to her, and they end up in an accident on the water and their rescue by a fisherman becomes the talk of the town. The breech between Avis and Philip is cracked open even more widely.

Ostrander resigns under pressure from the college and winters under doctor's orders in the south of France. Though he claims his damaged lungs need a change in climate, the trip is really nothing more than a veiled attempt to shield him from the consequences of his indiscretions. The family can hardly afford his European excursion with their reduced income.

Avis is "shocked to find her husband's absence a relief" (198), but her life is complicated by the illness of her son. He dies before Ostrander can return home. Upon his return, Ostrander's health continues to decline, and he and Avis decide to go south for the winter; Aunt Chloe will keep the baby. They go to Florida and live in the quiet harmony of those who have abandoned their passions but accepted the devotions of duty in a marriage. At Christmas, Ostrander has a vision of their dead son Van calling to him, beckoning him on. Soon after, Ostrander dies from a fall while riding. Avis returns home and wonders what her life and art could have been like "if her feeling for that one man, her husband, had not eaten into and eaten out the core of her life, left her a riddled, withered thing, spent and rent, wasted by the autocracy of a love as imperious as her own nature, and as deathless as her own soul" (244).

As Avis settles into her widowhood and almost frantic care of her daughter, her best friend, Coy, still cannot understand Avis's desire—even her need—for a life of her own separate from the constraints of marriage. In exasperation, she defends her understanding of women's role: "It is nature! Explain it how you will" (249). "But I," said Avis in a low voice, after an expressive pause, "*I* am nature, too. Explain me, Coy" (249).

References and Suggested Readings

Kessler, Carol Farley. "Phelps (Ward), Elizabeth Stuart." *The Oxford Companion to Women's Writing in the United States*. Ed. Cathy N. Davidson and Linda Wagner-Martin. New York: Oxford University Press, 1995.

Phelps, Elizabeth Stuart. *The Story of Avis*. New Brunswick, NJ: Rutgers University Press, 1985.

PIERCY, MARGE

Marge Piercy was born in 1936 to a Jewish mother and a Welsh father in a working-class neighborhood in Detroit. She received BA degree from the University of Michigan in 1957 and an MA degree from Northwestern in 1958. During the 1960s, Piercy was an organizer for the Students for a Democratic Society (SDS), and a political edge is still evident in her work. In an interview with John Rodden, she says,

> It's a very modern heresy that you can't have political poetry. . . . Politics is interwoven throughout discourse. If the attitudes that are spoken or implied agree with those you're used to, you don't consider them political. . . . If the attitudes expressed or implied are different, then it is seen as political or even polemical. (133)

Both a poet and a novelist, Piercy finds her subjects in everyday life, and her thematic concerns grow from her interest in environmentalism, myth, family and heritage, and feminism. For Piercy, the personal efficacy of art is to give "dignity to our pain, our anger, our losses" (188). But, as Piercy reveals, the function and power of poetry transcend the personal to the political:

> The farther you are from the centers of power in this society, the less likely you are to find validation of your experiences, your insights, and ideas, your life. It is more important to you to find in art that validation, that respect for your experiences that no minority expect the thin, white, and wealthy can count on. (188)

Piercy's *Woman on the Edge of Time*, a science-fiction utopian novel, is firmly situated in the politics of feminism and ethnicity. The novel features Consuela "Connie" Ramos, the titular woman on the edge of time but also a woman on the brink of an induced insanity. Her life is traumatized by the violent death of her young husband, the abusiveness of her second husband, poverty, her past drug use, humiliating encounters with the welfare system, the removal of her child, and her guilt and desire to reclaim her child. She thinks, "it was a crime to be born poor as it was a crime to be born brown" (54).

The narrative shifts between Connie's present, her past, and two futures—one utopian, one dystopian. Connie's present opens with a confrontation that leads to her commitment to Bellevue, a mental institution. Her niece, Dolly, seeks refuge at her door and is followed by her pimp, Geraldo. In an attempt to protect Dolly, Connie smashes Geraldo's nose, and he orchestrates an elaborate vengeance against her; Geraldo engages Connie's brother's considerable power and authority to have her institutionalized.

The humiliation and monotony of Bellevue are broken for Connie by visits from Luciente, a woman from the twenty-second century. Luciente is from a village in Massachusetts in the year 2137 and lives in a nonhierarchical world where the divisive issues of the twentieth century—race, gender, class, sexual orientation, capitalism, pollution—are not socially destructive. Luciente explains that Connie has been chosen for communication from the future because her "mind is unusual. You're what we call a catcher, a receptive" (34). Though Connie initially fears contact with Luciente, she comes to long for the visits that take her from the trauma of Bellevue. Although Connie does not leave the hospital in body, she drifts into another consciousness and visits Luciente's future.

Luciente claims that she needs Connie's help, but Connie cannot imagine that she has any purpose or necessary function. Connie describes herself as having a "police record and a psychiatric record, a fat Chicana aged thirty-seven, without a man, without her own child, without the right clothes, with her plastic pocketbook cracked on the side and held together with tape" (22). Her successful and powerful brother, Luis, has already once had her committed to a mental institution, and she feels helpless to survive this second institutionalization. She feels as if she is nothing more than "human garbage carried to the dump" (24).

As Luciente and Connie visit, we learn both about Connie's past and about the world Luciente is from. Connie has embraced the image that society holds of her and has no sense of self-worth any longer, but the more she reveals her history to Luciente, the more she and the reader come to see her differently. Her present situation is not so easily understood or categorized as the welfare workers and psychiatric case workers believe.

Connie was once young and in love with her first husband, Martín Álvarez, but he was an innocent victim of a barrio knife fight. She suffers from the poverty, the humiliation of welfare, and the suspicious watchdog attitude of the welfare workers. She longs for an education, the chance to make something of herself, but she cannot break out of the cycle that entraps her. Her second husband was abusive, and when she finally found a loving and healthy relationship with Claud, he died. After his death, lost in grief and alcohol and drugs, Connie does not provide adequate care for her daughter. She longs to regain custody of her daughter, Angelina.

As her name indicates, Luciente is "shining, brilliant, full of light" (28). She is a slight, androgynous person and explains that there are no gendered pronouns in her world, only the generic "per." The people have only first names, and those can change throughout life as they will.

The world where Luciente lives is not bound by our gender rules; people couple freely with male or female as it pleases them. Reproduction is a separate action from sexual expression. They have a brooder where genetic material is stored and embryos grow. Parenting is done by a group of comothers rather than by one or two persons. Every child has three mothers, "to break the nuclear bonding" (97). When a child is twelve, he or she is set down in the wilderness to earn "per" name.

Luciente's culture has made an effort to correct some of the ills of the twentieth century. She says,

> We decided to hold on to separate cultural identities. But we broke the bond between genes and culture, broke it forever. We want there to be no chance of racism again. But we don't want the melting pot where everybody ends up with thin gruel. We want diversity, for strangeness breeds richness. (96)

She continues, "We tried to learn from cultures that dealt well with handling conflict, promoting cooperation, coming of age, growing a sense of community, getting sick, aging, going mad, dying" (117).

After a number of visits to the world of the future, Connie starts to trust her new friends there. When she is back on the ward, she is able to reach out to others more compassionately. It is through the visits to the future, and not from her psychiatric care, that Connie is slowly changing and moving toward health. The dehumanization of the ward is in stark contrast to the validation she finds in the future world.

Connie is shown another vision of the future, a world of slavery, sexual barter, intolerance, environmental poison, and violence. All of the worst terrors of the twentieth century pale in comparison to the terrors of this alternative future. Still Connie does not understand how she can be of any help to the future. Luciente and her friends tell Connie that she is their ancestor and that the time she lives in is a "crux-time" where "probabilities clash and possibilities wink out forever" (170). Luciente's people are in a struggle with another group, the Shapers, who want to "breed for selected traits," and if Connie cannot slow the genetic manipulations of her time, the future is in danger and the alternative chaos will unfold. Suddenly Connie understands and commits herself to Luciente's aid.

Back on the psychiatric ward, Connie has been moved to a special ward for a special study she is tapped for. She turns herself into a model patient so that she can get a pass out of the ward for a Thanksgiving visit to her brother Luis's house in New Jersey. While out on pass, she visits Luis's nursery and finds some poisons to take with her to use against the doctors who are involved in the genetic alterations. Back on the ward, she puts the poison in their coffee and effectively stops the procedures. The last chapter of the book is clinical notes on her case. Connie has fulfilled her mission in the "crux-time."

References and Suggested Readings

Piercy, Marge. Interview with Bill Moyers. "Marge Piercy." *Fooling with Words*. New York: William Morrow, 1999. 170–94.

————. Interview with John Rodden. "A Harsh Day's Light: An Interview with Marge Piercy." *Kenyon Review* (Spring 1998): 132–43.

————. *Woman on the Edge of Time*. 1976. New York: Fawcett Crest, 1983.

Viles, Deborah. "Piercy, Marge." *The Oxford Companion to Women's Writing*. Ed. Cathy N. Davidson and Linda Wagner-Martin. New York: Oxford University Press, 1995.

PSEUDONYMS

Names are powerful agents of identity. At the very least, they evidence a particular lineage or group identity; at times, they are simply chosen by a person to denote association with a particular person, idea, or concept. The act of changing names, then, can either empower or disidentify a person. Poligaysi Qoyawayma, a Hopi woman, remembers that when she first went to school, the white men there changed her name immediately to "Bessie," printed it on cardboard, hung it around her neck, and sent her home with the new identity. Polingaysi's mother and grandmother took the name change as proof that "the white man was unfeeling." "'You had your beginning as a true Hopi,' Polingaysi's mother told her, fingering the cardboard. 'You were named in the Hopi way. Your true name is Polingaysi. That will always be your name'" (Qoyawayma 28).

The imposition of white identity onto Native children through renaming has been well documented, and the act of reclaiming a tribally given name has provided both personal fulfillment and political agency for the individual. Women writers have also had an identity imposed on them in a sense, though neither with the same severity nor with the same effects: Within a patriarchal system that has throughout history valued male more than female contribution, women have at times opted to "pass" themselves as men, particularly within the literary sphere. For some, a masculine pen name offered anonymity, while for others, it was a strategic choice that they hoped could enhance their marketability and subject them to criticism based on their abilities rather than on their gender. And beyond the gendered markers of names, some women have also found it professionally beneficial (and, at times, necessary) to erase also any markers of race or ethnicity in order to carve through the racism and sexism inherent in early literary criticism.

The overt political charge of pseudonymical writing has not always existed, though. As Susan Coultrap-McQuin has pointed out, eighteenth- and nineteenth-century writers, male and female, often took on a pen name in order to demonstrate that they intended their work for consumption of family and friends rather than for the sake of personal fame. This approach, long viewed as "proper," motivated some writers to use general names, as in the example of Anne Bradstreet, who wrote simply as "A Gentlewoman" (Coultrap-McQuin 716). But as women began to more openly contest sexism and patriarchy, they began, too, to hide their gender in order to point out that their works were being evaluated unfairly, as in the case of George Eliot. On the one hand, then, these writers were countering their subjugation; on the other hand, they were sometimes doing so within the confines of an outwardly male identity.

For contemporary woman writers, for whom some space has been made in the literary canon largely due to feminist intervention, the act of renaming constitutes a way of asserting rather than concealing identity, as exemplified by the likes of bell hooks, Toni Cade Bambara, and Elana Dykewomon. This shift in purpose demonstrates not only the generally greater agency of women but also their awareness of the various facets of identity that, along with gender, make up the individual.

References and Suggested Readings

Coultrap-McQuin, Susan. "Pseudonyms." *The Oxford Companion to Women's Writing in the United States*. Ed. Cathy N. Davidson and Linda Wagner-Martin. New York: Oxford University Press, 1995. 716–17.

Qoyawayma, Polingaysi. *No Turning Back: A Hopi Indian Woman's Struggle to Live in Two Worlds*. Albuquerque: University of New Mexico Press, 1964.

See also hooks, bell.

Lisa R. Williams

REGIONALISM

Women writers, such as Sarah Orne Jewett, Kate Chopin, and Willa Cather, were long dismissed by (male) critics as "regional" authors, the implication being that their writings had little universal appeal or impact. *Regionalism*, the term often used to describe these voices collectively, has been reclaimed in recent years: Judith Fetterley and Marjorie Pryse's 1992 text *American Women Regionalists, 1850–1910* establishes regional writers as powerful forces in the literary canon, noting that works grounded in place do much to broaden the traditionally East Coast–focused acknowledgment of what constitutes American literature. This sort of feminist-revisionist history allows regional writers to be billed as place-specific rather than idiosyncratic. In the United States, where regions differ dramatically from one another, few reasons other than sexism exist to explain the long-lived dismissal of these works; the category seems to have been less focused on literary characteristics than on the gender of the author recording those characteristics.

Regional writings, also referred to as texts of local color because of the way they "paint" a particular picture, are often characterized by extreme reliance on geography for plot as well as by the use of dialect. Willa Cather, for example, writes about life on the Nebraska prairie, whereas Sarah Orne Jewett writes about life in Maine. While many male authors also wrote about specific locales, the term *regionalism* was rarely applied to their work, leaving feminist scholarship to address the political implications of the term.

References and Suggested Readings

Fetterley, Judith, and Marjorie Pryse, eds. *American Women Regionalists, 1850–1910*. New York: W. W. Norton, 1995.

See also Chopin, Kate; hooks, bell.

Lisa R. Williams

RICH, ADRIENNE

Adrienne Rich's 2003 Bollingen Award for her lifetime of contributions to the field of poetry and for her latest volume, *Fox: Poems 1998–2000*, is another in the long stream of recognition that started very early in her career with the 1951 Yale Series of Younger Poets Award for her first volume, *A Change of World*. In her professional career of over fifty years, she has remained attuned to the demands of her craft and has evolved in her subject matter and style from a "striking allegiance to modernist aesthetic fathers," as noted by Gilbert and Gubar, to a clearly defined and unapologetic feminist dialectic.

Born in Baltimore, Maryland, on May 16, 1929, to a professional family—her father was a physician and teacher and her mother was a pianist—Adrienne Rich was first educated at home by her mother. She graduated *cum laude* from Radcliffe in 1951 and married Alfred H. Conrad in 1953. With Conrad, she had three sons and continued writing poetry while becoming more involved in the feminist movement. In 1970, her marriage ended and her husband committed suicide. Harriet Davidson suggests, "These two events remain great silences in Rich's work."

Rich's 1963 edition of *Snapshots of a Daughter-in-Law: Poems, 1954–1963* is generally viewed as the volume in which she makes the artistic leap from apprenticeship to a singular voice of her own. *Diving into the Wreck* (1973) continues with a feminist voice that some critics decried as too strident, too busily engaged in the same strategies of totalizing that she criticizes in male-gendered behaviors. But other critics welcomed the volume as significant and even-handed, and it was awarded the National Book Award in 1974.

As Rich's poetry increasingly embodied her belief that the "personal is political," deeply entrenched aesthetic conservatives such as Harold Bloom struck out at Rich. When Bloom edited *The Best of the Best American Poetry: 1988–1997*, he refused to note any poem from the 1996 collection edited by Adrienne Rich. He says,

> The 1996 anthology is . . . a monumental representation of the enemies of the aesthetic who are in the act of overwhelming us. It is of a badness not to be believed, because it follows the criteria now operative: what matters most are the race, gender, sexual orientation, ethnic origin, and political purpose of the would-be poet. (16)

In her essay "Blood, Bread, and Poetry," Rich comments on her growing political awareness. Born and raised in "white mainstream American culture," educated and privileged, Rich began to piece together for herself the "history of the dispossessed" (244). Tutored by the work of such writers as Mary Wollstonecraft, Simone de Beauvoir, and James Baldwin, Rich learned "'the way things are' could actually be a social construct, advantageous to some people and detrimental to others, and that these constructs could be criticized and changed" (245).

Rich's reputation could stand on her significant body of poetry alone—she has over twenty volumes published—but she has also made a significant mark on the social landscape with her prose. Her 1980 essay "Compulsory Heterosexuality and Lesbian Experience" challenges heterosexual feminists to "examine heterosexuality as a political institution which disempowers women" (203). She also introduces the notion of the *lesbian continuum* to encapsulate female experiences of "woman identification" while disengaging the idea from an eroticized, genital sexuality. All the while, Rich's agenda is to "find out where our common base is, to become educated in each other's realities, to search for and document the mistakes of the past so we can stop making them" (262).

Other important prose works by Rich include *Of Woman Born: Motherhood as Experience and Institution* (1976), *Women and Honor: Some Notes on Lying* (1977), *On Lies, Secrets and Silence: Selected Prose, 1966–1978* (1979), *What Is Found There: Notebooks on Poetry and Politics* (1993), and *Arts of the Possible: Essays and Conversations* (2001).

References and Suggested Readings

Davidson, Harriet. "Adrienne Rich." *Modern American Writers*. The Scribner Writers Series. 441–56. 25 January 1999 <http://127.0.0.1fastweb?link+Comp+!1470 ahtm>.

Gilbert, Sandra M., and Susan Gubar. *No Man's Land: The Place of the Woman Writer in the Twentieth Century*. Vol. 3: *Letters from the Front*. New Haven: Yale University Press, 1994.

Rich, Adrienne. "Blood, Bread, and Poetry." *Adrienne Rich's Poetry and Prose*. Ed. Barbara Charlesworth Gelpi and Albert Gelpi. New York: W. W. Norton, 1993. 239–52.

———. "Compulsory Heterosexuality and Lesbian Existence." *Adrienne Rich's Poetry and Prose*. Ed. Barbara Charlesworth Gelpi and Albert Gelpi. New York: W. W. Norton, 1993. 203–24.

See also Lorde, Audre; Marriage; Olsen, Tillie; Sexuality; Stefan, Verena; Wollstonecraft, Mary.

ROWSON, SUSANNA

Susanna Haswell Rowson was born in 1762 in Portsmouth, England, the only child of William Haswell and Susanna Musgrave Haswell, who died soon after childbirth. Her father, in service to the Royal Navy, was sent to America to work as a customs collector, and he remarried and settled in Nantasket, Massachusetts.

Haswell returned to England in 1767 to get his five-year-old daughter, and she lived in the Colonies for the next eleven years. But with revolution fermenting in the American colonies, the British Lt. Rowson was stripped of his property and returned to England in 1778.

Back in England, Susanna worked as a governess while she wrote her first novel, *Frankensteinia*. In 1786, she married William Rowson, by all accounts a less than satisfactory partner. The Rowsons moved to America and followed the stage where Susanna experienced not an immodest success both as an actor and a playwright. In 1797, she opened a school for girls, the Young Ladies' Academy, that became quite successful. Rowson exercised considerable control over the operations of the school and infused its curriculum with subjects that enlarged the traditional core for women at the time. Furthermore, Rowson wrote many of the texts used in her school in order to present a more balanced role of women in culture and history. In addition to her educational texts, Rowson wrote plays, poetry, and the following novels: *Frankensteinia* (1786), *The Inquisitor* (1788), *Mary, or The Test of Honour* (1789), *Charlotte: A Tale of Truth* (1791), *Rebecca, or The Fille de Chambre* (1792), *Trials of the Human Heart* (1795), *Reuben and Rachel; or, Tales of Old Times* (1798), *Sincerity* (1803), *Sarah, or The Exemplary Wife* (1813), and *Charlotte's Daughter; or The Three Orphans* (posthumously published in 1828).

Charlotte Temple (1791), earlier titled *Charlotte: A Tale of Truth*, is the novel on which Rowson's present reputation rests. Cathy N. Davidson notes that "*Charlotte Temple* became America's first best-selling novel in the earliest years of the Republic" (xi), and though a cautionary tale to young women, it appealed to a "broad cross section of American readers" (xiii).

The novel opens with a conversation between Montraville and his companion, Belcour, two officers in the army, as they discuss their desire to "take a survey of the Chichester ladies as they returned from their devotions" (9). With the narrative decision of focusing the reader's attention on the plans of Montraville and Belcour rather than on Charlotte, the titular character, Rowson establishes the social condition in which the novel takes place—where men, even if sometimes playfully, are in a predatory posture toward women. Montraville sets his attention on the fifteen-year-old Charlotte Temple who is under the care of Mademoiselle La Rue, the French teacher at the school where Charlotte is expected to finish her education. With a quick bribe to La Rue, Montraville secures an interview with Charlotte that will become the first step in her journey away from obedience to her parental expectations.

Charlotte Temple is the daughter of a man whose ideas about the rights of women are more progressive than those of his peers. Mr. Temple watched, as a young man, while "his sisters [were] legally prostituted to old, decrepid [sic] men" (12), and he determined that his behavior toward women would be different. He marries a woman whom he truly loves, even though she brings not a dowry but a widowed father who must also be supported. Into their loving and high-minded union is born Charlotte, who will ultimately fall into the snares that her parents hope to help her avoid.

Doubtless, left on her own, Charlotte would never have courted the danger she finds herself in, but under the derelict care of Mademoiselle La Rue, a woman who had "lived with several men in open defiance of all moral and religious duties" (26), Charlotte is torn between her passion and her principles. Though in her first rendezvous with the gentlemen soldiers Charlotte is disgusted by their crudities and by the "liberties Mademoiselle permitted them to take" (27), her acuteness is slowly dulled as she continues to join their company. Montraville picks Charlotte out for his special attention, though he knows he will soon be leaving for the American Colonies and that he has no serious intentions toward her even if he weren't. He continues to press her for appointments, and though she longs to refuse him, she is certain she has the moral strength to withstand his demands. Furthermore, she feels an unreciprocated allegiance to Mademoiselle La Rue and knows that any step she takes to extricate herself from her pattern of duplicitous behavior will implicate her guardian, La Rue. Torn between abstract moral principles, the immediate lesser danger of shielding La Rue, and her own inchoate sexual desires, Charlotte is paralyzed in her efforts to withdraw her connections to Montraville. When Montraville finally promises marriage upon reaching the American shore, Charlotte agrees to an elopement.

Meanwhile, back at her home, Charlotte's parents plan a birthday party for her, intending to pick her up at the school and return her home for the festivities. Charlotte receives a letter from her mother announcing their intentions, and it provides her with the resolve to break her relationship with Montraville. She goes to him one last time to deliver the news of her "triumph of reason over inclination," of her will to follow "religion, duty," but Montraville threatens to "put a period" to his existence, swearing that he cannot live without her (47). While Charlotte struggles with these new complications, Montraville "lift[s] her into the chaise" and effects her virtual kidnapping as she faints (47).

When Charlotte's grandfather arrives at school to pick her up for her birthday party, he is greeted with the grim news of her elopement. Fully aware that an elopement worked only to the advantage of the man and that for a young girl it was the first step to her inevitable social suicide and probable ruin, the grandfather laments, "My child is betrayed; the darling, the comfort of my aged heart, is lost. Oh would to heaven I had died but yesterday" (50–51). When Charlotte's mother hears of her elopement, she prays, "save her from the miseries which I fear will be her portion, and oh! Of thine infinite mercy, make her not a mother" (53–54).

Finding herself on board a ship soon to leave for America, Charlotte composes a letter to her parents but, rather than send it, Montraville tears it up. Once they are underway, all hopes for a speedy return and reconciliation to her parents evaporate. Accompanying Charlotte and her betrayer are Mademoiselle La Rue and Montraville's friend, Belcour. La Rue quickly recognizes that Belcour has no intentions of keeping faith with her and that she stands to gain nothing from an alliance with him, so she just as quickly sets her aim at a Colonel Crayton, "an officer of large unencumbered fortune and elevated rank" (57). Before the voyage is over, La Rue has extracted "a promise of marriage on their arrival at New York, under forfeiture of five thousand pounds" (59), and Belcour has determined he will claim Charlotte for himself when Montraville discards her.

Upon arrival in New York, Montraville settles Charlotte in a small house with a servant and a supply of funds; though he spends little time with her, she has become his acknowledged mistress, much to her own sorrow. She reflects on the legal protections that are offered a married woman and recognizes that she has none of them nor the esteem of "the very man to whom she has sacrificed every thing dear and valuable in life" (67). Soon the charms of Julia Franklin, a young woman of some property and a viable marriage candidate, capture Montraville. Charlotte can sense that her fortune is turning, but she is unable to recognize the machinations of Belcour as he turns his lascivious eye her way. Alone in a foreign land, now pregnant, soon to be deserted by her lover, and under the predatory intent of an even less principled man, Charlotte has little to cheer her until she is befriended by Mrs. Beauchamp, the daughter of the unfortunate Colonel Crayton, who has come to realize that he was duped by the scheming La Rue. Suspecting that Montraville has sabotaged Charlotte's attempts to contact her parents, Mrs. Beauchamp offers to deliver her letters.

On the verge of betraying Charlotte and marrying Julia Franklin, Montraville experiences some remorse; afraid that Montraville might yet do the honorable thing by Charlotte, Belcour convinces him that Charlotte is faithless and wanton in her affections. Montraville breaks all connections with Charlotte but pledges financial support for her and her child; however, he entrusts the account to the perfidious Belcour and, thus, unwittingly, plunges Charlotte into utter poverty.

Once Charlotte's parents receive word from her, her father hastens to America to rescue her; before he can reach her, though, Charlotte is cast from her house because she cannot pay the rent; she appeals to her former friend Mrs. Crayton, only to be turned out into the cold, and she gives birth to her daughter in a hovel. Mr. Temple arrives just in time to bestow a reconciling look on Charlotte and receive her child into his arms before she dies.

Montraville returns to New York to find that Charlotte has died, and as he uncovers Belcour's complicity in her death, Montraville takes vengeance against him. Belcour dies from his wounds, and Montraville suffers "severe fits of melancholy" for the rest of his days (118).

Temple returns to England with Charlotte's daughter, Lucy, and a nurse. Ten years later, while in London on business, the Temples come upon a woman in wretched condition sitting on the steps of a doorway. Mr. Temple assists her to a house and sees to her care. When the woman is able to speak, she reveals that she is Mrs. Crayton, the instrument of their beloved Charlotte's downfall and herself given over the last seven years to a life of dissipation, poverty, and vice. Nonetheless, the Temples move her to a hospital where she soon dies, "a striking example that vice, however prosperous in the beginning, in the end leads only to misery and shame" (120).

Rowson's novel strikes a note of caution as it warns young girls to take heed of Charlotte's fate and avoid it. But Rowson is never prudish in her moralizing; rather, she suggests that women must take care in a dangerous world, where they are vulnerable sexually, socially, and even legally, to a social construct that promulgates gender inequity.

References and Suggested Readings

Davidson, Cathy N. Introduction. *Charlotte Temple*. By Susanna Rowson. Ed. Cathy N. Davidson. New York: Oxford University Press, 1986. xi–xxxiii.
———. Introduction. *Charlotte Temple*. By Susanna Rowson. New York: Oxford University Press, 1986. Rpt. of *Charlotte: A Tale of Truth*. 1794.
Warhol, Robyn R., and Eve M. Lynch. "Susanna Rowson." *An Encyclopedia of British Women Writers*. Ed. Paul Schlueter and Jane Schlueter. Revised and Expanded ed. New Brunswick, NJ: Rutgers University Press, 1998.

S

SCHREINER, OLIVE

The South African novelist, feminist, anti-imperialist, pacifist, and Socialist Olive Schreiner is best-known for her novel *The Story of an African Farm* (1883), whose protagonist Lyndall is an outspoken feminist heroine and New Woman whose tragic end unfortunately belies her forward-looking attitudes on female equality. Like her American counterpart Charlotte Perkins Gilman, Schreiner was a leading feminist thinker at the turn of the century, the author of the feminist tract *Woman and Labor* (1911), which she referred to as her "sex-book" and suffragists hailed as their bible.

Born in Cape Colony, South Africa, in 1855, Olive was the ninth of Gottlieb and Rebecca Lyndall Schreiner's twelve children. Although her father, a deeply religious missionary of German descent, led the family into destitution, her mother never lost her sense of British superiority over both the Boer (Dutch settlers in Africa) and the native Africans. Olive's bleak childhood was spent wandering the karroo (South African plains), going from mission station to mission station. Although she lacked a formal education, she read widely and was especially influenced by the philosophical works of Herbert Spencer, Ralph Waldo Emerson, and John Stuart Mill, the champion of women's rights.

At the age of fifteen, she took the first of a series of governess positions with Boer farming families. Out of the loneliness and frustration bred from her position as a servant in other people's houses, Olive began to write novels. In 1881, she went to England to become a medical doctor, taking with her the manuscript of *The Story of an African Farm*. Although the chronic ill health that was to plague her for the rest of her life prevented her from completing her medical studies, her novel of South African life, published in 1883 under the pseudonym Ralph Iron, created a sensation in London and turned Schreiner into an instant celebrity. She became active in the Men's and Women's Club, an elite organization that met to discuss women's social, political, and sexual status in Victorian England, issues then referred to under the rubric of "the Woman Question." She befriended such intellectuals as Karl Marx's daughter Eleanor Marx and the sexologist Havelock Ellis with whom she maintained a decades-long correspondence and friendship, although their relationship never developed into a romantic one. Throughout the 1880s, she lived in London rooming houses, writing and speaking on topics including prostitution and birth control.

After returning to South Africa in 1889, Schreiner met and married Samuel Cron Cronwright in 1892. Her husband supported her writing endeavors and added his name to hers out of deference to her feminist sentiments. At the age of forty, she gave birth to a daughter who lived only one day. During the Anglo-Boer War (1899–1902), Schreiner was imprisoned for her radical political stance. An anti-imperialist as well as a feminist, she resigned her vice presidency of the Cape Women's Enfranchisement League when the group failed to support suffrage rights for black women. Many of her later writings address the multiracial struggle for South African independence from British colonial rule, expressing her staunch pacifism and concern for native African rights.

In later years, Schreiner spent long periods of time apart from her husband, returning to England without him shortly before World War I and remaining there until her return to South Africa just before her death in 1920. Her first novel, *Undine*, based on her own unhappy childhood, and an unfinished novel about prostitution entitled *From Man to Man* were published posthumously. Her work has had an enduring influence upon South African writers since. Doris Lessing has hailed *The Story of an African Farm* as one of "that small number of novels, with *Moby Dick*, *Jude the Obscure*, *Wuthering Heights* . . . which is on a frontier of the human mind."

When it was discovered that the best-selling novel, *The Story of an African Farm*, was written by a young female governess recently arrived in England from South Africa, its author became an instant celebrity, courted by London's elite intellectual society. Set on a farm in the desertlike South African plains in the late nineteenth century, *The Story of an African Farm* features one of the most memorable feminist heroines in literature. In her character Lyndall, Schreiner created an outspoken defender of women's rights and an unconventional New Woman, whose refusal to marry the father of her illegitimate child marks her defiance of Victorian moral codes and female socialization. Paradoxically, Lyndall's tragic demise at the end of the novel is at odds with her forward-looking ideas about women's liberation. Constrained by her historical moment, Schreiner was ultimately unable to grant her heroine the independence and freedom she so eloquently espouses in the novel.

The farm of the novel's title belongs to Tant' Sannie, a selfish, stupid, and obese Boer woman, who has in her care two girls, her stepdaughter Em, the child of her deceased English husband, and Em's orphaned cousin Lyndall. As children of twelve, Em dreams of marriage as an escape from the farm, but Lyndall confidently announces her intention to go to school. The other European inhabitants of the farm are Otto, the saintly German overseer, and his son, Waldo. Part One of the novel focuses on the arrival of a stranger named Bonaparte Blenkins, a confidence man who claims kinship with Napoleon and the Duke of Wellington. While the astute Lyndall can see through this impostor, Otto and Tant' Sannie are easily taken in by the tales he fabricates. Despite his ignorance, they install him as the children's schoolmaster. Bonaparte begins to court Tant' Sannie in order to get her farm but accuses Otto of having the very same intention, causing the Boer woman to cast Otto out. On the eve of his departure, however, the German dies. Bonaparte takes his place as overseer, acting with particular cruelty toward Otto's son, Waldo. Part One ends with Bonaparte's expulsion from the farm after Tant' Sannie catches him courting her wealthier niece.

In Part Two of the novel, the stories of Em and Lyndall, now of marriageable age, take center stage. Gregory Rose, who has leased part of the farm, arrives and promptly falls in love with the yellow-haired Em. In a comic parody of a lovesick male, Gregory pines over Em in letters to his sister, calling her "my affinity; the one love of my youth, of my manhood; my sunshine, my God-given blossom" (177). Because Em's "idea of love was only service" (180), her responses to his passionate suit leave Gregory feeling disappointed and cold. When her cousin Lyndall returns to the farm from school, Em tells Gregory he will see a truly beautiful woman whom he cannot help but love. While the sweetly conventional Em fantasizes about her impending marriage and her role as selfless wife, Lyndall returns from four years in boarding school afire with passionate feminist rhetoric. Although she wears a man's ring, she tells Em: "I am not in so great a hurry to put my neck beneath any man's foot; and I do not greatly admire the crying of babies" (184). Lyndall seeks out Waldo, whom she sees as a soul mate, sharing with him her anger about female socialization and her belief in women's equality. She rages against girls' boarding schools as "nicely adapted machines for experimenting on the question, 'Into how little space a human soul can be crushed?'" (185). Lyndall explains to Waldo the process whereby "the world makes men and women" out of the "little plastic beings" born into it, "To you it says—Work! and to us it says—Seem!" (188). Denouncing marriage as another form of prostitution, a "means of making bread," she imagines a time in the future when a woman will have "earnest, independent labor" and love will be "a strange sudden sweetness breaking in upon her earnest work" (195).

Tant' Sannie's marriage to a young widower, whose wife made him promise to marry a fat woman over thirty before she died, offers a further comic critique of the marriage institution. Gregory becomes increasingly taken with Lyndall, although he ostensibly disapproves of her independence. Lyndall expresses her love for Waldo, telling him: "When I am with you I never know that I am a woman and you are a man; I only know that we are both things that think. Other men . . . are mere bodies to me; but you are a spirit" (210). Following Tant' Sannie's wedding, Gregory drives Lyndall home, leaving Em to go with Waldo. Seeing his affection for Lyndall, Em tells Gregory: "It would be better if you and

I were never to be married" (222). Meanwhile, Waldo leaves to seek experiences in the world. Gregory professes his love for Lyndall, offering her the same kind of selfless service he had been so dissatisfied with in Em: "If I might but always be near you to serve you, I would be utterly, utterly happy. I would ask nothing in return!" (231). Lyndall, who is pregnant with another man's baby, agrees to marry him, making clear she desires only the protection of his "name" and nothing else. When the father of Lyndall's unborn child arrives, she tells him she would rather enter into the semblance of marriage with Gregory, whom she does not love, than to give up her freedom in marriage to him. She accuses her companion of wanting to marry her only because "you cannot bear to be resisted, and want to master me" (238). Although Lyndall refuses to marry him, she finally agrees to go with him and to let him take care of her until such time as they no longer love each other.

After Lyndall's departure, Gregory goes in search of her, tracing her movements through the countryside. Eventually, he finds Lyndall in a hotel, where she has been ill in bed for months. Her child lived only eight days, and her companion and she have parted ways, although he continues to send money. The feminine Gregory cross-dresses as a female nurse and, true to his words, serves Lyndall selflessly and anonymously until her death.

Returning to the farm with news of Lyndall's death, Gregory decides to marry Em, because Lyndall has told him to in a four-word note, written but never posted, which he has found on her desk. Waldo has returned from his travels, and Em laments to him, "we long for things, and long for them, and pray for them. . . . Then at last, too late, just when we don't want them any more, when all the sweetness is taken out of them, then they come" (296). The hollowness of Em's impending marriage to Gregory gives the lie to Tant' Sannie's exuberant praise of marriage as "the finest thing in the world" (293). As the novel ends, Waldo dies peacefully while sitting in the sun. Lyndall and her soul mate Waldo are, paradoxically, survived by the characters who do not rebel against the conventionality the novel so deliberately critiques. In Lyndall, Schreiner has created a representative New Woman, a character who defies conventional Victorian constructions of femininity. Unhappily, her tragic end belies the feminist ideals she and her author so ardently espoused.

References and Suggested Readings

Barash, Carol, ed. *An Olive Schreiner Reader: Writings on Women and South Africa*. New York: Pandora, 1987.

Gilbert, Sandra M., and Susan Gubar. *No Man's Land: The Place of the Woman Writer in the Twentieth Century, Vol. 2, Sex Changes*. New Haven: Yale University Press, 1989.

Lessing, Doris. "Introduction." 1968. *The Story of an African Farm*. By Olive Schreiner. New York: Crown, 1987.

Schreiner, Olive. *The Story of an African Farm*. 1883. Hammondsworth, England: Penguin Books, 1971.

See also Brontë, Emily; Gilman, Charlotte Perkins.

SEDGWICK, CATHARINE MARIE

Catharine Marie Sedgwick was born in 1789 in Stockbridge, Massachusetts, to a well-established family that emphasized education and anti-Calvinist religious leanings. Her father, Theodore Sedgwick, was Speaker of the House of Representatives during Washington's administration. Sedgwick's own spiritual journey led her to Unitarianism and the publication of her first work (1822), *A New-England Tale: or, Sketches of New-England Character and Manners*, a novel that calls for religious tolerance. Her desire for social justice and education led to Sedgwick's founding of the Society for the Aid and Relief of Poor Women and of the first free school in New York (47).

A prolific writer, Sedgwick's other works include *Redwood* (1824), *The Travellers* (1825), *The Deformed Boy* (1826), *Hope Leslie* (1827, reprinted 1987), *Clarence* (1830), *The Linwoods* (1835), *Letters from Abroad to Kindred at Home* (1841), and *Married or Single?* (1857).

Sedgwick's third novel, *Hope Leslie*, received favorable reviews, with the exception of critics concerned about her inclusion of Indians in her work, and secured her rank with Washington Irving and William Cullen Bryant as one of America's premier writers. Her intellectual circle included James Fenimore Cooper, Nathaniel Hawthorne, William Cullen Bryant, Ralph Waldo Emerson, and Herman Melville. By the twentieth century, however, Sedgwick's literary fortunes had fallen as the critical establishment generally neglected her work. Not until the 1987 reprint of her best novel, *Hope Leslie*, has Sedgwick once again garnered the attention due one of the founders of the American literary landscape.

Hope Leslie is a historical romance situated in a seventeenth-century Massachusetts colony and is singular in its sympathetic portrayal of Native Americans and of a strong female main character.

Hope Leslie and her sister, Faith, are the children of Alice Fletcher and Charles Leslie. Alice had been the beloved of William Fletcher, her cousin and heir to her father's fortune, but the younger Fletcher cannot accept his uncle's requirement that he must "abjure . . . the fanatical notions of liberty and religion . . . and pledge unqualified obedience to the king, and adherence to the established church" (10). Fletcher necessarily breaks his engagement to Alice and makes preparations to leave England. At the last minute, he is unable to forsake his love, and he returns to his uncle in an attempt to earn his favor and Alice's hand once more. But even at the cost of Alice's "total alienation of mind" (14), his uncle has married Alice off to another man, Charles Leslie. In despair and a measure of compliance with his fate, Fletcher marries a ward of Mr. Winthrop, who later becomes the governor of the Massachusetts colony.

Years pass in the colony, and Fletcher grows steadily uneasy with the hypocrisies and heresies of the Puritan founders until he removes himself and his family to a frontier settlement outside of Boston. Meanwhile, in England, Alice Fletcher Leslie's father and husband both die, and she makes her way to the colony with her two daughters, only to die en route. Just before Fletcher goes to Boston to greet the two girls at the end of their disastrous journey, a young Pequod Indian girl is sent to the Fletcher home by Governor Winthrop. Magawisca is fifteen, fluent in her language and in English, and soon becomes fast friends with Fletcher's four-teen-year-old son, Everell. The vision of the compassionate Mrs. Fletcher is none-theless blurred by ethnocentrism, and she assures Magawisca that she is blessed to be "taken from the midst of a savage people, and set in a christian [sic] family" (24). She further suggests that Magawisca "will soon perceive that our civilized life is far easier—far better and happier than your wild wandering ways, which are indeed . . . little superior to those of the wolves and foxes" (24).

With Magawisca situated in the bosom of his family, Fletcher leaves home for Boston to embrace the orphaned Leslie girls into his family. In Boston, the two girls are baptized by the Rev. Cotton Mather and are rechristened with Puritan names, Hope and Faith. Because he will be detained in Boston by business, Fletcher sends Faith on to his home in the company of several attendants and Oneco, the brother of Magawisca. He stays in Boston for nearly a year before re-turning home with Hope and her tutor. Just hours before his arrival home, Fletcher's house is set upon by three Indians, including the father of Magawisca and Oneco. Fletcher's family is killed, except for Everell and Faith Leslie, who are taken captive by the Indians.

Though happy to be reunited with her father, Magawisca does not approve of his murderous actions in effecting the rescue of her and her brother. Mononotto, chief of a decimated people, offers a wrenching response to her censure, "my people, my children, were swept away like withered leaves before the wind—and there where our pleasant homes were clustered, is silence and darkness" (75). Nonetheless, Magawisca is pitted between her father and Everell, her close friend from a family that only treated her with kindness. All the while that Oneco lov-ingly cares for the other captive, Faith Leslie, Everell is seeking an opportunity for their escape. Mononotto senses he must act quickly and readies his plan to kill Everell. Magawisca intervenes just at the moment that Mononotto swings his weapon at Everell, and while he is saved, her arm is severed. She bids Everell flee, and seven years pass before the narrative is resumed.

In the epistolary tradition of the early novel, Sedgwick covers the seven-year span with a long and detailed letter to Everell in England where he has been for the last five years. Hope Leslie is now a grown woman, Faith Leslie has remained a captive, and through a series of complicated plot diversions, Hope performs an act of heroism that frees Magawisca's grandmother from the charges of witchcraft and certain death. The old woman promises in return that she will arrange a meeting of Hope and her long-lost sister.

Before that meeting takes place, Everell returns from England, and the novel takes a decided turn to romance. Several new characters are introduced: Miss Downing, the best friend of Hope, and a middle-aged gentleman—Sir Philip Gardiner—and his page who have recently traveled from England. In a predict-able turn of events, Everell and Miss Downing become engaged, and Sir Philip sets his sights on Hope Leslie. Magawisca reenters the narrative to fulfill her grandmother's promise that Hope and Faith would be briefly reunited. Faith, however, has married Oneco and has no desire to return to white society. Hope is aghast that her sister has married an Indian, and Magawisca scolds her, "Think ye that your blood will be corrupted by mingling with this stream?" (188). Hope's disgust is somewhat tempered by the news that Faith and her husband have converted to Catholicism, believing that "any christian [*sic*] faith was better than none" (189).

A tangled set of adventures brings the novel to a satisfying close. Hope is nearly captured by pirates in her attempt to find her sister; Gardiner is unmasked as a papist scoundrel posing as a Puritan come to the colony only to marry Hope for her inheritance; his page is revealed to be a young woman and his cast-off lover, Rosa; the pirate ship containing Gardiner is blown up in Rosa's last act of vengeance; Miss Downing realizes that Hope and Everell are meant for each other and steps out of their way; and the dignified Magawisca returns to her people.

In *Hope Leslie*, Sedgwick gives us a novel unusual in its advocacy for women and its recognition of the dignity and humanity of the Indian, partial though it may be. Perhaps the character Mrs. Fletcher reflects Sedgwick's imperfect view of the Indian. On the one hand, she laments their primitive and inferior ways, but at other times, she passionately defends them, as in the following passage, "You surely do not doubt, Martha, that these Indians possess the same faculties that we do. [Magawisca] . . . has rare gifts of mind—such as few of God's creatures are endowed with" (21).

In her preface to the novel, Sedgwick reveals the same double-mindedness and lack of information about the Indian:

> In our histories, it was perhaps natural that they should be represented as "surly dogs," who preferred to die rather than to live, from no other motives than a stupid or malignant obstinacy. Their own historians or poets, *if they had such*, would as naturally, and with more justice, have extolled their high-souled courage and patriotism. (6) [italics mine]

Whatever her attempts to portray Indians in a positive light, the strident oft-repeated opinions of several characters offset that intent. The servant Jennet routinely proclaims the Indians to be the "crafty offspring of a race that are the children and heirs of the evil one" (39). And even the narrative voice, presumably reflective of the author's stance, is often derogatory. In one instance the narrator states, "Caution is the instinct of the weaker animals; the Indian cannot be surprised out of his wariness" (78). An even more telling narrative passage reveals Sedgwick's valorization of the European worldview; she castigates the Indian for obeying the laws of nature rather than "usurping her dominion" (83) and avows that

> it is not permitted to reasonable instructed man, to admire or regret tribes of human beings, who lived and died, leaving scarcely a more enduring memorial, than the forsaken nest that vanishes before one winter's storm. (83)

In her portrayal of Hope Leslie as a woman who chafes against the restrictions placed on her gender in her time, Sedgwick is a stronger reformer. She draws both Hope Leslie and Magawisca with intelligence and will and capability. And significantly, she closes the novel with this pronouncement, "marriage is not *essential* to the contentment, the dignity, or the happiness of woman" (350).

References and Suggested Readings

Blain, Virginia, Isobel Grundy, and Patricia Clements. "Sedgwick, Catharine Marie." *The Feminist Companion to Literature in English*. New Haven: Yale University Press, 1990. 31.

Giles, Jane. "Catharine Marie Sedgwick." *American Women Writers: From Colonial Times to the Present*. Ed. Lina Mainiero. Vol. 4. New York: Frederick Ungar, 1982.

Kelley, Mary. Introduction. *Hope Leslie*. By Catharine Marie Sedgwick. Ed. Mary Kelley. New Brunswick, NJ: Rutgers University Press, 1987.

Sedgwick, Catharine Marie. *Hope Leslie*. 1827. New Brunswick, NJ: Rutgers University Press, 1987.

SENTIMENTALISM

Used almost exclusively to describe women's writing, sentimentalism refers pejoratively to the supposedly excessive affect of the female authorial voice. In the Western tradition of distinguishing between reason and emotion, this concept serves to further the association of women with inferior reasoning and, thus, inferior intellect.

Uncle Tom's Cabin (1852) provides one example of a text long dismissed as sentimental in spite of its influence and popularity. Jane Tompkins points out that literary criticism has, at least since the 1940s, "identified formal complexity and difficulty of apprehension with literary merit," so that many women, whose access to education was limited and whose works, therefore, often wrote differently from their male contemporaries and so were dismissed (2309). Yet *Uncle Tom's Cabin* sold hundreds of thousands of copies in its first few years of publication and bore a distinct antislavery message, and while very much a product of a time that viewed African Americans as popular stereotypes, the text demonstrates the power of a well-written message as well as the irrelevance of its author's gender. As Nina Baym has suggested, Little Eva's tears in the text are far from being merely sentimental: They served to mobilize an entire nation that had yet to fully embrace abolitionism.

The relegation of women's writings to the "sentimental" sphere was, of course, merely a single manifestation of overarching gender divisions. The woman's place was in the home, where she raised the children; the man's place was outside of it, where he earned the wages. As a result, many women naturally took up writing, for it in many cases provided her with the only available means of earning a separate income. Louisa May Alcott exemplifies this phenomenon, so that it is no surprise that her protagonist in *Little Women* lives such a convincing struggle to succeed as a writer and breadwinner.

The term *sentimental* has been applied carelessly to women's writings from the nineteenth century without regard for their individual merit. Although the term is being reclaimed by some feminist revisionists who point to the inevitable social observations and criticism embedded in women's work, its history rests very much on a foundation of dismissal.

References and Suggested Readings

Davidson, Cathy N. "The Sentimental Novel." *The Oxford Companion to Women's Writing in the United States*. Ed. Cathy N. Davidson and Linda Wagner-Martin. New York: Oxford University Press, 1995. 786–88.

Tompkins, Jane. "Harriet Beecher Stowe." *The Heath Anthology of American Literature*. 3rd ed. Ed. Paul Lauter. Boston: Houghton Mifflin, 1998. 2305–9.

See also Stowe, Harriet Beecher.

Lisa R. Williams

SEXUALITY

Multiple explanations exist for the modern construct of sexuality. For Michel Foucault, sexuality as a concept emerged in the late nineteenth century, when same-sex acts began to be discussed in medical terms. Previously, Foucault argues, there were homosexual acts but no corresponding descriptors, such as "homosexuality" or "bisexuality" or "lesbianism" to talk about them. John D'Emilio disagrees, positing the emergence of capitalism as the beginning of sexuality as an identity. He argues that wage labor led to a shift away from the heterosexual family unit, which in turn made it possible for homosexual desire to become an identity rather than simply a practice. Both analyses, while focused predominantly on male sexuality, make a common and crucial point about sexuality: The very concept is a social construct.

Heterosexuality—that is, attraction to members of the opposite sex—is assumed by much of contemporary society to be "normal," largely as a result of Sigmund Freud's theories that posited same-sex attraction as a social and sexual immaturity. Poststructuralist scholars, however, argue that without a binary such as that of homosexuality/heterosexuality, heterosexuality itself does not exist. After all, heterosexuality, in order to be "normal," needs something against which it can define itself. As a result, women who identify as bisexual (attracted to both sexes) or lesbian (attracted to the same sex) have historically been relegated to second-class status by right of their deviant-deviant sexuality. Adrienne Rich attempted to point to this phenomenon by discussing what she calls compulsory heterosexuality. She writes, "The fact is that women in every culture and throughout history have undertaken the task of independent, non-heterosexual, woman-connected existence, to the extent made possible by their context, often in their belief that they were the 'only ones' ever to have done so" (231). And in order for those engaged in same-sex attractions or acts to think themselves the "only ones," they had to be kept invisible, according to Rich, by means of enforced heterosexuality.

The rigidity of gender categories became problematic for people who did not fit the heterosexual mold, and studies began to emerge that identified nonheterosexual individuals, most of them emphasizing the "invert" status of alternative sexualities. These studies did not emerge without recourse: When Magnus Hirschfeld spoke to a group of young men in Hitler's Germany about the "oneness" that existed "beneath the duality of sex," arguing that "every male is potentially a female and every female is potentially a male," everyone registered for the talk was sent to concentration camps. In the United States, a similar fear of difference manifested itself during the McCarthy era and led to the dismissal of nonheterosexuals from government service—in spite of the Kinsey report, which shortly before the McCarthy era had reported the existence of at least twenty million homosexuals.

Concern with deviance divided not only society at large but also those engaged in feminist work. More conservative activists wanted to dissociate themselves from lesbian women, who, by nature of their same-sex attractions, were often viewed as "militant" or "man-hating," while heterosexual women's demands were sometimes more palatable and certainly more likely to be met. Nonheterosexual women began to speak out about their unacknowledged (and sometimes actively hidden) presence in a movement that assumed heterosexuality to be normal. Monique Wittig, for example, wrote that the "discourses which particularly oppress all of us, lesbians, women, and homosexual men, are those which take for granted that what founds society, any society, is heterosexuality" (300). A group called Radicalesbians made much bolder assertions about the investments made in the concept of sexuality: "Lesbian is a label invented by the men to throw at any woman who dares to be his equal, who dares to challenge his prerogatives (including that of all women as part of the exchange medium among men), who dares to assert the primacy of her own needs." The group went on to say that "[u]ntil women see in each other the possibility of a primal commitment which includes sexual love, they will be denying themselves the love and value they readily accord to men, thus affirming their second-class status" (196).

Obviously, sexuality has been used and claimed for various reasons, but its use as an identity category seems to be largely a modern phenomenon. Same-sex acts alone often do not constitute a nonheterosexual identity; rather, such an identity seems to hinge on the assertion of those acts as primary and equal.

References and Suggested Readings

Before Stonewall: The Making of a Gay and Lesbian Community. Prod. Before Stonewall, Inc., in assoc. with Alternative Media Information Center. First Run Features, 1984.

Radicalesbians. "The Woman Identified Woman." *Feminist Theory: A Reader.* Ed. Wendy Kolmar and Frances Bartkowski. London: Mayfield. 195–98.

Rich, Adrienne. "Compulsory Heterosexuality and Lesbian Existence." *Blood, Bread, and Poetry*. New York: Norton, 1984.

Wittig, Monique. "The Straight Mind." *Feminist Theory: A Reader*. Ed. Wendy Kolmar and Frances Bartkowski. London: Mayfield, 2000. 299–303.

See also Rich, Adrienne; Wittig, Monique.

Lisa R. Williams

SHANGE, NTOZAKE

The African American poet, playwright, and dancer Ntozake Shange provocatively crosses boundaries among poetry, drama, and dance, as well as politics, aesthetics, and spirituality in her creative work. Catapulted to national fame with the 1976 Broadway production of her "choreopoem" *for colored girls who have considered suicide/when the rainbow is enuf*, Shange claimed for black women both a beauty and an artistic voice that had been previously denied them through her groundbreaking theatrical creation. Although subsequent work has never met with the acclaim accorded *for colored girls*, Shange, together with writers such as Alice Walker and Audre Lorde, is recognized for helping to establish a voice for women of color in the largely white, middle-class feminist movement of the 1970s and 1980s.

Shange was born Paulette Williams on October 18, 1948, to a middle-class African American family in Trenton, New Jersey. Her father, Paul T. Williams, was a surgeon and her mother, Eloise Owens Williams, was a psychiatric social worker. The oldest of four children, Shange was exposed to a wide range of African, African American, and European American cultural influences as a child. Raised in material security, Shange admitted in a 1976 *Village Voice* article that she later rebelled against the conservatism of her black middle-class background by adopting the speech patterns of the family's live-in maids. At the age of eight, Shange moved to St. Louis, Missouri, where she was among the first blacks to integrate the school system. She later fictionalized this experience in her novel *Betsey Brown* (1985). At age thirteen, Shange moved back to New Jersey, where she attended high school, eventually entering Barnard College in 1966.

At age nineteen, despondent over her separation from her law-school husband, Shange made the first of four suicide attempts that took place during her Barnard years. Nevertheless, Shange managed to graduate from Barnard in 1970 with honors in American Studies, moving to Los Angeles to enroll in a master's program in American Studies at the University of Southern California, where she earned her MA degree in 1973. In 1971, she was baptized in the Pacific Ocean by two South African friends and took her new name: Ntozake ("she who brings her own things") Shange ("one who walks with lions").

After moving to San Francisco in 1973, Shange taught humanities and women's studies at various Bay Area colleges and became involved with the burgeoning local third world and white women's arts scene. Numerous women's bars sponsored poetry readings and new small presses published women's writing. In addition to writing and reciting her poetry, Shange studied dance, performing with choreographer Halifu Osumare's troupe *The Spirit of Dance*. After leaving the troupe in 1974, Shange went on to collaborate with Paula Moss and various Bay Area musicians in a performance piece that would become *for colored girls*. Buoyed by the piece's wildly successful run in the Bay Area, Shange and Moss went to New York, where the play was optioned by Joseph Papp's Public Theater. Papp eventually brought the show to Broadway, where it opened at the Booth Theater in September 1976. The play, which went on to tour nationally and internationally, received the 1977 Obie, Outer Critics Circle, Audelco, and *Mademoiselle* awards, as well as Tony, Grammy, and Emmy nominations.

Between 1976 and 1982, the Public Theater produced numerous of Shange's plays, although none achieved the acclaim or attention that *for colored girls* had garnered. Her nondramatic works published during this period include *Natural Disasters and Other Festive Occasions* (1977), a collection of poetry and prose, *Nappy Edges* (1978), a book of poetry, *Sassafras* (1976), a novella later expanded into the novel *Sassafras, Cypress & Indigo* (1982), and *Liliane: Resurrection of the Daughter* (1995).

Remarried in 1977 to musician David Murray, Shange gave birth to a daughter in 1981 named Savannah Thulani Eloisa. In 1983, she left New York for Houston, where she held academic positions at Rice University and the University of Houston. She continued to publish several volumes of poetry and her autobiographical novel *Betsey Brown*. In 1989, Shange returned east to be nearer the New York art scene.

Shange's "choreopoem," *for colored girls*, combined poetry, drama, dance, and music to create an unconventional, nonlinear artistic form—a series of twenty danced poems performed on stage by seven actresses. Listed in the cast of characters as the Ladies in Brown, Yellow, Red, Green, Purple, Blue, and Orange, the women are distinguished chiefly by the color of their costumes. Out of their shifting portraits of multiple unnamed characters, a collective black female protagonist emerges to claim and celebrate her personhood. For many, performances of *for colored girls* became consciousness-raising events that claimed the relevance of feminism—seen primarily as a political movement of middle-class white women—to black women's lives. Like Zora Neale Hurston's *Their Eyes Were Watching God* and Alice Walker's *The Color Purple*, *for colored girls* was also the subject of controversy in some corners of the black community, criticized for representing abusive relations between black men and women rather than focusing on white men as the true source of black female oppression. Such controversy notwithstanding, *for colored girls* is widely recognized as a landmark text of the black feminist movement.

The opening poem, "dark phrases," promises to "sing a black girl's song" so that she may "know herself." Silenced and circumscribed by a hostile culture, the "black girl" cannot recognize her "infinite beauty" or "her own voice." "song of her possibilities" promises to bring her back to life. Subsequent poems trace scenes from the lives of black women, from a teenager's loss of her virginity in "graduation nite" to women's stormy love affairs with men to date rape and abortion.

The poem "sechita" evokes a carnival dance hall girl who performs for the local "rednecks" in Natchez, Tennessee, an act of humiliation in which "god seemed to be wipin his feet in her face." As the drunken men aim gold coins between her thighs, Sechita (egyptian/goddess of creativity/2nd millennium) manages to transcend her tawdry surroundings. In the light of the full moon, she conjures men and conjures the spirit: "sechita/egypt/goddess/harmony/kicked viciously thru the nite/catching stars tween her toes."

In "toussaint," a young girl finds a real-life adolescent male hero to match the hero she discovered in the adult reading room of the local library—Toussaint L'Ouverture, a black man "who refused to be a slave." In "i used to live in the world," a newcomer to Harlem finds herself in a constricted world where openness is an invitation to violation, "six blocks of cruelty/piled up on itself/a tunnel/closin." In the series of four "no more love poems," the collective protagonist proclaims both her need for intimacy and her desire to be accepted for herself: "ever since i realized there waz someone callt/a colored girl an evil woman a bitch or a nag/i been trying not to be that." One speaker demands: "lemme love you just like i am/a colored girl/i'm finally being real/no longer symmetrical & impervious to pain." One by one, the seven women proclaim their love too "beautiful," too "sanctified," too "magic," too "saturday nite," too "complicated," too "music" to "delicate" to have it "thrown back on my face."

In "somebody almost walked off wid alla my stuff," the speaker, addressing the male lover who fails to recognize and respect her personhood, claims ownership of the "calloused feet," "fried plantains," "pineapple pear juice," "tacky skirts," and "sun-ra" records—the "stuff" that together constitutes her self. In "sorry," the other women respond to the speaker's declaration of selfhood, by mimicking a range of familiar lame apologies that men use to justify their bad behavior and claiming for themselves the right to "do exactly what i want to/& i won't be sorry for none of it."

The penultimate and controversial poem "a nite with beau willie brown" recounts the tragic story of Crystal, whose childhood sweetheart Willie returns from Vietnam "crazy as hell." Plagued by Willie's use of alcohol and drugs and his domestic violence, Crystal obtains a restraining order against him, prohibiting his access to their two children, Naomi and Kwame. In a painfully misguided attempt to reunify the family, Willie breaks down the door to the apartment and dangles his two children out a fifth story window, demanding that Crystal marry him. When she doesn't respond quickly or loudly enough, he drops the children to their deaths.

Out of the wreckage of this tragic poem, the speakers rise again, evoking their own holiness and strength in the face of adversity. The lady in red, who has recited "a nite with beau willie brown," moves with the support of the other women from the recognition of "missin somethin" to the declaration, "I found god in myself/& i loved her/ . . . fiercely." This refrain is taken up by all the women, becoming a "song of joy," dedicated in the play's closing lines to "colored girls who have considered suicide/but are moving to the ends of their own rainbows."

References and Suggested Readings

Shange, Ntozake. *for colored girls who have considered suicide/when the rainbow is enuf: a choreopoem.* New York: Macmillan, 1977.
Smith, Valerie, ed. *African American Writers.* New York: Charles Scribner's Sons, 1991.
Tate, Claudia, ed. *Black Women Writers at Work.* New York: Continuum, 1983.

See also Hurston, Zora Neale; Lorde, Audre; Walker, Alice.

Lisa R. Williams

SHELLEY, MARY

Mary Wollstonecraft Shelley was born in 1797 in London and died there in February 1851. She was the daughter of William Godwin, the political philosopher, whose major work *Enquiry Concerning Political Justice* (1793) espoused anarchy and the moral theory of utilitarianism, and Mary Wollstonecraft, the feminist author of *A Vindication of the Rights of Women* (1792). Wollstonecraft died from complications in childbirth, and though Godwin remarried some four years later, Shelley never experienced the joys of a happy home life. When she was only sixteen, she met the poet Percy Bysshe Shelley, and they became lovers. Soon, she was pregnant, and, with the dissolution of the poet's first marriage, the two married in 1816.

Shelley was early and often acquainted with tragedy. Her first three children died before she was twenty-two; in 1816, her half-sister, Fanny Imlay, committed suicide; and in July of 1822, her husband, Percy Bysshe Shelley, died by drowning. Though she wrote prolifically throughout her life, her most admired work remains *Frankenstein; or, The Modern Prometheus*, published in 1818.

During the summer of 1816, Mary Wollstonecraft and Percy Bysshe Shelley were visiting with Lord Byron and his personal physician, a Mr. Polidori, and the four each decided to write a ghost story. Mary Shelley recounts in her 1831 introduction to the third edition of the book that the story was written during "a wet, ungenial summer," with "incessant rain" confining the group to the house. She cast about for a story that "would speak to the mysterious fears of our nature, and awaken thrilling horror—one to make the reader dread to look round, to curdle the blood, and quicken the beatings of the heart" (171). The genesis of her story is found in conversations between P.B. Shelley and Lord Byron in which "various philosophical doctrines were discussed, and among others the nature of the principle of life, and whether there was any probability of its ever being discovered and communicated" (171). Shelley confesses that she "was a devout but nearly silent listener" (171). Of the four, only she finished a story, and the result,

Frankenstein, is one of the most probing looks into the relationship between the creator and the creation.

Mary Shelley structures her novel in a complicated and somewhat strained nesting of stories and narrators. Robert Walton writes to his sister, Margaret Walton Saville, who, as Susan Wolfson notes, does not coincidently share the initials of Mary Wollstonecraft Shelley, informing her of his arrival in the cold northern streets of Petersburgh were he is preparing to gather a crew of whalers to embark on a northern exploratory expedition (59). Walton boasts of the "inestimable benefit which [he] shall confer on all mankind to the last generation" should he discover a passage "through the seas which surround the pole" (Shelley 8). Walton reminds his sister that he was raised by his uncle after the death of his father, whose "dying injunction" had forbidden him to "embark in a sea-faring life" (8). Though he tries to be a poet, Walton's experience is a disappointment and a failure, so he returns to his first and forbidden calling—the sea. The stilted epistle is clearly a narrative stage for the reader of the novel and not a realistic letter to Walton's own sister. The reminders to his sister of information that she surely knows is perhaps more distracting to the twentieth-century reader than it would have been to nineteenth-century readers steeped in the epistolary tradition.

Walton reports in a second letter that his expeditionary force is shaping up nicely but that he has a deep personal regret in the midst of his professional successes. He confesses that he has no friend to "participate [in his] joy" or to "sustain [him] in dejection" (10).

Nonetheless, Walton is anxious to leave on his journey, where he will go "to unexplored regions, to the 'land of mist and snow'" (11). Not long into their northern exploration, Walton and his shipmates are navigating an extremely close field of ice when they spy an unusual sight—a dog-drawn sledge driven by a man of gigantic stature. The next morning on an ice floe, they find a second man, a European, and not "a savage inhabitant of some undiscovered island" as the first man had seemed to be (13). Walton soon becomes fast friends with the stranger and grows to "love him as a brother" (15). As Walton's ship continues toward the North Pole, the stranger abides with him and gradually unfolds his tale of despair.

Shelley abandons the epistolary structure and substitutes another narrative strategy, the journal, as she begins chapter one with the shipboard stranger's first-person account recorded by Walton. The stranger, Victor Frankenstein, sees in Walton a life not yet blighted and uses his story as a cautionary tale:

> You seek for knowledge and wisdom, as I once did; and I ardently hope that the gratification of your wishes may not be a serpent to sting you, as mine has been. I do not know that the relation of my misfortunes will be useful to you, yet, if you are inclined, listen to my tale. (17)

Walton's hubristic motive in discovering a northern passage places him in a direct parallel with the character Frankenstein, for both long to become known by their exploits. Frankenstein's goal is just as overreaching as Walton's, for he longs to "banish disease from the human frame, and render man invulnerable to any but a violent death" (22).

Victor Frankenstein relates his origins from a respected and well-to-do family of Geneva. His tenderhearted parents readily take in his father's Italian niece, Elizabeth, when her mother dies. She comes to live with the family, and it is decided that one day she and Frankenstein will marry. With his supportive parents, his younger brothers—Ernest and William—and a dear schoolfellow, Henry Clerval, Frankenstein passes his early years.

He gives full devotion to his studies and has an interest in Cornelius Agrippa, a reputed magician; Paracelsus; and then Albertus Magnus, the occultist. His father steers him toward the more appropriate study of natural philosophy, and he continues to flourish under the care of his parents. When Frankenstein is seventeen, his parents decide that he should "become a student at the university of Ingolstadt" (24). Before he can leave, however, Elizabeth contracts scarlet fever, and in nursing Elizabeth, his mother too gets the fever. Elizabeth recovers, but his mother dies. Frankenstein goes off to school, leaving behind his family and dear friend, Henry Clerval. Frankenstein, who "had ever been surrounded by amiable companions," was now alone (26).

Frankenstein's teachers are astonished that he has spent his time studying the old alchemists, and they guide him into a fuller appreciation of contemporary science. Now an avowed acolyte, Frankenstein exclaims,

> None but those who have experienced them can conceive of the enticements of science. In other studies you go as far as others have gone before you, and there is nothing more to know; but in a scientific pursuit there is continual food for discovery and wonder. (29)

He becomes quite a good scientist, earns the respect of his teachers, and becomes obsessed with the question of the origins of life. He undertakes a study of anatomy, and after much study and labor succeeds in "discovering the cause of generation and life" and even becomes "capable of bestowing animation upon lifeless matter" (30). With the hope that "a new species would bless [him] as its creator and source; many happy natures would owe their being to [him]," Frankenstein begins the compilation of his creature (32). But as he nears completion of his eight-foot creature, Frankenstein recoils as "the beauty of the dream vanished, and breathless horror and disgust filled [his] heart" (34). He cannot bear to look on his creature and runs from him, wandering through the night. In the morning, quite by accident, Frankenstein is at an inn where a coach disembarks his friend Henry Clerval. Frankenstein will not tell Henry of his creation but falls ill and Henry cares for him. Certainly there is some measure of irony in Frankenstein's confession that "surely nothing but the unbounded and unremitting attentions of my friend could have restored me to life" (37–38), while he himself is unable or unwilling to provide that same attention to his own creation.

Once Frankenstein is nursed back to health, he and Henry take a walking tour of the environs of Ingoldstadt before returning home to Geneva. Frankenstein's renewed spirits are short-lived, however, as he receives a letter from his father informing him of the murder of his youngest brother, William. Frankenstein returns to Geneva but arrives too late to get inside the city doors and wanders during the night. In a flash of lightning, he sees an object, the "gigantic stature, and the deformity of its aspect, more hideous than belongs to humanity, instantly informed me that it was the wretch, the filthy daemon to whom I had given life" (48). It has been two years since Frankenstein has seen his creation, but he instinctively knows that the monster has killed his brother. Nonetheless, in an act of cowardice, he allows a young servant girl, Justine, to stand trial for the murder. Though Justine is innocent, her priest forces her into a confession, the court finds her guilty, and she is condemned to death.

In Volume Two of the novel, Frankenstein languishes in the knowledge that he, "not in deed, but in effect, was the true murderer" (61). His father is concerned over his mental anguish and exhorts him to travel to Mont Blanc for diversion and relief. There in the mountains, Frankenstein meets his creature, and greets him with inhospitable language, "Devil! Do you dare approach me? Begone, vile insect! or rather stay, that I may trample you to dust!" (65). The creature begs Frankenstein to do his duty as Creator or be subject to this threat:

> You purpose to kill me. How dare you sport thus with life? Do your duty towards me, and I will do mine towards you and the rest of mankind. If you will comply with my conditions, I will leave them and you at peace; but if you refuse, I will glut the maw of death, until it be satiated with the blood of your remaining friends. (65)

Though Frankenstein responds to the threat with violence, the creature returns with rational discourse and implores Frankenstein to "Remember, that I am thy creature: I ought to be thy Adam; but am rather the fallen angel. . . . Make me happy, and I shall again be virtuous" (66). What follows is another narrative nesting as the creature tells his story to Frankenstein.

For the first time, Frankenstein "felt what the duties of a creator towards his creature were" and listened to his tale (67). The creature describes his coming to awareness—he is first a creature of feeling and not thought, and tries to "express my sensations in my own mode, but the uncouth and inarticulate sounds which broke from me frightened me into silence again" (69). He finds a fire left by someone and delights in the warmth but burns his hands before learning to tend the fire. He also learns to gather foods and support himself. Though he still longs for companionship, his appearance frightens people, and he is once attacked by a whole village. The creature retreats to a hovel adjoining a cottage, seeking shelter from "the inclemency of the season, and still more from the barbarity of man" (71). There, peering in on the family that lives in the cottage, he receives his education. He experiences emotions, "sensations of a peculiar and overpowering nature: they were a mixture of pain and pleasure" (72). He comes to understand that the family suffers from poverty; he learns the relationship of the people and of their method of communication and begins to learn a few words. He spends the winter there in secrecy, sleeping during the day and observing the cottagers; then during the night and early morning hours, he performs chores for them—clearing their path of snow or carrying in wood for them. He hears their praise for the person who had performed such acts and is lured into the hope that they will not turn from him in fright when he reveals himself to them.

The unwitting source of the creature's education is the DeLacey family, recent immigrants who have suffered cruelly for their acts of generosity toward a family in danger. The father, his son, and daughter were imprisoned for five months before a trial in which they were exiled from France and deprived of their fortune. They now live in Germany where the essential Exile sits beyond their walls. Before he reveals himself to them and is cast out, he receives a considerable education as the children read such works as *Paradise Lost*, *Plutarch's Lives*, and *Sorrows of Werther* to their blind father. When the creature hears the story of *Paradise Lost*, he identifies first with Adam but then more fully with Satan, "for often, like him, when I viewed the bliss of my protectors, the bitter gall of envy rose within me" (87).

The creature learns to read and write, and finds Frankenstein's journal in the pocket of the clothes that he took from Frankenstein's room as he ran away into the night. From the notes, he more fully realizes how detestable his creator finds him. The double rejection, by his creator and by the DeLacey family, causes him to declare "everlasting war against the species, and more than all, against him who had formed me, and sent me forth to this insupportable misery" (92).

The creature requests of Victor Frankenstein that he build him a companion "of the same species" and with his "same defects" (97). Frankenstein immediately refuses, and the creature, though inclined to anger, emphasizes that he is willing to reason with Frankenstein. Frankenstein reluctantly consents once the creature pledges he and his companion will leave Europe and never be seen again. Frankenstein is noticeably shaken by the encounter with the creature, and though he has made a conciliatory gesture toward him, Frankenstein remains fixed in his physical and emotional abandonment of his creation.

As Frankenstein works on the companion for the creature, he begins to imagine any of several outcomes of his next creation. He grows aware that the first creature had promised not to threaten humans anymore but that the next creature had made no such promise. What he was creating was a sentient being, "she, who in all probability was to become a thinking and reasoning animal, might refuse to comply with a compact made before her creation" (114). He even imagines that they might hate each other or be repulsed by the other's deformity. He fears that they would have children, that "a race of devils would be propagated upon the earth" for which his actions would be responsible. Frankenstein asks, "Had I a right, for my own benefit, to inflict this curse upon everlasting generations?" (113). The questions that he proposes to himself reveal his initial lack of foresight and his abnegation of his duties as creator.

As Frankenstein is equivocating, the creature appears at his window, and Frankenstein responds by destroying the creature he is making. The creature acknowledges what Frankenstein has feared all along, "You are my creator, but I am your master;—obey!" (116). They have a heated discussion and the monster leaves with this threat, "It is well. I go; but remember, I shall be with you on your wedding-night" (116).

Meanwhile, Clerval has been murdered, and Frankenstein is arrested for the crime. As is characteristic of Frankenstein when he is confronted with disturbing situations, he falls into an illness. He "lay for two months on the point of death" (122) and languishes in prison for three months. A trial reveals that he is not guilty and he is released. During his illness, though, Frankenstein cried out in his sleep that he is guilty for the deaths of William, Justine, and Henry, but his father imagines that he is in a delirium. His cousin Elizabeth sends a letter affirming her love for him but releasing him from the promise of marriage should he so choose. He writes back to Elilzabeth and promises to tell his great secret the day after they are married.

On their wedding night, Frankenstein is worried that the creature will come for him and asks Elizabeth to go on to her room while he waits; when he hears a scream and runs to her room he finds that she has been killed. He returns to Geneva, and his father dies, "under the horrors that were accumulated around him" (137).

Frankenstein vows to pursue the creature until one or the other dies and calls on the "spirits of the dead" and the "wandering ministers of vengeance, to aid and conduct" his work (140).

Shelley closes the frame of the novel as the dying Frankenstein completes his tale to Walton who writes the story to his sister Margaret. Walton laments the loss of his newfound friend, Frankenstein, and nearly commits himself to the monomaniacal search for the creature in his stead, but his sailors threaten to mutiny if he does not promise to sail southward once the ice breaks. Frankenstein realizes that Walton is not unlike him in his potentially destructive ambition and leaves him with these last words before dying, "Seek happiness in tranquility, and avoid ambition, even if it be only the apparently innocent one of distinguishing yourself in science and discoveries" (152).

When Walton returns to Frankenstein's deathbed the next morning, he finds the creature standing over him, exclaiming, "Oh, Frankenstein! generous and self-devoted being! what does it avail that I now ask thee to pardon me? I, who irretrievable destroyed thee by destroying all thou lovedst" (153). The creature confesses his story to Walton and vows that he will kill no more, having no more reason. He will flee to the frozen north, build his funeral pyre, and "consume to ashes this miserable frame" (155). He believes that in his atonement, his "spirit will sleep in peace" (156). The creature then jumps from the cabin window and is "lost in darkness and distance" (156).

Beyond its continued attraction as a gothic science fiction story, *Frankenstein* offers much interpretative ground for feminist criticism. Barbara Johnson suggests that though the story centers on male figures, the novel is ultimately about female authorship, as demonstrated by the "story of a man who usurps the female role by physically giving birth to a child" (248). Susan Wolfson notes that "Elizabeth has no function that is not directed toward her male companions" (55), and Paula Feldman wonders if the tale isn't a metaphor for Mary Shelley's own conflicted views about motherhood (75). Doubtless, *Frankenstein* will provide rich discussions for feminists for some time to come.

References and Suggested Readings

Feldman, Paula R. "Probing the Psychological Mystery of Frankenstein." *Approaches to Teaching Shelley's Frankenstein.* Ed. Stephen C. Behrendt. New York: MLA, 1990.

Johnson, Barbara. "My Monster/My Self." *Frankenstein.* By Mary Shelley. Ed. J. Paul Hunter. New York: Norton, 1996. 241–51.

Ray, Anne-Marie. "Mary Wollstonecraft Shelley." *An Encyclopedia of British Women Writers.* Ed. Paul Schlueter and June Schlueter. Revised and Expanded ed. New Brunswick, NJ: Rutgers University Press, 1998.

Shelley, Mary. *Frankenstein.* Ed. J. Paul Hunter. New York: Norton, 1996.

———. "Introduction to *Frankenstein*, Third Edition (1831)." *Frankenstein.* Ed. J. Paul Hunter. New York: Norton, 1996.

Wolfson, Susan J. "Feminist Inquiry and *Frankenstein.*" *Approaches to Teaching Shelley's Frankenstein.* Ed. Stephen C. Behrendt. New York: MLA, 1990.

See also Wollstonecraft, Mary.

SILENCE AND VOICE

In its most general sense, voice can be defined as the reward for successfully battling oppressive systems that enforce silence, or it may represent the very means by which the battle was fought. White women, for example, often argue that to attain voice, they must free themselves from the constraints of patriarchy, and many have done so through the written word. As feminism has become more self-conscious in its ethnocentrism, however, women of color have complicated this definition by pointing out that no single woman's voice exists—and that minority women have often been silenced by the very movements credited with giving them voice. As a result, the binaries of silence and voice become ever more problematic, and women find that these terms apply both inside and outside of feminism. In other words, as Lugones and Spelman explain, "the concept of the woman's voice is itself a theoretical concept, in the sense that it presupposes a theory according to which our identities as human beings are actually compound identities, a kind of fusion or confusion of our otherwise separate identities as women or men, as Black or brown or white, etc."

Thumbnail sketches of women's progress point readers to the most overt ways in which women have won at least partial battles against the forces that would silence them: the right to vote, the right to own property, the right to earn equal wages; and, more generally, women's expanded control over marriage, education, and reproduction. These issues dismiss imbalances of power within the category of *woman*, though, and they also silence the various ways in which other issues, such as race, ability, class, religion, and gender, intersect with sex. For all women to have voice, then, much more is needed than access to the vote and a room of one's own: Women in greater positions of power need to acknowledge their privilege and the ways in which they have used that privilege to silence others. But simply asking a woman of less privilege to discuss the commonality of womanhood does not qualify as an invitation to speak. Lugones and Spelman note that

> [i]ndeed, many Hispanas, Black women, Jewish women—to name a few groups— have felt it an invitation to silence rather than speech to be requested—if they are requested at all—to speak about being "women" (with the plain wrapper—as if there were one) in distinction from speaking about being Hispana, Black, Jewish, working-class, etc., women. (19)

And bell hooks agrees:

> Again and again, black women find our efforts to speak, to break silence and engage in radical progressive political debates, opposed. There is a link between the silencing we experience, the censoring, the anti-intellectualism in predominantly black settings that are supposedly supportive . . . and that silencing that takes place in institutions wherein black women and women of color are told that we cannot be fully heard or listened to because our work is not theoretical enough. (32)

The binary of silence and voice, then, does not necessarily point one to patriarchal control. It also points to oppressions within the feminist movement itself that need to be addressed if the both terms are to be defined fully.

References and Suggested Readings

hooks, bell. "Theory as Liberatory Practice." *Feminist Theory: A Reader*. Ed. Wendy Kolmar and Frances Bartkowski. London: Mayfield, 2000. 28–33.
Lugones, Maria C., and Elizabeth V. Spelman. "Have We Got a Theory for You! Feminist Theory, Cultural Imperialism and the Demand for 'The Woman's Voice.'" *Feminist Theory: A Reader*. Ed. Wendy Kolmar and Frances Bartkowski. London: Mayfield, 2000. 17–27.

See also hooks, bell.

SPIRITUALITY

The biblical book of Genesis describes man as being made in God's image and provides him with "dominion over the fish of the sea, and over the fowl of the air, and over the cattle, and over all the earth, and over every creeping thing that creepeth upon the earth." When woman was created, however, she was fashioned after man as well as after God; her body was created literally from that of the man. Based on this story of bodily origin as well as on woman's biblical role as the temptress, woman has been made subservient to her male counterpart. This role has in many ways dictated the moral, legal, and personal relationships between women and men.

Recognizing and disagreeing with this pattern, Elizabeth Cady Stanton pointed out in 1895 that

> [t]he Bible teaches that woman brought sin and death into the world, that she precipitated the fall of the race, that she was arraigned before the judgment seat of Heaven, tried, condemned, and sentenced. Marriage for her was to be a condition of bondage, maternity a period of suffering and anguish, and in silence and subjection, she was to play the role of a dependent on man's bounty for all her material wants, and for all information she might desire on the vital questions of the hour, she was commanded to ask her husband at home. Here is the Bible position of women briefly summed up. Consequently, when women questioned their subjugation in any area of life, "they were referred to the Bible for an answer." (95–97)

In response to this exclusion, many women have turned to alternative spiritualities, a tendency that became apparent in the nineteenth century and is described in depth in Braude's *Radical Spirits: Spiritualism and Women's Rights in Nineteenth-Century America* (1989). Other women, still invested in more traditional forms of religion, did what Stanton did: They worked to reform Christianity rather than abandoning it altogether. Stanton penned a "Woman's Bible" in which she proposed alternatives, such as "an ideal Heavenly Mother" as well as Father. She also argued that, while man was given dominion over every living creature, he was not specifically given dominion over women, so that "[n]o lesson of woman's subjection can be fairly drawn from the first chapter of the Old Testament" (97).

Some women began by taking up Stanton's critical position and then moved to far more radical positions later in their lives. Mary Daly, for example, at first criticized the Catholic Church for its patriarchal center and then eventually proposed an entirely separate alternative to Catholicism. Cathy Davidson, in her survey of women's spirituality, points out that women from a variety of ethnic and religious heritages have proposed revised interpretations of their religions and cites authors such as E.M. Broner and Karla F.C. Holloway for their considerations of Jewish and African American traditions, respectively.

Paula Gunn Allen, a Laguna/Pueblo scholar and teacher, notes that many non-Western cultures rely less on a patriarchal system and so are less subject to these concerns. In talking about the nonhierarchical relationship between all living things ascribed by many Native groups, she quotes a Keres song:

> I add my breath to your breath
> That our days may be long on the Earth
> That the days of our people may be long
> That we may be one person
> That we may finish our roads together
> May our mother bless you with life
> May our life paths be fulfilled. (56)

Gunn Allen summarizes, "Christians believe that God is separate from humanity and does as he wishes without the creative assistance of any of his creatures, while the non-Christian tribal person assumes a place in creation that is dynamic, creative, and responsive" (56–57). And Alice Walker also points to the tenuous relationship between a patriarchal religion and a feminist (and even more particularly, a feminist of color): "In day-to-day life, I worship the Earth as God—representing everything—and Nature as its spirit. But for a long time I was confused. After all, when someone you trust shows you a picture of a blond, blue-eyed Christ and tells you he's the son of God, you get an instant image of his father: an older version of him" (9).

Patriarchal religions still wield a tremendous amount of power, as evidenced by the contemporary battle between gay and lesbian people and the more conservative churches. The arguments surrounding this issue are markedly similar to those surrounding the split between feminism and traditional spiritualities. Alice Walker's response in many ways summarizes the call made both by feminist and gay/lesbian reformers when she recommends a "decolonizing" of the spirit—that is, a departure from ways of being that oppress specific groups of people.

References and Suggested Readings

Davidson, Cathy N. "Spirituality." *The Oxford Companion to Women's Writing in the United States*. Ed. Cathy N. Davidson and Linda Wagner-Martin. New York: Oxford University Press, 1995. 838–40.

Gunn Allen, Paula. *The Sacred Hoop: Recovering the Feminine in American Indian Traditions*. Boston: Beacon Press, 1986.

Stanton, Elizabeth Cady. "From the Woman's Bible." *Feminist Theory: A Reader*. Ed. Wendy Kolmar and Frances Bartkowski. London: Mayfield Publishing Company, 2000. 95–97.

Walker, Alice. *Anything We Love Can Be Saved*. New York: Random House, 1997.

See also Walker, Alice.

Lisa R. Williams

STEFAN, VERENA

Author of the international feminist literary classic *Shedding* (1975), Swiss-born feminist writer and activist Verena Stefan is best known for this groundbreaking novella, which traces a young woman's transformation from heterosexual dependency to lesbianism as a political expression of female independence. One of the first literary works to emerge out of the German women's movement of the 1970s, *Shedding* experimented with writing as a form of feminist activism and helped inspire the development of a new genre of women's literature.

Born in Switzerland in 1947 to a Swiss mother and Sudeten German father, Stefan left her hometown of Bern in 1968 for West Berlin. Trained as a physical therapist, she cofounded the feminist women's health group Bread + Roses in the early 1970s. The collective wrote and published a health manual for women. Inspired by her work with the group, Stefan wrote and independently published *Shedding*, an autobiographically based fictional work that is usually described as a female bildungsroman. Based on word-of-mouth rather than commercial publicity, the book has sold more than 300,000 copies in Germany and has been translated into eight languages.

Shortly after the publication of *Shedding*, Stefan left Berlin to live in the countryside in southern Germany for the next eighteen years. The influences of ecofeminism and her experiences in rural living inform her volume of eight stories titled *Literally Dreaming* (1987), available together with *Shedding* in an English translation published by the Feminist Press in 1994. Together with Gabriele Meixner, Stefan has also translated into German Adrienne Rich's *Dream of a Common Language* and Monique Wittig and Sande Zeig's *Brouillon pour un dictionnaire des amantes*. Currently, she lives in Munich.

Shedding became a touchstone text of the German women's movement of the 1970s and an international literary classic. Combining feminist polemic with poetic lyricism, the book criticizes the 1970s German Left for its failure to theorize the sexual oppression of women and its insistence on viewing sexism as secondary to class and racial oppression. Focusing on sexuality as the primary location of women's oppression, *Shedding* traces the transformation of its first-person female narrator from her debilitating dependency on men to lesbianism as an expression of female liberation and independence. Stefan's linguistic experimentation in the original German—dividing words and refusing to capitalize nouns—also represents an important attempt to create a nonpatriarchal language capable of expressing a uniquely feminine aesthetic.

In "Shadow Skin," the first of the novella's four chapters, the protagonist notices the arrival of spring in Berlin, marked by a "cascade of greening birches." The sensual aliveness she experiences through nature is contrasted with her vulnerability to sexual violation in the street, as two men at a sidewalk café harass her with the words "Jesus, what knockers!" Enraged but helpless to react, the narrator goes home, feeling her breasts "hang against my ribcage, warm, sun-filled gourds," a naturalistic image that looks ahead to her empowerment in the final chapter, "Gourd Woman." The narrator describes various experiences with heterosexuality, characterized either as dependency or as sexual violation: "Men's glances assault me, claw their way into the creases of my jeans between my legs as I descend the stairs to the subway. Whistles and clacking tongues cling to me. In the evening all the bruisings of the day under the shower under the skin. Cars slowing down, windows rolled down, skid marks. A lone woman, still an alien, and still up for grabs." Gradually, the narrator begins to resist what she views as the "colonization" of her body. She longs to shed her scarred skin. Increasingly dissatisfied with her relationship to her lover Samuel, she becomes involved with a women's group called Bread + Roses and develops an intimacy with a married woman named Nadjenka. She wonders what would happen if "women broke free of men" and decides to experiment with living alone, without sexuality or a steady relationship with one person.

In "Withdrawal Symptoms," the narrator begins her experimental life, moving into an apartment with three women, each of whom has "shed her former life with a man." She begins to "lead a different life, speak another language." She characterizes her separation from Samuel and her life as one-half of a couple as "cutting the umbilical cord," "shedding the old skin," and going "through a period of withdrawal." She begins to develop an intimacy with a woman artist named Fenna, and the two women set about trying to imagine or create new forms of eroticism that don't just imitate old heterosexual patterns.

"State of Emergency" begins with a lengthy and didactic conversation/debate between the narrator and another woman concerning the politics of heterosexuality versus lesbianism. Meanwhile, the narrator continues to explore the "unmapped territory" of lesbian sexuality with Fenna: "Our intimacies were circumspect. In the time it took for us to exchange a single kiss, I would in the past have already had intercourse and found myself standing there fully clothed and ready to depart." She begins "to see myself for what I really am," "to assemble the separate parts to make one whole body."

In "Gourd Woman," the protagonist has learned to love herself and her body, including the breasts that were the focus of her sexual violation in the opening chapter. In the bathroom mirror, "two soft pale brown gourds nodded toward the basin." The narrator pronounces this "the year of the gourd woman!" Bearing the traces of the old skins she has shed, she "walks giggling through the streets," mouthing the words: "I am my own woman." *Shedding* ends on an ironic note that celebrates the narrator's newfound self-empowerment: "People turn and stare. To think that nowadays even young women have started talking to themselves!"

References and Suggested Readings

Kester-Shelton, Pamela, ed. *Feminist Writers.* Detroit: St. James, 1996.

Levin, Tobe. "Afterword." *Shedding and Literally Dreaming.* By Verena Stefan. New York: Feminist Press, 1994.

Stefan, Verena. *Shedding.* 1975. New York: Feminist Press, 1994.

See also Wittig, Monique.

STOWE, HARRIET BEECHER

Purportedly acknowledged by President Lincoln as the "the little woman who wrote the book that started this great war," Harriet Beecher Stowe was born in 1811 into a family that situated her for such an accomplishment. The intellectual and progressive family of Litchfield, Connecticut, was headed by the famed Congregationalist preacher and revivalist Lyman Beecher. Harriet's older sister and surrogate mother, Catherine—after the early death of Roxana Foote Beecher—was an educator and feminist who founded the Hartford Female Seminary and later the Western Female Institute in Cincinnati. Harriet's closest brother Henry Ward Beecher was also a renowned preacher, orator, and a supporter of women's suffrage and abolitionism. Harriet herself authored the best-selling novel of the nineteenth century, *Uncle Tom's Cabin*.

Her family moved from Connecticut to Cincinnati, Ohio, where her father accepted the presidency of Lane Theological Seminary in 1832. In 1836, Harriet married Calvin E. Stowe, a professor at Lane Seminary. With the widowed and childless Stowe, Harriet had seven children. In Cincinnati, just across the river from slaveholding Kentucky, Beecher Stowe's antislavery sentiments deepened. In addition to her intellectual apprehension of the issues of slavery, Beecher Stowe's understanding of the physical separations of the institution were heightened by the loss of her own favored child, Charley, to cholera in 1849 when he was only eighteen months old. Stowe's moral argument against slavery is augmented by the raw grief seen in such passages as this one from *Uncle Tom's Cabin*:

> And oh! Mother that reads this, has there never been your house a drawer, or a closet, the opening of which has been to you like the opening again of a little grave? Ah! happy mother that you are if it has not been so. (75)

When she began to write sketches for various magazines, including *Godey's Lady's Book*, Beecher Stowe complained to her husband, "If I am to write, I must have a room to myself, which shall be *my* room." Expressing such an opinion, she predates Virginia Woolf's longing for a *room of one's own* by nearly a century. Beecher Stowe's massive output of work is best remembered by *Uncle Tom's Cabin* (1852) but also includes such notable works as *A Key to Uncle Tom's Cabin: Presenting the Original Facts and Documents upon which the Story is Founded* (1853); *Dred: A Tale of the Great Dismal Swamp* (1856); *The Minister's Wooing* (1859); *The Pearl of Orr's Island: A Story of the Coast of Maine* (1862); *Pink and White Tyranny: A Society Novel* (1871); and *Palmetto-Leaves* (1873).

Stowe's reputation continues to rest on *Uncle Tom's Cabin*, but the novel is no longer simply viewed as an exemplar of sentimental and regional fiction. Since the recovery movement of feminist literature, Stowe has been reconsidered in light of her proactive stance against two of the most entrenched ideologies of her time: patriarchy and slavery.

After having no small part in quickening a nation to the immorality and trauma of slavery, Stowe died in her sleep in 1896.

Stowe's *Uncle Tom's Cabin* opens in Kentucky on the Shelby farm where the principle character, Uncle Tom, is enslaved under a tolerant but financially haphazard master who soon must sell him because of his own debts. In another of the multiple layers of irony surrounding the slave question in America, the word of honor of a Southern gentleman must be upheld to the lowest of slave traders of his own race but need not be upheld in social relations with blacks. Shelby's promise to Tom that he will never be sold to another master is quickly abrogated when he has gambling debts that must be paid to the unsavory Mr. Haley. For Mr. Shelby, custom, more than doctrine, dictates his morality, and he hides his culpability in the excuse of common practice. He complains to his disapproving wife, "I don't know why I am to be rated, as if I were a monster, for doing what every one does every day" (28).

In the Shelby household also resides the beautiful Eliza, a "petted and indulged favorite" (9) of Mrs. Shelby. Married to George Harris, enslaved on a neighboring plantation, the handsome couple has lost two infant children before the birth of their child Harry. When Mr. Haley comes to receive his property (Uncle Tom) from Mr. Shelby, he spies the young Harry and requests that he be included in the deal.

Meanwhile, George Harris, sorely mistreated by his master, is burning to flee to Canada and earn the money to buy his wife and child from slavery. When Eliza hears that Mr. Haley has bought Harry, she too decides to flee and take her son to safety. Because both Eliza and her son are "so white as not to be known as of colored lineage, without a critical survey" (45), they are able to make some progress in their flight to the Ohio River. Once there, though, the broken ice floes present an obstacle that Eliza must overcome, and, in doing so, Stowe presents the reader with perhaps the most dramatic and remembered scene in all of American literature: Eliza jumps into the river and maneuvers from floe to floe as she makes her way across the Ohio. In presenting Eliza as a mother willing to make any sacrifice to save her child, Stowe creates a rhetorical situation that resonates with the staunch maternal morality of her New England readers.

As Tom is taken away, Mrs. Shelby promises to keep track of him and to do her best to see that he is brought again to Kentucky and to his wife and children. On the boat on which Tom is shipped downriver are the young Evangeline St. Clare and her restless father. When Evangeline (Eva) falls into the water, Tom rescues her and she insists that her father buy Tom. A sincere bond grows between the little girl and Uncle Tom, and they pass many an hour engaged in reading the Bible.

Stowe uses the narrative shift to the Deep South to emphasize her political purposes in writing the text. In addition to the saintly Eva who questions the morality of slavery, there is her father who, having been raised in the web of the "peculiar institution," abhors it but feels paralyzed to challenge it. His wife, Marie, on the other hand, believes in the absolute inferiority of the slave and insists "there's no way with servants but to *put them down*, and keep them down" (149). St. Clare's cousin, Miss Ophelia, has come to the South from Vermont to help with the household for a time, and she provides a Christian and abolitionist self-righteousness that is initially tainted with an undercurrent of loathing for black people. The interplay of these four characters offers the reader a view of several prominent historical perspectives on the slave question.

Meanwhile, as the years pass, Eva weakens with consumption. Always a kind and thoughtful child, she grows increasingly pure in thought and desirous of freedom for the enslaved people on their plantation. She questions her calloused mother on why the slaves are not taught to read, only to be cut short by her sarcasm. Eva nonetheless expresses a wish to free the slaves, move them to free territory, and teach them to read and write. Her wishes do not come to fruition though before she dies.

Eva's influence lives past her life, and her father acts on her urgings to lead a more introspective life and to read the Bible. St. Clare and Tom engage in lengthy discussions about the condition of St. Clare's soul, and St. Clare comes to the place where he begins the legal process of Tom's manumission. Soon after, St. Clare suffers a fatal stabbing wound as he tries to separate two drunken fighters in a local social club. As he dies, he confesses his faith in God, but he leaves unfinished the emancipation of Tom and his other enslaved persons.

Tom and the other enslaved persons on the St. Clare plantation are sent to the slave warehouse where Tom is bought by the evil Simon Legree. Little wonder that the name Simon Legree has imprinted itself on the cultural consciousness of Americans who have never even read *Uncle Tom's Cabin*, for he is truly a harsh master. His rule of practice is to treat his servants like commodities and to use them as hard as he can. He says, "When one nigger's dead, I buy another; and I find it comes cheaper and easier, every way" (294). All evidence on the plantation seems to support the rumor that he freely kills any slave who dares defy him or tries to flee.

When Tom helps fill the cotton basket of another picker who is struggling in the field, he is punished. Legree further decides that Tom himself will administer a beating to the young woman. Tom refuses and is severely beaten. As he lies in utter pain and despair, he is visited by a young woman, Cassy, who provides water for him and warns him of Legree's depravity and unchecked lawlessness. She tells Tom, "Here you are, on a lone plantation, ten miles from any other, in the swamps; not a white person here, who could testify, if you were burned alive. . . . There's no law here, of God or man" (312).

But Legree does have an Achilles heel: He is haunted by his mother's dying desire that he repent of his evil ways and turn to "his soul's eternal good" (323). When Legree has Tom beaten, his servants bring him a locket with a curl of hair given to Tom by the dying Eva; the hair, so reminiscent of Legree's mother's lock of hair given to him at her death, pierces him with consuming fear. Though his heart is not open to the call of repentance, it is susceptible to the irrational fears of phantoms and ghostly reprisals.

Cassy realizes that Legree's weakness offers her an opportunity for escape. Above Legree's home is an attic never used, and she realizes that she could create a false diversion of escape and then hide in the attic with impunity. Whatever noise she might make would only confirm Legree's notion of "haunts."

Legree continues to find opportunities to taunt Tom's faith and to press him into more and more brutal physical service. Though Cassy suggests that Legree might be killed easily enough when he is in a drunken state, Tom will have no part of murder. Finding no help with her plan for dispensing of Legree, Cassy carries out her plan of escape, taking with her Emmeline, a young girl now being sexually used by Legree. When Tom refuses to tell Legree what he knows of the whereabouts of the two women, Legree beats him unmercifully.

Soon after Tom's beating, young George Shelby from Kentucky finally arrives at Legree's place, having finally fulfilled his mother's promise that they will keep track of him and buy him back. He watches as Tom utters his last words of forgiveness and joy at the prospect of Heaven. As Tom dies, George vows to "do *what one man can* to drive out this curse of slavery from [the] land" (365).

Cassy and Emmeline leave the Legree attic as "two white figures gliding down the avenue towards the high-road" (367) and impersonate a Creole lady with her servant. They board the same boat north that George Shelby is on, and George is "troubled with one of those fleeting and indefinite likenesses" (368) when he sees Cassy. She grows uneasy at his interest and decides to throw herself on his mercy and reveal her story. Another woman on board, Madame de Thoux, also strikes up a conversation with George and learns of the fate of her brother long separated from her. As the threads of the story are pulled into place, the reader learns that Cassy is the mother of Eliza, who was so long ago torn from her. Madame de Thoux is the sister of George Harris, Eliza's husband. All have a joyous reunion safely in Canada, where George and Eliza have lived for five years, finally free. Soon after the reunion, George Harris and his reunited family travel to Africa where they start a new life in Liberia.

It remains to George Shelby to reveal to Uncle Tom's wife that he did not survive being sold downriver. But true to his word, George does arrange for the emancipation of all of the enslaved persons on his plantation. And so the story of Uncle Tom ends with his pious life and tragic death serving as the catalyst for the reformation and freedom of many souls.

References and Suggested Readings

MacFarlane, Lisa Watt. "Stowe, Harriet Beecher." *The Oxford Companion to Women's Writing*. Ed. Cathy N. Davidson and Linda Wagner-Martin. New York: Oxford University Press, 1995. 856–58.

Ryan, Barbara. "Harriet Beecher Stowe." *Dictionary of Literary Biography, Volume 243: The American Renaissance in New England, Fourth Series*. Ed. Wesley T. Mott. The Gale Group, 2001. 303–19.

Stowe, Harriet Beecher. *Uncle Tom's Cabin*. 1852. New York: W. W. Norton, 1994.

See also Gilman, Charlotte Perkins; Jacobs, Harriet Ann; Sentimentalism.

SUFFRAGE

In spite of the criticism aimed at such categorizations, the phrase "first wave feminism" generally refers to women suffragists' efforts to get the vote, a task they achieved in 1920. This movement hinged on the belief that women's oppression took root in the denial of access to certain rights and representations, a philosophy often referred to as liberal feminism.

Elizabeth Cady Stanton, a leading figure in the suffragist movement, hardly seemed a candidate for the propagation of a "liberal" ideology. She was born into an extremely conservative family, and as a female child, she was reminded constantly that male children were preferable. Even so, Stanton, along with Lucretia Mott, led the fight for women's suffrage and, at the Seneca Falls Convention wrote the "Declaration of Sentiments." The introduction to the Declaration explained the justification for such a text:

> When, in the course of human events, it becomes necessary for one portion of the family of man to assume among the people of the earth a position different from that which they have hitherto occupied, but one to which the laws of nature and of nature's God entitle them, a decent respect to the opinions of mankind requires that they should declare the causes that impel them to such a course. (2035)

These "causes" included some fifteen indictments of men, beginning with "He has never permitted her to exercise her inalienable right to the elective franchise" (2035) and ending with "He has endeavored, in every way that he could, to destroy her confidence in her own powers, to lessen her self-respect, and to make her willing to lead a dependent and abject life" (2036).

Suffragists' assertions hinged on a belief in women's rights as natural and God-given, which directly paralleled many of the abolitionist arguments of the same period. As a result, women began to fight for universal suffrage and founded the American Equal Rights Association. At its first annual meeting in 1881, Sojourner Truth spoke of the Fifteenth Amendment, which had granted African American men the right to vote in 1870. Her words hinted at what many women saw as the injustice of a sexist extension of suffrage: "Now colored men have the right to vote. There ought to be equal rights now more than ever, since colored people have got their freedom" (2052). Her words hinted too at the emerging division between abolitionist and feminist philosophies, and the two thereafter became more self-consciously distinct. This division forced many African American women to choose one movement over the other—an enforced split identity for which even contemporary mainstream feminism is criticized.

Fractures began to appear in the leadership of the suffrage movement as well, and eventually, an antisuffragist movement emerged in response to such disagreement. A number of organizations were developed in order to accommodate women's differing priorities: One encouraged black women to pursue the vote; another endeavored to link working- and middle-class women; yet another relied on images of women as domestic workers in order to emphasize the centrality of women's roles. These differing emphases disseminated the group's power and made it vulnerable to attacks from antisuffragists, who thought women, as mere homemakers, incapable of managing the right to vote. Nonetheless, after more than seventy years of struggle, women finally gained the right to vote in 1920 through the Nineteenth Amendment. The longevity and difficulty of this battle had been predicted by Stanton in 1898; she foresaw that there would be "no small amount of misconception, misrepresentation, and ridicule," but she also knew well that this undertaking was a way of addressing women's feelings of being "aggrieved, oppressed, and fraudulently deprived of their most sacred rights" (2036).

References and Suggested Readings

Borish, Linda J. "Suffrage Movement." *The Oxford Companion to Women's Writing in the United States*. Ed. Cathy N. Davidson and Linda Wagner-Martin. New York: Oxford University Press, 1995. 860–62.

Stanton, Elizabeth Cady. "Declaration of Sentiments." *The Heath Anthology of American Literature*. Ed. Paul Lauter. Boston: Houghton Mifflin, 1998. 2035–37.

Truth, Sojourner. "Address to the First Annual Meeting of the American Equal Rights Association." *The Heath Anthology of American Literature*. Ed. Paul Lauter. Boston: Houghton Mifflin, 1998. 2051–52.

Lisa R. Williams

T

TAN, AMY

Born in 1952 in Oakland, California, Amy Tan is a Chinese American novelist, and the tensions surrounding her split/doubled identity occupy a large place in her fiction. She earned a BA degree from San Jose State University in 1973, an MA degree in linguistics in 1974, and went on to do postgraduate work at the University of California, Berkeley, from 1974 until 1976. She worked as a freelance technical writer before she moved to short stories and, finally, her first novel, the award-winning *The Joy Luck Club* in 1989. Her startling success with *The Joy Luck Club* was almost immediately followed by *The Kitchen God's Wife* in 1991. In 1993, Tan coauthored the screen play for the film version of *The Joy Luck Club*, and in 1995, her third novel, *The Hundred Secret Senses*, was published. She has written two children's books, both illustrated by Gretchen Schields, *The Moon Lady* (1992) and *The Chinese Siamese Cat* (1994). In 2001, Tan published another novel centered on the theme of generational conflicts, *The Bonesetter's Daughter*. In 2003, Tan's first nonfiction work, *The Opposite of Fate: A Book of Musings*, met with an audience eager to see the woman behind the fiction. Tan has found a consistent and appreciative audience both in popular and critical circles, and though her first two novels have become standard fare in many college courses, it is *The Joy Luck Club* that has garnered the larger audience. Tan came upon the strategy for *The Joy Luck Club* in 1985 when she read Louise Erdrich's *Love Medicine* and recognized that her pattern of multiple voices and tangled narrative would be well suited to her own cross-generational saga.

Tan comments freely on the position in which she is often placed—that of a representative for Chinese culture. The role is "an onerous burden. . . . There's also a danger in balkanizing literature, as if it should be read as sociology, or politics." She further comments that she does not write "about cultural dichotomies, but about human connections. All of us go through angst and identity crises. And even when you write in a specific context, you still tap into that subtext of emotions that we all feel about love and hope, and mothers and obligations and responsibilities."

The Joy Luck Club is such a book about "human connections," about "love and hope, and mothers and obligations and responsibilities." It is the story of a fierce and unspoken love between mothers and daughters and the desire of the mothers to teach their daughters how to "lose [their] innocence but not [their] hope, [h]ow to laugh forever" (239).

The polyphonic narrative of *The Joy Luck Club* opens and closes with the voice of Jing-mei (June) Woo. Sandwiched in between the narrative frame are the voices of three sets of mothers and daughters and even a brief narration by Suyuan, June's deceased mother, filtered through the voices of her daughter and husband. As is suggested by the divided narrative, the novel is about the conflicting voices of mothers and daughters, about the concealed truths of their own lives. With the exception of the controlling consciousness abiding in June, none of the first person voices is privileged over the others. Embedded in each voice is a truth that delineates the characters' identity and that, in the act of storytelling, offers alternate versions of that identity. As Rose relates in her narrative, "To each person I told a different story. Yet each version was true" (210). In the sense that the novel is a gathering of stories, the act of storytelling itself is foregrounded.

The novel is presented in four sections, each beginning with an italicized parable. This story establishes the theme for the set of four narratives that follow. The parable that introduces the first section, "Feathers from a Thousand Li Away," tells of a woman who immigrates to America from China with a beautiful swan and "all [her] good intentions" to give her daughter. She dreams that her daughter "will always be too full to swallow any sorrow!" and that "[s]he will know my meaning" (3). But the immigration officials take her swan and ask her to "fill out so many forms she forgot why she had come and what she had left behind" (3). All of the women's "good intentions" are silenced by the severance from China and by the often painful integration into a new country.

In the first section, the mothers' narrations all recount childhood experiences in China wherein they experience a separation from their own mothers; the parable forecasts the strained relationships the women will have with their own daughters and adumbrates the personalities into which the characters will grow.

"The Twenty-Six Malignant Gates," the second section of the novel, gives voice to the four daughters who narrate significant events from their childhood. The parable that introduces the second section tells of a girl who refuses to heed her mother's warning and suffers an accident as a result. This parable also illustrates the missed or absent communication between the mother and daughter, a theme that resonates throughout the novel.

The third section, "American Translation," again features the narrative voices of the daughters, now as young women who have encountered difficult passages in their lives. The introductory parable shows a mother visiting her daughter's home and hanging a mirror in the bedroom so that the daughter's "peach-blossom luck" will be multiplied (159). Correspondingly, the stories in this section all show the mothers stepping into their daughters' lives to reflect a restorative truth.

The parable in final section of the novel, "Queen Mother of the Western Skies," relates the story of a grandmother playing with her granddaughter. The grandmother thinks back to the time when she was "once so free and innocent" and remembers that she "threw away" her innocence in order to protect herself and that she taught her daughter to do the same. Now she wonders if she has done the right thing. She calls her granddaughter the Queen Mother of the Western Skies and requests, "come back to give me the answer," and in the child's laughter, the grandmother hears the lesson that she must "lose [her] innocence but not [her] hope" (239).

The restoration of balance is the imperative of the novel; as the story opens, we learn that there is a vacant corner at the mah jong table of The Joy Luck Club. The club was formed forty years ago by Suyuan Woo, modeled after a similar club she had formed in China during the Sino-Japanese War. The first mah jong club provided an opportunity for Suyuan and her neighbors to come together and forget for a short while all the miseries of the war. Suyuan started the American version of the Joy Luck Club with a group of women from the First Chinese Baptist Church who "also had unspeakable tragedies they had left behind in China and hopes they couldn't begin to express in their fragile English" (6). When Suyuan Woo dies "quickly and with unfinished business left behind" (6), her daughter June is expected to fill the corner and restore balance to the mah jong club. But insofar as June restores balance to the group of four in her mother's generation, she unbalances the group of four daughters. Thus, early on we see that June is a pivotal character who must be the linchpin between both generations. In a wonderful scene at the ending of the book, June transcends her roles as daughter and as a substitute in the group of mothers. She travels to China to meet her older half-sisters, where in the first moment of recognition, all three sisters utter, "Mama, Mama" (331). June must reassure herself, "I know it's not my mother, yet it is the same look she had when I was five and had disappeared all afternoon" (331). In her twin sisters, she sees the face of her own mother, and she is again a daughter. Likewise, in the face of June, the twins see a replication of the photo of their own youthful mother left with them as babies, and she becomes the representation of their mother. In the doubled role of mother and daughter, June is able to restore balance to both groups of mothers and daughters.

Another reason the "aunties" call June to the east corner of the mah jong table is to present her with an airline ticket to China so that she can fulfill her mother's intention to reunite with her long-lost daughters. June has never heard the full story of how her mother came to lose her twin daughters until her father relates the tragic ending when they arrive in China. The pattern of delayed information is another stumbling block in the mother/daughter relationships. The aunties charge June with the task of telling the twins about their mother. June is uncertain, "What will I say? What can I tell them about my mother: I don't know anything. She was my mother." The aunts are shocked and not a little fearful, "Imagine, a daughter not knowing her own mother!" (31). June realizes then that they are fearful that their own daughters are "just as ignorant, just as unmindful of all the truths and hopes they have brought to America" (31). All three of the aunts have had childhoods in which they suffered terrible separations from their own mothers, and the idea that a daughter would not cherish the gift of her mother's presence and life with her is unthinkable. Doubtless, they are resentful that the first-generation daughters have the gift of their mothers and can't seem to appreciate that gift. All of the mother/daughter relationships are fraught with misunderstanding, lack of communication, and sometimes a contest of wills.

June believes that her mother is always "displeased" with everyone; "Something was always missing. Something always needed improving. Something was not in balance. This one or that had too much of one element, not enough of another" (19). It does seem as if June cannot meet the expectations of her mother, and, a result, she becomes an underachiever. She will not practice her piano, she drops out of college, she takes a job at a second-rate company and can only excel in small ways. The fault may rest in part with Suyuan who hopes too strongly for June and who places her expectations for three daughters on June alone.

Before Suyuan's death, she and June do come to some understanding. Suyuan praises June for her humbleness in refusing to grasp for the best quality crab at a Joy Luck Club dinner. She says, "Everybody else want best quality. You think different." June notes, "She said it in a way as if this were proof—proof of something good" (234). On that night, her mother gives June a jade necklace: "For a long time, I wanted to give you this necklace. See I wore this on my skin, so when you put it on your skin, then you know my meaning. This is your life's importance" (235). June accepts the gesture, recognizing it is fraught with a meaning that she can't yet understand.

After the death of her mother, June sits down to play a selection from the childhood recital when she willfully disappointed her mother. She notices that opposite her old recital piece, "Pleading Child," is a piece on the right-hand side of the page, "Perfectly Contented." As she plays both pieces, she notes "they were two halves of the same song" (155), and she comes to an acceptance of her mother's love.

Ying-Ying St. Clair and her daughter, Lena, move through long-term patterns of silence and passivity to achieve an empowering and articulated love. A series of betrayals in China and the stripping of her identity and voice in America leave Ying-Ying unable to be an active and healthy presence in the life of her daughter. Lena grows up with the burden of her mother's depression and develops an eating disorder and a low self-esteem. Even in her marriage, Lena cannot find a voice, and her husband, Harold, largely ignores her, as he turns their marriage into nothing more than a financial arrangement. When Ying-Ying sees the danger Lena is in, the way that Harold is turning her into a nonperson, she decides, "now I must tell her everything about my past. It is the only way to penetrate her skin and pull her to where she can be saved" (274).

Like Lena, Rose Hsu Jordan is in a marriage that is shaky. Her husband is committing adultery and demands that Rose leave their house so that he and his new wife might move in. He sends her a check for ten thousand dollars and demands that she accept it and sign the divorce papers. An-mei helps Rose to see that "ten thousand dollars was nothing to him, that [she] was nothing to him" (214). Rose remembers that her mother once told her, "A girl is like a young tree. You must stand tall and listen to your mother standing next to you. That is the only way to grow strong and straight" (213).

Rose has grown into a woman who cannot make decisions because of a tragedy in her youth. While their family was at the beach, her little brother, Bing, wandered out on the reef. Rose had been put in charge of Bing, but at just the moment he most needed her careful eye, her mother called her to break up a fight between two other brothers. Bing was swept away by the tide and lost. Ever after, Rose dwells in a place of guilt and indecision. It is only in her adulthood that, with her mother's help, she is freed from the past.

Of all the Joy Luck women, Lindo Jong and her daughter Waverly are the characters with the strongest wills. Lindo is the only one of the four women from the older generation who was able to exercise some measure of control over her experiences in China. With that control came personal triumph, which reinforced Lindo's sense of competence and esteem. Her experiences in America have been less marred by tragedy than those of the other Joy Luck Club women. It is no surprise then that her daughter is the most aggressive and strong-willed. Waverly is a nationally recognized chess champion when she is just a girl, and she grows up with a sense of power and entitlement that serve her well as a tax attorney but not as a supportive friend. Waverly and Lindo both treat all encounters as competitions, games to be won by skillful strategy. But even they experience a new level of understanding in the course of the novel.

Though the mothers and daughters find a way to understand each other, they remain partially trapped in the questions that trouble both sides of the generation gap: "How do you know what is Chinese, what is not Chinese?" (228) and "How to lose your innocence but not your hope?" (239).

Tan's second novel, *The Kitchen God's Wife*, revisits the topic of mother/daughter relationship and conflict but in a less complicated narrative structure than in *The Joy Luck Club*. Winnie and her daughter Pearl come to a greater understanding of each other through shared secrets. Tan examines the relationship between a Chinese American woman, Olivia, and her elder Chinese sister, Kwan, in *The Hundred Secret Senses*. The relationship is laden with cultural misunderstandings that are brought into some focus when the two sisters make a trip to China together. Both novels share the strengths of Tan's earlier work: a crystal clear style, a dead-on dialect, sharp insight, and a loving humor.

References and Suggested Readings

"The *Salon* Interview: Amy Tan." *Salon* 12 November 1995. 28 Jan. 1999 <http://www.salon1999.com/12nov1995/feature/tan.html>.

"Tan, Amy." *Contemporary Authors: New Revision Series.* Vol 54. Detroit: Gale Research, 1997.

Tan, Amy. *The Hundred Secret Senses.* 1995. New York: Ivy-Ballantine, 1996.

————. *The Joy Luck Club.* 1989. New York: Ivy-Ballantine, 1990.

————. *The Kitchen God's Wife.* 1991. New York: Ivy-Ballantine, 1992.

Wang, Dorothy. Review of *The Joy Luck Club.* By Amy Tan. *Newsweek* 17 April 1989: 69.

See also Erdrich, Louise.

TRUE WOMAN

Barbara Welter's 1966 essay "The Cult of True Womanhood" explained the way womanhood had been defined in America during the nineteenth century. Proper women, according to Welter, were pure, pious, focused on domestic life, active outside of the home only when the work related to the church, and submissive to their men; women were, according this model, men's subordinates, and they were not permitted to desire equal status. This social position was supported and justified by Christianity, which described even the origin of woman as dependent on man. The true womanhood ideal also furthered the emphasis on women's sexual purity at the time of marriage; unchaste women were considered tainted or fallen. The ideal woman, supposedly unconscious of her own erotic capabilities, was expected to maintain her innocence and simultaneously help men to become less sexual, since men's focus on sexual activity was seen as "natural."

Women writers during this time period often created characters who fulfilled the ideals of true womanhood; many slave narratives catered to this definition of womanhood in order to try and establish a common humanity. Harriet Jacobs, while willing to discuss directly the injustices dealt her, also emphasizes her own true womanhood. In keeping with the emphasis on piety, she explains that "[m]y mistress had taught me the precepts of God's Word" (1841). She also describes her love for her child by writing, "As I held her in my arms, I thought how well it would be for her if she never waked up; and I uttered my thought aloud" in order to point out to white women that she, too, possessed the qualities of a loving (human) mother (1850). Similarly, Frances Ellen Watkins Harper, although born to free parents, wrote a poem entitled "The Slave Mother," which exemplifies this tendency. When in the poem a slave mother's child is taken away to be sold, she responds as any mother would, with her heart "breaking in despair." Harper does not in her text emphasize the rights of the mother; rather, she draws attention to the universality of maternal grief.

Gradually, as rights-based campaigns, such as abolition and suffrage, gained momentum, though, the concept of the ideal woman leaned more toward the valorization of independence, and the more modern new woman became the feminist ideal instead.

References and Suggested Readings

Harper, Frances Ellen Watkins. "The Slave Mother." *The Heath Anthology of American Literature*. 3rd ed. Ed. Paul Lauter. Boston: Houghton Mifflin, 1998. 2055–56.

Jacobs, Harriet Ann. "From *Incidents in the Life of a Slave Girl*." *The Heath Anthology of American Literature*. 3rd ed. Ed. Paul Lauter. Boston: Houghton Mifflin, 1998. 1839–63.

Welter, Barbara. "The Cult of True Womanhood." *American Quarterly* 18 (1966): 151–74.

See also Jacobs, Harriet Ann.

Lisa R. Williams

WALKER, ALICE

One of the most prolific, versatile, and acclaimed of contemporary African American feminist authors, Alice Walker has earned widespread recognition for her considerable achievements as a fiction writer, poet, and essayist. Born in Eatonton, Georgia, in 1944, Walker was one of eight children of Willie Lee and Minnie Tallulah Grant Walker, both sharecroppers. Although her childhood of rural poverty was a difficult one, Walker gained strength and empowerment from her mother, whom she has honored as an important source of artistic inspiration in her essay "In Search of Our Mothers' Gardens." An important feminist statement akin to Virginia Woolf's *A Room of One's Own*, Walker's essay situates her own work within a black matrilineal literary and artistic tradition.

Walker attended Spelman College in Atlanta and received her BA degree from Sarah Lawrence in New York in 1965. Between 1965 and 1968, she was extremely involved in the Civil Rights Movement, working on voter registration drives in Georgia, at a Head Start program in Mississippi, and at the Department of Welfare in New York City. In the 1960s and 1970s, she also taught at various colleges and universities. In 1967, she married Melvyn Roseman Leventhal, a white civil rights lawyer, with whom she had one daughter, Rebecca. They were amicably divorced in 1977.

In 1968, Walker published her first volume of verse, *Once*, based on her experiences in civil rights work and her travels to Africa, and she has continued to publish volumes of poetry, including: *Revolutionary Petunias* (1973); *Good Night, Willie Lee, I'll See You in the Morning* (1979); *Horses Make a Landscape Look More Beautiful* (1984); *Her Blue Body Everything We Know: Earthling Poems, 1965–1990 Complete* (1991); and *Absolute Trust in the Goodness of the Earth: New Poems* (2003).

Although her early volumes of poetry met with critical praise, Walker first gained national prominence as contributing editor to *Ms. Magazine*, where she published such landmark essays as "In Search of Our Mothers' Gardens" (1974) and "Looking for Zora" (1975), about her journey to mark Zora Neale Hurston's grave and to honor this important yet neglected African American literary foremother. In 1979, Walker edited a Zora Neale Hurston reader, entitled *I Love Myself When I Am Laughing . . .* , published by the Feminist Press. Walker has been one of the key people credited with rescuing Hurston's work from obscurity and securing her place in the American literary canon.

Above all, Walker has received recognition for her achievements as an inspired fiction writer. Her first novel, *The Third Life of Grange Copeland*, was published in 1970—the same year as Toni Morrison's debut novel, *The Bluest Eye*. Critics have seen these two works as inaugurating the astonishing outpouring of black feminist writing that has continued unabated ever since. Her second novel, *Meridian* (1976), was followed by her breakthrough work, *The Color Purple* (1982). Winner of the American Book Award and the Pulitzer Prize for Fiction in 1983, *The Color Purple* earned Walker enormous praise and also brought her accusations of male bashing because of its honest and unflinching representation of the sexual oppression and domination of black women by black men. In 1985, *The Color Purple* was adapted to a movie, directed by Steven Spielberg and starring Whoopie Goldberg as Celie. Walker has written about her mixed encounter with Hollywood in *The Same River Twice: Honoring the Difficult* (1996). Her fourth novel, *The Temple of My Familiar* (1989), was followed by the powerful and controversial novel *Possessing the Secret of Joy* (1992), an indictment of the patriarchal practice of performing clitoridectomies on African women. Walker has also written two critically acclaimed volumes of short stories: *In Love and Trouble* (1973) and *You Can't Keep a Good Woman Down* (1981).

In her nonfiction prose writing, Walker articulates the sensibility she designates "womanist," a term she defines as a "black feminist or feminist of color" (xi) in the beginning of her essay collection *In Search of Our Mothers' Gardens: Womanist Prose* (1983). Walker's "womanism" has been embraced by women of color who have felt marginalized by the racial blindspots of mainstream (white) feminism. Walker's other essay collections include *Living by the Word* (1988); *Warrior Masks: Female Genital Mutilation and the Sexual Blinding of Women* (1993), a volume coauthored with Pratibha Parmar concerning the sexual oppression faced by women in African countries; and *Anything We Love Can Be Saved: A Writer's Activism* (1997). Walker lives in Northern California, where she continues to write.

Walker received the prestigious 1983 Pulitzer Prize for fiction for her third novel *The Color Purple*. Since its publication in 1982, the novel has enjoyed enormous popularity, received serious critical attention, and inspired a Hollywood film adaptation. Written as a series of letters by the central protagonist, Celie, and her sister, Nettie, this epistolary novel honestly and unflinchingly explores the damaging effects of male domination upon Celie's spirit and her eventual redemption through the love of her husband's mistress, Shug Avery. Breaking the silence surrounding such taboo subjects as incest and lesbianism, *The Color Purple* both explores the theme of sexual oppression of black women by black men and situates its frank treatment of sexism within the black community in the context of white racial oppression of blacks both in the United States and in Africa in the period between the turn of the century and the Second World War.

The novel's opening sentence indicates the taboo nature of its subject matter: "You better not never tell nobody but God. It'd kill your mammy" (1). Thus silenced, the fourteen-year-old Celie writes a series of letters to God, confiding the painful facts of her life: her repeated rapes and abuse by her father, the death of her mother, and the birth of her two children (subsequently taken from her by her father) as a result of incest. Protective of her younger sister, Nettie, Celie encourages her sister to keep studying, even though she herself has been taken out of school because of her pregnancies. When she nears the age of twenty, her father arranges her marriage to a man Celie refers to as Mr. ———, a widower with four children for whom Celie has no feeling. Mr. ——— beats Celie "cause she my wife" (23) and in order to survive, she makes herself "wood": "I say to myself, Celie, you a tree. That's how come I know trees fear man" (23).

While in town one day, she spies a girl who looks like her daughter, Olivia, who is being raised by a minister and his wife. When Nettie comes to visit, she recognizes her sister's broken spirit and urges her to fight; however, Celie contents herself with merely staying alive. Cruelly, Mr. ——— sends Nettie away when she refuses his advances. As Nettie prepares to leave, Celie encourages her to seek out the minister's wife for help and makes her promise to write.

Soon Mr. ———'s lover, Shug Avery, a flamboyant blues singer with whose picture Celie has fallen in love, arrives in town. When Shug takes ill, Mr. ——— brings her home to live, and Celie nurses her back to health. As a member of this love triangle, Celie writes: "For the first time in my life, I feel just right" (60). Shug's influence begins to change Celie, as she sees that Shug doesn't bow to Albert (Mr. ———) as she does. Whereas previously Celie had advised Albert's son Harpo to beat his wife, Sofia, unquestioningly repeating Albert's attitudes toward her, now she tells him: "Some womens can't be beat. . . . Sofia one of them" (66). When Celie confides to Shug that Albert beats her, Shug promises: "I won't leave . . . until I know Albert won't even think about beating you" (79). Appalled to learn that Celie is still a "virgin" (81), having never experienced sexual pleasure, Shug begins to teach her about her body.

Shug leaves and returns at Christmas time with a new husband, Grady. While Albert and Grady are off together, Celie confides to Shug that her two children were fathered by her father. Moved to tears, Shug makes love to Celie. Shug learns that Albert has been hiding the letters that Nettie has been sending over the years and secretly obtains them for Celie to read. Through Nettie's letters, whose standard English contrasts with the folk idiom of Celie's letters to God, Celie learns that her sister has gone to Africa to work as a missionary with the minister and his wife, Samuel and Corrine, along with their two children, Olivia and Adam, actually Celie's biological children. Enraged by Albert's deception, Celie wonders:

"How I'm gon keep from killing him" (150). Shug channels Celie's anger into creativity, encouraging her to sew pants to wear in lieu of the impractical dresses she uses to do her chores. Celie experiences equality and reciprocity in her relationship to Shug and gradually develops a sense of her own personal autonomy and power, something she has never experienced in her oppressive relationships with men.

Every day, Celie reads Nettie's letters with "a needle not a razor in my hand" (153). The letters detail Nettie's experiences living in an Olinka village and suggest parallels between the sexual oppression of African women in traditional tribal culture and the treatment of African American women in the southern United States. Nettie also describes the Olinkas' displacement from their village by a British rubber manufacturer, exploring colonial oppression as an analog to racial oppression in the South. Nettie informs Celie that she has learned from Samuel and Corrine that the man they knew as their father is actually their stepfather and that their real father was lynched by white men. She describes Corrine's jealousy because Olivia and Adam resemble Nettie, and her confession to Samuel and Corrine that she is the children's aunt. Corrine dies shortly thereafter.

Celie begins to address her letters to Nettie instead of God. When she confides her loss of faith in God to Shug, Shug tells her that God is not the old white man you hear about in church but something in nature and "inside you and inside everybody else" (202). Shug says: "I think it pisses God off if you walk by the color purple in a field somewhere and don't notice it" (203). Shug returns to Memphis taking Celie with her. Here, Celie blossoms under Shug's loving care and begins to sew special custom-designed pants for everyone she knows, eventually creating a flourishing business. One of her employees tries to teach her standard English, but Celie believes "only a fool would want you to talk in a way that feel peculiar to your mind" (223).

Nettie's letters contain the news that she has married the now widowed Samuel and describe her disillusionment with the Missionary Society in England, where their appeal on behalf of the Olinka falls on deaf ears. Returning to Africa, they must also contend with their pain that Tashi, Adam's beloved, has received ritual scarification and plans to submit to a female circumcision ceremony. Meanwhile, in America, Celie learns "the man us knowed as Pa is dead" (250). She and Nettie have inherited the land, house, and store that belonged to their real father. Her joy is lessened, however, when she learns that Shug "got the hots for a boy of nineteen" (255) with whom she runs away.

Celie receives a telegram from the United States Department of Defense, claiming that the ship bringing Nettie's family back from Africa has been sunk by German mines. All of her letters to Nettie are returned unopened the same day; however, unwilling to believe that Nettie is dead, she continues to write to Nettie, telling her "being alive begin to seem like a awful strain" (262).

Back home, Celie and Albert reconcile, finding a bond in their common love for Shug. "It don't surprise me you love Shug Avery," Albert says, "I have love

Shug Avery all my life" (277). Albert confesses that he beat Celie because she wasn't Shug and that Shug castigated him for "mistreating somebody I love" (277). Celie and he embrace, "two old fools left over from love, keeping each other company under the stars" (278). Together, they "sit sewing and talking and smoking our pipes," (279) an image of androgyny that suggests the newfound gender parity in the relationship. The new Albert, softened and repentant, asks Celie to marry him again "in the spirit as well as the flesh," but she refuses preferring to "be friends" (290). Shug returns, betraying a little jealousy about Celie and Albert's friendship, but Celie assures her: "Us talk bout you. . . . How much us love you" (291). In Celie's final letter, addressed to God once again, Celie gives thanks for the safe return of Nettie, Samuel, Olivia, Adam, and Tashi from Africa, describing her emotional reunion with her sister after some thirty years. Rejoined to her loved ones at the novel's conclusion, Celie's spiritual redemption is complete.

Walker's 1983 nonfiction collection *In Search of Our Mothers' Gardens* gathers essays, articles, and reviews written between 1966 and 1982. The volume opens with multiple definitions of *womanist*, including a "black feminist or feminist of color," deriving from the black folk expression "womanish," used by mothers of female children to describe "outrageous, audacious, courageous or willful behavior" and "a woman who loves other women, sexually and/or nonsexually" (xi). Coined by Walker as an alternative to "feminist," a label some women of color have seen as belonging to white women, Walker's "womanism" has been embraced by many who have felt excluded from the feminist community on the basis of race. The volume includes essays on the achievements of African American women such as Zora Neale Hurston and Coretta Scott King, as well as personal reflections on Walker's own life as a mother and writer.

The title essay, "In Search of Our Mothers' Gardens," is an important statement of Walker's notion of a matrilineal artistic tradition. Walker poses the question: "How was the creativity of black women kept alive, year after year and century after century, when for most of the years black people have been in America, it was a punishable crime for a black person to read or write? And the freedom to paint, to sculpt, to expand the mind with action did not exist" (234). Revising and extending Virginia Woolf's *A Room of One's Own*, Walker emphasizes the enormous constraints placed on black women's creativity, constraints that make the achievements of artists, such as the African American poet Phyllis Wheatley, an eighteenth-century slave, all the more astonishing. Honoring the extraordinary gifts of anonymous black women, of quiltmakers and root workers who created art with whatever medium was available to them, Walker pays tribute to her own mother's creative genius, which found expression in her enormous gift for gardening. Describing how "her memories of poverty are seen through a screen of blooms" (241), Walker redefines black women's artistic achievements, honoring her maternal forebears who preceded and empowered her, enabling her own artistry to bloom.

References and Suggested Readings

Evans, Mari, ed. *Black Women Writers (1950–1980): A Critical Evaluation*. Garden City, NY: Anchor, 1984.

Gates, Henry Louis, Jr., and K.A. Appiah, eds. *Alice Walker: Critical Perspectives Past and Present*. New York: Amistad, 1993.

Gilbert, Sandra M., and Susan Gubar, eds. *The Norton Anthology of Literature by Women: The Traditions in English*. 2nd ed. New York: Norton, 1996.

Walker, Alice. *The Color Purple*. New York: Washington Square, 1982.

———. *In Search of Our Mothers' Gardens: Womanist Prose*. New York: Harcourt, 1983.

See also Hurston, Zora Neale; Morrison, Toni; Woolf, Virginia.

WALKER, MARGARET

Margaret Walker was born in Birmingham, Alabama, in 1915. She completed her undergraduate work at Northwestern University at only age nineteen and later studied creative writing at the University of Iowa where she received her MA degree in 1942. Her first volume of poetry, *For My People*, won her the Yale Series of Younger Poets Award. She completed her PhD degree at University of Iowa in 1965.

She married and had four children with Firnist James Alexander. Walker has taught at colleges and universities throughout the South, but held a long-term appointment at Jackson State University in Jackson, Mississippi, from 1946 until 1979. Throughout and following her teaching career, Walker has continued to write in several genres. Her body of work includes *Richard Wright: Daemonic Genius* (1988), *This Is My Century: New and Collected Poems* (1989), *How I Wrote* Jubilee *and Other Essays* (1990), as well as her important novel *Jubilee* (1966).

Given the obstacles she faced, it is a wonder that Walker wrote at all. Her essays tell of the difficulties she had in finding time to write, juggling her family, home, and career. The prejudices she faced as a woman, as a black woman, and as a Southerner are staggering. Though she labored for decades in higher education, her external successes exacerbated her tenuous relationships with administrators and colleagues.

Walker says she had three aims in writing *Jubilee*: "(1) to hew to the line of my simple folk story during the war, (2) to maintain historical accuracy and to relate the importance of the war to my characters, plus (3) to point up the significance of the Negro people and their role during the war."

Margaret Walker's *Jubilee* is a sweeping historical novel based on the oral history of her own family and prodigious amounts of research. The novel centers on the character Vyry, the unacknowledged child of the plantation master, John Dutton. Vyry is patterned after Walker's own great-grandmother. From her earliest days on the plantation in Dawson, Georgia, to the ending of the book when she is a woman who has lived through "birth and death, flood and fire, sickness and trouble" (408–9), Vyry triumphs in body and spirit over seemingly insurmountable circumstances.

Because she is very light skinned, and can indeed pass as white, Vyry's parentage is no secret, and Big Missy, the master's wife, sets her mind against the child from her earliest days. Vyry is close in age to Big Missy's daughter, Lillian, and strangers often mistake the two girls for sisters or twins. The confusion only increases Big Missy's hatred of Vyry, and when the child is moved to the Big House to be the personal servant of Lillian, her life of torment escalates.

The book is peopled with two very different but engaging men, Innis Brown and Randall Ware, the two husbands of Vyry. Randall Ware is a free man of Georgia, a blacksmith who is strong in his sense of individuality and independence. As Walker says in her essay, "How I Wrote *Jubilee*," Ware "was not of the plantation life and culture, and he could not be shaped by such forces. He belonged to an artisan class of free laborers and had neither the slave mentality of Innis nor the caste notions of Vyry" (63).

Jubilee is divided into three sections, each comprising multiple chapters or "incidents" whose titles reflect folk sayings and "exact repetitions of [her] grandmother's words" (54). Section One focuses on the Antebellum Years, Section Two on the Civil War Years, and Section Three on Reconstruction.

The book opens with the death of Hetta, the enslaved mistress of John Morris Dutton, the plantation master. Only twenty-nine, Hetta is used up by the hard life of slavery and by giving birth fifteen times in those brief years. Her last wish before she dies is to see once again her baby, Vyry. Left motherless in infancy and unacknowledged by her father, John Morris Dutton, Vyry is raised by Mammy Sukey until she is pressed into service in the Big House at age seven. There, Vyry is the personal maid for her half-sister, Lillian, to whom she bears such a resemblance that Big Missy cannot abide her presence.

John Morris Dutton is largely an absentee landlord, ceding the daily running of the plantation to his wife and his overseer, Grimes, while he himself rides, hunts, and politics. Though Dutton has a streak of humanity in him, his wife and overseer take delight in their cruelties to the slaves. Vyry is immediately selected for merciless treatment from Big Missy, including such indignities as having the contents of a chamber pot thrown in her face and the painfulness of being hung by her thumbs in a closet. Before long, Vyry is pressed into service in the kitchen, helping Aunt Sally, the cook. It is Aunt Sally who, as a surrogate mother, instructs Vyry in the ways of womanhood and who teaches her to value her strength as a woman. When Vyry is about fifteen, Aunt Sally is sold, and Vyry becomes the primary cook on the plantation.

It is about this time that Vyry meets Randall Ware, a free black who owns property and his own blacksmithing business. Ware is immediately stricken with Vyry and promises her he will buy her freedom if she will "marriage" with him. As a born free man, Ware came to Georgia with his Quaker friend Randall Wheelwright, who moved from Virginia in order to be more active in the Underground Railroad. With his independent wealth, his freedom, and literacy, Ware stirs the heart of Vyry and quickens her thirst for freedom. She asks permission of John

Morris Dutton to marry Ware, but he refuses, knowing that by law, she would become a free woman.

With Ware, Vyry gives birth to three children, though only two live. For her stillborn second child—doomed to enslavement—Vyry cannot grieve. Her hopes of freedom, even through the efficacy of Randall Ware, have dimmed to a dull acceptance of her life as a slave. Ware's own status is growing more precarious as Georgia considers a law to regulate free blacks, so he urges Vyry to escape with him. Vyry cannot fathom leaving the children behind to be collected later, as Ware's plan necessitates, and makes her flight with the toddler and infant in tow. She and the children are caught, and she is given seventy-five lashes on her bare back.

The second section of the novel is given over to the Civil War Years and shows rupture of the Southern plantation structure and the disintegration of the Dutton family. On his way home from the Georgia Legislature, John Morris Dutton is injured in the wreck of his carriage, and he does not survive. Before his death, he reminds Vyry that he has promised to set her free upon his death, but the promise proves to be hollow, either as neglect on his part or a violation of the will on Big Missy's part. Once more, Vyry's hopes for freedom have been raised and dashed.

Both Big Missy's son and son-in-law join the Confederacy, but neither survives the war. Within three years, the Dutton family has suffered the loss of its three men. As the war continues and the resources of the South diminish, the overseer, Grimes, joins the army, leaving the Dutton plantation without the harsh discipline that he had imposed. A laxity presides over the plantation even though Big Missy reaches new heights of strident hatred for the black race. When she prays that she will never live to see the day when blacks "are free and living like white folks" (220), she little suspects that only her own death will answer her prayer. She dies from a massive stroke as the guns of the Union forces can be heard not far from her plantation. Miss Lillian, Vyry's half-sister and the only adult Dutton left on the plantation, spirals into madness, and Vyry is left to run the household. When the war comes to a close and the enslaved persons are freed, Vyry is twenty-eight. Though remaining friends leave the Dutton Plantation and seek another life, Vyry stays on, remembering the promise of Randall Ware that he would return for her after the end of the war. She lingers until all the Duttons have gone and the plantation is boarded up.

A transient former slave, Innis Brown, has lingered at the plantation for months, helping out and providing protection for Vyry's family. He is immediately taken with Vyry and urges her to marry him and leave for a better life. Only after all hopes of Ware's return are diminished does Vyry consent to marry Brown and leave Georgia for a life elsewhere. The new family meets the worst kind of opposition as they attempt to make a home and establish a farm. They find an abandoned piece of river-bottom land and build a log house, and in the first blush of freedom, "everything seemed possible" (267).

The first fruits of freedom are soon spoiled for the Browns as the river-bottom floods and they lose most of their possessions and the efforts of their hard work.

The children, Jim and Minna, contract malaria, and finally recover after Vyry's careful folk doctoring.

When the children are well enough to travel, the Browns leave their flooded home and look once again for a spot to settle. They find a farm just being vacated by a poor white family and are lead to believe that the land is abandoned and available to them on squatter's rights. They soon learn that they can stay only if they agree to a sharecropping contract with the owner of the land, and they unwittingly enter into a relationship of exploitation and deceit. When it becomes clear that they will never be treated fairly, the Browns, with their new baby, leave the situation and are once again homeless.

For the third time, the Browns find what promises to be a place to settle, and for the second time, they build a new home for their family. But again, their hopes for a peaceful life are shattered as the Ku Klux Klan burns them out, and they must flee.

Meanwhile, since his flight from Georgia and his seven-year absence from Vyry, Randall Ware has been working with the Union Army as a blacksmith. At the end of the war, he makes his long way back to Georgia, stopping in Atlanta for the First Convention of Colored People in Georgia. He castigates himself with the idea that perhaps his stop at the convention delayed him just enough to miss Vyry. In any event, Vyry is gone when Ware returns to Dawson, Georgia, and he sets up his smithy once again. There he determines that he will exercise his new freedoms by becoming a part of the local political process. He attends the Freedman's Convention, becomes a charter member of the Georgia Equal Rights Association, and soon is perceived as a threat by the white establishment.

By 1870, Innis and Vyry have found a place to settle down, but before they build once again, Vyry is determined to test the community to see if they have a chance of survival there. Because she is so light, and is mistaken for white, she overhears conversations that help her get a sense of the racial climate of the county. She learns just enough to convince her that once more, the family should move on. Through a fortuitous incident, however, Vyry gains the reluctant trust of the community. She meets a very young white couple just having their first child, and they have no one to help with the delivery. Unwilling to let the young girl deliver alone, Vyry steps in and acts as the "granny." Her generosity is acknowledged and repaid when the white men of the community ask her to stay and be the local midwife; they even offer to help build the Brown's new house. Innis is in awe of Vyry for her ability to change the hearts of the community, but she deflects his praise, "I figgers with a little time the good Lawd'll show us which a way the wind gwine blow. I done prayed hard, and them folks is done had a change of heart" (365).

Meanwhile, Randall Ware learns of Vyry's whereabouts and he searches her out. He realizes that he has intruded upon a delicate situation, given that her children are his, but that she is married to Innis Brown. Ware invites his son, Jim, to go with him and finally receive the education that he has longed for. He makes provision for Jim's sister, Minna, to go to school as well. In the course of his visit,

Vyry, Innis, and Randall all come to a new understanding and respect for each other. When Ware learns of the hardships Vyry endured in his absence and the unpolluted respect she still had for humanity, he realizes, "She was only a living sign and mark of all the best that any human being could hope to become" (407).

In telling Vyry's story, Walker reinscribes the historical record and validates the oral tradition; her accomplishment in *Jubilee* is significant.

References and Suggested Readings

Campbell, Jane. "Walker, Margaret." *The Oxford Companion to Women's Writing in the United States*. Ed. Cathy N. Davidson and Linda Wagner-Martin. New York: Oxford University Press, 1995.

Walker, Margaret. "How I Wrote *Jubilee*." *How I Wrote* Jubilee. Ed. Maryemma Graham. New York: The Feminist Press, 1990.

———. *Jubilee*. 1966. New York: Bantam, 1967.

WHARTON, EDITH

Born in 1862 in New York City as Edith Newbold Jones, Wharton was the youngest child of a wealthy couple and enjoyed a privileged childhood. From the ages of four to ten, Wharton lived in Europe with her family, and the transformative experience deeply imprinted her with a European sensiblilty. Her marriage to Edward "Teddy" Robbins Wharton was one of incompatibility and sexual frustration, which she largely blamed on her mother. She divorced Teddy in 1913 and never remarried. She did, however, have a two-year long, passionate affair with journalist Morton Fullerton (Funston 111).

Her first novel was *The Valley of Decision* (1902) and her second, *The House of Mirth* (1905), gained her the attention of Henry James, with whom she became fast friends until his death (Funston 110). Wharton's 1911 novel *Ethan Frome* has as its subject a love triangle. Her *Age of Innocence* won the Pulitzer Prize in 1921.

With the approach of World War I, she actively urged America to help France; her work with Belgian refugees was recognized by the King of Belgium, and she was named a Chevalier of the Legion of Honor by the French (Funston 111). According to Funston, "Her themes—the necessary price an individual pays to be a part of society, and the conflict between stability and change—continue to remain relevant to the American experience" (112). Wharton died in 1927.

Wharton's *The House of Mirth* is the story of Lily Bart, a hothouse flower able to survive in a controlled environment but who flounders when that controlled climate is altered. Lily Bart, a New York socialite born to parents who by birth, training, and temperament, belong to the outer fringes of New York's ostentatious circle of conspicuous consumers, is moved even more precipitiously to the edges of that culture when her father suffers financial reverses and dies. Her mother dies afterward, and, as a young woman, Lily is cast onto the care of an unwilling aunt, Mrs. Peniston. Though her needs are met by the sporadic generosity of her aunt, Lily has no dependable income to secure her place in a society that demands the keeping up of appearances above all else. Gifted by her social graces and extraordinary beauty, Bart maintains for a time the delicate dance of social viability and the harsher necessities of securing her future through a pragmatic marriage by living quite beyond her means.

Her pressing needs to find an income precipitate a series of social *faux pas* that begin the machinations of her decline. The novel opens when Lily Bart is twenty-nine and pushing the limits of her most important asset—youthful beauty. She shudders at the appearance of the first telltale wrinkles that presage her ultimate fall from the social machinery that values her only for her beauty and quick wit. Her instincts of social intercourse are acute, and she is perceptively aware of the motivations and intrigues woven into the tapestry of the social elite. However, she makes a series of missteps that set in order the slow unraveling of her own life and, ultimately, the discovery of her own soul. The price is a very high one, and the period of tutelage dangerously long. Lily Bart's material and social descent is made sympathetic only by the corresponding quickening of her moral dimension.

Gertie Farish, Lily's foil and only true friend, becomes the portal for Lily's growth. Farish is the moral center for Lily's life and holds up to her a model of prudence and philanthropy, meager though her resources are. Gertie recognizes that Lily can only escape the dangers she is in if she is to leave the worldview that is pulling her under. Lily, however, has the vision only to make enough money to get back into the artificial culture of "society." The inability of Lily to recognize, let alone embrace, a different view of what is important in life is a major blockade in her growth. She has no appropriate models before her; her two most likely candidates, Lawrence Selden and Gertie Farish, are both in reduced but genteel circumstances, and each has made the adjustments necessary to exist in that world. Selden, as a man, has greater opportunity than does Gertie, for he lives in a world that valorizes the male with both opportunity, moral laxity, and privilege. Selden works as a lawyer; he too has had indiscretions more serious than Lily's, though they do no harm to his reputation. Lily notes quite accurately that the difference between men and women is that "a girl must [marry], a man may if he chooses" (12).

The irony of Lily's downfall is not that she violates the moral code but that she violates the social code, not that she does the wrong thing but that she gives the appearance of having done the wrong thing. In a society based on the flimsy moral infrastructure of appearances, even the *appearance* of violation is enough to tumble a most carefully built house of cards. For Lily, once the first card falls, the collapse of the entire structure is inevitable. Always, Lily's missteps seem to happen as a result of her resistant willingness to step fully into the demands of the social game. Her first mistake is to take tea in the apartment of Lawrence Selden, a single man, where she mines him for information that may help her seal a marriage with Percy Gryce. As she leaves his apartment, she is seen by a social climber, Simon Rosedale, whose insinuating curiosity puts her on the defensive. She covers her slip with a lie that is innocent enough but one that further pulls her into Rosedale's sticky web. Soon, she is unable to extricate herself. She longs to have the opportunity, as men do, to make business arrangements, to invest in the market, to make money. But her one attempt to forge a business alliance results in a further degradation of her social barometer. When she appeals to Gus Trenor, the husband of her friend, to invest some money with him, he reads the situation as a winking admission that Lily is willing to enter a liaison with him. Though she never concedes to him, even in the frightening instance when he lures him to his empty house and threatens her with his overpowering physicality, her reputation is marred beyond repair. Her correctives to earlier mistakes only hasten her on the descending spiral to the status of social pariah. She leaves the circle of the Trenors and Dorsets to enter the social circle of the Gormers, but the result is a further downgrading of her social capital. In a culture of cutthroat intrigue and betrayal, Lily Bart has no stomach for the game; she has the chance to mend her social standing by bringing Bertha Dorset down with a series of letters she has written revealing her affair with Selden. Lily's moral courage is more innocent and natural, accidental almost; she is not trained in morality but comes to it with a simplicity and ease that characterizes none of her familiars save Gertie Farish.

Lily's moral courage will not mend her frayed social fabric, however; and by thirty, she lies dead of an overdose of chloral.

References and Suggested Readings

Funston, Judith E. "Wharton, Edith." *American National Biography*. Ed. John A. Garraty and Mark C. Carnes. Vol. 23. New York: Oxford University Press, 1999.

Waid, Candace. "Wharton, Edith." *The Oxford Companion to Women's Writing*. Ed. Cathy N. Davidson and Linda Wagner-Martin. New York: Oxford University Press, 1995. 916–19.

Wharton, Edith. *The House of Mirth*. 1905. New York: Norton, 1990.

WINTERSON, JEANETTE

The adopted daughter of Pentecostal Evangelists, Jeanette Winterson was born in 1959 in Manchester, England. She earned a BA degree in English from St. Catherine's College, Oxford University, in 1981. Both her family and Church disapproved of Winterson's lesbianism, and it became the reason of her break with the Church. Winterson downplays its influence and connection to her work. She says, "I am not interested in gay/lesbian literature *for its own sake*. I am interested in literature. I am an experimental writer and a sophisticated one. My personal life is *not* a way into my work and never has been."

Winterson's first novel, *Oranges Are Not the Only Fruit* (1985), an autobiographical coming-out story featuring a main character named Jeanette, won the Whitbread Prize for a First Novel. Other works include a screenplay of that novel in 1990, *Boating for Beginners* (1985), *The Passion* (1987), *Sexing the Cherry* (1989), *Written on the Body* (1992), *Arts & Lies: A Piece for Three Voices and a Bawd* (1994),

Gut Symmetries (1997), and *The PowerBook* (2000). Winterson has also written short stories and essays.

The Passion is located in the early nineteenth century during the Napoleonic wars and is narrated alternately by Henri, a young French peasant who joins the army out of an intense devotion to Napoleon, and Villanelle, a cross-dressing, web-footed, gambling Venetian woman. Henri begins his career in the army as the neck-wringer of Napoleon's daily chicken, but is soon elevated to Napoleon's personal server. Henri's change in status will cause him trouble later as it arouses the jealousy and vengeance of the cook. Napoleon's "passion" for chicken, announced in the first sentence of the novel, is the first of the many passions that drive the narrative.

Henri would like to be an intellectual, but as a peasant boy who rejects the priesthood because he demands a God who can "meet passion with passion" (10), he joins the passionate Napoleon. In the army, he becomes friends with Domino, the midget groom of Napoleon's horse, and Patrick, a defrocked Irish priest with an eagle eye. When Henri goes to war, a little village girl asks him if he will kill people, and he tells her no, "just the enemy" (8). Henri soon has cause to question his early naïveté as the exigencies of war intrude upon his devotion to Napoleon. Nothing is as clear as it once was, and in an attempt to combat the erasures of a fading and forgiving memory, Henri starts keeping a journal. Domino scorns his efforts and says, "The way you see it now is no more real than the way you'll see it [later]" (28). The difference in the attitudes of Henri and Domino reveal their essential approaches to life. Henri lives for the future, but Domino lives only in the present. He warns Henri, "every moment you steal from the present is a moment you have lost for ever. There's only now" (29). Henri narrates his story from a distance of time, and as the novel progresses, we learn that he narrates from a prison for the criminally insane. Thus, we can make some sense of his apparent narrative equivocation in his frequent injections of the phrase "I'm telling you stories. Trust me." Do we trust the story as truth or mistrust it as prevarication? The phrase takes on greater significance, as it is the final word of the novel. Winterson's following comment from a *Salon* interview reveals the postmodernist impulse of her work:

> I don't believe in happy endings. All of my books end on an ambiguous note because nothing ever is that neatly tied up, there is always another beginning, there is always the blank page after the one that has writing on it. And that is the page I want to leave the reader.

The second section of the novel is narrated by Villanelle, equally as passionate as Henri but nonetheless his foil. Where his passion roots him in a passive devotion to Napoleon, Villanelle's passion opens her to the dangerous life of the gambler. Though the daughter of a boatman and born with the webbed feet of all Venetian boatmen, because of her gender, Villanelle is not allowed to enter that profession. She instead becomes a casino worker and pickpocket. Her narration is marked by the repetition of her signature phrase, "You play, you win, you play, you lose. You play." She first learns the bitter lesson of the gambling life when she falls in love with the beautiful Madame Clicquot. They have an affair of nine passionate days, but the tenth day never comes, and Villanelle metaphorically and literally loses her heart in the gamble of love. She learns that "[s]omewhere between fear and sex. Somewhere between God and the Devil passion is and the ways there is sudden and the way back is worse" (68).

At the casino, Villanelle is daily confronted by a flabby rich man with "fingertips that had the feel of boils bursting" (96) who wants to marry her. His business of supplying meat and horses to Bonaparte's army provides him with unlimited wealth. Having lost her heart already, and being willing to gamble, Villanelle marries and spends the next two years traveling around the capitals of Europe before stealing her husband's money and leaving him. When he finds her, her husband suggests a wager. If she wins, Villanelle can have her freedom; if he wins, he can do with her as he wants. Villanelle loses against a fixed pack of cards, and her husband gives her to a French army general who forces her into the role of a vivandière. The vivandières, who "serviced" the men of the army, were "runaways, strays, younger daughters of too-large families, servant girls who'd got tired of giving it away to drunken masters, and fat old dames who couldn't ply their trade anywhere else" (38).

In the third section of the novel, the narrator is once again Henri, and the trajectories of Henri and Villanelle bring them together in the "zero winter" of the war in Russia. Though growing more disillusioned, Henri still is devoted to Napoleon. He has lost an eye at Austerlitz; his friend Domino is wounded, and Patrick has spiraled into an alcoholic haze. Henri wonders if he should simply vanish out of the war. He realizes that his own need for a father has brought him through mindless devotion to this place in the war and in his life. In an act of self-preservation, Henri says, "To survive the zero winter and that war we made a pyre of our hearts and put them aside for ever. There's no pawnshop for the heart. You can't take it in and leave it awhile in a clean cloth and redeem it in better times" (82). His decision to desert is solidified; he can no longer stay with Napoleon. On that night, he starts to hate Napoleon and to hate himself for ever having loved him. He notes, "If the love was passion, the hate will be obsession" (84).

Henri enters his tent to invite Domino and Patrick, his companions of eight years, to desert with him, and in his tent is a vivandière, Villanelle. He falls immediately in love and asks her to join them. Domino, who does not believe in a future, refuses to go, but Patrick and Villanelle join Henri, and they make their way on foot to Venice. Along the way, Villanelle tells her story, Henri falls deeper in love with her, and Patrick dies. Their optimism dies with Patrick, and they feed their survival only with stories. As they near Venice, Henri pledges his help to retrieve Villanelle's heart. When they arrive in Venice, they go to Villanelle's parents' home where they welcome Henri as a son. Though he has never fully understood the literalness of her request, Henri fulfills his promise to retrieve Villanelle's heart.

When Villanelle's husband finds her with Henri, it is revealed that he is also the vengeful cook of Henri's early days in the army. He threatens them both, and their encounter soon turns violent. Villanelle hands Henri a knife, and he kills the husband/cook. In the moment that he kills, something snaps in Henri, and he moves far beyond self-defense as he cuts out the heart of the husband/cook.

Henri is declared insane and is convicted for the murder and imprisoned in "the Rock." Villanelle visits him faithfully and tries to effect his release. But Henri retreats to his own world, refuses to leave his sanctuary, and spends his days writing in his journals and planting flowers. Even still, he comes to a kind of sanity in his insanity; he says, "I think now that being free is not being powerful or rich or well regarded or without obligations but being able to love" (154). The novel ends with the ambiguous phrase, "I'm telling you stories. Trust me."

References and Suggested Readings

Allison, Terry. "Jeanette Winterson." *Gay and Lesbian Literature*. Ed. Sharon Malinowski. Vol. 1. Detroit: St. James Press, 1994.

Doan, Laura L. "Jeanette Winterson." *An Encyclopedia of British Women Writers*. Ed. Paul Schlueter and June Schlueter. Revised and Expanded ed. New Brunswick, NJ: Rutgers University Press, 1998.

Miller, Laura. "Jeanette Winterson, England's Literary Outlaw, Talks about the Erotics of Quantum Physics and the Horrors of the British Press." *Salon* April 1997: 1–2. 19 January 2001 <http://www.salon.com/april97/winterson970428.html>.

Winterson, Jeanette. *The Passion*. New York: Grove Press, 1987.

WITTIG, MONIQUE

The 2003 death of Monique Wittig silenced a singular voice that worked for decades to deny the silences imposed on women by social constructs, such as politics, economics, and ideology. Born July 12, 1935, in Dannemarie on the Upper Rhine in France, Wittig lived in Paris before immigrating to the United States in 1976. While still in Paris, she was instrumental in the founding of the French Women's Liberation Movement in 1970, though she broke with the group in 1976. She was also a member of the group of women who made a deliberate statement by attempting to lay a wreath dedicated to the Wife of the Unknown Soldier at the Arc of Triumph.

Wittig found an artistically compatible publisher in Les Editions de Minuit and was awarded the Prix Médicis in 1964 for her work *L'Opoponax*. Central to Wittig's work is a body of three experimental novels: *Les Guerillères* (1969—translated under the same title in 1971), *Le Corps Lesbien* (1973—translated as *The Lesbian Body* in 1975), and *Virgile, Non* (1985—translated as *Across the Acheron* in 1987).

Les Guerillères opens with an impressionistic poem that adumbrates the thematic concern of the novel: the struggle, rebirth, and ultimate victory of women. The next page features only a thick-lined circle set in the upper center of the page; the circle is repeated twice more throughout the text and suggests both a visual wholeness and a containment. Wittig places in the text a singing siren whose song is "nothing . . . but a continuous O" that evokes "the zero or the circle, the vulval ring" (14).

The remainder of the text comprises two other stylistic maneuvers. Wittig uses short poetic narratives that provide glimpses of the women warriors who are featured in the text, generally followed by lists of women's names set boldly in all capital letters and centered on the page. The women's names particularize the story that is otherwise set in a nonspecified time and place, perhaps a utopian future. Most of the narrative vignettes contain copious lists that suggest Homeric strategies and a nod toward myth-making that Wittig addresses more directly in *Brouillon pour un dictionnaire des amantes*. Coauthored by Sande Zeig and translated by them as *Lesbian Peoples: Material for a Dictionary*, the book, in part, valorizes the mythic mothers who have been erased from cultural history.

The women of *Les Guerillères* carry books that they call *feminaries* and in which is the wisdom of the community. Female genitalia are mentioned often and with great celebration and pride. The women "take a proper pride in that which has for long been regarded as the emblem of fecundity and the reproductive force in nature" (31). But the women also learn that "they must now stop exalting the vulva. They say that they must break the last bond that binds them to a dead culture" (72). A celebration of the vulva that escalates to a centrality that marginalizes others is not morally superior to phallocentrism that came before.

While the first part of the book if given over to the celebration of the vulva-centric community of women, the second part is devoted to a more active war against the ideologies—including language—that have traditionally imprisoned women. The narrative suggests "those who call for a new language first learn violence" (85). Furthermore, the women are reminded that "men in their way have adored you like a goddess or else burned you at their stakes or else relegated you to their service in their back-yards" (100). As Jean Duffy suggests, the movement in the text is appropriate and accurately reflects the steps necessary in a revolution of any kind: First there must be a "reassessment of the effects of male ideology" followed by "an attack on male-centered symbolism." What is at risk is substantial; the narrative voice reminds the women, "Better for you to see your guts in the sun and utter the death-rattle than to live a life that anyone can appropriate" (116).

When the war is over and the women have accomplished their purpose, they can say, "truly is this not magnificent? The vessels are upright, the vessels have acquired legs. The sacred vessels are on the move" (142).

In addition to her novels, Wittig has a small but significant body of prose that has broken theoretical ground for feminists. Her major contributions are gathered in *The Straight Mind and Other Essays* (1992). While not a separatist, she nonetheless suggests that

lesbianism provides for the moment the only social form in which we can live freely. Lesbian is the only concept I know of which is beyond the categories of sex (woman and man), because the designated subject (lesbian) is *not* a woman, either economically, or politically, or ideologically. (20)

References and Suggested Readings

Duffy, Jean. "Monique Wittig." *Dictionary of Literary Biography, Volume 83: French Novelists Since 1960.* Ed. Catharine Savage Brosman. Gale Group, 1989. 30 August 2003 <http://galenet.galegroup.com/>.

Reynolds, Margaret. "Monique Wittig: Radical French Writer at the Cutting Edge of Feminist Philosophy." *The Guardian* 5 February 2003. 31 August 2003 <http://books.guardian.co.uk/print/0,3858,4598718-103684,00.html>.

Wittig, Monique. *Les Guérillères.* 1969. Trans. David Le Vay. Boston: Beacon Press, 1985.

See also Sexuality; Stefan, Verena.

WOLF, CHRISTA

Born in Landsberg an der Warthe, Germany, in what is now Gorzow Wielkopolski, Poland, in 1929, Christa Wolf once enjoyed acclaim as one of Europe's finest literary voices. Her work and integrity as an artist came under serious criticism when she published a 1979 manuscript, *What Remains and Other Stories,* in 1990, after the reunification of Germany. According to *Contemporary Literary Criticism,* "Critics writing for conservative German newspapers considered the delayed publication an act of cowardice, contending that Wolf should have published the story in 1979, when it may have served a political purpose." The volume is critical of the East Germany secret police (the Stasi), and the literary world was even further shocked when it was revealed in 1993 that Wolf had worked for the Stasi from 1959 to 1962. Still, Wolf has supporters who insist that the incidents must be put in perspective with the body of her important work.

Wolf's first work of fiction was a novella entitled, in translation, *Moscow Novella* (1961). Her next two novels, *Divided Heaven* (1965) and *The Quest for Christa T.* (1968), were well received across Europe and gained a following in the United States. Her memoir, *A Model Childhood* (1976), concerns her youth as she grew up under the growing power of Hitler's Nazism.

It is in *Cassandra* (1983), however, that Wolf hits her stride as a feminist writer. The novel is a retelling of Aeschylus's *Oresteia* that reconfigures the story by bringing the seer Cassandra from the margins of the text to its center as a first person narrator. Set during the Trojan War, Priam's daughter, Cassandra, has the bitter gift of prophecy that will be believed by no one. She knows that men would "rather punish the one who names the deed rather than the one who commits it" (14). And indeed, Cassandra narrates her ruminations about the political situation and the war in her father's kingdom as she sits in a dungeon awaiting execution. To counter her own fear and to gain power over her own interior situation, Cassandra tells her story and insists on speaking before the council. As she tells the truth that Paris "gravely violated the right of hospitality . . . when he abducted Helen," she is deemed mad by the council (75). The voice of the prophet is never easily received, and Cassandra's vulnerability as seer is redoubled by her gender. When critic Edith Waldstein asks the question, "How can the individual who is capable of viewing society from a utopian perspective integrate these perceptions within a society whose history has proven harmful, if not devastating, to humanity?" (196), she suggests that the rhetorical purpose of *Cassandra* goes beyond the retelling of the Greek myth and squarely addresses Wolf's historical present as well.

As the doomed seer, Cassandra nonetheless contends, "I will continue a witness even if there is no longer one single human being left to demand my testimony" (22). Scorned, abandoned, raped, and sentenced to death, Cassandra remains true to her role even though the gift is not one she would have desired. Awaiting death, she asks the only sensible, if tautological, question, "Why do I go on living if not to learn the things one learns before death?" (97). One thing that she has learned is that the patriarchal order is too invested in maintaining its rigid posture to yield to the prophecies of a woman. Cassandra say, "we have no chance against a time that needs heroes" (138). In the midst of the war, it is only in the voices of the women that we hear the logic of "[b]etween killing and dying there is a third alternative: living" (118).

Published in the same volume with the novel *Cassandra* are four essays that were originally written as a series of lectures on poetics, delivered by Wolf at the University of Frankfurt. In the essays, Wolf offers an account of how she became intrigued with the subject of Cassandra and how her novel evolved.

Wolf has most recently written *Medea: A Modern Retelling* (1998) and is seeing a rebuilding of her literary reputation. Wolf has lived recently in California where she has served as a Getty Scholar in Residence at the Getty Center for the History of Art and the Humanities in Santa Monica.

References and Suggested Readings

"Christa Wolf." *Contemporary Literary Criticism*. Gale Group, 2003. 31 August 2003 <http://galenet.galegroup.com/>.

Waldstein, Edith. "Prophecy in Search of a Voice: Silence in Christa Wolf's *Kassandra*." *The Germanic Review* 62 (1987): 194–98.

Wolf, Christa. *Cassandra: A Novel and Four Essays*. 1983. Trans. Jan Van Heurck. New York: Noonday Press, 1988.

WOLLSTONECRAFT, MARY

Best known as the author of the polemical feminist classic *A Vindication of the Rights of Woman* (1792), Mary Wollstonecraft was born in London on April 27, 1759. Her father, Edward John Wollstonecraft, had inherited a large fortune from his father—a wealthy manufacturer—and subsequently lost it through unsuccessful attempts to establish himself as a gentleman farmer. The second of five children and the oldest daughter, Wollstonecraft witnessed firsthand the tyranny of her father and the submissiveness of her mother, Elizabeth Dickson. Mary later recalled how she tried to protect her mother from her father's drunken abuse, often sleeping outside the door to her parents' bedroom so that she might intercede.

At the age of nineteen, Wollstonecraft escaped this unhappy household by hiring herself out as a companion to a widow in Bath and later returning home to nurse her dying mother. Following her mother's death in 1782, she went to live in the home of her most cherished friend, Fanny Blood, where her needlework helped with the financial situation of the struggling Blood family. In 1784, Wollstonecraft went to attend to her sister Eliza, who was suffering from a nervous breakdown after the birth of her daughter. Convinced that Eliza's mental anguish was due to the cruelty and abuse of her husband, Wollstonecraft persuaded her sister to flee husband and child, hiding her while she awaited a legal separation. The child, who remained legally in the custody of the husband, died when less than a year old.

Together with Fanny Blood, Eliza, and their other sister Everina, Wollstonecraft established a school at Newington Green. After Blood went to Lisbon to marry her longtime suitor Hugh Skeys, she sent for Wollstonecraft to attend the birth of her first child. Fanny died in her arms during childbirth, throwing Wollstonecraft into despondency. When Newington Green was forced to close for financial reasons, she wrote her first book, *Thoughts on the Education of Daughters* (1786), and became a governess for the daughters of the Anglo-Irish family of Viscount Kingsborough. Dismissed from this position, she returned to London, where she began for the first time to earn a living by writing. In 1788, her friend and publisher Joseph Johnson issued her first novel, *Mary, a Fiction*, which she had composed while a governess, as well as a children's book, *Original Stories from Real Life*. Associated with the revolutionary movements in France and America, Johnson introduced her to the men in his circle, including the mystical romantic poet William Blake, who illustrated the second edition of *Original Stories*. With her earnings, Wollstonecraft helped to support her two sisters and father, as well as the indigent family of Fanny Blood.

In response to Edmund Burke's *Reflections on the Revolution in France* (1790), an attack on the French Revolution and its British sympathizers, Wollstonecraft composed *A Vindication of the Rights of Men* (1790). Her defense of revolutionary ideals focused particularly on the wrongs faced by the British working classes. As the first book-length response to Burke, it met with instantaneous success; however, it was soon followed and overshadowed by other works, especially Thomas Paine's classic *The Rights of Men* (1791–1992). In a sequel, *A Vindication of the Rights of Woman* (1792), Wollstonecraft turned to a defense of the oppressed of her own sex, the work for which she is most famous today. Extending her enthusiasm for revolutionary ideals, Wollstonecraft argued passionately that by excluding women, the goals of liberty, equality, and fraternity would be undermined.

Wollstonecraft's romantic life was characterized by storminess. In December 1792, she went alone to France to view the revolution firsthand. There, she met and fell in love with an American, Gilbert Imlay, the author of a book on the Kentucky backwoods, who had fled America to avoid prosecution for debt.

Although she refused to marry Imlay legally, she was registered as his wife at the American Embassy for the protection American citizenship offered. In 1794, their daughter, Fanny, was born, and Imlay returned to London for what became a protracted stay, abandoning his wife and daughter in Paris during the Reign of Terror. Upon reuniting with him in London and discovering his infidelities, Wollstonecraft tried to commit suicide, an attempt that was discovered and prevented by Imlay. He sent her on an extended trip to Scandinavia as his business envoy. When Wollstonecraft returned to find him living with an actress, she again attempted suicide, this time throwing herself from a bridge into the River Thames.

After Imlay left London for Paris with the actress, Wollstonecraft used the letters she had written to him during her trip to write a book, *Letters Written during a Short Residence in Sweden, Norway, and Denmark* (1796). Wollstonecraft renewed an earlier acquaintance with the famed radical writer William Godwin, the author of *Inquiry Concerning Political Justice* (1793) and of *Caleb Williams* (1794), a novel that gave fictional form to his social views. The two became lovers. Despite the fact that he had attacked the institution of marriage in his *Inquiry*, Godwin married Wollstonecraft after she became pregnant with her second child. Despite their happiness, the marriage lasted less than a year. In 1797, Mary died of complications from childbirth, eleven days after birth of their daughter, Mary Wollstonecraft Godwin. Their daughter, Mary, later married the poet Shelley and wrote the classic novel *Frankenstein*.

After her death, Wollstonecraft's grieving husband published *Memoirs of the Author of "A Vindication of the Rights of Woman"* (1798) and edited her *Posthumous Works* (1798), which included her unfinished novel, *The Wrongs of Woman: or Maria, A Fragment*, as well as her love letters to Imlay. Godwin's frankness about Wollstonecraft's personal life—her love affairs with him and Imlay, her suicide attempts, and her free thinking on matters of religion and sexuality—resulted in a scandal. For more than a century, her colorful personal life overshadowed her philosophical and intellectual achievements. Victorian advocates of women's equality, such as John Stuart Mill, studiously avoided reference to her work. In the twentieth century, however, Mary Wollstonecraft has been revered as an important foremother in the feminist polemical tradition that includes such figures as Margaret Fuller, Charlotte Perkins Gilman, Olive Schreiner, Virginia Woolf, and Adrienne Rich. Indeed, the feminist poet Adrienne Rich pays homage to Wollstonecraft in her poem "Snapshots of a Daughter-in-Law" (1955), quoting from *Thoughts on the Education of Daughters*:

> "To have in this uncertain world some stay
> which cannot be undermined, is
> of the utmost consequence."
> Thus wrote
> a woman, partly brave and partly good,
> who fought with what she partly understood.
> Few men about her would or could do more,
> hence she was labeled harpy, shrew and whore.

The groundbreaking work by Wollstonecraft, *A Vindication of the Rights of Woman*, is recognized today as a classic polemical argument on behalf of women's social, legal, political, and economic equality. Published in 1792 and inspired by Wollstonecraft's enthusiasm for the ideals of the French Revolution, *A Vindication of the Rights of Woman* argues that the democratic goals of liberty, equality, and fraternity can only be achieved if women as well as men are included in the revolutionary era's ground swell of social reform.

A number of polemical tracts about women's rights had preceded it—among them Catharine Macaulay's *Letters on Education* (1790), which Wollstonecraft had reviewed enthusiastically upon its publication two years earlier. Although *A Vindication of the Rights of Woman* was primarily seen and received at the time as a treatise on behalf of women's education, its scope exceeds that issue. *A Vindication* is admired by contemporary critics and readers as one of the earliest critiques of misogynist literary representations of women, as a radical assertion of women's existence as an oppressed class that cuts across social stratum, and as a cogent analysis of how women, denied social and economic equality, have been forced to use coquetry and deception to obtain male protection—an arrangement that creates them as an inferior class, that corrupts both men and women, and that interferes with the sexes' common humanity.

Although the work suffered neglect in the two centuries after its publication while its author was excoriated for her unconventional personal life and radical views, *A Vindication*, in fact, paved the way for the feminist polemical tradition in English carried on in the nineteenth and twentieth centuries. Today, both work and author have been restored to their rightful places of honor in feminist literary history.

Wollstonecraft's unfinished novel, *The Wrongs of Woman: or Maria, a Fragment*, fictionalized the arguments of her classic feminist polemic *A Vindication of the Rights of Woman*. Wollstonecraft's husband edited and published the work posthumously in 1798. Portraying a heroine wrongly imprisoned in a madhouse by her husband who desires to control her considerable property, *The Wrongs of Woman* explores women's enslavement by the legal and domestic codes of the day. The novel makes the poignant argument voiced by the heroine herself in the opening chapter, "Was not the world a vast prison, and women born slaves?" Didactic in tone, the novel's purpose, expressed in the author's preface, is to represent "the misery and oppression, peculiar to women, that arise out of the partial laws and customs of society" and to show "the wrongs of different classes of women, equally oppressive, though, from the difference of education, necessarily various."

In chapter one, we meet the heroine Maria, confined in a private insane asylum, a "mansion of despair." Separated from her four-month-old baby, she "mourned for her child, lamented she was a daughter, and anticipated the aggravated ills of life that her sex rendered almost inevitable." Unjustly confined by her tyrannical husband although she is sane, Maria attempts to enlist the sympathies of her guard, Jemima, "an outcast of society," who values her position and the wages she receives as her "only chance for independence." Nevertheless, having suffered injustice herself, Jemima determines to do everything within her power to aid the wronged Maria, bringing her "books and implements for writing."

After "six weeks buried alive," Maria struggles with her despondency but becomes cheered when Jemima brings her a parcel of books belonging to a fellow inmate. She especially appreciates the marginal notes, which indicate a sensibility and values "perfectly in unison with Maria's mode of thinking." Certain the owner of the books is no more mad than she, Maria longs to meet him. A correspondence soon ensues between Maria and the other inmate, Henry Darnford, aided by Jemima who acts as a go-between and protector. Darnford bribes his keeper and manages to arrange a clandestine visit to Maria's cell, soon followed by other meetings. Darnford recounts his history, confessing that he had been a "thoughtless and extravagant young man" who squandered his patrimony and traveled abroad. Upon returning to England, he was forcibly confined in the asylum without knowing the reason why. The passion between Darnford and Maria grows: "A magic lamp now seemed to be suspended in Maria's prison, and fairy landscapes flitted round the gloomy walls, late so blank." Maria confesses to her lover that she is married: "You must be told who I am, why I am here, and why, telling you I am a wife, I blush not to."

Jemima, softened by the tender love she witnesses between Maria and Darnford, gives them an account of her own life. Her mother was a servant girl, who was seduced, then rejected, by a fellow servant in the house and who died nine days after Jemima's birth. Growing up in hunger and neglect, Jemima is eventually seduced and impregnated by her master at the age of sixteen. Turned out of the house by her jealous mistress, she induces an abortion by drinking a potion, hoping but failing to kill herself as well. Jemima turns to prostitution, "detesting my nightly occupation, though valuing . . . my independence, which only consisted in choosing the street in which I should wander, or the roof, when I had money, in which I should hide my head." Eventually, as the mistress of a libertine, she acquires a taste for literature and fine conversation. After his death, however, she discovers that only the most menial labor is open to women. Taking work as a washerwoman, she suffers an injury on the job, which renders her unable to work. Imprisoned for thievery and sent to a workhouse for begging, Jemima eventually accepts the offer of forty pounds a year to work in this "private receptacle for madness," run by a "villain." Grateful for a measure of financial independence, she has hardened her heart to the suffering she witnesses until meeting Maria.

In chapter six, Maria reflects on Jemima's fate and her own, considering the "oppressed state of women" and again lamenting having given birth to a daughter. She persuades Jemima to go and inquire about the fate of her daughter, and Jemima returns with the news that her child is dead. Stricken with grief, Maria sends Darnford the memoirs she has been writing for her daughter, which comprise chapters seven through fourteen. Maria recounts how she grew up in a household ruled by the tyranny of her father and older brother, for whom her mother had an "extravagant partiality." Maria becomes a favorite of an uncle, who possesses a great fortune and a romantic sensibility, which influences Maria.

Soon, a merchant named Venables moves to the neighborhood, and his son George develops an interest in Maria. Unaware of his libertinism, Maria is flattered by his attentions. Following the death of her mother, Maria's father takes a mistress, a former servant who now exerts an "illegitimate authority" over the family. Maria complains that by "allowing women but one way of rising in the world" and by "fostering the libertinism of men," society turns women into "monsters" and then points to their "ignoble vices" as "proof of inferiority of intellect." Desperate to escape from her father's household, Maria seeks the advice of her uncle, who encourages a marriage to George Venables. Thinking "more of obtaining my freedom, than of my lover," Maria doesn't know that her uncle has promised Venables five thousand pounds; thus, she remains ignorant that greed is his motive for marriage.

Following her marriage, Maria becomes aware of her husband's true character. She regrets that "in my haste to escape from a temporary dependence, and expand my newly fledged wings, in an unknown sky, I had been caught in a trap, and caged for life." She becomes aware of her husband's financial embarrassments and his womanizing, and she learns that he has an illegitimate child. Believing "personal intimacy without affection" to be "degrading," Maria withdraws to her own separate quarters. Determined to win her back, Venables softens in his behavior toward Maria, and, yielding to him, she becomes pregnant. Addressing her daughter directly, Maria writes: "The greatest sacrifice of my principles in my whole life, was the allowing my husband again to be familiar with my person, though to this cruel act of self-denial . . . you owe your birth; and I the unutterable pleasure of being a mother." Observing that a woman who leaves her husband is despised and shunned, Maria laments her enslavement: "Marriage has bastilled me for life."

Soon Maria becomes an object of the attention of a wealthy visitor to her husband's house. When the gentleman attempts to seduce her, she learns that her husband has encouraged the seduction, advising him that all women have a price. Enraged that her husband has virtually sold her into prostitution, Maria determines to leave him, removing her wedding ring; however, her husband locks her in the house. Resisting her husband's efforts to force her to return to their marriage bed, the pregnant Maria finally flees the house and finds other lodging. Her husband pursues her from lodging to lodging, hunting her like an "infected beast," and she is haunted by nightmares of him. Three days after the birth of her daughter, Maria learns of the death of her uncle, who has left her a large fortune. Maria determines to leave England; however, her plan is thwarted by her husband, who drugs her and confines her to the asylum where she now resides.

The novel's remaining three chapters consist of incomplete sketches, which Godwin pieced together from his wife's drafts following Wollstonecraft's death. Darnford returns the memoirs to Maria, decrying the absurdity of the laws of matrimony that lead to such bondage as she has suffered. Maria now receives

Darnford as her husband, defying conventional moral codes. Darnford learns that the keeper of the asylum has been part of a conspiracy to confine him and rob him of an inheritance. The asylum keeper abruptly departs, and Maria flees with Jemima, leaving word for Darnford to come and find her. They learn that Venables has brought legal suit against Darnford for seduction and adultery. Desiring to be lawfully wedded to Darnford, Maria instructs him to plead guilty to adultery but not to seduction. She writes an impassioned statement summarizing the wrongs she received at the hands of her husband and arguing for the dissolution of their marriage bond. However, the judge declares it is "her duty to love and obey the man chosen by her parents and relations." Reaffirming the legitimacy of the legal oppression of women, he opines:

> Too many restrictions could not be thrown in the way of divorces, if we wished to maintain the sanctity of marriage; and, though they might bear a little hard on a few, very few individuals, it was evidently for the good of the whole.

The few contradictory hints for the remainder of the novel suggest that Wollstonecraft conceived of a dark outcome for Maria's story, including her betrayal by Darnford and her possible suicide. A passionate chronicler of the "wrongs of woman," Wollstonecraft, unfortunately, was unable at the time of her death to imagine a positive resolution of those wrongs.

References and Suggested Readings

Abrams, M.H., et al., eds. *The Norton Anthology of English Literature*. 5th ed. Vol. 2. New York: Norton, 1986.

Gilbert, Sandra M., and Susan Gubar, eds. *The Norton Anthology of Literature by Women: The Traditions in English*. 2nd ed. New York: Norton, 1996.

Kelly, Gary. Introduction. *Mary and the Wrongs of Woman*. By Mary Wollstonecraft. New York: Oxford University Press, 1976.

Wollstonecraft, Mary. *A Vindication of the Rights of Woman*. 1792. New York: Norton, 1988.

———. *The Wrongs of Woman: or Maria, a Fragment*. 1798. *Mary and the Wrongs of Woman*. New York: Oxford University Press, 1976.

See also Gilman, Charlotte Perkins; Rich, Adrienne; Schreiner, Olive; Shelley, Mary; Woolf, Virginia.

THE WOMAN QUESTION

"Many women are considering within themselves, what they need that they have not, and what they can have, if they find they need it," wrote Sarah Margaret Fuller. "Many men are considering whether women are capable of being and having more than they are and have, and, whether, if so, it will be best to consent to improvement in their condition" (1718). These questions—what women could and did have in the nineteenth century, when Fuller was writing—comprise "the woman question." Far from being a singular question, this concept encompassed the various political, economic, and social challenges women were facing around the time of the emergence of the suffrage movement.

Sarah Moore Grimke also addressed the woman question by pointing out that men deliberately denied them access to power by providing them only with inferior educations. "In most families," Grimke laments,

> it is considered a matter of far more consequence to call a girl off from making a pie, or a pudding, than to interrupt her whilst engaged in her studies. This mode of training necessarily exalts, in their view, the animal above the intellectual and spiritual nature, and teaches women to regard themselves as a kind of machinery, necessary to keep the domestic engine in order, but of little value as the intelligent companions of men. (2025)

As Grimke suggests here, inferior education and relegation to the domestic sphere were means of keeping women "in their place." As women became more aware of and willing to challenge these injustices, their concerns were often lumped together and referred to by men as "the woman question." The phrase not only references the (acknowledged) beginnings of feminism, it also evidences the ways in which men have trivialized, even linguistically, the concerns of women. Because of this patronizing dismissal, Sarah Moore Grimke knew that women could not rely on men to contribute any solutions to the questions being raised. "I feel that I am calling upon my sex to sacrifice what has been, what is still dear to their hearts, the adulation, the flattery, the attentions of trifling men," she wrote (2030). In other words, according to Grimke, women would only find an answer to the woman question when they undertook its study for themselves.

References and Suggested Readings

Fuller, Sarah Margaret. "Woman in the Nineteenth Century." *The Heath Anthology of American Literature*. Ed. Paul Lauter. Boston: Houghton Mifflin, 1998. 1714–35.

Grimke, Sarah Moore. "Letters on the Equality of the Sexes, and the Condition of Woman." *The Heath Anthology of American Literature*. Ed. Paul Lauter. Boston: Houghton Mifflin, 1998. 2024–31.

Lisa R. Williams

WOOLF, VIRGINIA

The noted British novelist, essayist, critic, and diarist Virginia Woolf is considered by many to be the foremother of twentieth-century feminist literary criticism. She was born Adeline Virginia Stephen in London on January 25, 1882, into a well-to-do and highly intellectual Victorian household. Her father, the biographer, philosopher, and literary critic Sir Leslie Stephen, had a vast library and introduced her to a steady stream of distinguished literary and intellectual visitors. Woolf's mother, Julia Jackson Duckworth, also had artistic connections and had a book published on nursing entitled *Notes from Sick Rooms* (1883).

Her parents' marriage was a second one for both of them; they were widow and widower when they met. Woolf's large family included a retarded half-sister from her father's first marriage to the daughter of Victorian novelist William Thackeray and three half-siblings—Stella, George, and Gerald—from her mother's first marriage to the lawyer Herbert Duckworth. Woolf's childhood experiences apparently included unwanted sexual advances from her two older half-brothers, George and Gerald. The Stephens had four more children together: Vanessa, Thoby, Virginia, and Adrian. In keeping with the standards of the day, the boys were sent away to school, while the girls were educated at home. Woolf later expressed great bitterness over this inequitable situation.

The first of a series of mental breakdowns, which were to plague Woolf until her death by suicide, occurred in 1895 with the death of her mother, whom she later immortalized in the character of Mrs. Ramsay in her 1927 novel *To the Lighthouse*. This tragedy was followed in 1897 by the death of her half-sister Stella. Although she loved her father, his presence cast a long shadow in the years following her mother's death; in 1904, Woolf experienced his death as a liberation of sorts. She later wrote in her diary that had her father lived, there would have been "no writing, no books—inconceivable." Following her father's death, she settled in Bloomsbury with her sister Vanessa and brothers Adrian and Thoby (whose sudden death from typhoid in 1906 was another traumatic event of this period). Here, she became acquainted with a circle of her brother Thoby's friends from his University days at Cambridge, which included such brilliant men as the biographer Lytton Strachey, the economist John Maynard Keynes, the art critic Roger Fry, the painter Clive Bell—who shortly married her painter sister Vanessa—the political theorist and man of letters Leonard Woolf, and the novelist E.M. Forster. Known as the Bloomsbury Group after the district of London where they gathered, this intellectual and artistic circle was infamous for its frank discussions of sexuality, including homosexuality, and its bohemian rejection of conventional Victorian sexual mores and standards.

Like many of the artists and intellectuals associated with the Bloomsbury Group, Woolf was bisexual. In 1909, she was engaged very briefly to the homosexual Lytton Strachey, but both immediately changed their minds. She married Leonard Woolf in 1912, a union that lasted until her death. The marriage was an extremely happy one, although the couple remained childless and their compatibility was primarily intellectual rather than sexual—indeed their union seems to have been largely a platonic one. In the 1920s, Woolf carried on a passionately erotic love affair, lasting several years, with the writer Vita [Victoria] Sackville-West, a lesbian poet and novelist from an aristocratic family background, who was married to the bisexual diplomat and author Harold Nichols. Both the marriage to Leonard and the relationship with Vita had, in their different ways, profound and positive influences on her writing.

Following her marriage to Leonard, Woolf was able to focus her energies on publishing her first novel, *The Voyage Out* (1915), followed by *Night and Day* (1919), both fairly traditional, linear narratives that reflect Victorian aesthetic standards. In *Jacob's Room* (1922), *Mrs. Dalloway* (1925), and *To the Lighthouse* (1927), Woolf broke from Victorian realist narrative forms and perfected her stream-of-consciousness technique; by the mid-1920s, she had established herself as one of the most innovative and experimental novelists of the modernist period. Woolf's experimental style finds its fullest expression in *The Waves* (1931), followed by *The Years* (1937) and *Between the Acts*, published posthumously in 1941.

During the same time period in which she was honing her craft of fiction, Woolf and her husband founded the Hogarth Press in 1917, a hobby that became an extremely successful and important publishing venture. The Press brought out such notable works as the poems of T.S. Eliot, the short stories of Katherine Mansfield, and English translations of Sigmund Freud's writings, in addition to Woolf's own novels. Woolf was also a prolific literary critic, an active letter writer, and a passionately committed diarist—her diaries are an outstanding literary achievement in their own right.

Although she had long demonstrated an interest in feminist issues, her relationship with Vita Sackville-West inspired her best-known and most direct treatments of these themes: *Orlando* (1928), *A Room of One's Own* (1929), and *Three Guineas* (1938). In the novel *Orlando*, Woolf wrote a tribute to Sackville-West in the form of a parodic biography of a four-hundred-year-old character, who starts out as a young aristocratic man in the Elizabethan age, changes from male to female in the course of the seventeenth century, and winds up as a modern woman driving a motor car in the "present moment"—October 11, 1928. Satirizing both the history of literature and the history of sexuality, Woolf playfully suggests both might be a matter of style. The novel was adapted into a popular film in 1994. *Orlando*'s sister text, *A Room of One's Own*, is an extended essay on the subject of women and fiction, focusing particularly on the material conditions necessary for women to develop as writers and artists. Many consider it to be the first major achievement in feminist literary criticism in the English language. *Three Guineas* is the second of Woolf's major nonfiction works and her most radical feminist work. Conceived as a sequel to *A Room* and written during the rising tide of Fascism in Europe, it is a significant statement about feminism and pacifism.

As the Germans were bombing England in World War II, Woolf began to feel signs of the psychic distress returning. The fact that Leonard was of Jewish origin must have only added to her anxieties. Her brother Adrian, a physician, had provided them both with the means to poison themselves in case of German invasion. Nevertheless, on March 28, 1941, fearing that she was once again going mad and would be a burden to Leonard, Virginia Woolf filled her pockets with stones and drowned herself by walking into the River Ouse in Lewes, Sussex.

Published in 1929, the literary essay *A Room of One's* Own has become a classic of twentieth-century feminist literary criticism and remains one of the most frequently read and debated statements on the subject of women and literature. Composed of six chapters, the essay was revised and expanded from papers delivered at Newnham and Girton, two women's colleges in Cambridge in October

1928. Written in the form of a lecture on the topic of "women and fiction," the essay addresses its female audience directly, ostensibly the audience of the lecture hall but also the larger female reading audience toward which the book is aimed. Much more than a discussion of women and fiction, *A Room of One's Own* is actually a feminist analysis of the material conditions—social, political, and economic—in which women struggle to become creators of literature.

In chapter one, Woolf asserts her thesis that "a woman must have money and a room of her own if she is to write fiction" (4). To explain this contention, Woolf imaginatively recounts the story of the two days leading up to her lecture, "making use of all the liberties and licenses of a novelist" (4) and insisting that "'I' is only a convenient term for somebody who has no real being" (4). First, she describes her visit to the town of "Oxbridge" (the name is a combination of the two most prestigious universities in England, Oxford and Cambridge). Here, her entry into the library, which houses the great manuscripts of English literature, is barred because of her sex. Descending the steps in anger, Woolf meditates on the "unending stream of gold and silver" (9) that endowed the great university, amply providing for lectureships, chairs, fellowships, libraries, and laboratories. She describes in detail the lavish luncheon spread, further evidence of the university's great wealth and abundance.

Leaving Oxbridge, where gate after gate locks behind her as the "treasure-house was being made secure for another night" (13), Woolf walks to Fernham, a fictional women's college nearby. Unlike the lavish luncheon, dinner at Fernham is very poor and plain, reminding her of "bargaining and cheapening and women with string bags on Monday mornings" (17). She laments the "reprehensible poverty of our sex" (21) and wonders "what had our mothers been doing that they had no wealth to leave us?" (21). While men had been making money and leaving great sums to endow all-male universities, women had been bearing and raising children. Even if a woman had earned money, until very recently it would have been her husband's property. Woolf ends by pondering the relative effects of poverty and wealth on the mind.

Woolf visits the British Museum in chapter two seeking answers to the question of why women are so poor and what effect this has on the creation of fiction. Here, she finds shelves and shelves of books by men about women. Despairing of finding any answers in these books, Woolf sketches a caricature of "Professor von X., engaged in writing his monumental work entitled *The Mental, Moral, and Physical Inferiority of the Female Sex*" (31). The books are useless, because "they had been written in the red light of emotion and not in the white light of truth" (32–33). By insisting on women's inferiority, Woolf concludes, angry male professors like Professor von X. reinforce their own feelings of superiority and preserve their patriarchal power. Women serve as "looking-glasses possessing the magic and delicious power of reflecting the figure of man at twice its natural size" (35).

In a nearby restaurant where she lunches, Woolf pays the bill with money left to her by an aunt. She ponders how this legacy of five hundred pounds has freed her from doing menial labor typically open to women or from being financially dependent on a man. She deems this financial independence infinitely more important than the vote. She imagines the day one hundred years hence when "women will have ceased to be the protected sex" (40) and will be free to earn their livings in all the occupations once denied to them.

In chapter three, Woolf wonders why no women wrote a word of the extraordinary literature of Elizabethan England. She laments how little is known about the lives of middle-class women before the eighteenth century. Would it have been possible for a woman to write Shakespeare's plays? She imagines that "Shakespeare had a wonderfully gifted sister, called Judith" (46). Woolf can only imagine an unhappy ending to Judith's story. Kept from school for a life of domestic drudgery and marriage, she runs away to the London theater, only to end up seduced, pregnant, and dead by her own hand. The truth in this fictional story, Woolf says, "is that any woman born with a great gift in the sixteenth century would certainly have gone crazed, shot herself, or ended her days in some lonely cottage outside the village, half witch, half wizard, feared and mocked at" (49). The material conditions did not then exist, and to some extent still do not exist, to permit the development of the woman artist. No woman in those historical circumstances could have achieved the "incandescent, unimpeded" (57) mind of Shakespeare.

Woolf establishes the possibility of a female or matrilineal literary tradition in chapter four. She begins with the aristocratic Lady Winchilsea, born 1661. Following her conclusions in the previous chapter about the historical limitations on the woman artist, Woolf claims her poetry suffers because it is suffused with anger and bitterness at the position of women. Similarly she finds the Duchess Margaret Cavendish's writings "disfigured and deformed by the same causes" (61). In Dorothy Osborne's letters, she finds evidence that "even a woman with a great turn for writing has brought herself to believe that to write a book was to be ridiculous" (63). But with Aphra Behn, "we turn a very important corner" (63). A middle-class woman, "forced by the death of her husband and some unfortunate adventures of her own to make a living by her wits" (63–64), Behn set a precedent for women to make a living by writing. At the end of the eighteenth century, "the middle class woman began to write" (65)—a change Woolf deems more historically important that the Crusades or the Wars of the Roses.

By the nineteenth century, the shelves are full of novels by women. The novel becomes the genre of women, Woolf hypothesizes, because women wrote in the common sitting room and were frequently interrupted; the novel required less concentration than poetry or plays. Moreover, the novel genre was well-suited to women, who received their "literary training" in the "observation of character" and the "analysis of emotion" (67) in the common sitting room. Woolf discusses the four great women novelists of the nineteenth century: Jane Austen, Charlotte Brontë, Emily Brontë, and George Eliot. Woolf admires Austen, because, like Shakespeare, her mind "had consumed all impediments" (68). Although Charlotte Brontë has "more genius in her than Jane Austen" (69), Woolf complains that she writes "in a rage where she should write calmly" (69). George Eliot, too, is limited by the mores of the times, which forced her into isolation and seclusion for the sin of living with a married man. Had Tolstoy been similarly ostracized, she argues, he could hardly have written *War and Peace*. Only Jane Austen and Emily Brontë, in Woolf's view, succeeded in maintaining their "integrity" as artists, rather than being caught up in apologizing for or defending their sex: "They wrote as women write, not as men write " (74–75). Since "we think back through our mothers if we are women" (76), the absence of a well-developed female literary tradition must have taken an enormous toll on the writing of women. Women had to invent a new way of writing, since a "man's sentence" was "unsuited for a woman's use" (76). Perhaps another reason women wrote novels, theorizes Woolf, is that "the older forms of literature were hardened and set by the time she became a writer. The novel alone was young enough to be soft in her hands" (77).

In chapter five, Woolf brings us to her present day, when there are almost as many living women authors as male ones. Taking a random title off the shelf, Woolf begins to read from a hypothetical novel entitled *Life's Adventures* by "Mary Carmichael." To her astonishment, she turns the page and reads the sentence "Chloe liked Olivia" (82). Woolf is struck by the immense change: "Chloe liked Olivia perhaps for the first time in literature" (82). Before, women had been shown only in relation to men or (in the case of Cleopatra and Octavia for instance) in competition with each other. Now they not only liked each other, but "they shared a laboratory together," suggesting, "that women, like men, have other interests besides the perennial interests of domesticity" (83). She thinks of all that has been "left out" (83) in literature about women and all the "infinitely obscure lives" of women that "remain to be recorded" (89). She also thinks about the task of describing for men that "spot the size of a shilling at the back of the head which one can never see for oneself" (90). In short, she imagines literature that brings women's perspectives to the representation of both sexes.

In chapter six, Woolf looks up from her reading and sees an "ordinary enough" (96) sight below her window: a girl and a young man come together in the street and get into a taxicab. She thinks back to her contention that "a woman writing thinks back through her mothers" (97), her argument for a matrilineal literary tradition. She wonders if thinking of the two sexes as separate from each other, as she has been doing, "interferes with the unity of the mind" (97). Perhaps, the soul is comprised of two powers, male and female; "in the man's brain the man predominates over the woman, and in the woman's brain, the woman predominates over the man" (98). She compares this with Coleridge's contention that the great mind is androgynous. Praising Shakespeare as an exemplar of this androgynous mind, Woolf complains about the "virility" of contemporary men's writing: "Men, that is to say, are now writing only with the male side of their brains" (101). She states that "it is fatal for anyone who writes to think of their sex. It is fatal to be a man or woman pure and simple; one must be woman-manly or man-womanly" (104).

Woolf ends by returning to her image of Shakespeare's sister, who has become a frequently cited symbol of the silenced and unrealized woman poet. She imagines the day one hundred years hence when women will have five hundred pounds a year and rooms of their own. She urges her female audience to continue to write, even in poverty and obscurity, so that Shakespeare's sister can be reborn.

One of the most beloved novels by Virginia Woolf, *Orlando* is "an homage to her love for Vita Sackville-West" (Blain et al. 1186). Published in 1928, the novel was dedicated to and based on the aristocratic family history of Vita Sackville-West, a lesbian poet and novelist with whom Woolf had a serious and passionate love affair between 1923 and 1928. Sackville-West posed for several of the photographs accompanying the original text. Subtitled "A Biography," this witty, playful, and exuberant piece of fiction simultaneously parodies the conventions of academic historical writing, the history of English literature, and the nature of relations between the sexes. Recounting the life of Orlando, a nearly four-centuries-old transsexual character freed from traditional constraints of time and gender, Woolf's novel is a feminist utopian fantasy that presents gender roles as a matter of fashion rather than biology—as fluid and changeable as literary and historical styles.

The narrator introduces Orlando as an aristocratic boy of sixteen in Elizabethan England—"for there could be no doubt of his sex, though the fashion of the time did something to disguise it" (13). The narrator rhapsodizes about Orlando's "shapely legs" (14) and "eyes like drenched violets" (15). A poet who writes volumes of verse in the style of his age, Orlando is also a favorite of the aging Queen Elizabeth, an admirer of his legs, violet eyes, and manly charms. She bestows many houses, lands, and favors upon him. In the spirit of the age, Orlando lustily pursues trysts with young women, inciting the jealousy of the Queen. He is engaged to be married to a woman with a family tree "as old and deeply rooted as Orlando's itself" (33).

Soon the Great Frost settles over London, and King James turns the frozen river into a pleasure ground. Here, Orlando first spies and falls in love with a figure of ambiguous gender who turns out to be a Moscovite princess named Sasha. Their intimacy creates a scandal in the court, and they plan to run away together. Sasha ends by betraying him, however, setting sail in the Russian ambassador's ship when the Great Frost thaws and leaving Orlando, knee deep in water, to hurl "at the faithless woman all the insults that have ever been the lot of her sex" (64).

In chapter two, Orlando is exiled from court over his scandalous affair with Sasha. Retiring to his house in the country, he falls into a deep sleep for seven days, awaking with "an imperfect recollection of his past life" (66). Pining for Sasha, he takes up a life of solitude, reading, and writing. He discusses the great literary figures of the age—Shakespeare, Marlowe, Ben Jonson, Browne, Donne—with the poet Nicholas Greene, an occasion for the narrator to satirize the history of English literature. Greene insults Orlando's writing and person, causing Orlando to burn "in a great conflagration fifty-seven poetical works, only retaining 'The Oak Tree'" (96). By the age of thirty, Orlando has concluded: "Love and ambition, women and poets were all equally vain. Literature was a farce" (96). Orlando continues to write "The Oak Tree: A Poem." The passage of time does nothing to age Orlando in the conventional sense, but the "historian of letters" might note "he had changed his [literary] style amazingly" (113). One day, while at work on his poem, "a very tall lady in riding hood and mantle" (113) appears, introducing herself as the Archduchess Harriet. Overcome by passion, Orlando realizes that it is "Lust the vulture, not Love, the Bird of Paradise" (117–18), which has seized him. In order to extricate himself from the vulture's grip, he asked King Charles to send him to Constantinople as Ambassador.

While in Constantinople, Orlando is promoted from Ambassador to Duke. He also falls into another deep sleep, and this time—extraordinarily—awakens as a woman. As Orlando gazes at himself in the mirror, the narrator emphasizes his androgyny: "No human being, since the world began, has ever looked more ravishing. His form combined in one the strength of a man and a woman's grace" (138). Moreover, although "Orlando had become a woman. . . . [I]n every other respect, Orlando remained precisely as he had been." Nevertheless, "for convention's sake," the narrator now substitutes "she" for "he" and "her" for "his" (138). Dressed in "those Turkish coats and trousers which can be worn indifferently by either sex" (139), Orlando leaves Constantinople and spends some time with a gypsy tribe, before determining to return to England on an English merchant ship.

Dressed as a young Englishwoman of rank, Orlando sits on the deck of the *Enamoured Lady* and realizes "with a start the penalties and privileges of her position" (153). Orlando's sex change gives her a unique perspective on the nature of the sexes, and her ruminations about male and female roles in the course of the voyage wittily unsettle traditional assumptions about gender. Orlando also recalls Sasha, for "though she herself was a woman, it was still a woman she loved; and if the consciousness of being of the same sex had any effect at all, it was to quicken and deepen those feelings which she had as a man. For now a thousand hints and mysteries became plain to her that were then dark" (161). Upon returning to England, Orlando learns she is a party to various lawsuits, charging among other things: "(1) that she was dead, and therefore could not hold any property whatsoever" and "(2) that she was a woman, which amounts to much the same thing" (168). Starting afresh upon "The Oak Tree," she is interrupted by the reappearance of the Archduchess Harriet, who now reveals himself to be a gentleman rather than a lady. The Archduke Harry begs forgiveness for the deceit he had practiced upon Orlando previously, and the two of them "acted the parts of man and woman for ten minutes with great vigour and then fell into natural discourse" (179). Orlando now occupies herself with avoiding the persistent marriage suit of Archduke Harry. She is caught up in the swirl of eighteenth-century society, hobnobbing with "wits" and men of genius like Pope, Addison, and Swift, whose attitudes toward women are satirized. Dressed as a man of fashion, Orlando picks up a prostitute named Nell and returns to her lodging. Revealing herself to be a woman, Orlando spends an enjoyable evening talking with Nell and some fellow members of her "tribe," whose company she finds far superior to the so-called "wits." Her thorough enjoyment of female society also disproves the male notion that "women are incapable of any feeling of affection for their own sex and hold each other in the greatest aversion" (220).

For the duration of the century, Orlando enjoys the freedom of transvestism: "From the probity of breeches she turned to the seductiveness of petticoats and enjoyed the love of both sexes equally" (221). As the chapter ends, "light," "order," and "serenity" give way to "dark," "doubt," and "confusion" (225–26). "The Eighteenth Century was over; the Nineteenth Century had begun" (226).

In chapter five, "a great cloud" (227) hangs over Great Britain, an indicator of the enormous change in the climate of the times. As dampness spreads over everything, the Victorian age becomes swaddled and smothered in all manner of things. Likewise, "love, birth, and death were all swaddled in a variety of fine phrases. The sexes drew further and further apart" (229). Orlando finds herself pregnant, takes to blushing, and "was forced at length to consider the most desperate of remedies, which was to yield completely and submissively to the spirit of the age, and take a husband" (243). In a parody of the gothic romance style, Orlando is rescued by a man on horseback while she lies on the moor with a broken ankle: "A few minutes later, they became engaged" (250). Her fiancé, Marmaduke Bonthrop Shelmerdine, cuts a passionately romantic figure, his name recalling the poet Shelley, "whose entire works he had by heart" (261). The theme of androgyny continues as Orlando accuses Shel of being a woman, and he accuses her of being a man: "For . . . it was to each . . . a revelation that a woman could be as tolerant and free-spoken as a man, and a man as strange and subtle as a woman" (258). Orlando marries Shel, a sea captain, whose "life was spent in the most desperate and splendid of adventures—which is to voyage round Cape Horn in the teeth of a gale" (252).

In chapter six, Orlando ponders her situation:

> She was married, true; but if one's husband was always sailing round Cape Horn, was it marriage? If one liked him, was it marriage? If one liked other people, was it marriage? And finally, if one still wished, more than anything in the whole world, to write poetry, was it marriage? She had her doubts. (262)

Having achieved, nevertheless, a "dexterous deference to the spirit of the age" (266), Orlando is free to continue to write and finishes her manuscript, "The Oak Tree," "just in time to catch the eleven forty-five" (272) to London, the railway train having been invented in the interim. In London, she meets her old friend Nick Greene, now "the most influential critic of the Victorian Age" (277), who pronounces her poem instantly publishable. Having completed her manuscript, Orlando gives birth to a baby boy. In the very next sentence Orlando stands looking out the window, but it is not "by any means, the same day" (296). The women have grown "narrow," and "the men's faces were as bare as the palm of one's hand" (297). It is the "present moment"—October 11, 1928 (298). Orlando, now age thirty-six and driving a motor car, goes shopping in a department store and spies the apparition of her first love, Sasha. The "present moment" is infused with past moments, just as our selves are "built up, one on top of another, as plates are piled on a waiter's hand" (308). Orlando "change[s] her skirt for a pair of whipcord breeches, and leather jacket" (315) and contemplates her literary prize for her poem, "The Oak Tree." Touring the house and grounds she has lived in for close to four centuries, she seeks out the oak tree she has known since she was a lad in 1588; like her, it is still in the prime of its life. An airplane appears in the sky overhead delivering her husband, Shel, the sea captain, who leaps to the ground as the novel closes on the twelfth stroke of midnight, October 11, 1928.

References and Suggested Readings

Abrams, M.H., et al., eds. *The Norton Anthology of English Literature*. 5th ed. Vol. 2. New York: Norton, 1986.

Blain, Virginia, et al., eds. *The Feminist Companion to Literature in English*. New Haven: Yale University Press, 1990.

Crawford, Anne, et al., eds. *The Europa Biographical Dictionary of British Women*. Detroit: Gale, 1983.

Gilbert, Sandra M., and Susan Gubar. *No Man's Land: The Place of the Woman Writer in the Twentieth Century, Vol. 2, Sex Changes*. New Haven: Yale University Press, 1989.

———. eds. *The Norton Anthology of Literature by Women: The Traditions in English*. 2nd ed. New York: Norton, 1996.

Kester-Shelton, Pamela, ed. *Feminist Writers*. Detroit: St. James, 1996.

Rose, Phyllis, ed. *The Norton Book of Women's Lives*. New York: Norton: 1993.

Summers, Claude J., ed. *The Gay and Lesbian Literary Heritage*. New York: Henry Holt, 1995.

Woolf, Virginia. *Orlando: A Biography*. 1928. New York: Harcourt, 1956.

———. *A Room of One's Own*. 1929. New York: Harcourt, 1957.

See also Austen, Jane; Behn, Aphra; Brontë, Charlotte; Brontë, Emily.

YAMAMOTO, HISAYE

Born in 1921 in Redondo Beach, California, to *issei* (Japanese immigrant) parents, Hisaye Yamamoto gives eloquent voice to the *nisei* (second-generation Japanese American) experience in her short fiction. Her most frequently anthologized story, "Seventeen Syllables" (1949), explores the complex relationship between an *issei* mother and her *nisei* daughter, subtly mapping the gaps in understanding created by linguistic, cultural, and generational differences. The frequently anthologized story is also a tragic and unsentimental portrait of the sacrifices, particularly of autonomy and creativity, demanded of women in marriage.

During World War II, Yamamoto and her family were incarcerated in an internment camp in Poston, Arizona, where her short story "The Legend of Miss Sasagawara" (1950) is set. There, she was a reporter and columnist for the camp newspaper, *The Poston Chronicle*. Following the end of the war, Yamamoto was one of the first Japanese American writers to gain national recognition despite continued anti-Japanese sentiment. Her story "Yoneko's Earthquake" (1951) was included in the *Best American Short Stories: 1952*. In the early 1950s, she received a John Hay Whitney Foundation Opportunity Award and worked as a volunteer on a Catholic Worker rehabilitation farm on Staten Island, New York.

After marrying Anthony DeSoto, Yamamoto returned to Los Angeles, where she devoted time to raising five children. Like other women who have divided time between writing and family responsibilities, Yamamoto did not publish a book until *Seventeen Syllables and Other Stories* (1988), a collection of previously published stories written over the preceding four decades. A recipient of the Before Columbus Foundation's 1986 American Book Award for Lifetime Achievement, Yamamoto resides in Southern California.

In the context of the Japanese American immigrant experience, the story "Seventeen Syllables" explores the limitations placed on artistic creation because of social conditions of gender, race, and class—what the working-class feminist writer Tillie Olsen has called in her book *Silences* "the unnatural thwarting of what struggles to come into being, but cannot." In an interview with King-Kok Cheung, Yamamoto has called Olsen's "Tell Me a Riddle" "the most perfect short story I've read," further suggesting the strong thematic links between these two writers. Like "Tell Me a Riddle," "Seventeen Syllables" is also a strikingly unsentimental portrait of marriage and an exploration of the troubling surrender of self it entails for many women.

Narrated in the third person from the point of view of the daughter, Rosie Hayashi, "Seventeen Syllables" revolves around two interlinked plots: Rosie's adolescent sexual awakening with Jesus Carrasco, the son of the Mexican family employed by the Hayashis to assist in the tomato harvest, and her mother's, Tome Hayashi unfulfilled passion for writing haiku, a Japanese poem consisting of seventeen syllables. The distance between Rosie and her mother is established in the opening scene in which Rosie's mother reads a haiku she has composed. Rosie "pretended to understand it thoroughly and appreciate it no end, partly because she hesitated to disillusion her mother about the quantity and quality of Japanese she had learned" (8). Rather than struggle to communicate with her mother across the barrier of language and culture, Rosie finds it "so much easier to say yes, yes, even when one meant no, no" (8).

Rosie's awakening passion for Jesus, realized in a secret rendezvous and first kiss, is juxtaposed against her father's growing jealousy about his wife's passion for haiku. This jealousy eventually erupts in violence when an editor from a San Francisco Japanese newspaper arrives to present Tome with a landscape portrait, the first-place award for a haiku she has submitted. When Tome lingers in the house over tea with the editor instead of returning to the fields, her husband abruptly sends him away and angrily burns and destroys the portrait.

As mother and daughter stand watching the dying fire, Rosie's mother shares the truth of her past, revealing her betrayal by a lover in Japan and her subsequent arranged marriage with Rosie's father. In the story's dramatic final paragraph, Rosie's mother kneels on the floor, in the posture of a suitor proposing marriage, and begs her daughter: "Promise me you will never marry!" (19). Caught up in her memory of Jesus, Rosie utters her "familiar glib agreement" and, when she finally begins to cry, her mother's "embrace and consoling hand came much later than she expected" (19). Yamamoto's ending captures both Tome's bitter disillusionment with men and marriage and Rosie's painfully conflicting loyalties.

References and Suggested Readings

Cheung, King-Kok. Introduction. *Seventeen Syllables and Other Stories*. By Hisaye Yamamoto. Latham, NY: Kitchen Table, 1988.

———, ed. "Seventeen Syllables." By Hisaye Yamamoto. New Brunswick, NJ: Rutgers University Press, 1994.

Davidson, Cathy N., and Linda Wagner-Martin, eds. *The Oxford Book of Women's Writing in the United States*. New York: Oxford University Press, 1995.

Gilbert, Sandra M., and Susan Gubar, eds. *The Norton Anthology of Literature by Women: The Traditions in English*. 2nd ed. New York: Norton, 1996.

Yamamoto, Hisaye. "Seventeen Syllables." 1949. *Seventeen Syllables and Other Stories*. Latham, NY: Kitchen Table, 1988.

YEZIERSKA, ANZIA

The year of Anzia Yezierska's birth is uncertain, but she immigrated to the United States with her family in 1890 when she was about nine years old. Her short stories and novels are infused with the people of her Polish-Russian-Jewish family and neighbors from the Lower East Side of New York City where they lived. Yezierska graduated from Columbia University Teachers' College in 1904 and taught school for ten years before beginning her career in writing. Though she married twice and had a daughter in her second marriage, neither marriage was long-lived. Her relationship that generates the greatest interest is a lately uncovered affair with educator John Dewey. Confirmed by Yezierska's daughter, the affair occurred during 1917 and 1918 when Dewey was dean of Columbia's Teachers' College and she was a recent graduate seeking employment.

Her works include *Hungry Hearts and Other Stories* (1920), *Salome of the Tenements* (1923), *Child of Loneliness* (1923), *Bread Givers* (1925), *Arrogant Beggar* (1927), *All I Could Never Be* (1932), and *Red Ribbon on a White Horse* (1950). Though Yezierska and her work fell into obscurity during the middle of the century, she achieved considerable recognition early in her career and once again since the 1970s. In 1919, her short story "The Fat of the Land" was selected as the Best Short Story of the Year by Edward J. O'Brien. Both her first two books were bought by Hollywood; *Hungry Hearts* earned her ten thousand dollars from Samuel Goldwyn. Her riches were not lasting, and she died in poverty in 1970.

Bread Givers is a fictional account of Yezierska's life and is a classic immigrant story of the pressures of survival and assimilation. The novel is structured in three parts, each reflecting a stage in the protagonist's journey from the Old World to the New World. The novel relates the story of the recent immigrants, the Smolinsky family. Reb Smolinsky, the patriarch, is a student of the Holy Torah and is strongly grounded in the Old World traditions that honor his role. Four daughters, all of whom present a challenge of dowry to the family, shoulder the burden of supporting the family financially.

Reb Smolinsky is unreasonable in his expectations about how their life will be in America: "But my books, my holy books always were, and always will be, the light of the world. You'll see yet how all America will come to my feet to learn" (9). He also has very traditional Old World views of women; he believes "the prayers of his daughters didn't count because God doesn't listen to women. Heaven and the next world are only for men. Women could get into Heaven because they were wives and daughters of men" (9).

Rigidly devoted to God, Reb Smolinsky is imperious with his family and neighbors. Even though the family struggles financially, he will not seek work but prefers to stay home and absorb himself in his studies. When his landlady comes to collect the rent, he slaps her for disrespecting the Torah and suggesting that he work to earn his rent. She has him arrested and jailed, but his charges are dismissed, and the men of the community treat him like a king.

The mother is a mere shadow of her former beautiful and spirited self. Her marriage to Reb Smolinsky was arranged by a matchmaker and shows signs early of being a disaster. She is from a wealthy family, but when her father dies, Smolinsky is given control of the business. He runs it into the ground, and the family comes to America with hopes of survival. So changed is Mrs. Smolinsky that her daughters can't recognize her in the stories of the past.

The novel opens when the first-person narrator, Sara Smolinsky, is ten years old. Already she feels the pressures of adulthood as she expresses, "always it was heavy on my heart the worries for the house as if I was mother" (1). Called *Blut-und-Eisen* (blood and iron) for her strong will, Sara makes a profit peddling herring when the family has nothing to eat; humiliatingly, she also collects coal from other people's ashes so the family can stay warm. Her three older sisters, Bessie, Mashah, and Fania, all suffer differently under their father's stern rule according to their personalities and rank in the family.

The three older daughters are of marriageable age, but Bessie, the oldest, has no immediate prospects of marriage. As the "burden bearer" of the family, Bessie works and gives all her money to the support of the family. One night Bessie does have a suitor come over to meet the family. Berel Bernstein offers her marriage even though she has no dowry. Her father steps in to negotiate the marriage, demands too much, and loses the opportunity for Bessie. Within six weeks, Bernstein marries another, and Bessie is heartbroken.

Mashah is called the "empty-head" by the family. Mashah looks fresh as a doll and does not show the effects of the grinding poverty they live under because "[t]he pride in her beautiful face, in her golden hair, lifted her head like a diamond crown" (4). She falls in love with Jacob Novak, a piano player, but neither father approves of the match. Mr. Novak disapproves of the impoverished family from which Mashah comes; Reb Smolinsky disapproves of Jacob because he plays piano on the Sabbath. He forbids Mashah to see Jacob, but with a letter from Mashah and the urgings of little Sara, the lovers are reunited. Again, Smolinsky drives Jacob away, and Sara notes, "each time he killed the heart from one of his children, he grew louder with his preaching on us all" (65).

Fania, the third daughter, is courted by Morris Lipkin, an impoverished poet. Reb Smolinsky is incensed and determines that he will find proper husbands for his daughters by using the matchmaker, Zaretzky. As her father forces his will upon his daughters, Sara thinks, "how grand it would be if the children also could pick out their fathers and mothers" (76). Smolinsky brings Moe Mirsky to the house to look at his daughters. Mirsky is reputedly a diamond dealer, and Mashah is forced into a date with him. Soon they are engaged but only because Mashah longs to escape her father. The father also brings in Abe Schmukler, in the cloaks-and-suits business, from Los Angeles for Fania. There is a double wedding for the two girls, but Mashah is soon back to report that Mirsky is not a diamond dealer at all but a salesmen in a jewelry store who was fired for using company diamonds to flash before her. She comes home only because she has not eaten. Her father's only response is to revile her for her bad judgment in men.

Six months later, Fania reveals that Abe Schmukler is a gambler and that she wants to come back to New York. Fearful that he will be disgraced by his daughter's situation, Smolinsky refuses to allow her to come home. He blames her for the poor match and reminds her of the precarious place a woman holds in his Old World order:

> And don't forget it, you are already six months older—six months less beautiful—less desirable, in the eyes of a man. Your chances for marrying again are lost for ever [sic], because no man wants what another turns down. (85)

With two daughters out of the house, the family's income is diminished. Sara now works in a paper-box factory and helps support the family. Her father takes her wages and spends them on his fraternal organizations, societies, and lodges; he gives a tithe to charities but nothing to his own family. He declares himself a matchmaker now, and when Zalmon the fishmonger comes to him looking for a wife, he sees the opportunity to give him Bessie. Bessie is furious and rejects Zalmon until he comes courting with his youngest son, Benny. Benny is able to "unlock the love that [Zalmon's] fur coat and the gold watch and chair and all his thought-out love-bargaining speeches had failed to do" (107). As the wedding day nears, Bessie confides in Sara that she will not marry, that she will run away. When little Benny becomes violently ill, Bessie nurses him and, thus, passively finds her way into the marriage. It is simply a marriage of resignation in which "the burden bearer had changed her burden" (110).

With the five hundred dollars that Zalmon has paid for the marriage arrangements, Reb Smolinsky decides to go into business for himself by buying a grocery in Elizabeth, New Jersey. He refuses to allow his wife to participate in the decision, makes a fool's bargain, and loses the family's money. Mrs. Smolinsky is furious with yet another poor decision of her husband, and she tries to throw him out of the house. She cries, "[People] think I got a bread giver when what I have is a stone giver" (127). Smolinsky refuses to leave, and his wife is left only with the solace that they have a roof over their heads.

Now seventeen, Sara is bored and listless; she misses the rush of the city and her work with "[t]he joyous feel of money where every little penny was earned with your own hands" (129). She tells her mother, "I can't respect a man who lives on the blood of his wife and children. If you had any sense, you'd arrest him for not supporting you" (130).

Sara watches her sisters give in to the will of their father and decides that she cannot; she says, "I want to learn something. I want to do something. I want some day to make myself for a person and come among people" (66). Against her father's protests, she rebelliously leaves for New York, affirming, "My will is as strong as yours. I'm going to live my own life. Nobody can stop me. I'm not from the old country. I'm American!" (138).

In New York, Sara finds her sisters in desperate straits. Bessie is under the tyrannical rule of Zalmon, the fishmonger. Mashah lives in poverty with a husband who flaunts his fine clothes while his children starve. Neither brother-in-law will allow her to stay, and Sara is turned out into the streets.

In the second part of the novel, "Between Two Worlds," Sara establishes an independent life. After a difficult search, she finds both a private room where she can study and a job in a laundry. She works ten hours a day and then attends two hours of night school. By the time she studies and catches a bit of sleep, the next day arrives with its demands. Her life is lonely and difficult, and she learns that, even in America, men are privileged over women. One night she goes into a cafeteria, starving for a piece of meat, and the portion she is given is much smaller than the one given to the man in line before her. When she contests her portion, she is simply told that men always get more.

Sara maintains communication with her mother and sisters, and though they urge her to marry, Sara insists that she must become a person in her own right first. When she refuses a match arranged by her sister Fania, Sara believes that her father will be proud of her for her devotion to her studies. Instead, he reviles her, and Sara is reconciled to their locations in two different worlds: "I saw there was no use talking. He could never understand. He was the Old World. I was the New" (207).

Meanwhile Sara flourishes in the academic environment of college though she struggles socially. The award is announced at the ceremony, she wins a contest for the best essay, "What the College Has Done for Me" (232). The thousand-dollar prize enables her to start the next chapter of her life. She buys nice clothes and finds a good apartment, all in preparation for her new job as a schoolteacher.

Sara returns home after a six-year absence to find her mother dying. Within thirty days of his wife's death, Mr. Smolinsky marries the widow Feinstein. The daughters are heartsick when they see that the money given by four lodges on their mother's death has been lavished upon Mrs. Feinstein. Their former home is refurnished with gaudy new furniture, and the new Mrs. Smolinsky wears new clothes. But Reb Smolinsky is an unchanged man, and once the lodge money is gone, he contributes nothing more to the household. His new wife writes a scathing letter to Sara's principal demanding that half of her wages be sent for the upkeep of her father.

The letter only serves to bring Sara and her principal together in a relationship of growing respect and intimacy. Hugo Seelig is also a first-generation American whose parents emigrated from a village near the Smolinsky's home village in Poland. One night as they are going out for dinner, Sara and Hugo bump into a street vendor. It is Sara's father, forced into a job by his new wife. Sara steps in to take care of her ill father and, in doing so, begins the journey to reconciliation. Hugo wins his favor by asking for instruction in Hebrew.

Sara's journey away from the Old World of her father equips her to reenter that world on her own terms and to take care of him out of love and not duty. Together, she and Hugo forge a new life in the New World of America.

References and Suggested Readings

Harris, Alice Kessler. Introduction. *Bread Givers*. By Anzia Yezierska. New York: Persea Books, 1975. v–xviii.

Henriksen, Louise Levitas. "Yezierska, Anzia." *The Oxford Companion to Women's Writing in the United States*. Ed. Cathy N. Davidson and Linda Wagner-Martin. New York: Oxford University Press, 1995.

Shapiro, Ann R. "The Ultimate Shaygets and the Fiction of Anzia Yezierska." *MELUS* 21.2 (1996): 79–88.

Yezierska, Anzia. *Bread Givers*. 1925. New York: Persea Books, 1975.

Index

Note: Page numbers in **bold** type indicate main entries.

About the Author

KATHY J. WHITSON is Professor of English at Eureka College. Her previous books include *Native American Literatures: An Encyclopedia of Works, Characters, Authors, and Themes* (1999).